Redeemers

ALSO BY ENRIQUE KRAUZE

Mexico: Biography of Power

REDEEMERS

Ideas and Power in Latin America

ENRIQUE

KRAUZE

Translated by Hank Heifetz
and Natasha Wimmer

HARPER

An Imprint of HarperCollins*Publishers*
www.harpercollins.com

HarperCollins books may be purchased for educational, business, or sales promotional use. For information, please write: Special Markets Department, HarperCollins Publishers, 10 East 53rd Street, New York, NY 10022.

FIRST EDITION

Grateful acknowledgment for permission to reproduce illustrations is made to the following:

Courtesy of LatinstockMexico/Corbis: page 2 (Martí); page 272 (Péron). Courtesy of the National Library of Uruguay, literary file: page 22 (Rodó). Courtesy of CONACULTA-INAH-MEX; authorized reproduction by Instituto Nacional de Antropología e Historia: page 48 (Vasconcelos). Courtesy of Ricardo Salazar: page 118 (Paz). Courtesy of AFP/Roger Viollet: page 292 (Guevara). Courtesy of Rodrigo Castaño: page 332 (Castro and García Márquez). Courtesy of Fiorella Battistini: page 364 (Vargas Llosa). Courtesy of Notimex: page 404 (Ruiz). Courtesy of AFP/José Uzon: page 432 (Marcos). Courtesy of Reuters: page 450 (Chávez).

Designed by Fritz Metsch

Library of Congress Cataloging-in-Publication Data

Krauze, Enrique.
Redeemers : ideas and power in Latin America / Enrique Krauze; translated by Hank Heifetz and Natasha Wimmer.—1st ed.
p. cm.

ISBN-13: 978-0-06-621473-3 (hard)
ISBN-10: 0-06-621473-4 (hard)
ISBN-13: 978-0-06-093844-4 (pbk.)
ISBN-10: 0-06-093844-7 (pbk.)

1. Intellectuals—Latin America—Biography. 2. Politicians—Latin America—Biography. 3. Revolutionaries—Latin America—Biography. 4. Latin America—Intellectual life—19th century. 5. Latin America—Intellectual life—20th century. 6. Latin America—Politics and government—19th century. 7. Latin America—Politics and government—20th century. 8. Political science—Latin America—History—19th century. 9. Political science—Latin America—History—20th century. 10. Power (Social sciences)—Latin America—History. I. Title.

F1407.K73 2011
980.03—dc22
2010052591

11 12 13 14 15   ov/rrd   10 9 8 7 6 5 4 3 2 1

For Andrea

Contents

PART V

Religion and Rebellion

PART VI

The Postmodern Caudillo

The Revolution has been the great Goddess, the eternal Beloved and the great Whore of poets and novelists.

— OCTAVIO PAZ

Acknowledgments

I am particularly grateful to Hank Heifetz, who was not only the translator of most of this volume but also an editor with whom I closely discussed every section, every idea, and, at times, page and sentence.

I am also grateful to my editor Tim Duggan and to my former editor at HarperCollins, Cass Canfield, Jr., who helped me formulate the first conception of this book; to my friend Leon Wieseltier, who continually aided my work by publishing earlier versions of some of these chapters in *The New Republic*, and to the late, gracious Barbara Epstein, who published me in *The New York Review of Books*.

My thanks also to Julio Hubard, Rafael Lemus, Miruna Achim, Fernando García Ramírez, Humberto Beck, Ricardo Cayuela, Ramón Cota Meza, and Mauricio Rodas, for their help in the research for some of these chapters; to Guillermo Sheridan, who provided an important part of the correspondence of Octavio Paz; to Juan Pedro Viqueira, who was of considerable help in solidifying my views on Chiapas. And to my Venezuelan colleagues Simón Alberto Conzalvi, Germán Carrera Damas, Elías Pino Iturrieta, Teodoro Petkoff, and the recently deceased Manuel Caballero, who taught me the history of their country and have steadily defended, with equal zeal, democracy and truth. And to my Venezuelan friend, the late Alejandro Rossi, who lived and worked for many years in Mexico. Also to Mario Vargas Llosa, for suggesting the title *Redeemers*. And finally, to Gabriel Zaid, for our constant conversation.

Preface

Redeemers is a history of political ideas in Latin America during the late nineteenth and twentieth centuries. It is inspired by Isaiah Berlin's books on Russian thinkers of a somewhat earlier period and Edmund Wilson's mixture of analysis and biography in his *To the Finland Station*. The ideas are my major protagonists but I do not approach them as abstractions. I deal with them as expressed in the lives of human beings for whom—as with Berlin's nineteenth-century Russians—these ideas were developed or adopted with a religious, almost theological seriousness. All these thinkers (and men of action) have their historical importance but I have not included figures who were merely politicians, however powerful, or great writers who never ventured out of their ivory towers. My selection of men (and one woman) is certainly not exhaustive. But they were chosen as representatives of the major themes of Latin American politics. There are great differences among them but this variety is in itself one of my subjects, because the ideas that have formed the modern Latin American political mind arose from a broad and highly varied range of human beings. And they are all figures whose lives were marked by a passion for power, literature, history, and revolution and, for the most part, by love, friendship, and family. Real lives, not walking ideas. The course of Latin American political speculation has been like traffic in two directions on the giant highway of time, from nineteenth-century liberalism toward revolutionary commitments and then back toward modern, more democratic versions of liberal thought. (The word "liberal" in Latin America has a traditional meaning somewhat different from its American usage. The nineteenth-century Liberals, as opposed to the Conservatives, favored individual liberties and democracy, the separation of church and state, freedom of commerce, and gradual social reforms. The liberal route was the foundation—at least in theory and values—of the original Latin American states.)

The religious overtones of the title are intentional. In Latin America, the religious background that stems from an overwhelmingly Catholic culture has always suffused its political reality with moral categories and paradigms. The prophets in my first section (though they all had some religious beliefs) were essentially proponents of important secular ideas. The four Josés (the Cuban Martí, the Uruguayan Rodó, the Mexican Vasconcelos, the Peruvian Mariátegui) configure the revolutionary vocation of the continent with an apostolic zeal and a spirit of sacrifice that arose from a culture intent on the salvation (and domination) of the Indians, established in the sixteenth century by the missionary fathers. These four men were like a torch passed from hand to hand, changing its nature but not its fire as it moved along, from the quandary of the republican Martí (who tried to persuade the United States to abandon its imperial designs on the countries of "our America") to the Hispano-American nationalism of Rodó (whose book *Ariel*, stimulated by the trauma of the Spanish-American War, marked a multiple shift in the intellectual history of our countries), to the cultural crusade of Vasconcelos, which spread from Mexico throughout Latin America, to the highly original vanguard Marxist and indigenist Mariátegui. All of these men believed in the communion between reader and author through the written word. As intellectuals they were not professors (though Rodó was more so than the others) but made their ordinary living as writers and editors of magazines and books.

As a young man, Octavio Paz wanted to be a "redeemer" and a "hero" and thought that the liberal and democratic order, irremediably lost in the Great War, could be reestablished on morally superior foundations, through socialist revolution. His embrace of Marxism in the year 1930 (Mariátegui would die in the same year) was an intermediate stage for him but also a natural continuation of the lives of his grand-father, the Liberal, Ireneo Paz, and his father, Octavio Paz Solórzano, a follower of Emiliano Zapata. In the 1930s, much of the Latin American intelligentsia moved strongly to the left, in repudiation of fascism and through a natural sympathy with the embattled Republic in the Spanish Civil War. The alternative of liberal democracy seemed out-of-date. But in Paz's later years (across more than two decades during which I worked very closely with him), he would rediscover it. I treat him at considerable length in this book, using him as a kind of central spine and reference, because he intellectually confronted, for and against, most of the major revolutions of the twentieth century. His books and essays, and the various journals he founded and directed, are fundamental chapters in the intellectual and cultural history of modern Mexico and often of Latin America. His personal and family history is very much a voyage, of going and coming on that highway of ideas, from democratic liberalism to the Mexican Revolution, from the Mexican Revolution to the Russian, from the Russian Revolution back to the Mexican and then back to democratic liberalism. And though Paz took strong anticlerical positions, Christianity is also one of the keys to understanding his trajectory.

The shadow of Plutarch's *Parallel Lives* presides over the next sections. The ideas of my first four prophets and the themes of Octavio Paz weave in and out of their lives. The first pair are secular saints, whose images live on in the collective memory of Latin America and much of the world: the meteoric careers of the former actress Eva Perón and the archetypal twentieth-century guerrilla fighter, Che Guevara. In the second pair of lives, I discuss our two greatest contemporary novelists, the Colombian Gabriel García Márquez and the Peruvian Mario Vargas Llosa, focusing on their very different viewpoints around the classical theme of Latin American dictatorship. Next I consider the marriage of theology and revolutionary liberation in the lives of two Mexican redeemers of the Indians: the late bishop of Chiapas, Samuel Ruiz, and Subcomandante Marcos, the guerrilla in the mask.

And finally, appearing alone, is a complicated figure, a mélange of influences, Hugo Chávez of Venezuela, who is trying to turn the history of his country into his personal biography. He is not a man of ideas but neither is he a man without ideas. He is an authoritarian Latin American leader, a *caudillo*. He is not primarily (though he may seem so) a vulgar *caudillo* but, more precisely, a leader for the modern mass media age, a preacher, a redeemer through television or Twitter, a post-modern *caudillo*, a product of the curious Latin American devotion to the idea of the "Great Man" derived in large part from the Scotsman Thomas Carlyle.

Redemption or democracy? This is still the central dilemma of Latin America. Most of our peoples and countries seem to have chosen democracy, a return to the republican and liberal origins of these countries. But if it is to last, democracy in Latin America must have a clear and effective social vocation. If it does not, the region will begin to return to a search for redemption, with all the suffering that may move along that road.

On the Translation

Redeemers is translated from the Spanish by Hank Heifetz (including all poems and prose selections presented in Spanish, even if drawn from another language, except of course for citations in the original English), but the following exceptions should be noted.

The chapter on García Márquez appears essentially in a translation by Natasha Wimmer. It has been somewhat edited and revised by the author and by Hank Heifetz (and includes a small amount of new material).

The chapter on Hugo Chávez contains substantial material (especially at the beginning, though revised and with a number of additions) from an earlier translation by Wimmer, as does the chapter on Subcomandante Marcos and a portion (also edited) of the chapter on Vargas Llosa.

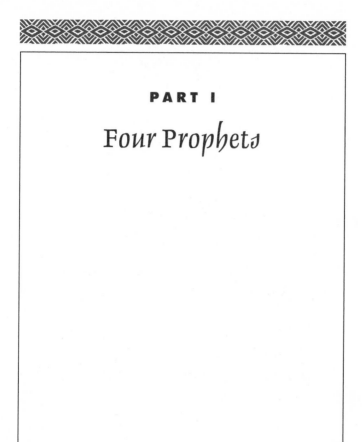

PART I

Four Prophets

1

José Martí

THE MARTYRDOM OF THE LIBERATOR

The history of the modern ideas of revolution in Latin America begins with the life, work, and martyrdom of a New Yorker named José Martí. He was born in 1853 in Cuba, an island that, along with other islands (Puerto Rico and the Philippines), was the last bastion of the Spanish Empire. Both of his parents were Spanish. His father, from Valencia, was a sergeant in the army and his mother had been born in the Canary Islands. He had endured poverty as a child and exile since his adolescence. "I have learned how to suffer," he wrote from the prison of La Criolla, at the age of sixteen, to Rafael María de Mendive, a teacher who had inspired his political awakening. Martí's prison time was spent at hard labor in a quarry, which left him with a permanent and often painful inguinal hernia for the rest of his life. His precocious commitment to the cause of Cuban independence had landed him behind bars. Some months earlier, he had expressed his newfound faith in a one-act drama, adolescent in style, premonitory for its content. In *Abdala*, a Nubian warrior confronts the Egyptian Empire for the purpose of redeeming his people:

> *I am Nubian! All my people*
> *await me, to defend their liberty!*
> *A foreign people treads our land*
> *and threatens us with vile slavery;*
> *they boldly display their powerful pikes*
> *and honor commands us and God commands us*

to die for the fatherland, rather than see it
a cowardly slave to the barbarous oppressor!

And with his mother, Espirta, Abdala debates a vital question: What is the deepest kind of love?

ESPIRTA: And is that love greater than what your mother awakens in your breast?
ABDALA: Perhaps you believe there is something more sublime than the fatherland?

Abdala's words would resound along the course of Martí's life. They would be an essential part of his myth, but the myth would also obscure the luminous side of his personality, as a masterful poet; a bold, original, and surefooted writer of prose; a man of limitless energy and curiosity and a heart overflowing with creative delight and love, above all love.

Deported to Madrid, he took a degree in law and published *El presidio político en Cuba* (The Political Prison in Cuba), demonstrating that freedom of speech was much greater in Spain itself than in its American colony. He wrote a poem on the execution of medical students in Cuba falsely accused of subversion and, when the first Spanish Republic was proclaimed in 1873, a prose piece titled *La República Española ante la revolución cubana* (The Spanish Republic Compared to the Cuban Revolution), referring to the failed Cuban revolt of 1868. And there for the first time he applied his idea of the Republic and his conception of liberty to the criticism of imperial domination:

And if Cuba proclaims its independence through the same right that the Republic has proclaimed itself, how can the Republic deny Cuba its right to freedom, the very same it has exercised in order to exist? How can the Republic deny itself to itself? How can it dispose of the fate of a people, imposing a condition upon it where its complete and free and most evident will does not enter?

The words impressively anticipate the statements of American anti-imperialists in 1898—men like Carl Schurz, William James, and Mark Twain—faced with the American annexationist war in Cuba and the occupation of the Philippines. A republic cannot suffocate another republic, without denying its own essence. The idea of the Republic is a constant refrain in Martí's concept of revolution. From 1873 on, he would always be a classic republican, committed to democracy, to civilian (not military) rule, and a sworn enemy of tyranny and personalist power (*caudillismo*).

His concept of revolution was a legacy of the American Revolution and the later Latin American wars of independence against Spain. Years later Martí would write, with passion and sympathy, about the Martyrs of Chicago (the execution of innocent anarchists after the "Haymarket Riot," when a bomb-throwing incident in 1886 killed a policeman). And earlier, in 1883, he mourned, discreetly, the death of Karl Marx, but never applying partisan terms nor the concept of revolution itself that would later become common usage. And he would use the occasion to warn against violence:

> Karl Marx is dead. He deserves honor, because he stood with the weak. But he does not do well who points to harm and burns with generous anxiety to relieve it, but rather he who teaches a gentle remedy for that hurt. The task of launching men against men is frightening. Turning some men into beasts for the good of others is unworthy. But one has to find an outlet for indignation so that the beast may halt in its tracks, before it leaps, and be frightened away.

Until the moment (in 1882) when he chose to settle down in New York City, Martí was a wandering Cuban across "great America." He was a short, slender man, with a passionate and hyperactive temperament. He considered living in Mexico or Guatemala, where he wrote for journals, gave lectures, and collected admiration and fame. In both countries he left loyal friends, evasive or enamored women (one who languished and died when he moved on), but he left both countries behind, disdaining their dictators or their local luminaries, men always uneasy with the presence of a man without a country who proclaimed himself the citizen of a greater country, the "country of America." Martí then thought he might go to Honduras or to Peru. "It's very hard, wandering this way, from land to land, with so much anguish in my soul," but in that same soul a certainty "was seething": "In my head I carry my unhappy people and it seems to me that one day their freedom will depend on a breath from me."

In Mexico, he met (and would later marry) Carmen Zayas-Bazán, a Cuban of aristocratic descent. And Martí decided to return to Cuba with her. It was a discreet return, using only his middle name and his matronymic as a semi-pseudonym (he would enter Cuba as Julián Pérez). He tried, briefly, to settle into his native land, where his son, José Francisco, was born in November 1878. But the call of his conscience drew him rapidly into conspiracy against the government and he was deported again to Spain, where he remained very briefly.

In 1880 he came to New York and began to solicit funds for a second Cuban attempt at independence, the so-called "Little War" (*La Guerra Chiquita*). With a force of twenty-five men, General Calixto García set sail for Cuba, only to meet with another defeat. Martí remained in New York, as interim president of the Cuban Revolutionary Committee.

He was living at 51 East Twenty-ninth Street, in the home of Manuel Mantilla, a Cuban exile who was very ill and would die a few years later. With Mantilla were his wife, María Miyares, a Venezuelan, and their two children. When his own wife and son arrived from Cuba, Martí rented a house in Brooklyn. But Carmen never comprehended nor came to terms with her husband's political passion (her father thought he was a "*loco*"). In October she returned to Cuba. One month later, María Miyares de Mantilla gave birth to a daughter she named María. Her father was not Manuel but José Martí, who became the girl's godfather. Martí then spent a brief time in Venezuela, María's native land, where he founded an ephemeral publication (the *Revista Venezolana*) and announced "I am a son of America . . . Give me, Venezuela, a way to serve you; in me she will have a son." But the supremely vain Venezuelan president, Antonio Guzmán Blanco (disgruntled because Martí had not mentioned him in a public speech), decided to expel him. Martí returned to New York. His mother requested, his wife demanded that he come back to Cuba. He would write to Carmen,

> You say I should come back. If it meant dying when I arrive, I would gladly give up my life! I don't have to force myself to go, but rather to not go back . . . That you don't value it [Martí's political work], that I know. But I don't have to commit the injustice of asking you to value a grandeur that is merely spiritual, secret and unproductive. . .

It was a marital tension that could not be resolved: Carmen did not understand his mission and would never support it.

The contours of the drama were established. Exiled from his country in order to serve the revolution, estranged from his wife and bereft of the son he adored, consoled by his secret affair with a married woman and walks in the park with his "goddaughter," Martí would live only thirteen years more. Carmen and his son, José Francisco, would still alternate long periods in Cuba with time in New York until the final break in August 1891, after which he would never see his son again. All through that decade he would lessen his personal anguish with the dedicated passion of his work, as an active strategist, ideologue, orator, prophet, and, in the end, moral *caudillo* of the Cuban independence movement. He would publish short, beautiful books of poetry. He would translate novels, edit books and journals; and he would let himself be carried away by a voracious desire to understand and make others understand the marvels of this strange and dizzying city that had accepted him.

New York was now his home, or at least his home away from home. Dealing with this environment into which he had settled, "struggling to dominate the beautiful and rebellious English language," Martí would become the innovator, in Spanish, of the journalistic column in the form of an extended letter. As he wrote to Bartolomé Mitre, editor of the major Argentine newspaper, *La Nación*, he wanted to write from New York neither to denounce nor to praise but to offer a lively and intelligent vantage point from which to observe a reality that was important for Latin Americans to understand.

Everything astonished him. His copious accounts are a primary source for the study of a decade of life in the United States, not only of the transition from a more or less peaceful application of the Monroe Doctrine to active and militarily aggressive imperialism but also and mainly about everyday matters and national events: the trial of President Garfield's assassin, the inauguration of President Cleveland (and the trousseau of his fiancée), the opening of the Brooklyn Bridge, the bustle of a Sunday at Coney Island, the fashions of Fifth Avenue, diversions (dances, sleigh rides, regattas, boxing matches, baseball games), the crimes and criminals of New York, the death of Jesse James, the wonderful bouillabaisse served by Madame Taurel in Hanover Square, which was then the center of the financial district; art exhibitions, openings of plays, details of the Oklahoma land boom and the wars out west against the Sioux. And in one of these long epistolary pieces, written for *La Nación* in 1886, on the installation of the Statue of Liberty in New York Bay, he writes the kind of encomium that generations of immigrants would feel, though less eloquently, as their ships slowed down to enter the great harbor of the Land of Hope:

> There she is finally, on her pedestal higher than the towers, magnificent as the tempest and as kind as the sky! Any dry eyes in her presence once again learn what tears are. It seemed that souls were opening and flying up to shelter themselves in the folds of her tunic, whisper in her ears, settle on her shoulders to die, like butterflies in the light! She seemed alive; smoke from the steamboats enveloped her: a vague clarity crowned her. She was truly like an altar, with the steamboats kneeling at her feet! . . . She has been created by all the skill of the universe, as freedom is created from all the sufferings of men.

He saw the faults and the virtues of the Colossus of the North. And the dangers for Latin America. The overwhelming emphasis on money did not seem to him "a sound basis for a nation, this exclusive love, vehement and uneasy, for material fortune that ruins people here, or polishes them only on one side, giving them the appearance of being simultaneously colossi and children." And stemming from these values, "a cluster of avaricious thinkers" yearned for expansion at the cost of the territories of "our America." Certainly it seemed to him that it was "a deeply painful thing to see a turtledove die at the hands of an ogre." But one should not confuse "a circle of ultra-'eagleites' [*aguilistas*—a word Martí coined from the symbol of the eagle and applied to American chauvinists]" with the thought of a "heterogeneous, hard-working, conservative people, occupied with itself, and because of these same varied strengths, well-balanced." And faced with the cultural inertia of Spain in America, Martí felt an urgent need to explain the United States "to bring into the light all its magnificent qualities, and to highlight, with all its positive strengths, this splendid struggle of men."

For a decade, Martí's columns appeared every week in *La Nación* and later in as many as twenty Latin American newspapers. Although he was an electrifying speaker, the orator's quality of rousing rhetoric barely appears in his articles. An observation he made in 1881, about a single interesting word, reflects his sense of the proper style for his innovative journalism: "The bare word, vigorous, colloquial, natural, colorful, the sincere word, candid, simple, the word 'yankee,' this was the word used by Henry Ward Beecher." And, in fact, it was in New York that Martí began to change the language of Latin American Spanish, shifting away from what he termed metaphors replete with "suffering and victimhood," expressions like "to write our history with blood," toward descriptions and structures that rely on demonstrative logic. In the North American press and literature he discovered a freedom without fear and without the need to harangue. Speaking up, writing, publishing cease to be merely forms of rebellion and become a profession, "lively, simple, useful, human conversation," a public discussion. Martí has stopped thinking in abstract terms or delivering lessons from on high. He speaks directly with the reader. He pours the old wine of the highest Spanish literary tradition (the poets and dramatists of the sixteenth and seventeenth centuries, the Golden Age, which he knew in vivid detail from his period in Spain) into the new wineskins of North American journalism. Viewed from that perspective, Martí was the first modern writer of Latin America.

And not only as a journalist. Devoted as he was to the cause of Cuban liberation, Martí had no conscious, aesthetic intention of renovating the language but he did just that through three channels: his columns, his books of poetry, and his letters. Journalism in the Spanish language had never before reached the artistic level Martí achieved and his best-known book of poetry, *Ismaelillo*, predated and anticipated, by nearly a decade, the first modernist currents of poetry in Spanish.

The fifteen poems of *Ismaelillo* (published in 1882) are inspired by the deprivation he felt after the departure for Cuba of his son, known affectionately as Pepito. The language is simple, elegant, totally free of nineteenth-century romantic rhetoric yet threaded with sudden, often surprising images, looking forward to modernism and back to the Spanish poets of the seventeenth-century Golden Age (*El Siglo de Oro*). Not only his absent and longed-for son, but his quest for political and expressive freedom enter into the verses:

> *The air is inhabited*
> *by diminutive eagles:*
> *They are ideas soaring up,*
> *their prisons shattered!*

Yet everywhere (perhaps even with the choice of a word like "diminutive") a remembered infant pervades the brief, influential collection:

> *Is what swathes him*
> *flesh or mother-of-pearl?*

His laugh, as if in a cup
of Arabian onyx,
bubbles up in triumph
on his unmarred chest
Here you are! pale bone
here! alive and everlasting!
I am the son of my son!
It is he who renews me!

The Spanish philosopher Miguel de Unamuno—who compared José Martí to the high priest of Italian unification, Giuseppe Mazzini—said about Martí that he was "a man of feeling as much or more than a man of thought." In Martí's letters (to friends and political partisans, and which were published years after his death) Unamuno saw the mark of two illustrious Spanish predecessors in letter-writing as art—the Roman Seneca and St. Teresa de Ávila.

New York would always both fascinate and disturb him. Writing to his most frequent correspondent, the Mexican Manuel Mercado, Martí would say, "Everything binds me to New York, at least through some years of my life; everything binds me to this cup of poison." Distant from his family and not drawn to the provocative life available to a man alone in the great city, he had to work at meagerly paid and uninspiring jobs for various business houses. The idea of becoming an editor offered him a hope for improving his life, a possibility that seemed to flow naturally from his positive evaluation of the work ethic that surrounded him. He would write, "Here a good idea always finds welcoming, soft, fertile ground. One must be intelligent, that is all. Do something useful and you will have everything you want. Doors are shut for those who are dull and lazy; life is secure for those who obey the law of work." Martí saw himself as someone who could translate North American culture for Latin Americans and build a bridge of understanding between the two Americas. He had been surprised to see (like the Argentine Sarmiento on his travels in 1847) that everybody here seemed to read, and he thought of inspiring a broader spectrum of

Latin Americans to adopt the same practice. He had done a brief stint as editor of a scientific journal (*La América*, where he had published pieces on the advantages of some types of fertilizer and the excellence of certain cheeses). Based on this limited experience, he floated a plan in 1886 to establish, with some of his Mexican friends, "a noble and extensive American enterprise" that would publish "cheap and useful books . . . human and highly topical, to instill character and prepare people for practical work."

Martí's attempt to create a publishing venture for all Latin America, beginning with Mexico, coincided with a parenthesis in the urgency (though never in the commitment) of his political activity. In the middle of the 1880s, after two failed attempts to overthrow the Spanish colonial government, Martí advised his followers to wait until internal Cuban conditions could mature to a point when the revolutionaries might be received with sympathy and efficiency—to ensure that a war would be conducted with minimum suffering and maximum benevolence, setting the stage for a free and harmonious republic. He was especially disturbed by the personalist *caudillismo* of the men who had led the two previous wars, Antonio Maceo and Máximo Gómez. He had come to know both of them in 1882 in New York. In 1884, he had written to Gómez:

> But there is something beyond any personal sympathy that you can inspire in me . . . and it is my determination not to contribute—through blind love of an idea that dominates my life—even an iota toward bringing a regime of personal despotism to my land, which would be more shameful and ill-fated than the political despotism it now endures, and graver and more difficult to uproot, because it will arrive with the excuse of certain values, embellished by the ideas it would incarnate, and legitimized by triumph . . . The fatherland belongs to no one and if it does—this only in spirit—it will be his who serves it with the greatest detachment and intelligence . . . [Such a person] might very likely be you,

or it might not be you. To respect a people who love us and place their hopes on us, is the height of grandeur. To make use of their suffering and their enthusiasm for one's own private benefit; that would be the height of ignominy.

His project for producing "cheap and useful books" is never accepted by his Mexican friends. They see no possible market for the venture. Nor does he succeed in getting a Mexican publisher for his translation of the novel *Ramona* by Helen Hunt Jackson, even though "it is a good book, on a Mexican theme." The parenthesis of relative political inactivity has begun to close. On the tenth of October 1886, a day on which the Cuban community honored the outbreak of the first unsuccessful war against Spain, Martí returns to giving public speeches, and his words circulate through the Cuban community from New York to Florida. His office at 120 Front Street becomes a meeting place not only for Cubans but for other Latin Americans: "it's come to be like a stock market of nations." In 1887, his father, the former Spanish army sergeant, dies; Martí admits to having never understood him. To his oldest Cuban friend he writes: "I will die here, Fermín, without being able to put this ardent activity to use, other than indirectly and unhappily." He meant of course his dedication to the freedom of Cuba: "The truth is . . . I live now only for my country."

Martí had long been impressed with the writings of Ralph Waldo Emerson and the poetry of Walt Whitman. Like both of these writers (but especially Whitman) he was a man of insight and emotion, not a builder of systems. But both Americans contributed to what became one of Martí's central tenets: freedom is a resource you must secure for yourself. No one else can give it to an individual or to a nation. For Cuba he was concerned (at least as much as for its freedom) with creating conditions that would permit his country to govern itself democratically. And he gave his opinion (in a letter to his friend Gonzalo de Quesada in 1889) on the proposal of José Ignacio Rodríguez for a negotiated and peaceful grant of independence mediated by the United States:

... it is guided by the confidence, for me impossible, that the nation
that has need of us (for reasons of geography, strategy, property
and politics) will pull us out of the hands of the Spanish government and then give us our freedom, so that we may conserve what
we did not acquire and that we could use against the interests of
those who have granted it to us. Confidence of this kind is a generous feeling but as for its being rational, I cannot concur . . . And
once the United States is in Cuba, who will get them out of there?

For Martí there were four problems to be addressed: the danger
of *caudillismo*; the methods for winning independence; the pressure
toward annexing Cuba to the United States, favored by some Cubans as
well as North Americans; and finally the general attitude of the United
States toward the island. Martí was compelled to discuss, analyze, and
mediate between various, conflicting forces. He knew very well that
the Cubans were confronting a bureaucratic Spanish Empire, sclerotic
and tyrannous, under whose reign there were no citizens but only subjects. Yet Martí would insist that the struggle was for independence, not
a war against the Spaniards: "We Cubans began the war and we and
the Spaniards will finish it. Let them not maltreat us and we will not
maltreat them. Let them show respect and we will respect them. Steel
responds to steel, friendship to friendship."

The American press was beginning to discuss the pros and cons of
annexing Cuba. On the island, many well-off Cubans approved of the
idea. Annexation, they believed, would transform them into large-
scale businessmen and vastly enhance the value of their landholdings.
(They pointed to the example of Texas, where a few decades earlier,
barren and unused Mexican land had become highly valued American properties.) The rumors kept spreading, under the growing influence of the "yellow press" powered by William Randolph Hearst,
the newspaper mogul who could perhaps create a war. Martí immediately recognized the importance of a public discussion. In a letter
to New York's *Evening Post* on March 21, 1889, titled "A Vindication of

Cuba," he spoke up for Cuban workers in the United States and their love of freedom:

> They admire this nation, the greatest that freedom has ever established; but they do not trust the disastrous elements that, like worms in the blood, have begun their work of destruction in this marvelous Republic. They have made the heroes of this country their own heroes and they yearn for the ultimate success of the North-American Union as the greatest glory of humanity; but they cannot honorably believe that the excessive individualism, the adoration of wealth and the prolonged jubilation over a terrible victory are preparing the United States to become the nation that typifies freedom, which must be a country without opinions based on the immoderate appetite for power or acquisition or triumphs that are opposed to goodness and justice.

Confronted with the new ideology of American expansionism ("We are the Romans of this continent," said the jurist Oliver Wendell Holmes), Martí, always a prudent man, was shedding his original admiration. At first he felt estranged, then wounded, betrayed, trampled by a monster. And he did not know how to reconcile the irreconcilable. The United States had accepted him as an equal, a free man within its public life (an unaccustomed welcome for the wanderer), but the machinery of power was priming to crush his dream of a fatherland without even taking it into account. They seemed about to concede Cuba an existence within a North American agenda but to absolutely ignore the Cuban point of view. "What almost pulls the ground out from under my feet is the danger I see of my land falling bit by bit into hands that must stifle it." And not only Cuba had to endure this affliction but also "peoples of the same origin and composition as mine."

In July 1889, a remarkable monthly journal began to appear, directed by Martí. It was called *La Edad de Oro* (The Golden Age) and was his final attempt at salvation through the culture of the printed word. The magazine published stories, parables, poems, and other writings of interest to children. But it lasted only four issues, until Martí rejected his sponsor's insistence on including religious themes. By then, thoughts of departure and death reappeared, as in the poem to his friend and fellow militant Serafín Sánchez:

> . . . as if there had entered within me
> Storms of silence, precursor
> Of that much greater silence
> Where all of us are equal. . .
> And after baking the bread
> With the pain of every day,
> The pen gone dead in my hand,
> I enfold myself in the hurricane . . .
> And about me I have to tell you
> That in proceeding I am serene.
> Without fear of thunder or lightning,
> I am preparing the future.

His pronouncements also grew in intensity, disappointment, and anger: " . . . the United States, instead of strengthening its democracy and saving itself from the hatred and misery of monarchies, is growing corrupt and diminishing democracy; and hate and misery, with all their menace, are reborn." At the beginning of 1891, he would write "Our America," the cornerstone of Latin Americanism in the twentieth century.

He began the piece with a statement of pride in what Latin America had achieved, countries that "with their silent masses of Indians" had advanced to create "compact and progressive nations." But the future did not lie in imitating the United States or following the fashionable patterns of French-inspired thought. "You cannot parry a weapon thrust at a plainsman's horse with a decree from Alexander Hamilton. A sentence from Sieyès [the philosopher of constitutionalism in the revolutionary and Napoleonic eras] will not loosen the clotted blood of the

Indian race . . . Neither the European nor the Yankee book hold the key to the Latin-American enigma." Martí now uses the word *yanqui* with a new negative weight. He still feels that the form of a republic is "the logical government" but now he adds, "If the republic does not open its arms to everyone and move forward for the benefit of everyone, the republic will die."

In April 1892, he joined with other Cuban leaders in founding the Cuban Revolutionary Party. Among them was Máximo Gómez, the general to whom Martí had written his letter rejecting *caudillismo*. (Gómez was a Dominican who had joined the cause of Cuban liberation, just as many Latin Americans would transcend national boundaries to enter revolutionary movements in the twentieth century.) The party's statement of basic principles, written by Martí, contained a commitment to "the absolute independence of the Island of Cuba" and support for the independence of Puerto Rico. The necessary war for independence must be brief and "generous"; all factions must unite to create, "through a war of the spirit using republican methods," a durable nation that would attend to the well-being of its citizens and be "duly conscious of its difficult . . . geographical situation." And after winning the war, the party was not to stay in power and mimic "the authoritarian spirit and bureaucratic composition of the Colony" but encourage the development of "a new country, sincerely democratic," aware of the need for a "balance of social forces" and "the dangers of sudden freedom in a society created by slavery."

Toward the United States, Martí does not preach hatred, nor does he show any ideological prejudice against the country that had been his home for thirteen years. Because he knew them well, he writes to warn the Americans, not to attack them. North American ignorance and greed are the problems; they must be replaced by respect for Latin America.

Martí is not yet forty years old but his letters are full of thoughts of his mortality and of the impending war. With the formation of the party, he resigned his various positions as consul in New York for Uruguay, Argentina, and Paraguay and as president of the Hispanic Literary Society. He began to travel widely again, pursuing economic and political support for the revolutionary venture. He went to the Cuban communities of Florida, then to the Caribbean, Central America, and Mexico, where the perpetual president Porfirio Díaz himself would donate twenty thousand pesos to his cause. In March 1895, along with General Gómez, who would lead the expeditionary force, Martí would sign and issue, from the Dominican Republic, the famous Manifesto of Montecristi. More than a declaration of war, it was a preliminary plan for the future constitution of the Republic of Cuba. And he sent a letter (to the Dominican writer Federico Henríquez y Carvajal) that is often considered his political testament:

> . . . it will never be triumph but agony and duty. My blood is burning. Now is the time to give respect and a human feeling to sacrifice, to make war viable and indelible . . . I will rouse the world. But my single desire would be to stand firm there, cling-ing to the last trunk . . . the last fighter: to die in silence. For me the hour has come.

In his letters and poems, Martí says good-bye to almost everyone. A few, stern lines to his son. Nothing to his wife. To his mother, a sen-tence almost identical to the conclusion of his adolescent drama *Abdala*: "You mourn, with the anger of your love, the sacrifice of my life; and why did you give birth to me as a life in love with sacrifice?" To my "very good Carmita," the elder daughter of María Miyares, he says that he loves her as if she were his own daughter and urges her to care for her mother and her brother. And he writes to "my María," his own natural child who was then fourteen, and takes the time to advise her on scientific readings, and offer some subtle thoughts on the essence of love and practical ideas about her possible future vocation. He counsels her to put her trust in language: "Learn from me. I have life on one side of the table, death on the other, and my people on my shoulders: and see how many pages I am writing!" At the end of his letter, he asks her to feel "cleansed and weightless, like the light" and "if you never see me again . . . place a book . . . on my tomb. Or on your breast, because there

I will be buried if I die somewhere that men will not discover. Work. A kiss. And hope for me."

On April 1, 1895, a boat sailed for Cuba from the Dominican Republic, carrying leaders of the Cuban Revolutionary Party, including the writer and former New Yorker José Martí. The exiles landed on April 11 and connected with resistance forces on the island. José Martí began his war. For others it would go on for years, till the Americans invaded in 1898 and Spain was finally defeated. For Martí it lasted little more than a month. He had time to reencounter the beautiful island he had yearned to see again. It was an epiphany for him, and his *Diary* was a literary consecration of the experience. He sees and names and re-creates the natural world and the Cuban people and their customs in memorable and moving detail.

His death was due to a mixture of military ineptitude, foolhardy bravery (he may have been intent on refuting slurs about his lack of fighting experience), and the abandonment to the prospect of a martyr's death clearly evident in his writings. He had a special guard assigned to him (his name was Ángel de la Guardia, literally "guardian angel") but he did not listen to his warnings. On May 19, at Dos Ríos, where two rivers meet, he moved ahead of the rebel troop emplacement and, with only one man mounted beside him, charged a small squad of Spanish soldiers. They shot him off his horse. A Cuban "mulatto" serving as scout for the Spanish army came upon his dying body and recognizing him, cried out, "You here, Don Martí!" The scout then gave him the coup de grâce. The Spaniards moved forward to empty his pockets, loosely bury the body, and then dig it up and bury it again after confirming the identification. All his life, Martí had expected, even craved such a death that could be the beginning of redemption for himself and for his people.

On the day before he was killed, he had written a letter—one more that would become famous—to his close friend Manuel Mercado:

> Every day now I am in danger of giving my life for my country and for my duty . . . to prevent in good time, with the independence

of Cuba, the United States spreading across the Antilles and falling, strengthened by its conquests, on our territories of America.
What I have done up to now, and will do, is for that [purpose]
. . . to prevent—through annexation by those imperialists and the
Spaniards—a road opening up in Cuba, one that has to be sealed
off—and we are sealing it off with our blood—toward the annexation of our peoples of America to the turbulent and brutal North
that has contempt for us . . . I have lived inside the monster and I
understand its entrails—and my sling is that of David.

A few years later, in the streets of Havana, a song of mourning, in
the syncopated Afro-Cuban rhythm of the clave, began to be heard:

> *Martí, he should not have died*
> *Ay, his dying!*
> *If Martí had not died*
> *a different rooster would crow,*
> *the fatherland would be saved*
> *and Cuba would be happy.*
> *Martí should not have died!*
> *Ay, his dying!*

In his future as a myth, Martí had not died. Nor would he ever
die. His body now rests in the Santa Ifigenia Cemetery in Santiago de
Cuba. Before 1959, all Cubans remembered him as the redeemer who
gave his life for the independence of the island, which was accomplished according to some, partial or thwarted according to many
others. After 1959, the revolutionaries in power claimed him as one
of their own. They saw themselves as the new "sling of David" and
believed they had completed his work. Many in the growing body of
Cuban exiles focused on his warning that a *caudillo* could overthrow
a tyranny "to replace it, through all the prestige of triumph, with his
own." They also saw themselves in the mirror of that man in constant
exile, who had labored for the independence of Cuba. In a sense he

belongs to them both, the redeemers and those who reject their version of redemption. And he belongs, with great distinction, to the history of Spanish literature.

Martí had initiated the new era of revolutionary thought in Latin America. Other, and different, voices would soon be heard.

2

José Enrique Rodó

THE HISPANIC-AMERICAN HOMILY

The first ideologue of Latin American nationalism was a taciturn Uruguayan man of letters named José Enrique Rodó. Born in 1871, he was the son of a Catalan businessman wealthy enough to own a house in the colonial quarter of Montevideo. He began his education by reading in his father's extensive library of Latin, Spanish, and Hispanic-American classics. In a certain sense, he never left that library.

The walls of his natural reserve would grow even higher as the family's fortunes declined and, when already an adult, additional financial setbacks were inflicted upon him. According to all reports, he remained stubbornly single, distant, and spectral, close only and always to his mother and his brothers. And though in time he would enter the heated realm of politics, his ideal would always be the cultivation of "the divine religion of thought."

As a high school boy in the Elbio Fernández Lyceum, he did his first critical writing. He was already dealing with themes that would pervade his later work, like the cult of heroes, then represented for him by Bolívar and, curiously, also by Benjamin Franklin. The death of his father, in 1885, began some anxious years for Rodó. He broke off his studies and took jobs like that of a secretary in the office of a notary public, or as a clerk in a bank that specialized in cashing checks. Turning back to the university, he earned the highest distinction in literary studies but never finished the work for a degree. Finally, in 1895, he founded a journal, the *Revista Nacional de Literatura y Ciencias Sociales* (National Review of Literature and Social Sciences), dedicated to "shaking loose the stagnation in which for the moment the living forces are mired" of Uruguayan intellectual activity. In his journal, Rodó writes literary criticism, exhumes and interprets Spanish and Latin American classics, and exhibits the first, broader aesthetic tendencies of his thoughts.

The civil war in his country mattered less to him than his own emotional crises. In 1897 he wrote to a friend, "When the resonance of battle overwhelmed hearts with grief or electrified them with enthusiasm, mine was weighed down with anxieties far removed from the struggle of the parties and barely shared the interest and emotion of others." In that same year, his journal ceased publication: "Every one of us is a fragment of a great corpse. As for me, the disappointments, the rude experiences, the bitter tastes of life have always had the value of fortifying my devotion to art and study, where low, miserable things do not reach." In 1898 the victorious Colorado Party offered him a guaranteed employment in the Office of Military Appraisals. With resignation, Rodó accepted that "desperate recourse that we term a public employment in our country." In the same year, he was named an interim university professor of literature (he gave a course in intellectual history that ranged from Plato to Spencer) and also accepted an interim post as director of the National Library. One of his contemporaries described him then as "a tall young man, quite thin . . . who moved stiffly, his arms dangling, his hands open—flaccid and dead hands that felt as cold as something inanimate when shaken . . . and if there was anything circumspect about him, it was his forehead, a broad forehead, that seemed even broader because he used to brush his hair straight back; a smooth cold forehead, behind which there already nested thoughts that were his own, haughty, the will of a *conquistador*, self-absorbed and serene."

Suddenly, at the end of the century, two events rattled him, one for the better, one for the worse. A maternal aunt left him a substantial inheritance and the United States defeated Spain in the Spanish-American War. The war angered and saddened him. As the son of a Catalan émigré, he loved Spain though, as a Latin American, he was in favor of Cuban independence. But a humiliated Spain, a Cuba that seemed only to have changed its master—Rodó hated both results. And he responded with a small book that was really a moral homily directed to Latin American youth. He called it *Ariel* and it would change the ideological history of Hispanic America to such a degree that it was still required reading in Latin American secondary schools when the son of a Galician soldier defeated in that war, Fidel Castro, triumphantly entered Havana to close, in various ways, the cycle initiated in 1898.

For the government of the United States and ample sectors of public opinion, the skirmish at the end of the century seemed to confirm a Destiny that was not only Manifest (the program for American expansion formulated in 1839) but clearly manifested, first in the war against Mexico of 1846–48 and then again, a half century later, in the war against Spain. Only rags were left of the worn-out Spanish Empire, and the United States, with humiliating ease, proceeded to reorder the map of the world. The Philippines and the islands of Guam, Cuba, and Puerto Rico changed hands, from the dominant naval power of the sixteenth century to the dominant naval power of the twentieth century. They were no longer colonies, now they were "protectorates."

Not all Americans were convinced by the new nomenclature. In that critical year of 1898, as America followed the exhortations of William Randolph Hearst into its war against Spain, Mark Twain founded the Anti-Imperialist League of the United States. With his sharpened weapon of irony, the great writer fought against the menace he saw in his country's transformation into an empire: "And as for a flag for the Philippine Province, it is easily managed. We can have a special one— our States do it: we can have just our usual flag, with the white stripes painted black and the stars replaced by the skull and cross-bones."

Latin Americans for the most part reacted like survivors of an earthquake. The United States was unaware and disdainful (as José Martí had noted) of the reality of life and feeling in Spanish-speaking America. It could not recognize the historic impact of its actions on those countries to the south, little understood by most Americans. *Ariel*, that meditative book by an intellectual of the end of the nineteenth century, was a natural product of the Hispanic reaction. It came at an opportune moment, as an expression of the unfortunate encounter between the two Americas that had been brewing all along the nineteenth century, and it foreshadowed a more extensive conflict that would last till nearly the end of the twentieth.

THE CYCLE of admiration and disenchantment had begun long before 1898. At least three generations of Latin American Liberals had turned toward the United States as a model. They were eager to create a constitutional and secular republic distinct from and opposed to the absolute and Catholic monarchy from which they had seized their independence (and whose inheritance was defended, with differing nuances, by the political groups, clergy, soldiers, and intellectuals known as Conservatives). In some cases, the respect for the United States veered close to a total assimilation of what were seen to be its virtues. The Mexican Constitution of 1824, the first to declare the Mexican nation a federal republic, included an introduction in which the legislators, headed by the brilliant journalist Lorenzo de Zavala, took pride in their emulation of the North Americans. The Mexican Congress, it affirmed, "is happy to have had a model to imitate in the flourishing Republic of our neighbors to the north." (Consistent federalist that he was, Zavala would end his days composing the constitution of the Republic of Texas and becoming its first vice president.)

Simón Bolívar, the Liberator of Latin America, was much more cautious and suspicious of the United States, which, unlike England, had remained neutral during the wars of independence. Bolívar thought it was preferable for these new republics to build strong connections with England, the major naval power of the period. In the English (and other European) systems, he saw more of the balance he favored between order and freedom, with a strong executive power and centralized government. But even Bolívar admired the "promising" example of the United States of America:

Who can resist the victorious attraction of the full and absolute enjoyment of sovereignty, independence, freedom? Who can resist the love that inspires an intelligent government to simultaneously unite private and general rights; that erects the supreme law of the individual will upon the common will? Who can resist the authority of a benevolent government that, with a skillful, active and powerful hand, directs, always and everywhere, all its resources toward social perfection, the sole goal of human institutions?

Halfway through the nineteenth century, the admiration on the part of the Liberals (commonly called "progressives") was almost continental. In the far south the distinguished writer Domingo Faustino Sarmiento (who would later become president of Argentina) liked to call himself *Franklincito* ("little Benjamin Franklin"). His praise for the United States knew no bounds. He spent six months traveling through the country in 1847, after a long trip to Europe, and would constantly compare it, very favorably, to France:

> I am convinced that the United States has the most educated people on earth, the ultimate result of modern civilization . . . The only nation in the world where the masses read, where writing is used for every necessity, where 2000 newspapers satisfy the curiosity of the public . . . where education, like well-being, is disseminated everywhere, within reach of those who wish to obtain it. Is there anywhere else on earth where one or the other has reached such a point? France has 270,000 people who can vote, in a nation of the most ancient civilization in the world, with a population of 36,000,000 . . .

In Mexico, not even the loss of half its territory to the Colossus of the North lessened the faith of its Liberals in the United States. In 1864, Walt Whitman marveled that, in difficult moments for his country, it was "Mexico, the only one to whom we have ever really done wrong, and now the only one who prays for us and for our triumph, with genuine prayer. Is it not indeed strange?" There were two reasons for this continued adhesion. One was political: the Conservatives who supported the imposition of the emperor Maximilian (with the aid of

French troops and Austro-Hungarian backing) favored the Confederacy and the destruction of the unified American nation. But there was also an ideological element—the United States was the mother country of the Liberals.

After the triumph of the liberal Republic under Benito Juárez, with the French driven out and Maximilian executed, Juárez's successors, Sebastián Lerdo de Tejada and Porfirio Díaz, had their apprehensions about the United States. The American union, buoyed by its victory in the Civil War, might decide to attack Mexico and absorb even more of its land. Lerdo de Tejada would say, during his period in office (1872–76), "Between strength and weakness, [it's a good thing that there is] the desert," and Díaz, during his long reign over Mexico (1876–1911), may have said: "Poor Mexico, so far from God, so near the United States." Both launched diplomatic battles (Mexico is still renowned for the skills of its diplomats) to counter the pressures from its neighbor—commercial, military, political—and avoid any further loss of territory. But the general Mexican attitude continued to be positive and sometimes overwhelming. The Liberals had taken refuge in the United States to conspire against the dictator Santa Anna or to strengthen their resources against the French invasion. Lerdo de Tejada had gone into exile in New York after the coup d'état of Porfirio Díaz in 1876. Díaz himself had visited New York under happier circumstances in 1881, for his honeymoon. And Díaz was amenable to the "peaceful penetration" advocated by the U.S. senator James Blaine. He allowed the American-built railroad to mediate "between strength and weakness" and—taking care to balance the American presence with European participation—relied on American investment in mines, agriculture, and oil wells for much of the impressive material progress in Mexico toward the end of the nineteenth century. But the general picture changed radically with the growth of imperialist sentiments within the United States.

Around 1897, one of José Martí's friends, the most prominent Mexican intellectual of his time, Justo Sierra Méndez, traveled to the United States. Sierra was a jurist, an historian and journalist, an orator, and a major theorist and innovator in the field of education. In his youth he

had heard Benito Juárez argue—in accord with the pure liberal canon—
that Mexico could benefit considerably from protestant immigration,
because Mexicans could learn habits of frugality, hard work, and the
value of education. But Sierra had abandoned a strictly liberal point
of view, not only to adopt the fashionable positivist and evolutionary
philosophy (primarily the ideas of Auguste Comte and later Herbert
Spencer) but also through distrust of American foreign policy and an
incipient cultural nationalism that would carry him closer to conservative positions. (For cultural, political, and religious reasons, the
Conservatives had rejected Mexico's English-speaking, protestant, and
liberal neighbor.) Actually, Sierra already considered himself a "conservative liberal." His travel diary *En tierra yanquee* (On Yankee Land)
reflects the balance sheet that liberal and positivist thought at the end
of the century was now beginning to assemble about that country with
its two contrasting faces: democracy and imperialism. And the balance
was tilting toward the negative. Standing before the Capitol building in
Washington, D.C., he wrote:

> I belong to a weak people, who can pardon but should not forget
> the frightful injustice committed against them half a century ago;
> and I want to retain, in the face of the United States (that astonish-
> ing work of nature and good fortune) the proud and silent resigna-
> tion, like that of my people, that has allowed us to become, with
> dignity, masters of our own destiny. I do not deny my admiration
> but I try to explain it to myself, I bow my head but it does not
> remain bowed; then it straightens up, better to see.

On the one hand suspicion, resentment before that blind mechanism of ambition and power; on the other hand admiration in the face
of "the peerless labor of the Capitol . . . soaked with constitutional law
down to its least little cell . . . How can we not bow before it, us, poor
nameless atoms, when history itself bows before it?"
    Just as it did within the mind of Justo Sierra (who in 1894 had tried
to persuade his friend "Pepe" Martí to remain in Mexico and dedicate

himself to the work of education), everything changed in Latin America with the defeat of Spain in 1898 ("that splendid little war," wrote Secretary of State John Hay, one of the first theoreticians of U.S. imperialism). The Mexican and Latin American liberals stopped "bowing their heads." It was a moment of rupture in the history of Latin American thought. An alternative had to be created. No longer should we be *like them*, and even less *be them*. It wasn't enough to be *far from them* and it seemed useless to *move closer to them*. A general consensus among intellectuals was that they had to be radically *different from them*. As Martí had foreseen, many Latin Americans refused to recognize a liberty imposed by foreign arms and the independence granted to Cuba so that it might become a protectorate.

What had happened in Cuba clarified, to many minds, the meaning of various nineteenth-century episodes. It was the most recent chapter in an already lengthy history that included the annexation of Texas, the Mexican-American War, the "filibuster" actions of ambitious American mercenaries in Central America, and certain explicit intentions (like those of Senator Henry Cabot Lodge, Sr.) to set the Stars and Stripes waving from the Rio Grande to Tierra del Fuego. After this collective change of consciousness, it was natural that the liberal admiration for United States democracy—though it never totally vanished—would cede the foreground to a fear of what the next blow of Teddy Roosevelt's "big stick" might precipitate in the Caribbean and Central America. Liberal circles began to agree (in relation to the United States) with their longtime conservative rivals. It was a sea change in the history of Latin American political ideas. A new Latin American nationalism began to take clear shape. And its contours were explicitly anti-American. *Ariel* would become its bible, the work of a writer who never set foot in the United States, born in a small and turbulent but educated and prosperous country that felt itself to be, like its neighbor Argentina, the Europe of Latin America, the only possible bulwark against the arrogant power far to its north.

———

THE SHOCK of 1898 was more than just political. It sent a violent tremor through the whole terrain of Spanish self-confidence. It seemed to question the very meaning of Hispanic civilization. The world was moving at a febrile pace and Spain could not keep up. It was a year of trauma so severe that it activated a system of spiritual survival within the Spanish language itself. The Spanish philosopher and diplomat Ángel Ganivet wrote to Miguel de Unamuno, who would become the most important and influential writer in that group of Spaniards—the Generation of '98—who were in the process of awakening to a new reality:

> The invention of the steamboat was a mortal blow to our power. Only recently have we learned how to build a warship, and until very recently our machinists were foreigners . . . Let us also admit the lack of adequate docks for our boats and, also something of the greatest importance, no money to pay for our squadrons, funds that had to be gained by exploiting those colonies we were trying to defend . . . It made more sense to let ourselves be defeated "heroically."

Its imperial dream (and centuries-old reality) now vanished forever, Spain could take comfort (and it was no small thing) in the fact that Latin America, after almost a hundred years of cold relations, rushed to a reconciliation with the humiliated "Maternal Fatherland." The two halves of the sphere of the Spanish language joined against the same adversary and the influence of its language. The extraordinary Generation of '98 shook Spanish culture awake from two centuries of intellectual somnolence. The defeat triggered an examination of consciousness that led these writers to renew "the genius of the race," to "rediscover" their own country, to travel its roads and reflect on the past and destiny of Spain. Their names would resound along the troubled and often tragic years of the Spanish twentieth century: Ortega y Gasset, Ganivet, Unamuno, del Valle-Inclán, Machado, Baroja, Maeztu.

In practical terms, the problem seemed evident: we do not have adequate access to technology, we are left out of that competition, but we do have our "spirit." Spain's "awakening of the soul" took on flesh in a renewed devotion to the work of Cervantes. Don Quixote, defeated by the technology of windmills, was immortal at the height of the human soul. In Latin America, the same kind of awakening had a different, surprising focus. It was more of a frontal assault and it made use of Shakespeare, or rather a few simplified characters from his last known play, *The Tempest.*

The new imperialists felt that the Hispanic peoples, some of whose lands they had just seized, were backward, barbarous, in need of guidance and supervision. The poet laureate of an older imperialism, Rudyard Kipling, wrote his famous (or infamous) poem "The White Man's Burden" explicitly as an encouragement and justification for the new American masters of the Philippines:

> Take up the White Man's burden—
> Send forth the best ye breed—
> Go bind your sons to exile
> To serve your captives' need;
> To wait in heavy harness,
> On fluttered folk and wild—
> Your new-caught, sullen peoples,
> Half-devil and half-child.

The last line recalls the way in which Prospero—sage, magician, and master of a tropical island—regards and treats his servant Caliban, who is a misshapen monster (at least according to the descriptions Shakespeare puts into the mouths of two of his minor characters), a creature of the island on which Prospero and his daughter Miranda and other scattered characters have been intentionally shipwrecked by Prospero for purposes of his own. Though Caliban is given a few moving speeches, he is presented essentially as a brute (and a dangerous one, since he has tried to rape Miranda). The play itself—and even the character of Caliban—has its complexities but it is easy to see in

Caliban a version of what American (or English or European) racists might stereotype as a typical member of the darker-skinned, presumably "inferior" races that are the "white man's burden."

But Latin American intellectuals at the turn of the century produced an inverse reading of the play, using Caliban on his native tropical island to represent not the victims of the new imperialism but the oppressors themselves and thus spin a kind of origin myth for their burgeoning anti-Americanism. The Nicaraguan Rubén Darío—in his day the greatest poet the Spanish language had produced since the seventeenth century—was the key figure in this conversion of Caliban. In a long diatribe against "the Yankees," first published in the newspaper *El Tiempo* of Buenos Aires on May 20, 1898, and then widely reproduced in many newspapers throughout Latin America, Darío represents them as beasts:

> No, no I cannot, I cannot support those buffaloes with their silver teeth. They are my enemies, they are those who hate Latin blood, they are the Barbarians . . . I have seen those Yankees in their oppressive cities of iron and stone and I have spent the hours I have lived among them with an indefinable sense of anguish. It seemed to me that a mountain was weighing upon me, I felt I was drawing my breath in a country of cyclopses, eaters of raw meat, bestial blacksmiths, inhabitants of houses of mastodons. Heavy people, with reddened faces, foul-mouthed, they move through their streets pushing and scraping against each other like animals, on their hunt for the dollar. The ideal of these Calibans is delimited by the stock exchange and the factory . . . No, I cannot be with them, I cannot be for the triumph of Caliban . . .

The identification of Caliban with capitalist democrats, lacking in spirit and elegance, was an old theme for Darío (he had already used it writing about Edgar Allan Poe in 1894). The usage may have originated with Ernest Renan and his play *Caliban* but it was salvaged and elaborated and given a distinctly antidemocratic form by the

Franco-Argentine historian and librarian Paul Groussac. He used it in a one-act play, yet another product of the crucial year of 1898. For Groussac, too, the Americans are beasts and he throws the American Civil War and the very different issue of the country's westward expansion into one malformed mass: "since the War of Secession and the brutal invasion of the West, one can freely extrapolate the Yankee mind from its shapeless and 'Calibanesque' body, and the old world has observed, with uneasiness and terror, this newest of civilizations which claims to supplant ours, deemed decrepit."

Groussac equates barbarism with democracy and in his thinking there is a heavy dose of conservative aesthetic snobbery and a hatred of the inevitable process of change, for good or bad, that is the very nature of life. In his text titled "Mexico" he writes:

I fear at times that this ultra-modern democracy consists of every people erecting its dwellings according to the mode of the day and tearing down those of its predecessors, so that each human generation leaves no more traces on the earth than a wandering herd of cattle. This leveling democracy, that loves blank slates and is the great fabricator of *self-made men* [English in the original]—we now contemplate it in its acute form, in this breathless and febrile occupation of the Far West, in the midst of all these practical innovations, a moral regression to the ancient migrations, to Asiatic nomadism, the shepherd's tent lit up with electric light.

Aside from the fact that Martí knew America well, Groussac barely at all, the attitude here (Groussac was known as a mordant writer) has nothing of Martí about it. There is neither ambivalence nor any attempt at comprehension. It is the simple rejection of a culture. Excerpts from "Mexico" were published in Montevideo, where José Enrique Rodó surely read them.

It was not by chance that ideological anti-Americanism arose in the Southern Cone or, more specifically, in Argentina and Uruguay. In both countries, the influence of France was not only a question of

literary taste. France came to them with a complex impact: a very powerful philosophical, literary, and political tradition and a confrontation
from on high with the Americans, whom the French of the nineteenth
century generally considered to be crude, even savage as a people.

The southerners had also received (especially Argentina) the idea of
a socialism that fought to improve the economic, cultural, and educational level of the poor, while generating a nationalist state. It was an
idea that barely existed in the United States, and where it did, it was
very far from the halls of power. In this respect, the specific attraction
of the writer Ernest Renan was central. His *What is a Nation?* outlined
a conception of "race" and "spirit" and a body of ideas both literary and
political. It is an idealism whose origins date back to German Romanticism, to those philosophers, especially Johann Fichte, who saw a particular "spirit" at the origin of every nation, specific to its culture and
more profound than the accidents of time and the changes brought on
by "progress." German philosophical thought came to rely heavily on
this idea of "the Spirit," and its acceptance in Latin America would partially explain the later sympathy felt, especially in the Southern Cone,
for the Germany of the Third Reich.

According to Renan, a nation is "a great solidarity" whose existence
is endorsed by "a daily plebiscite," and the spirit of a nation resides "in
the erudite consciousness of its inhabitants," located in a group who
must provide guidance and illumination for the rest of the country's
people. This shared ideal requires, of course, understanding and harmony among the people, and it includes the entire population. Which
is to say that a single language is necessary and that a nation embraces
all those who speak that language. For his Spanish-speaking readers
(and certainly for Rodó), this linguistic requirement led to the same
conviction asserted by Bolívar and Martí, though from a different point
of origin: all Latin America was a fatherland.

To the "youth of Latin America [he says simply 'America']," Rodó,
in the words of the Dominican writer Pedro Henríquez Ureña, "insisted on the need to protect the human personality as a whole against
the abuses of specialization or any other form of impoverishment; on

the lesson of Greece, with its comprehensive humanity, as opposed to Phoenicia and Carthage; on faith in the democratic way of life which, rightly interpreted, will work to safeguard spiritual freedom." Rodó was calling attention to "the outbreak of Mania for the North (*nordo-mania*)" in some areas of Latin American opinion. And Rodó would achieve and far surpass the objectives of his instruction.

These various influences (from Renan, Groussac, and Darío) all came together in Rodó's *Ariel*, the classic work that postulated a radical opposition between the collective essence of Spanish-American and Anglo-Saxon cultures. Although the image of American democracy in *Ariel* is nuanced, rich, and even (for the moment) positive, Rodó did create his own mythical reading: they are Caliban; we are Ariel (the sage Prospero's other servant, but an attractive one, light as the air); they, not us, have trouble understanding things, are insensitive and even deficient in "spirit." It was not merely the portrait of North Americans as wild beasts projected by Darío (who would later write kinder poems on the fearsome northern colossus). The publication of *Ariel* in 1900 set the confrontation within a context of didactic elegance, the product of a measured and reflective philosopher. Though various proclamations of Latin American unity already existed (political, historical, linguistic, and racial), the idea of cultural distinction expounded in *Ariel* would become the most active, influential, and long-lasting argument for that unity, perhaps the only one still current.

RODÓ SAW the book as an attempt to unite "the two segments of a great fatherland . . . that after the shattering of its political unity should always retain its spiritual unity." It was greeted with enormous enthusiasm in Spain. The historian Rafael Altamira commented, when he published the text of *Ariel* in his *La Revista Crítica* of 1901: "What Rodó asks of Latin Americans is that they always should be, or rather that they are, Spaniards, children of the classics and of Christianity." Miguel de Unamuno was more skeptical. He saw the book as too derivative of Renan and refused to identify himself with the Catholic perspective of Rodó. (His preference was for cultural independence, as reflected by his own Basque people, and for the broader spiritual freedoms he saw in Protestantism.)

But the greatest impact of this small book was of course on the Latin American continent. In 1901 it was reprinted in the Dominican Republic and Venezuela. In 1905 it appeared in Cuba. It was published in Mexico in 1908, an edition of five hundred copies edited by the progressive general Bernardo Reyes, governor of the state of Nuevo León, with a prologue by Pedro Henríquez Ureña, who was then living in Mexico and whose friends and disciples called him, still young, "el Sócrates." Henríquez wrote in his prologue: "His intention is to make a contribution toward forming an ideal for the governing class, of which they are very much in need." Alfonso Reyes, friend and disciple of Henríquez and the son of Governor Reyes, wrote of Rodó: "To him we owe an awakening of consciousness, the precise notion of American fraternity." When Alfonso Reyes and José Vasconcelos became two of the most distinguished men of letters in the first half of the twentieth century—for Mexico and for Latin America—both would enthusiastically accept the message of aesthetic and cultural "salvation" expounded in *Ariel*.

It was a message that did not conflict with the fashionable philosophy of positivism, another contribution of French (and Catholic) thought that had displaced classical liberalism in the intellectual circles of Latin America through the final decades of the nineteenth century and the beginning of the twentieth. Positivism was a "religion" of progress. It recognized the value of science but not of Anglo-Saxon "utilitarianism." Actually *Ariel* gave positivism new life in Latin America. Based on the racist theories current at the turn of the century, various positivist thinkers in Latin America (Carlos Octavio Bunge, Graça Aranha, Francisco Bulnes) had written works of gloomy pessimism about the future of the Latin American "race," supposedly weighed down by the maleficent mixture of a genetic Indian spinelessness and the intolerant psychological legacy stemming from Spain. *Ariel* offered a way out of this "dilemma." Our apparent weakness was really our greatest strength.

Two primary emphases emerge from the arguments of *Ariel*. First, the superiority of Latin culture over the mere utilitarianism espoused by the Caliban of the North. It was a claim that became a militant slogan for many. Latin Americanism, especially in the South, was also anti-Yankeeism. The other constant preoccupation was on the idea of youth as the strength of the fatherland and, therefore, the need for education as an indispensable tool for achieving the ideal. (The character who speaks for Rodó, all through *Ariel*, is Prospero, who is essentially a teacher.)

The current of Latin American cultural superiority would have a long and powerful presence in twentieth-century literature. In 1904 Rubén Darío would publish his famous poem "To Roosevelt":

> *Be careful. Long live Hispanic America!*
> *A thousand cubs have issued from the Spanish Lion.*
> *You would need to be, Roosevelt! the terrifying Rifleman*
> *the powerful Hunter through the will of God himself,*
> *to be able to retain us in the hold of your iron claws.*
> *And, though you can count on everything, you lack one thing: God!*

Darío would later moderate his position. Other partisans of *Ariel* (*arielistas*), like Pedro Henríquez Ureña and José Vasconcelos, would stress the affirmation of Spanish culture (and its roots in the Latin and Greek classics) rather than political and ideological harangues against the Yankees. But in Argentina, so close to France and so far from the United States, *Ariel* would fuel a belligerent antagonism toward the Yankee Caliban.

Alfredo Palacios, the first socialist legislator in Latin America, would argue for (and achieve) considerable improvement in the condition of Argentine workers but (though he was essentially an *arielista*) his explicit criticism of the United States dealt with concrete political issues, especially (in the 1920s) his defense of President Plutarco Elías Calles of Mexico when the latter was threatened with the possibility of an American invasion to defend U.S. financial interests. But another

Argentine socialist, Manuel Ugarte (1875–1951), was an early representative of *arielista* belligerence.

He came from a well-off family and so was able to study in Paris (in 1897 and, the critical year of 1898). He was deeply impressed by the pacifist socialist Jean Jaurès and his defense of Albert Dreyfus against the falsified anti-Semitic charges that split France between right and left during the Dreyfus Affair. (The effects of the Dreyfus Affair would soil French history all the way into World War II and Jaurès himself would be assassinated by a French nationalist in 1914.)

Ugarte, like so many others, was disgusted by the Spanish-American War. It would leave him not only pro-Spanish but fiercely antagonistic toward the United States. In 1901 he published an article titled "The Yankee Peril," which echoed Groussac, Darío, and Rodó, as well as including a lament for the U.S. annexations of Mexican territory in the previous century. His prestige as a writer (and his personal inheritance) permitted him to travel as a representative of Argentine socialism. In 1907 he attended the proceedings of the Second International Congress in Stuttgart, where he met figures like Lenin, Karl Kautsky, Georgi Plekhanov, Jean Jaurès, who had so impressed him in Paris, and Rosa Luxemburg. All of them were militants and authors published much later in Mexico by another Argentine socialist, Arnaldo Orfila Reynal, who would live to be a hundred years old (1897–1997), was a key figure in the dissemination of Marxist literature throughout Latin America, and was incidentally an acquaintance of yet another fiercely anti-Yankee Argentine, Ernesto "Che" Guevara.

Between 1912 and 1914, Ugarte would tour Latin America, performing a series of widely acclaimed public presentations (orations, commemorative visits to important historical sites, etc.), continually inflaming Latin American political passions and warning against the Yankee peril. When Woodrow Wilson took office in 1913, Ugarte published his "Open Letter to the President of the United States," which was in a sense a palimpsest of history, combining Latin America's longstanding liberal admiration for the achievements of the United States with apprehension and, in this case, restrained anger about its present and future course:

> You represent a civilization that was born from a choice, that substituted, as a point of departure, moral law for brute force, that flowered in the warmth of our ideals, like a reaction against the old errors of the world; and it would not be logical that you should commit, against us, assaults as grievous as those that Europe has committed in Asia and in Africa, because if you behave in that way, you would declare that your greatest, most illustrious predecessors were mistaken when they claimed to establish a new nation based on justice, and you would instead proclaim the bankruptcy of human perfection and of God's will.

Ugarte's activities were seminal in various ways. He was in constant written contact with two intellectual leaders of Peru in the twenties (Víctor Raúl Haya de la Torre and José Carlos Mariátegui) and he directly influenced the Nicaraguan general Augusto César Sandino, leader of the first guerrilla uprising against a Yankee presence in Latin America.

RODÓ'S EMPHASIS on youth and education was in part a spiritual reaction to Manifest Destiny, although in reverse. Almost all the great European theories of history and politics (Hegel, Marx, Lenin, and, in practice, imperialism and colonialism) assumed as a given that the great European nations would end up absorbing the so-called backward countries. It was the inevitable march of civilization and was the reason Marx and Engels had written in favor of the U.S. war against Mexico. Annexationism was not only a North American ideology. The European world of the nineteenth century (and of the beginning of the twentieth until the Great War) shared it as well.

But in the political and social thought of Latin America, rightists and leftists, liberals and conservatives converged in a symmetrically opposed theory. These countries abusively termed backward should raise themselves up and stop being captives. The proper route was to climb toward higher intellectual heights. Education then became the major obsession of Latin American nationalisms (even more than its already elevated importance within the currents of liberalism and positivism). And the universities were the front lines for this historic advance. The universities were already staking out a position as the heirs to the hegemony of the church, the new source of legitimacy and of men trained for responsibility and power. Now they were to fill an even higher function. Education had to be the means for drawing people out of their lacerating poverty. Moreover, the consensus affirmed that the distance between our nations and those more powerful rested not so much on the quantity of resources as in the knowledge of how to use them. The university was the highway to progress. And so the nationalist idea had to include a politics of education at the very heart of the conception of the Nation.

All across the continent, new ministries of education surged into being. National educational policy was of vital concern everywhere. Many liberals, both classical and positivist, had already stressed the importance of education: Justo Sierra in Mexico; Manuel Montt, the president of Chile; and, above all, the Argentine Domingo Faustino Sarmiento, who, during his presidency, had been swept into a succession of conflicts that made governing the country almost impossible but never slowed his commitment to opening schools and training teachers. With the turn of the century, the role of the teacher had taken on a new luster. The teacher began to be seen as the prototypical intellectual, the standard-bearer of moral and political redemption. But there was an even greater protagonist. The long-awaited savior of Latin America was to be the young university student.

The exhortation of Marx "Workers of the world, unite!" could well have had a new formulation to express a new reality. With its force due largely to Rodó, it could well have become "Students of all countries, unite!" The first great proof of its validity is the famous University Reform of 1918 in Córdoba, Argentina. The students went on strike in what was a conservative city. Their objective was nothing less than to dislodge the forms, hierarchies, and clerical content that dominated their instruction. They sought political autonomy for the university, for the first time in Latin America; the condition is now the norm in the public universities of Latin America (though not under dictatorships). Autonomy means among other things that the armed power of the state cannot blithely invade the precincts of the university. The students of Córdoba, powered by the new transnational respect for their status, were fighting for that goal, and they were also demanding the right to participate in the government of the university. They experienced those days of struggle as if they were living through the October Days of revolution in Russia in the previous year. The students of Córdoba were victorious, and their triumph accomplished even more, initiating a movement of university reform throughout the continent, spearheaded by students who were willing to take to the streets.

There were three major intellectual architects of the reform in Córdoba. The socialist politicians Alfredo Palacios and Manuel Ugarte and the student leader Deodoro Roca, who would later formulate his theory of the "complete man" (*hombre íntegro*), a conception of human improvement and possible perfection. They were all affected by the impulse of *arielismo*. The countries of Latin America, though technologically backward, would not peacefully accept the role of mere material nourishment for the great powers. At least in this wave of student assertiveness that crossed national borders, the intellectual tide of anti-Yankeeism had succeeded in uniting liberals and conservatives, Catholics and freethinkers, and an incipient left of socialists, anarchists, and Marxists. Latin American nationalism was beginning to set its stakes down on the table of an entire continent. Shared race and culture were the motivating value it drew from Rodó's brief and thoughtful book. The conception was a hopeful, even glorious one: a brotherhood that could not be denied.

DESPITE THE rhetorical pulse of some of his pages, José Enrique Rodó was certainly not an opponent of democracy. The tone of *Ariel* is one of lofty, professorial reflection, not invective. Some of its passages can be read as eulogies of American democracy, seen as a form of progress that must be complemented, purified, elevated through culture. Moreover, Rodó, in his later parliamentary career (he was elected three times to the Uruguayan Congress), gave ample evidence of democratic coherence and social sensitivity. But an aristocratic sensibility dominates *Ariel*. There is no political criticism of democracy. The criticism is more precisely aesthetic:

> The opposition between the regime of democracy and the elevated life of the spirit is an unfortunate reality when that regime comes to mean a disregard of legitimate inequalities and the substitution of a mechanical conception of government for the faith in *heroism*—in the sense meant by Carlyle. Everything that is more than an element of material superiority and economic prosperity takes on, within civilization, a prominence which will not fail to be leveled when moral authority belongs to the spirit of mediocrity.

In his cultural homily Rodó's inspiration was Renan but in his political ideas it was the Scottish rhetorician of inequality, Thomas Carlyle. The considerable prominence of Carlyle in the history of Latin American thought may seem surprising to those raised in the American (or even English) intellectual tradition. It is a predilection associated with Latin American authoritarianism and especially the cult of the leader. In Rodó's *El mirador de Próspero* (Prospero's Balcony), which he published in 1913, he offers literary portraits of various heroic figures of Spanish America, among them Garibaldi, that "visionary of action" (who took part in the Uruguayan Civil War); Juan Carlos Gómez, the Uruguayan journalist and representative of the classic republican tradition; and the legendary Ecuadorian journalist Juan Montalvo (whose liberal writings against the theocratic government of Gabriel García Moreno were so efficacious that they led to the assassination of the autocrat). But, from his tower, Prospero contemplates his primary hero: the Liberator Simón Bolívar.

In his essay on Bolívar, Rodó did not need to quote Carlyle. The inspiration is clear. Though the style of Rodó is nowhere near as torrential as that of the Scotsman, the shadow of Rodó's model drifts through his elegant modernist prose. In the style of Carlyle's *On Heroes and Hero Worship*, Rodó undertakes an exegetical journey through the major episodes of Bolívar's life. Few men other than Bolívar, he writes, "subjugate with such violent authority the sympathies of the heroic imagination." Nothing better illustrates Rodó's view of Bolívar as a *chosen one* than the comparison he draws with other leaders of the wars for Latin American independence, especially with San Martín: "Bolívar is a *Hero*, San Martín is not a *Hero*. San Martín is a great man, a great soldier, a great captain, an illustrious and extremely beautiful figure. But he is not a *Hero*." So deep were the aftereffects of Rodó's portrait of Bolívar that, almost a hundred years later, Julio María Sanguinetti, twice president of Uruguay, could recite a fragment of the essay by memory: "Great in thought, great in action, great in glory, great in his great misfortune that served to magnify the impure aspect latent in the soul of great men and great for taking upon himself, in his abandonment and his death, the tragic expiation of his greatness."

A year before the publication of *El mirador de Próspero*, another Latin American devotee of Carlyle, the Peruvian Francisco García Calderón (whom the Chilean poetess Gabriela Mistral would later call "the effective heir of Rodó"), had published, in Paris, *Les démocraties latines d'Amerique* (The Latin Democracies of America), with a prologue by the future president of France, Raymond Poincaré. It was a treatise on the political history of Latin America based on a fusion of fashionable evolutionist theories and the complete reduction of history to biography, in emulation of Carlyle. Following the lead of Rodó, García Calderón moves away from the classic republican viewpoint and tries to present a way to better understand the politics of the continent. Dissenting from Sarmiento (who, in his *Facundo*, the biography of a gaucho soldier and politician, had defined the fundamental dilemma of Latin America as the violent encounter "between civilization and barbarism"), García Calderón's variation of the new Latin American idealism would dissolve Sarmiento's antinomy through an equalizing vindication of the civilizers (like Sarmiento or his fellow Argentine Juan Bautista Alberdi) and the fierce backwoods *caudillos* who seemed to have risen from the soil to ride at the forefront of their marauding armies. In Argentina, the classic republican Bernardino Rivadavia had been (here he quotes Groussac) "the ardent forger of utopias." Opposing him had arisen the terrifying "caliph" Facundo with his "mystical barbarism." And finally the dictator Rosas arrived. His "fecund despotism," his "necessary terrorism" finished off "war and terror." The formula was almost dialectical: Rivadavia the thesis, Facundo the antithesis, Rosas the synthesis. With the same simple measure, García Calderón judged all the strong and constructive presidents of Hispanic America, excluding those who were only tyrants and no more. The Peruvian Ramón Castilla was the "necessary dictator of an unstable republic." Other dictatorial *caudillos* to whom he accorded his respect were the Bolivian general Andrés Santa Cruz ("heir to the unifying ideal of Bolívar"), the Chilean Diego Portales, and the Mexican Porfirio Díaz. These were, for him, the representative men of the Latin democracies, superior democracies, democracies of the spirit, not produced through the vulgar process of free elections. The cult of heroes floated in the air of the age. So much so that a young Argentine writer would learn German to read some of the intellectual antecedents of Carlyle. And the youthful Jorge Luis Borges found a famous sentence of the Scottish author to be perfectly reasonable: "Democracy is chaos furnished with electoral urns."

BY 1904, Rodó had become famous and enormously respected throughout the entire continent. But his psychic life was still an unending struggle between desolation and confidence. In that year he would write to Miguel de Unamuno, "I do not regard the immediate future of these countries with the pessimistic criterion many adopt." But the financial crisis that descended upon him in the "terrible year" of 1905 drove him to despair. A severe oscillation of feelings was his burden and he knew it: "Each one of my moments of hope is the upshot of a previous and intricate interior struggle with despair and pessimism. So that the ripened moments I offer of admonition and art are exceptional,

not the ordinary moments which, in me as in everyone, involve doubt
and sometimes desperation."

Rodó disapproved of radical actions and movements, both new and
old. He criticized the removal of crucifixes from hospitals in Uruguay
as a Jacobin abuse, and he feared the rise of working-class socialism,
this "great roar that is mounting." His way was one of moderation:
religious tolerance and social reforms. But not even politics calmed his
inner torment. After he had been elected twice to Congress, his political future played out in a rivalry with the popular president Batlle, who
would sometimes treat him with contempt. A portion of his profile, in
El Mirador de Próspero, of the Ecuadorian Montalvo, reads like an unconscious personal complaint:

> There remains isolation and spiritual abandonment, which is
> truly painful; there remains the common lack of understanding:
> from the moment that the thorns spring up of opposition to supe-
> riority, a passion of insignificant democracies, until shoulders are
> shrugged with an uncouth disdain toward all disinterested labor
> of style and investigation and, even within such work, there is
> deafness to the new and personal, a pretension of understanding
> where there is no understanding . . . ; there remain, finally, these
> lingering flavors of the village in relation to which, for lofty mat-
> ters of the spirit, all of Latin America has been, on a greater scale,
> a solitary back-water hamlet . . .

With the outbreak of the First World War, Rodó resigned from
the board of the newspaper *La Razón* because of the underlying pro-
German sentiments of the newspaper. His personal anguish takes on
a universal coloring. He feels the collapse of the western order as a
personal assault, the destruction of a world for which he had projected
a future that would include Latin America as an equal partner.

Some verbal portraits of the time describe him as more than ever
austere and withdrawn: "his face was like a mask without emotion or
intelligence." An Argentine journalist described a meeting with Rodó:

"we spoke in a small, unlit room; we said good-bye to each other without him crossing to the illuminated vestibule, and I only remember having seen, as if in a dream, among the shadows that blurred the edges of the furniture, a tall stooped figure and two hands moving in the mist."

The final passage through life of this solitary scholar was, as always for him, tortuous. It would be a final image of "the volatile soul," wandering in the world, nostalgic only for an era when Athens (or rather its leading minds) was a living force on the earth. He considers "laying down roots . . . having my own hut; forming a family; waiting in sanctified peace for the disappearance of this great illusion we call life." In July 1916 he made the grand gesture of abandoning the Latin American "hamlet." He traveled to Lisbon, Madrid, Barcelona. In 1917 he arrived in Italy, already feeling ill. He stayed for a month in Florence, where he composed a dialogue between two inanimate substances, "Bronze conversing with marble." He spent time in Rome, where he went to see the statue of José Artigas, the founding father of his country, commissioned to an Italian sculptor by the Uruguayan government. In April he arrived in Palermo. There he died of meningitis on the first of May. One of his last, unrealized projects had been to write an essay on José Martí.

3

José Vasconcelos

THE CULTURAL CAUDILLO

The Mexican Revolution, which erupted in November 1910, would be remembered in Latin America as the first assault on the heritage of nineteenth-century liberalism. Eventually (though by a complicated route) it would become an early element of the "great roar that is mounting," so feared by José Enrique Rodó and destined to grow ever louder across the twentieth century. It began as a liberal reproach, and then armed rebellion, against a dictator who had once been the military leader of the Liberal republican victory over the monarchy of Maximilian in 1867. Porfirio Díaz had retained much of the economic program of liberalism but completely jettisoned its commitment to electoral democracy. Francisco I. Madero, a rich businessman from the north of the country, educated in Europe and in California, had begun his campaign against Díaz's three decades of personal power with a book published in 1908 (*The Presidential Succession in 1910*) and passed reluctantly, step by step, toward revolution, after the aged dictator, who had finally promised to hold a genuinely free election, defrauded him of his presidential victory in 1910. Among his most ardent supporters was the young co-editor of the newspaper *El Antireeleccionista* (The Anti-Reelectionist), which spoke for the political party formed to support Madero in 1909. He was a lawyer and philosopher named José Vasconcelos.

Madero was not an intellectual at the level of Martí or Rodó, but he was imbued with a similar devotion to redemption. He was "the Apostle of Democracy" and the victory of his forces against the armies of Díaz came quickly. His difficult but dedicated term as the democratically elected president of Mexico was cut short by a military coup in February

1913, carried out by a coalition of conservative forces, encouraged and assisted by the American ambassador to Mexico, Henry Lane Wilson.

But the murder of Madero and his vice president, José María Pino Suárez, would unleash a far more complicated, violent, and confusedly social revolution than the idealistic Madero had ever imagined with his slogan geared to classic liberal premises: "Valid voting! No reelection! (*Sufragio efectivo, no reelección*)." When Madero had entered Mexico City in triumph after his victory, a tremor had shaken the unstable lake bottom on which Hernán Cortés had raised his colonial city. An earthquake of men at arms would now shake all of Mexico.

The renewed revolt, now directed against the military government of General Victoriano Huerta, involved a coalition of leaders and armies with different interests, antecedents, and ultimate objectives. And all through the country, there were also localized uprisings and confrontations of forces, some of them social, some of them personalist (centered around loyalty to a specific leader), some of them a mere settling of old grievances.

On the major stage of the Revolution (now entitled to the capital R it would retain for the rest of the century), Huerta was defeated and fled into exile in July 1914. But the anti-Huerta alliance dissolved into rival alliances and the fiercest battles of the Mexican Revolution were yet to be fought. The agrarian revolutionaries under Emiliano Zapata (from the state of Morelos, south of Mexico City) and the much more modern army (though heavily dependent on cavalry) of hardened frontiersmen from the north under the former bandit Pancho Villa faced off against forces whose leaders had more middle-class roots and values, first led by Venustiano Carranza and later by Álvaro Obregón and his subordinate generals from the border state of Sonora (like Obregón himself).

The various groupings were defined by the names of their leaders: Zapatistas, Villistas, Carrancistas, Obregonistas. The loyalties and origins of the common soldiers cannot be automatically and rigidly defined, but at this massive stage of confrontation within the Mexican Revolution, Zapata and Villa—both unlettered men of the people—represented (in their different modes) aspects of social revolution.

(Intellectuals were drawn to side with and sometimes to advise the various leaders, those influenced by anarchist ideas often to Zapata, the more socialist to Villa.)

But with the ultimate victors still undecided, the new state of things was beginning to be defined and legitimized from an unexpected source—the cultural originality of the Mexican Revolution, the specific nature of the amalgam of old and new that was already coming into being. The civil war between the revolutionaries had already turned intense by 1915. When the new Mexican Constitution was drafted, in 1917, the faction headed by Venustiano Carranza was well on its way to victory. The constitution shows the effects and includes the perspectives of a broad gamut of ideological currents (agrarianism, labor unionism, nationalism, socialism, more extremist and anticlerical "Jacobinism," and the embryonic corporate emphasis of the future Mexican state). All these trends were a modification—and often a correction—of the nineteenth-century liberal perspective. But in cultural terms, the Revolution was born and nourished, like the maguey plant, by the soil of Mexico. It sought its true face not outside and ahead, but within and facing toward its past. And the awakening first took shape precisely in that violent year of 1915.

II

The material isolation of Mexico during World War I and the constant pressure of its own raging civil war had, perhaps paradoxically, encouraged a process of concentration and introspection that many experienced as a "discovery of Mexico." The intellectual Manuel Gómez Morin, who was a student at the time, remembers (with affection) the year 1915:

. . . with optimistic stupor we took account of unsuspected truths. Mexico existed. Mexico as a country, with capacities, with aspiration, with life, with its own problems . . . And the Indians, and the mestizos and the creoles, they were living realities, men with every human attribute. The Indian was no mere substance fit for war or work, nor was the creole, nor was the mestizo . . . Mexico existed and the Mexicans!

During the years of war, hundreds of thousands of people, men and women, old and young, abandoned their plots of land, the haciendas they worked on or the "tiny fatherlands" of their villages, willingly or against their will, and traveled by train through their country on a kind of revolutionary tourism, at once frightening and hallucinatory. Like a giant encampment or an endless pilgrimage, making the Revolution or fleeing from it, the Mexican people entered the foreground of history. Artists began to mingle with the people and absorb their passions and their conflicts. It was natural that this migration should be intensely reflected in their art.

At the ground level of humanity, artists would discover the true landscape of Mexican life. In the year 1915, the painter Saturnino Herrán began to paint the common people and their customs, especially Indians, when he saw them in the city streets or in the villages. The historian Manuel Toussaint began to publish a series of "Colonial Sketches" of the Mexico City Cathedral, the chapel of El Pocito in Guanajuato, the houses of the sixteenth century (in the aftermath of the Conquest). The musician Manuel M. Ponce harmonized the songs he heard from the blind beggars who sang and twanged their rhythms on the jaw harp or played their harmonicas. The poet Ramón López Velarde wrote deeply moving modernist poems on life in the provinces, voices and sentiments of "a Mexico we all have lived in and did not know."

Years later, in 1921, in an essay titled "Fresh News of the Fatherland," López Velarde would describe the Revolution in almost religious terms, the revelation of a fatherland very different from the *Porfiriato* (age of Porfirio), a "new, intimate fatherland," "Castilian and Moorish, streaked with the Aztec." He went on more precisely: "The material repose of the country, through thirty years of peace, supported the idea of a pompous fatherland, a nation worth many millions, honorable in the present, epic in the past. These years of suffering were needed to conceive of a fatherland less external, more modest and probably more valuable." López Velarde died that same year (he was only thirty-three years old) when the real significance of that "Fresh News of the Fatherland" was barely emerging. It would be the creation of the most powerful myth of redemption in the first half of the Latin American twentieth century, and it would resonate far beyond the Spanish-speaking world. It was the myth of the Mexican Revolution, and its fundamental creator would be that same young newspaper editor who had written fiery articles in favor of Francisco Madero's electoral campaign. José Vasconcelos would become the cultural *caudillo* of the Revolution.

III

He was born in 1882 in Oaxaca, capital of the state with the same name, home to one of the largest and most varied Indian populations in Mexico, who had evolved an impressive pre-Columbian civilization. Both Benito Juárez and Porfirio Díaz had been born in Oaxaca: Juárez was a pure Zapotec Indian, Porfirio Díaz a Mixtec from his mother's side. Vasconcelos's mother was a very pious Catholic much beloved by the young José. Her relatively early death (in 1898) left a wound that never completely healed.

His father was a Mexican customs official and, as a child, Vasconcelos lived in the border town of Piedras Negras in Coahuila, where he would cross the border daily to a school in Eagle Pass, Texas, where he first began to acquire his excellent English. His later education would eventually lead him to the best high school in Mexico, the Escuela Nacional Preparatoria (National Preparatory School), and then to law school at the Escuela Nacional de Jurisprudencia. In 1905 he formally became a lawyer but his broader intellectual pursuits would always consume much of his energy. He was early known for his interest in philosophical speculation (and his arrogant temperament). He was a reader of Schopenhauer and was led, through him, to a serious interest in Hinduism. A circle of young intellectuals, soon to be very influential, welcomed his participation. The Ateneo de la Juventud (Athenaeum of Youth), with its affectedly classicist self-description, was led by the young Dominican Pedro Henríquez Ureña, that young "Socrates" who had become part of Mexican culture, who had praised Rodó's *Ariel* in 1905, whose father would become president of the Dominican Republic in 1916 and to whose uncle Federico, José Martí had written his famous letter of farewell. For all the members of the Ateneo, the message of Rodó opened the way to new values in philosophy and literature. Henríquez Ureña would write of the fresh emphases:

Greek literature, the writers of the Spanish Golden Age, Dante, Shakespeare, Goethe, the modern artistic orientations of England . . . [and] relying on Schopenhauer and Nietzsche one already began to attack the ideas of Comte and Spencer.

As part of an influential sequence of lectures organized by the Ateneo, Henríquez Ureña discussed the meaning of Rodó's *Ariel*. All these young men were *arielistas*, not so much from the anti-Yankee perspective (more characteristic of the Southern Cone) but in the redemptive power they ascribed to books, art, education, and culture in general. In September 1910, during the grandiose celebrations for the hundredth anniversary of Mexican independence, Vasconcelos gave a speech in which he criticized the philosophy of positivism, which had reigned triumphant over the intellectual life of Porfirio's long reign. It immediately established his reputation as the most original and powerful thinker among young intellectuals. Two months later, the fireworks of the Centenary Celebrations metamorphosed into the fires of war, as the first shots of the Mexican Revolution resounded. They were no surprise to José Vasconcelos, who had been working toward them since the fraudulent electoral defeat of Madero.

Vasconcelos had been a Maderista from the first moment. After the triumph of Madero's revolution in 1911, he returned to his lucrative practice, where his major client was an American oil company. During Madero's fifteen months of democratic government, Vasconcelos spent little effort on the academic labors of the Ateneo (they were trying to create a People's University). According to the first volume of his memoirs, he devoted much of his time to making love, with the "flexible Venus" he had met during the Madero revolution. Though he was married with two children, Vasconcelos began a relationship that, with its ups and downs, would last for almost a decade. She was the first of many lovers in his life but certainly his most intense and madly beloved liaison. Her name was Elena Arizmendi and, during the first stage of the Revolution, she had been a nurse in the neutral White Cross.

The assassination of Madero and the long chain of conflicts that followed (especially the civil war that really began in 1914, pitting the Villista-Zapatista alliance against the Carrancistas) dispersed the members of the Ateneo. Many intellectuals went into exile, among them Henriquez Ureña himself and Alfonso Reyes, whose father had been a leader of the uprising against Madero and was killed on the first day of fighting. Others chose internal exile, remaining in Mexico and waiting for the fury of the wars to die down. One of these men, the philosopher Antonio Caso, tried to keep the small flame of culture alive, giving classes in philosophy and evoking Renan and the spirit of Christianity while the battles swirled across the country. Caso wrote to Reyes:

We live in an infernal derangement . . . higher academic studies have nothing to do with a country in which barbarism is spreading as perhaps it has never done before in our history . . . To be an educated Mexican is one of the most unquestionable maladjustments in the world. Nothing to be done!

And yet it was a time of cultural and artistic introspection, rather similar to what happened in Spain after the shock of Spanish defeat in 1898. Vasconcelos did not live through it passively. After the assassination of Madero, completely ignoring his wife Serafina Miranda (who adored him) and his infant children José Ignacio and Carmen, he set off with his beloved Elena and joined the insurrection against the new dictator, Victoriano Huerta. He was sent to the United States, as a representative of the Revolution. On his return to Mexico, he allied himself with the fragile coalition between Villa and Zapata. He appears, smiling broadly, in the famous photograph of Villa and Zapata and some of their followers seated at a banquet in the Palacio Nacional after their armies had entered Mexico City. The differing character of the two great *caudillos* of the people could not have been better depicted. Zapata looks wary and distrustful, Villa festive and aggressive. And with them is the future cultural *caudillo* of Mexico, who will be centrally responsible for how both men (later assassinated) will come to be remembered.

In 1915, when General Álvaro Obregón defeated the forces of Villa and Zapata (known collectively as the Convencionistas), Vasconcelos went into exile, with Elena, first to the United States and then Peru. In Lima he began to talk about himself as a new "Ulysses" and the metaphor (if it was that, rather than a solid conviction) would become the title of the first volume of his autobiography, *Ulises Criollo* (The Creole Ulysses). The voluminous autobiography (after decades of a voluminous life) would eventually run to four volumes, all published in the 1930s. (The others, in translation, would be *The Storm, The Disaster,* and *The Proconsulate.* As literature, they are a collective masterpiece, unequaled in Mexican autobiographical writing.)

But now in Lima, nearer the beginning of his odyssey, he delivered a lecture titled "When the Eagle Destroys the Serpent," an image on the flag of Mexico based on the Aztec legend of the founding of their capital city Tenochtitlan, supposedly built by the wandering Nahua tribesmen at the sight of an omen, an eagle with a serpent in its claws, near the lake that now lies under Mexico City. In the lecture, he summarizes the history of Mexico and gives his list of its dark ages and its villains: "The Colony, cruel, small-minded, distressing, gloomy"; Iturbide (the short-term emperor immediately after independence), the Porfirista dictatorship, Huerta, and in the last and most recent place, the thievery, the usurpation, the supposed underhand arrangements of Carranza with the United States. And beside this gallery of "serpents" Vasconcelos presents another list, his own, of "magnificent eagles." They include "the founding heroes [of a sovereign, independent Mexico], Hidalgo, Morelos, Guerrero, Mina [a Spaniard who fought for the independence of Mexico] . . . The heroic dozen, with names like Ocampo, Lerdo, Prieto, Ramírez, Juárez [each one an especially dedicated, democratic and socially conscious Liberal], all unselfish, resolute, good and free men." They were the historical expression of Vasconcelos's ideology in that period, when he was as impeccably liberal as Madero. "Give us"—he said, invoking God—"another legion of heroes . . . and let them govern us." He was sketching out the program of his future public life: the education of "heroes" (or at least those prepared for the role) and their democratic ascent to power.

IV

When the moment came to return to Mexico and launch his own re-newed flight of a "magnificent eagle," his lover Elena Arizmendi had broken off their relationship. The passion between them is the central obsession of his second volume of autobiography, *La tormenta* (The Storm), a title that refers both to the "storm" of the Revolution and to Vasconcelos's intimate storm of love and desire. As described by Vas-concelos, the passion and tortured intensity of his long connection with "Adriana" (the name he gives her in his memoirs) is the most famous depiction of "mad love" in Mexican literature. For him, in the Mexico of the early twentieth century, a divorce had always been out of the question. From the beginning, he had felt that he would lose Adriana but the thought had never restrained his desire. "Only the infinite suits me," he would often say, and in love, it seems to have meant that what he wanted should go on and never end. Elena was his companion, his intellectual friend, his lover, of course, and his *soldadera* (the term for the women who followed their men—and sometimes fought beside them—on the roads of the Revolution). About her he wrote, "It was terrifying not to be able to give her all the protection, all the fervor that her extraordinary nature required." Toward the end of 1916, in the city of Lima, she left him.

It was a devastating blow for Vasconcelos. He was thrown back upon his own inner resources and he grasped at an old idea for support, his belief in the "autonomy" and invulnerability of the deepest part of the human being, his "soul." He would seek a higher truth, beyond the claims of the body. He had always been interested in philosophical pathways outside the main stream of the Western tradition. In Lima, he now returned to these interests, within the limits of the knowledge (and prejudices) of his time. His *Estudios Hindostánicos* (Hindustanic Studies), first published in 1920, consists of well-written, very short essays that are summaries from books by noted scholars, cognizant of the immensity of the Indian worldview and its resonances but without any living knowledge of India or the East in general, which he never visited. It is interesting that these summaries show the conventional disdain for those Hindu (and tantric Buddhist) practices that seek to value and use the body as a means to a higher goal, a dismissal imbibed from the Puritan values of English colonizers and other Western scholars and communicated to many more Westernized Indians (a dismissal combined—during the centuries of English domination—with similar, though not identical currents from their own ancient culture). A man with the physical vitality and overweening personality of José Vasconcelos might have found a natural home in such ideas. Instead (at least mentally) he would flee from the body that still yearned for his "Adriana." He would decide (in theory for a lifetime, in practice very briefly) that "he who serves the flesh becomes useless for the spirit."

He turned his attention to the pre-Socratic philosopher Pythagoras, none of whose writings have survived but who is credited (a tradition continued and developed by his followers) with elevating the harmonies of mathematical relations, and their offshoot of musical composition, to the heights of cosmic importance. Pythagoras is also supposed to have traveled far to the East—probably to India—from which he brought back the indigenous belief in the transmigration of souls, which (along with other concepts associated with Pythagoras) strongly influenced Plato. Vasconcelos was to become, more than anything, an apostle of beauty and art, and drawing on Pythagoras, he understood the central importance of rhythm to all art and perhaps to all life: "rhythm is at the essence of all things."

But at this moment of great anguish in his life, the search for beauty surely involved an attempt to replace "the flesh" of his lost Elena with an equal but abstract beauty of the spirit, something very close to a religion that could be his forever. He turned to Plotinus (205–270 A.D.), the founder of Neoplatonism, and his emanationist and mystic metaphysics. For Plotinus, ultimate reality is "the One," an eternal monistic unity to which no qualities can be ascribed. Various emanations ultimately produce the world and its individuals, though the system is far less cumbersome than in later Neoplatonists who introduce a great complexity of mythological forces within the process that descends to the human. In the teachings of Plotinus, a human being may be able, through contemplation, to grasp the eternal residue within himself (though it is very hard to do) and rise through the various spheres of celestial being, to an experience of mystical union with "the One," described—in the magnificent phrase of his treatise the *Enneads*—as "the flight of the alone to the Alone." It is a process very similar to what is taught in the earliest Upanishads and later in the more abstract philosophies of Advaita Vedanta, less the emphasis on celestial geography. (It may even ultimately be derived from the same source, carried westward by Protagoras or some other wandering Greek thinker.)

With his reading of Plotinus, Vasconcelos thought he could retain what he most prized in Elena Arizmendi (or her semi-mythicized form of Adriana): her beauty. "Plotinus," wrote Alfonso Reyes, "has left us imperishable pages about beauty . . . and it is explained as the victorious expression of the spirit in apparent objects of the senses . . . At the final hour of ecstasy and when the human soul returns to the highest heaven it appears that . . . the good itself has been surpassed by another qualification purer and higher, which is not the good but beauty, and [the soul] ends by conceiving of God in terms of beauty." About Plotinus, his ultimate values and the nature of the Plotinian experience of mystical union, Reyes is utterly wrong. "The One" has no characteristics, beauty no more than any other (though beauty is to be deeply appreciated as a gateway toward ultimate being); it is certainly not "God"; and the ultimate rapture is one of the complete loss of individual identity in a union with the all-embracing essence of the universe. (According to his disciple Porphyry—whose polishing may be largely responsible for the literary value of the *Enneads*—Plotinus himself only attained this state four times, which Porphyry seems to regard with awe.) But in regard to Vasconcelos (who is unlikely to have ever set aside his insistent personal self), the attraction of Plotinus's "pages about beauty" must have been very strong because, despite his more spiritual aspirations toward transcending the physical, it was beauty, and eventually power, that truly enthralled José Vasconcelos. Of course, the rapturous appreciation of the beautiful—and the intensity of sexual union—may be far closer to mystical union than more puritan sensibilities would care to admit.

In Lima he announced, "I follow the straight line of Plotinus." It was the first time that his diffuse interest in mysticism seemed to have found a clear channel. The reading of Plotinus had converted him to a kind of "aesthetic monism" that also provided the title of one of his articles, proposing the experience of beauty as an alternative mystical path, preferable to Christian love. Everything should lead away from the body and aspire to the divine. His interpretation of Beethoven's Seventh Symphony is an example of this vertical model, from "anguish at desire" and "the painful passion of a specific love" to the sentiment of detachment that triumphs over every misfortune. In the choreographic interpretation of passages from the Seventh by the Isadora Duncan ballet troupe, Vasconcelos imagines that "the feet draw the substance from the earth and raise it . . . toward celestial adventures." The final symphonic theme "advances proudly . . . wounds and rectifies, coordinates and adapts without squandering itself as life is squandered in so much useless exertion."

But for Vasconcelos, Plotinus was much more than just a philosophical authority. He wanted to translate what he saw as the doctrine of Plotinus into practical behavior, rather than merely preach to an educated audience. He thought he might write a major philosophical work modeled after the *Enneads* about "Good and Evil, Fortune, immortality, studied in successive treatises . . . according to the pattern of the Neo-Platonic master."

And then he thought he should practice the ideas of contemplation he saw in Plotinus: for him, above all, the contemplation of nature. He left Lima, attempted a rapprochement (unsuccessfully) with Elena in New York, and then began to travel across the American West, with all its astounding natural beauty. (Elena soon married an American businessman and would later become a pioneer Mexican feminist.) Vasconcelos wrote his first lyrical sketches, readings of nature against the background music of his feelings about Plotinus. They foreshadow the great descriptions of nature that are scattered through his volumes of autobiography. Predictably, the landscapes tend to become no more than reflections of Vasconcelos's past experiences or present ideals: stones "that carry discord in their breasts, like worn-out human loves," the sun imprisoned by its karma, ""trees that elevate their yearning," panoramas in which nature, contrasted with man, "completes its mission without failures."

He also imagines landscapes of the soul, more directly connected with Plotinian thought, as in his short story "El Fusilado" (The Executed Man), in which a military ambush and a lover's betrayal—inspired by the Revolution and Adriana—merely set the stage for the liberation of a man after death, the new life as the soul rises through the astral spheres. The *fusilado* no longer suffers when he remembers his days on earth or his children now orphaned, because "the pure spirit only knows joy."

In 1920, the rebellion of Agua Prieta, by generals from Sonora under the leadership of Álvaro Obregón, overthrew the government of Venustiano Carranza, who was hunted down and died in a surprise nocturnal attack. The leader that Vasconcelos had included in his list of "serpents" was dead and the way was open for Vasconcelos's return to Mexico. He became the rector of the National Autonomous University of Mexico (a position of considerable power and public prestige to which he would add much more of both), and later President Obregón appointed him Secretary of Education. In a letter to his friend Reyes, Vasconcelos says:

My body today can suffer as a slave and at times does suffer, but my soul is living a celebration. This, I tell you now, is the grace that I have found through the triple path of suffering, study and beauty. Suffering obliges me to meditate, thought reveals the inanity of the world and beauty shows me the path of the eternal. At those times when it is not possible to meditate or enjoy beauty, one must complete a work; a terrestrial work, a work that prepares the way for others and allows us to follow after ourselves.

He has accepted "a terrestrial work." Just as Plotinus wanted to perpetuate his own interpretation of Plato, so Vasconcelos will "complete a work" based on his aestheticized version of Plotinus. It will be a work of spiritual creation but very concrete in its results and its influence, an educational *Ennead*.

v

Vasconcelos designed a new emblem for the National University during his period as rector. It is a simply drawn map of all Latin America from the Rio Grande to Tierra del Fuego at the utmost southern tip of Patagonia. A phrase runs across the map, reflecting the obvious influence of Rodó's *Ariel: Por mi raza hablará el espíritu* ("The spirit will speak for my race"). The map is protected by two "magnificent eagles" and in the background rise the volcanoes of the Valley of Mexico. "I have not come," he said, "to govern the University but to ask the University to work for the people."

To accomplish his goal, so that the institution "might pour out its treasures and work for the people," one of his first ideas was to translate the classics and distribute them at no cost. Dazzled by Vasconcelos, the new generation hurried to his office and enrolled in his new educational crusade. The future editor, historian, and essayist Daniel Cosío Villegas was one of those young men. "Look, my friend," Vasconcelos said to him, "I'm not thinking of governing the University with the University Council. That's of no importance to me. I'm going to govern the University in a direct and personal way. If you care to participate in this government, come here, starting tomorrow and right here we will settle the problems of the University." The next day Cosío Villegas showed up on time and Vasconcelos gave him the job of translating the *Enneads* of Plotinus from French into Spanish.

In those years, Vasconcelos published dozens of authors under the imprint of the university. They were beautiful editions in green binding and they were given away in public places, like the Fountain of Quixote in Chapultepec Park, where ordinary Mexicans often spent Sundays relaxing with their families. President Obregón, a fearsome man of action but also well-known for his sense of humor, observed all this with ironic indulgence. What sense did it make to publish the dialogues of Plato for illiterate and poverty-stricken peasants? To Vasconcelos, it all made good sense. He was convinced that the uplift of the people had to begin with books. It was the old idea that José Martí had proposed, the salvation of Latin America through reading but now actually carried out by a revolutionary government. In October 1921, Obregón made Vasconcelos his Secretary of Education.

Setting aside the question of the actual value of Plato to the illiterate, Vasconcelos's program also jump-started, for the first time, a massive publishing industry in Mexico. He would later say that it had been "the first flood of books in the history of Mexico." They were all published in translation and Vasconcelos favored and disfavored (in other words, did not publish) authors according to his personal preferences and partly according to a general criterion that reflected his own taste and temperament. He liked to distinguish between what he called "books that you read sitting down" and "books that you read standing," by which he meant inspiring, "prophetic" books that could stir men's minds and emotions and theoretically change their lives. French rationalism or English and German Enlightenment literature interested him not in the least; nor did the more aphoristic sort of classical writer. Homer yes, Greek literary classics yes, Dante's *Divine Comedy* "because it was a confirmation of important celestial messages," some of the classic Spaniards as well as Latin American and Mexican writers, the gospels because "they represented the greatest miracle in history and the supreme law among all those that regulate the spirit," and only "as a condescension to current opinion" a few plays of Shakespeare.

"Truth is only expressed in prophetic form," he would say, but the decision on what constituted prophecy, what might lead to human redemption, was entirely to be decided by Vasconcelos. He published volume after volume of his own personal selection of "mystics," including Plotinus, who of course was one; Plato, who may have been; the somewhat odd choices of the novelists Romain Rolland and Benito Pérez Galdós (the great Spanish liberal novelist); and then Leo Tolstoy, because he represented the "genuine modern incarnation of the Christian spirit."

In this profusion of the written word that included so many writers of the highest worth, excluded others equally great, and perhaps spent too much publishing ink on Vasconcelos's personal hobby horses, certain patterns can be seen, apparently innocuous in the midst of all this immense cultural contribution, but signs of the great man's limitations and even of the truly dark road he would choose to descend in his later middle years. Despite his interest in non-Western cultural trends, for instance, he remains squarely within the Christian (and specifically Catholic) tradition, with no doubts about its cultural and moral superiority. On Buddhism, he recommends incorporating in his project "a reference to Buddhist morality, which is like an annunciation of Christian morality," an assumption that Vasconcelos, with his fluent English, could already have seen refuted in studies already available on southern (Theravada) Buddhism or even within the somewhat Westernized semi-religion of Theosophy. As for Shakespeare, the picture is a little more complicated. The notion of the absolute literary supremacy of Shakespeare has always been a position less acceptable to Latin cultures than to those strongly influenced by England (most Italian thought, for instance, ranks Dante Alighieri far above Shakespeare in literary skill and useful wisdom). Raised in a culture very committed to primary colors of feeling and morality (though capable of considerable rhetorical overkill), Spaniards and Latin Americans may often be daunted, even bewildered by Shakespeare's profusion of themes, characters, and language (his archaisms, of course, require a bit of study even for educated English-speakers). But in José Vasconcelos, this hesitation before Shakespeare suggests an instinctual rejection (which will become much stronger) of the Anglo-Saxon tradition and its affection for complexity and humor, its implicit democratic view of humanity, even in aristocratic England and of course much more clearly in post-revolutionary America.

And most important, the arrogance of his literary decisions (and the personal authoritarianism of his leadership, even as Rector of the University) reflects an enormously inflated sense of self that, despite his very great intellectual and artistic gifts, easily could lead him into errors of action and judgment. In the same way Plotinus distorts Plato, so Vasconcelos's Plotinus is a truncated Plotinus, with a magnification of the aesthetic—which most mattered to him and occupies only a portion of the *Enneads*—and lip service to the rest. And ultimately derived from Plotinus's revered Plato, a much more equivocal and in part sinister figure than the teacher Socrates begins to emerge as the daimon—Heraclitus's "presiding spirit" too easily translated as "fate"—ruling over Vasconcelos's character: the "philosopher king" of Plato's *Republic*.

Meanwhile, the massive educational adventure continued. He included in his project of publication many "books on the social question that help the oppressed, and that will be chosen by a technical committee along with books of practical application on the arts and industries." Vasconcelos wanted education to be the job of "crusaders," of "fervent apostles" filled with the "zeal for charity" and "evangelical ardor." A campaign against illiteracy began and young intellectuals strode into the slums. Cosío Villegas was one of these "apostles":

And we began to teach them to read and it was a spectacle to see the poet Carlos Pellicer arrive, Sunday after Sunday, in some neighborhood of some poor *barrio*, plant himself in the middle of the main square and begin to loudly clap his hands, after shouting as loud as he could for the people to come out, and when he had gotten all of them out of their hiding places, men, women and children, he would begin his litany: the dawn of the new Mexico is already in sight, which we all have to build, but more than anyone, them, the poor, the true support of every society ... and then the alphabet, the reading of a good piece of prose, and in the end verses, an unequivo-cal demonstration of what could be done with a language that one knew and loved. Carlos never had an audience that was more atten-tive, more sensitive, and that came to venerate him.

The educational mission "to the people" also involved a huge ex-pansion in public education. Between July and November 1922, for instance, the thirty-five professors of the Department of University Ex-tension and Exchange within the National University (headed by Pedro Henríquez Ureña—the "Sócrates" of the Athenaeum of Youth who had returned from exile) gave three thousand lectures to workers, at their work sites or union halls, on the most varied themes, ranging from the narrowly utilitarian issues of health and hygiene to such subjects as his-tory, patriotism, astronomy, and grammar.

Libraries were another Mexican void that Vasconcelos felt the need to fill. The Porfiriato had left an illiteracy rate of nearly 80 percent among the common people. In the Mexico of 1920, with its 15 million inhabit-ants, there were only 70 libraries and only 39 of those were public. In 1924, when Vasconcelos left the Ministry of Public Education, there were 1,916 libraries, and 297,103 books had been distributed among them. In the words once again of Cosío Villegas, nostalgically remembering his youth as a devoted participant in this mission of education:

Then one had faith in the book, and the book of lasting quality; and the books were printed in their thousands and they gave thou-sands away. To found a library in a small and remote village seemed to have as much meaning as building a church and decorating its dome with brilliant mosaics that, for the traveler, would announce that a place was nearby where he could rest and gather his senses.

Vasconcelos, who would be given the honorific of *Maestro de América* (Teacher of America), thought that "the schools are not creative institutions" and that the most important teachers were "the mission-ary teachers" who would travel through the country (like the Fran-ciscans and Dominicans after the Conquest) carrying with them the good news of a government concerned with the most needy among its people and anxious to offer them the benefits of culture. The good news now was not a sermon but a collection of books. The teachers car-ried traveling libraries with them. Jaime Torres Bodet, Vasconcelos's private secretary, described how it was done: "Some fifty volumes were carried around in a wooden crate that could be loaded on the back of a mule, to reach places far from a railroad line."

In the main quadrangle of the building that housed the Ministry of Public Education, Vasconcelos erected four statues, representing Greece, Spain, the Buddha—"as a suggestion of how, in . . . this Indo-Iberic race the East and the West, the North and the South have to unite . . . in a new amorous and synthesized culture"—and in the fourth corner, the figure of an Aztec warrior "to remember the refined art of the indigenes and the myth of Quetzalcoatl."

Meanwhile, the highly selective disciple of Plotinus devoted much of his free time to the cultivation of beauty with a list of lovers. When Berta Singerman, the famous Argentine *declamadora* (public performer of poetry, a profession then much valued), came to visit Mexico, Vas-concelos seduced her and paid his homage to the "refined art of the in-digenes" through an act of love somewhere within one of the pyramids of the ancient temple complex of Teotihuacan.

V I

The foundation myth of the Mexican Revolution was created most cen-trally through the visual arts under the patronage of José Vasconcelos and as another, highly important and original feature of his educational mission. He had spent much of his time in exile absorbing the master-pieces in American and European museums. His philosophical essays would interpret the world as a dance of the spirit, rising toward a musi-cal, "Pythagorean" harmony. He saw himself as the restorer of a higher aesthetic. In architecture he argued for a return to the old colonial tradition, especially the Mexican eighteenth century. Aesthetics dominated his entire outlook, including his sometimes idiosyncratic but impressive assemblage of literary heroes. In those days he thought that opera was destined to disappear (though not Wagner), and that music and dance—like Isadora Duncan interpreting Beethoven—would be the unified art of the future.

For the good of his native Mexico, Vasconcelos took hold of the aesthetic ferment dating back to 1915 and helped to give it an unexpected dimension, above all in the new mural painting. He coordinated the work of the three great muralists—Orozco, Rivera, and Siqueiros—as well as lesser talents and he gave them the walls of public buildings so that they might present the cultural rebirth of the country to the widest possible audience. Around 1931, in his short essay on "Mexican Painting"—with its subtitle of "The Maecenas," presumably comparing himself to Virgil's famous patron—he allows God Himself to speak in support of his project, as if to praise a cosmically sanctioned cultural *caudillo* in distinctly authoritarian terms:

> In the breast of all this anarchic humanity there will periodically appear those men who make order: to impose my law, forgotten because of the dispersal of paradisiacal faculties. They will be unified men, born chiefs . . . Through them the rhythm of the spirit will be victorious! Sometimes illuminated Buddhas, sometimes coordinating philosophers, their mission will be to unite the dispersed faculties, to give complete expression to the epochs, the races and the worlds.

Like many patrons, he overstates his own purely artistic importance. Without his plan, his "religious" doctrine that he had transmitted to them—as an intermediary of God (rather like the Plotinian demiurge who is an intermediary for the featureless One without qualities)—he asserts that these great painters would have remained only "noisy mediocrities."

What is true—above and beyond all that Vasconcelian noise—
is that their patron gave them the support and venues that opened
the gates to the golden age of Mexican muralism. To decorate the
centuries-old walls of the National Preparatory School (the former
College of the Jesuits) Vasconcelos contracted José Clemente Orozco,
a powerful painter of anarchist predilections who participated in the
Revolution. His murals would reflect the pain and striving and tragedy that Orozco had witnessed, including moments of redemption
but with little propagandistic charge. For the corridor of his Ministry
of Public Education, Vasconcelos wanted a festive, hopeful vision and
so he invited "our great artist, Diego Rivera." The role of the Maecenas, according to José Vasconcelos, necessarily involved a measure of
interference: " . . . the Maecenas not only gives . . . money but also the
plan and the theme."

Rivera arrived with sketches of women in costumes typical of each
state in the republic and a plan for the stairway that Vasconcelos described as an "ascending frieze that, starting from sea level with its
tropical vegetation, would change into the landscape of the high plains
and end with the volcanoes." These might have been Diego's responses
to the initial guidelines laid out by Vasconcelos but from then on it was
all Diego, there and elsewhere, including the 239 panels (within a space
of 17,060 square feet) in the corridors of the ministry. The specific subjects that he set beside each other, from 1923 to the completion of the
project in 1928, were not dictated by Vasconcelos, who was capable of a
more modest presence before the creation of great art: "The best artistic epochs are those in which the artist works with personal liberty, but
subject to a clearly defined philosophical or religious doctrine."

The doctrine was the Mexican Revolution, interpreted by Diego
Rivera with a weight of social idealism and historical (and aesthetic)
materialism, very different from the inclinations of Vasconcelos, who
might be termed a mystic of the flesh but hardly of the details of daily
living, which Diego reveled in: the world of work (women spinning,
men working in the fields, miners, dye workers) and the fiestas of
Mexico with all their energetic movement and local color. Yet perhaps

the most significant mural deals directly with education, depicting a female teacher in a rural setting instructing a class of Indians, while an armed revolutionary soldier stands guard to protect them. Even in his richly descriptive memoirs, Vasconcelos rarely condescends to the description of everyday activities. His themes are nature and the heavens, the environments of God, untouched by human beings. Or one man alone, himself, in touch with passion and the absolute. And yet there was a connection, a current of sympathy, between Diego Rivera and José Vasconcelos. Both of them, the philosopher and the artist, believed in social redemption through art.

As a spiritual architect, a patron of morally charged spectacle, José Vasconcelos touched a deep vein in Mexican history. The so-called Spiritual Conquest, the conversion of the Indians in the sixteenth century, had been accomplished not through sermons or books but by visual means. One of the sources of inspiration for Vasconcelos had been the wealth of mural paintings on the walls of so many Mexican convents, executed by Dominicans and Franciscans, sometimes with the help of Indian artists they had trained. Vasconcelos knew very well that the Mexican Indians had learned the conquerors' sacred history through these paintings and later from the sumptuous façades and altarpieces of the Mexican Baroque, which, like indigenous art itself, would crowd the available surfaces with rich, expressive detail. He was not interested in founding a religion but he did try to carry a message of universal culture (both Western and what he believed to be Eastern) throughout the country. And he complemented this message with a new and powerfully expressive valuation of Mexican culture, drawing from all its past histories: Indian, Viceregal, and Liberal. The Revolution in education represented a new order, a catholicity of culture.

"May the light of these bright walls be like the dawn of a new Mexico, of a splendid Mexico," José Vasconcelos said, concluding his speech on that morning of July 1922, when he inaugurated the building of his Ministry of Education in its new, dazzling colors. Despite his personal (and national) commitment to cultural splendor, he could never have suspected the tremendous historical and political significance that the corpus of Mexican mural painting would acquire. The murals of Rivera, Orozco, and Siqueiros would be the visual gospels that created the myth of the Mexican Revolution. Instead of the complicated pattern of contending and sometimes stubbornly local forces that it was, the Revolution as well as the previous history of Mexico took on— especially through the later work of Rivera—an idealized form, in clear stages, a new sacred history. First there was the Indian arcadia, then the trauma of the Conquest, the dark centuries of the Viceroyalty, the first redemption through independence from Spain, the second redemption (against the Catholic Church) of the Reform under Benito Juárez, the dictatorship of Porfirio Díaz, and the final redemptive advent of the Revolution. Orozco's interpretation is less linear, more ambiguous, deeper and often pessimistic. But in the richly flowering, lavishly colored textures of Rivera, the Revolution becomes not what it was but what it would have wished to be, what it sought to be, above and beyond all the differences of groups with differing ideologies resolving their quarrels on the fields of battle. The Revolution became an epic in which the Mexican people took their destiny into their own hands to correct the errors of the past and build a new order of social justice, in the fields and in the cities, marked by democracy, a healthy nationalism, universal education, and pride in their cultural roots.

It was a message that attracted intellectuals and artists from all of America and even Europe. They came to Mexico to photograph its people, to appreciate its landscape, its popular arts, its gastronomy. To translate its poems, to respect its hard-earned national self-esteem, admire its many schools for Indians and for the urban poor (inspired by the American philosopher John Dewey, who also came to Mexico). And in some cases (such as D. H. Lawrence, who wrote *The Plumed Serpent* after visiting the country), they even came to identify with, participate in, and artistically re-create its bloodiest mythical traditions. For some years, Mexico was a magnet for the world and, especially for the political left, a possible utopia.

Martí and Rodó applied their imagination to ideas and worked in the field of letters toward the unity of Latin America. Vasconcelos went a step further. Despite all his talk about higher planes of being, he was always, essentially, a man of the body. He proceeded to bring Latin America to Mexico and in his own person brought Mexico to Latin America. In September 1921, while still Rector of the National University, he organized the First International Convention of Students. Representatives arrived from all the countries of Hispanic America, including Venezuela, then governed by the dictator Juan Vicente Gómez. Vasconcelos gave a fiery speech attacking Gómez. Then he and the student representatives produced a declaration of Latin American nationalism that expanded its wording to include the entire world. All of them, of course including Vasconcelos himself, felt themselves to be apostles, saviors and "socialists of honor." In their resolution, signed by the president of the convention, Daniel Cosío Villegas, they declared:

> The youth of the universities proclaims that it will struggle for the advent of a new humanity, based on modern principles of economic, social and international justice [and affirms] its optimism before the grave problems that are shaking the world and its absolute confidence in securing a new social organization for the renovation of the economic and moral values of humanity that will permit and further the achievement of the high spiritual goals of man.

Many young people (including a number of writers), attracted by the educational experiments of Vasconcelos, would come to Mexico. One of them during his time in the country, the young Peruvian idealist Víctor Raúl Haya de la Torre, would found the A.P.R.A, a movement inspired by a Latin American vision. Later (as APRA without periods), it would have a long history as a political party in Peru. And among the renowned authors who arrived in Mexico, the Chilean poetess Gabriela Mistral (Nobel Prize for Literature in 1945) would accept the position of general editor for a *Collection of Readings for Women*.

Between August and December 1922, Vasconcelos carried the good news of the Mexican Revolution to Brazil, Argentina, Chile, and Uruguay. He was accompanied by some old friends from the Ateneo de la Juventud (like the writer Julio Torri), young collaborators like Carlos Pellicer, the opera singer Fanny Anitúa, a military band, a folkloric orchestra with dancers dressed in the conventional Mexican styles of a *tehuana* (an indigenous woman from the Isthmus of Tehuantepec) or a *china poblana* (a semi-mythical figure from the seventeenth century whose dress had become one of the standards of Mexican kitsch), as well as by cadets from the military college. In September, "Socrates," Pedro Henríquez Ureña, joined the traveling troupe. At every step they encountered aesthetic fragments, of the past or of the present, that for Vasconcelos seemed to foreshadow a common future. In Rio de Janeiro he thought he had encountered not only the traces of "Iberia, the common fatherland" but also "a religious unction derived only from the power of its beauty." In São Paulo, they welcomed him at the Teacher's College with songs and dances performed by the students. The city of Ouro Preto reminded him of Guanajuato: "the mineral leaves monuments, buildings and, in a short time, ruins." It pleased him to see that no single politician or "hero" in Brazil "incarnates the fatherland" as in (Spanish-speaking of course) Venezuela.

On the sixteenth of September 1922 (Mexican Independence Day), he delivered a special gift from Mexico to the people of Brazil, a statue of the last Aztec hero, Cuauhtémoc. (The original now stands on the Paseo de la Reforma in Mexico City.) In Uruguay, Vasconcelos (still politically the democrat) lamented the use of power by the former president José Batlle but appreciated his moderation. He and his entourage spent a month in Buenos Aires. Alfredo Palacios, the first Argentine socialist legislator, whom he described as "the Argentine patriarch of Iberoamericanism" and "apostle of every noble cause," gave him an impressive reception at the University of La Plata. Vasconcelos was profoundly impressed by the teachers' colleges Sarmiento had founded and he asked Pedro Henríquez Ureña to deliver a lecture on "The Utopia of America." His subject: in its cultural nationalism, in its return to origins, "despite how much tends to uncivilize it, despite the terrifying emotions that shake and disturb it to its very foundations . . . Mexico is creating a new life." Latin America should follow the example of Mexico.

In October he visited the spectacular waterfalls of Iguazú and was enraptured: "the vital nerve of Latin America and the propulsive center of a civilization without precedent in History . . . the people that will control Iguazú will be the people of America." In Chile he was received by a multitude of students and looked for trouble by criticizing the power of the military. He included a reference to Mexico: "The misfortune of Mexico, the misfortune of Chile, the misfortune of Latin America is that we are governed by the sword and not the intelligence."

He returned from his long voyage across the body of America convinced of three things: militarism is the central evil of Latin America, power should devolve to the intellectuals, and Latin America will be the cradle of a new civilization.

VIII

The presidential election of 1924 was on the horizon. Vasconcelos suggested himself as a candidate for president. The Sonoran generals in power had other plans. He resigned his position at the Ministry of Education and, as a test for his higher ambitions, ran for governor of Oaxaca and lost. Once again he went off into exile.

From then on his dream was to become a "new Sarmiento." As president of Argentina from 1868 to 1874, Domingo Faustino Sarmiento had constructed hundreds of schools, libraries, astronomical observatories, botanical and zoological gardens, parks, roads, railroads, ships, telegraph lines, and even new cities. Vasconcelos would be a new, modern Mexican Sarmiento. But in his farewell address to the teachers whom he had inspired and trained, he spoke of another antecedent (to him), one of greater significance to Mexico, no less than Quetzalcóatl, the mythological god-man who brought civilization to the Toltec culture, was then driven out of his homeland by Huitzilopochtli, the god of war, but promised to return, from the east where he had gone: "Quetzalcóatl, the principle of civilization, the god who constructs, will triumph over Huitzilopochtli, the demon of violence and evil, who for so many centuries has held destructive and insolent power!"

In 1925, Vasconcelos wrote his most exaggerated fantasy, *La raza cósmica* (The Cosmic Race). On reading it, Miguel de Unamuno said, and not with respect, "The great fantasizer!" Along with Spain, Vasconcelos declared, the Latin American race had fallen into a theological abyss long before 1898, in fact since the Battle of Trafalgar in 1805, when a league of European powers, spearheaded by the British fleet, defeated the alliance of Napoleonic France and Spain. While it seemed that God favored "Anglo-Saxonism," the Iberian race fragmented its geography into small republics and lost its "spirit" to two extremes, dogma and atheism. But destiny would offer a surprise. Using the lens of "race" typical of his time, Vasconcelos discerned a divine design: we Iberians would become a fifth race, the final race, which would fuse the four racial fragments of our planet. Near the Amazon, a city for the ages would arise, Universopolis he called it, where men would live totally suffused with love and beauty. In the glory of the tropics, humanity would be transformed, much for the better.

It was a vision of a future aesthetic empire. Vasconcelos united the philosopher Comte's division of history into three stages with the Neoplatonic myth of the hierarchical, sphere-by-sphere ascent of the soul. At the lowest level was the economic or warrior stage, then the intellectual or political, and, at the summit, the spiritual or aesthetic. The first level was no more than a law of the jungle, a trivial matter of ballistics and economics (Vasconcelos once defined the latter as "the kitchen of the intelligence"). The second level apparently was his view of the modern age, Western culture in its Aristotelian version, the tyranny of rules and reason. The third stage embodied Vasconcelos's version of the Plotinian heights, a very material paradise full of fantasy, inspiration, amorous joy, the miracle of divine beauty. In that state (or place), to be less than beautiful would be a desecration. "The ugliest will not procreate, they will not want to procreate . . . Matrimony [and here we hear the echoes of his autobiography] will cease to be a consolation for misfortunes . . . and will be transformed into a work of art."

Around 1926, the fantasist turned political again, within the restrictions of this stage of the world. The next Mexican elections would be in 1928. Vasconcelos did not participate in them, but when Álvaro Obregón, the president-elect, was assassinated in July 1928, new elections were called for 1929. Vasconcelos decided to launch his candidacy. He gave a speech in Chicago asking for support from the American government and American public opinion. The United States should stop supporting dictators and offer effective and respectful aid to liberal and democratic movements on the southern continent. He argued (for once Vasconcelos actually argued rather than declaimed) that, without democracy, the result will have to be either military or bureaucratic dictatorship: Latin American *caudillismo* or the dominance of a bureaucratic caste, as in Russia. He called for moral regeneration but associated it with the process of authentic democracy: "It is only fair to discuss and criticize democracy once we have installed it." While still in exile, he built up a following, especially among the young, through ferocious articles published in the newspaper *El Universal*.

His return to Mexico City was his own Palm Sunday, 1929. He would be the modern Quetzalcóatl, a liberator like Madero but far more cultured. Through the electoral process, the people should react as they did with Madero, only now their choice will transfigure the country for good and all. He would offer the chance to "purify the Revolution" and return it to its proper channel. He began to refer to himself, for the first time, as a "prophet." He had a new "Adriana," a dominating impassioned love, Antonieta Rivas Mercado, to accompany him on his great adventure.

But as he advanced in his quest, the signs of impending defeat grew stronger and the notes of Old Testament prophecy more frequent in his speeches: indignation, agitation, violent outbursts, dithyrambs on evil and injustice, anguish at the mistaken preferences of society. An observer mentioned "the sharp sword" of his words. Another saw the language of Vasconcelos descending in "naked phrases, luminous bursts." He himself dubbed them "spiritual dynamite." It was not mere rhetoric when Vasconcelos said of his campaign: "The Ten Commandments are my program above and beyond the Constitution." He was speaking more incisively than he may have realized. His campaign was all admonition, rather than a program. As in the Old Testament, it expressed almost no positive message.

But its negative criticisms were clear enough. His political rivals, the Sonoran generals, had enriched themselves through the Revolution. They had carved out new personal estates, they were brazenly sacking the banks, they were conspiring with the American ambassador Dwight Morrow to assure the victory of their candidate, Pascual Ortiz Rubio. Vasconcelos grew increasingly impatient with the masses of Mexico. Weren't the same people who cheered for him in the morning capable of going to the bullfights in the afternoon and applauding a matador who was in league with the government? Perhaps because he realized that he would lose the election, he gave orders for a reaction to the expected fraud. This included armed revolution, of course, as well as other means that partially contradicted his call to arms and resembled the methods of Gandhi: peaceful resistance involving the refusal to pay taxes, to use or to run any public transport, and so on. Vasconcelos now saw himself as the conscience of Mexico. Thanks to him the country had a new and final opportunity for salvation. "Your destiny, Mexico! is at stake." Vasconcelos or the abyss.

Once again, his uncompromising temperament—fierce, inflexible, convinced of his own magnanimity—spilled over into the lives of people he may have considered "all too human." And the result was to be expected. Young students who adored him were killed in the streets for his cause. He was surrounded by an entire generation of potential martyrs, his young apostles, the students. One of his followers, Andrés Henestrosa, a Zapotec Indian who had studied in Mexico City thanks to the program of scholarships established by Vasconcelos, wrote:

We all believed we were destined for sacrifice because we believed that our hearts were clean and immaculate. And so we ardently embraced *Vasconcelismo*. We came to this fight not to live nor to triumph but to leave, on the barricades of Mexico, on the asphalt of Mexico . . . that existence that would only take on meaning if we sacrificed it for that which is most desirable of all things: freedom, which we believed was threatened.

After he lost at the polls (in an election heavily marred by fraud but one that the generals would never have allowed him to win), Vasconcelos could have founded a new political party based on something more than his personal charisma. He refused to do it, and he also decided at first (despite his previous rhetoric) not to call for armed resistance. Only two options remained: exile or the sacrifice of his own life. Leaving the country would have the value of an historical stimulus. "Prometheus enchained" not by the jealousy of the gods but through the apathy of his own people. And yet a martyr's sacrifice would be by far the more dramatic statement. Not a suicide but the death that might come to him in battle or at least in defiance of the possibility of death. It was something he had asked of others. And they had given their lives, for him. After all, a new Madero should continue, right up to the end, faithful to the memory of Madero. And to that of José Martí.

To Andrés Henestrosa he confided that he was ready to resort to arms: "For the first time in the history of this damn country," he said, "Intelligence will mount a horse . . . I have enjoyed life, Andrés, I have been a lover of glory, as D'Annunzio has said . . . and I have played with death, during the years of the Revolution. So that for me, now is the hour."

With this last phrase, Vasconcelos was directly quoting José Martí, though it is interesting, given the future course of Vasconcelos's life, that he also quoted Gabriele D'Annunzio, the John the Baptist of Italian fascism, who would be honored and eventually sidelined by the "savior" Mussolini. (D'Annunzio was a man in some ways similar to Vasconcelos, much concerned with the supremacy of beauty and power and the serial seduction of women.) But when the day to set out on his armed rebellion arrived, with a small group of men ready to risk their lives, Henestrosa, who had awakened prepared for the fight at five o'clock in the morning, received no word from his *caudillo*. At seven o'clock he went to see Vasconcelos and was told, "After you went to sleep, we changed our plans."

Vasconcelos had decided it was not his hour. Some three months later, on February 14, 1930, between twenty and forty Vasconcelistas, accused of plotting against President Ortiz Rubio, were summarily executed by the army. Like the student Germán de Campo, who was shot by General Gonzalo N. Santos in the streets during the campaign, they had stood with Vasconcelos and he had now abandoned them. And he would bear the guilt of this final decision, at least in some measure, until his death thirty years later.

When Vasconcelos decided to leave, Mexico lost a secular saint, but did gain something more lasting. Outside of Mexico, from Spain and from the very belly of the beast he most hated, living and writing his memoirs in Austin, Texas, he would compose the four volumes of his great autobiography and various works of philosophy, including his *Aesthetics*, which he (though not posterity) considered his most important work. He would also produce other books, one on *Bolivarism and Monroeism* (1934), where he pursued the old theme of the irreconcilable differences between the two Americas, and a *Brief History of Mexico* (1936), in which he completely rejected the liberal vision of Mexican history he had thoroughly supported years earlier, plus at least two pamphlets: *What Is the Revolution?* and *What Is Communism?*

Accompanying him throughout his period of exile were his wife and his children.

I X

———

He would return to Mexico in 1938, after spending nearly a decade of mostly self-imposed exile in Europe and the United States. In Paris, in the early 1930s, together with the highly talented Antonieta Rivas

Mercado, he founded a journal, *La Antorcha* (The Torch), with the same name as an earlier journal he had directed in 1924–25. (In 1931, Antonieta would cause an enormous scandal when, isolated and desperate, lacerated by her love for two married men, one of them Vasconcelos, she entered the precincts of Notre Dame Cathedral and shot herself in the heart, using Vasconcelos's own pistol, in defiance of God and implicitly Vasconcelos.)

The journal, which survived for thirteen issues, was poorly produced, small in format, with errors in its French pieces and strewn with epigraphs in Spanish that are continual examples of the sin of pride: "God punishes and tests those he loves," or "Solitude is the fatherland of the strong and silence is its prayer." Even the advertisements in *La Antorcha* were marked by Vasconcelos's new and all-consuming ideological passion, which he would cultivate for the rest of his life: hatred of the Yankee, represented most vividly for him in the person of the American ambassador to Mexico, Dwight Morrow, whom he accused of orchestrating his defeat. It would not be the last conspiracy theory that would tarnish the later years of a man who had contributed so much to his own country and to Latin America.

La Antorcha was meant to "defend the moral and material interests of Spanish America," purifying the "degraded consciousness" of its people. He admitted that Spanish Americans had lost their earthly empire. But the spiritual realm remained, left vacant by the emptiness of Anglo-Saxon thought. One had to follow the example of the Hebrews or the ancient Iberians, oppressed by the Romans but immune to their philosophy. "Let us take the machine from the Yankee, not his metaphysics."

La Antorcha is the variation on one note of a man who refuses to forget. He had not been defeated. He had won "all the votes." Over and over he would keep on repeating: "It wasn't me who gave up the fight but a tired people who could not make good on their promise to fight in defense of the vote." If 14 million Mexicans "had forgotten the outrage," Vasconcelos would "think in flames" to burn away any trace (at least in himself) of forgetfulness. In his rage, in his elitist devotion to the idea of the superior man, the philosopher king, and his right to rule, he is no longer a democrat. And his tastes in reading have become even more idiosyncratic. This enormously intelligent man turned willfully ignorant and, already in 1933—as demonstrated by one of his short stories on a "rabbinical" conspiracy between Wall Street and Moscow to dominate the world—he had begun to accept a clumsily forged document produced by the Czarist secret police as truth, though fortunately he was no longer in the position to distribute thousands of free copies to the Mexican people. But *The Protocols of the Elders of Zion* had already received the blessings of a government risen to power, only one year earlier, in Germany. And Vasconcelos would soon bestow his praise on yet another book intimately connected with that government.

In 1940, shortly after the outbreak of war in Europe with Hitler's surprise assault on the Polish nation, Vasconcelos accepted a position as editor of *Timón* (Rudder), a journal funded by the German embassy. It would last for only seventeen issues because the Mexican government, resolutely neutral but strongly inclined toward the Allies (and later to enter the war against Germany), did not allow it to continue. *Timón* published virulently anti-Semitic propaganda (in two articles signed by Vasconcelos himself, others contracted by him), "information" direct from Joseph Goebbels's Ministry of Propaganda, and an article by Vasconcelos dealing with themes long familiar to his readers, how "Intelligence Imposes Itself" and the supreme value of a specific book:

Hitler, though he disposes of absolute power, is a thousand leagues from Caesarism. Hitler's force does not come from the barracks but from the book [*Mein Kampf*] inspired by his intelligence. Hitler does not owe his power to soldiers, nor to battalions, but to his own speeches that won him power in democratic competition with the other leaders and aspiring leaders that Germany developed after the First World War. To sum up, Hitler represents an idea, the German idea, that had been earlier humiliated by the militarism of the French and the perfidy of the English . . .

In other words, Hitler had won office through the same kind of peaceful and admirable campaign conducted by Vasconcelos. It was the merit of the German people to have responded well, unlike the ungrateful Mexicans, who had not been fully able to appreciate "intelligence" (for which Vasconcelos, in the above passage, uses the highly erudite classicism *cacumen*).

When the Allied counteroffensive on the eastern and western fronts began the pincer assault on Hitler's armies, Vasconcelos was devastated. He would turn his affection toward other dictatorial regimes. During the 1950s he would be received with respect by Franco in Spain and Perón in Argentina and Batista in Cuba. Invited to the Dominican Republic by Rafael Trujillo, he would write an appreciative prologue to a book of poems by the Caribbean dictator's wife.

In Mexico he would be honored for his luminous past. In 1941 he was made Director of the National Library and, some years later, put in charge of another great collection of books, the Biblioteca de México. He was lavishly honored at home and abroad as a writer and philosopher. His autobiographies, with their masterful style, had been welcomed with enormous praise and material success. But he was not consoled. The Mexican people had not risen as one to install him in the Presidential Chair. And he had not died heroically, like Madero or Martí. Along with his own wounded ego, he would sometimes dwell on the memory of those who had died in the streets, during his campaign. He would always want to be recognized, in retrospect, as the legitimate president of Mexico:

> . . . still pending is an act of justice for those who died in the electoral campaign of 1929 . . . The national conscience knows, or should know, that we won the elections of 1929 and while this is not recognized publicly, and perhaps officially, I would not be able to accept any honor without the feeling that I was betraying

truth and justice . . . Consequently, if my country does not decide to honor me as a political figure (which it should do) I prefer that it not concern itself with me in any way . . .

But he would accept every honor offered him. And it was clear that he no longer believed in democracy. In another one of his articles for *Timón*, writing of the benefits that would shower upon Latin America with the victory of Nazi Germany over the democracies (especially of course over the "perfidious" Anglo-Saxons), he said:

> And in this new era the peoples of America will find renewed opportunity to organize in conformity with their tradition and their blood, and according to their Christian antecedents . . . An outcome that would award victory to the Allies would be the worst possible calamity for the inhabitants of this continent. It would simply immerse us in an odious and enslaving state of colonialization.

His growing fascination with dictatorships converged with a return to the religiosity of his youth (and of his mother). He would turn to a rigid version of Catholicism that now replaced his former loose, aestheticized conception of Plotinus. In 1943 he became a Franciscan lay brother, praising the contributions of that order "to the construction of New Spain and what is today our Mexican Fatherland."

But the Franciscan principles were "too soft" for him. He switched over to the Jesuits: "At one time, I professed Franciscan exclusivism. But now I have understood that, for the brutality of the struggle we have to wage, San Ignacio de Loyola is superior." He would later conflate his return to Catholicism with the principles and activities of his period of true grandeur, many years ago in the 1920s:

> In reality, there is no difference between my position during the period, for example, during which I acted as a Minister of the Revolution and I often declared myself "a Christian in the manner of

Tolstoy" and my earlier position, as a Catholic (which is the same as being a better Christian than Tolstoy) and my return to the orthodox truth.

On the fourteenth of March 1942 his long-suffering wife, Serafina Miranda, died. For almost forty years they had been united only through love for their children. His daughter Carmen would remember the funeral:

> Vasconcelos had to rent two buses to carry all the people . . . She had always wanted to be loved by humble people. When the coffin was lowered into the ground, Vasconcelos sobbed bitterly. At that moment he must have known and felt who he really had as a wife; perhaps they were tears of belated repentance.

That same year, he remarried, to a much younger woman, the pianist Esperanza Cruz, with whom he had a son he named Héctor. The marriage would collapse, due to Vasconcelos's displays of jealousy and also because his daughter Carmen never accepted the new wife.

He would insist, more than once, that he had never been a Nazi sympathizer: "Me, a Nazi! I laugh at those who make that charge against me, because I am one of the few Mexicans who has struggled all his life against dictatorships. I sympathized with the cause of Germany because it had much to do with the liberation of a great people from the injustices of the Treaty of Versailles." It was a claim that did not prevent him—in 1955, only four years before his death—from contributing an enthusiastic preface to the second edition of *Derrota Mundial* (Worldwide Defeat), a justification of Nazism (and denial of the Holocaust) by the notorious Mexican Nazi Salvador Borrego Escalante. The preface, using the conventional, slightly coded language of neo-Nazi revisionism, showed no doubts about the value Vasconcelos placed on yet one more book, this one brimming for him with new "information":

> The lie achieved its objective. Entire populations were swept away to participation in the conflict, moved by sentiments based

on information that, as was afterwards learned, were deliberately fabricated by the band that controlled world communications.

As for what had been the real center of his purely personal life, the love of women, he would respond to a reporter's question by saying: "I have lived by fleeing questions about sex," and later, in his final years, to a friend, "The women I was involved with were total whores."

He was ferociously anti-Marxist and yet, in the last year of his life, his obsession with the figure of the *caudillo* and with the abstract affection for brutality and courage he had not shown in his critical hour of 1929 led him—still brandishing the banner of the Mexican Revolution and his own disappointment—to write to Fidel Castro, "Do not follow the example of Madero's weakness. Be hard; because, if not, you will have to swallow the reality of a people that will not respond to you."

He would spend much of his final years in the garden and small library of a large house south of Mexico City. He used to remind people who visited him that he was the real president of Mexico. He would tell the beads of his rosary under the table and murmur occasional prayers. His new life of relative abnegation (a Plotinian recommendation he had always ignored) did not extend to his enjoyment of food and drink. He especially favored Chinese dishes, because they gave him the impression that they required "a thousand years of preparation." The memory of 1929 pursued him to the end. He would never reconcile himself to his country, which, in his opinion, had lost so much by losing him. The cultural caudillo of the 1920s would die, still greatly honored and deeply embittered, on June 30, 1959, on the brink of the 1960s and a new decade of change and of upheaval.

4

José Carlos Mariátegui

INDIGENOUS MARXISM

In the 1920s, young Peruvians turned to Mexico, searching for a model they could apply to modify the outworn and unacceptable stratification, social and racial, that burdened their country. They were drawn by a social revolution, a nationalist constitution, an educational and cultural project that had rescued and revalued the Indian inheritance and presence in Mexico. And much of it was due to the efforts of a brilliant Mexican intellectual who had impressed the Peruvians and made many friends in Lima, during one of his periods of exile in 1916. He had now become the "Teacher of America," and in October 1925 the admiration of young Peruvians for José Vasconcelos would be sealed in blood.

José Santos Chocano (1875–1934) was known in Peru as the representative of modernism in poetry. He was a heavily built man with a bristling mustache and an extraordinary opinion of his own worth ("Walt Whitman has the north, I have the south"). He was known as the Bard of America (*El Cantor de América*) and had become a very public supporter of the militarist and antidemocratic ideas that another modernist poet, the Argentine Leopoldo Lugones, had enunciated some months earlier. "There has sounded again, for the benefit of the world, the hour of the sword," Lugones had said. In Mexico, José Vasconcelos had parted ways with the military and he severely reproved Chocano's position: "we have lost a poet and gained a buffoon." The polemic between "the Bard of America" and the teacher of Latin American youth resonated throughout the intellectual life of the continent. The Federation of Peruvian Students defended Vasconcelos with an open letter published in the press and titled "Poets and Buffoons": "We, the under-signed writers and artists feel a duty to declare *our intellectual and spiri-tual solidarity* with José Vasconcelos and our profound admiration for his work as a thinker and teacher." Among the signers were the young writer Edwin Elmore and his friend, the already famous José Carlos Mariátegui. A few months later Mariátegui would begin to publish *Amauta*, one of the most important intellectual and literary journals in the history of Latin America.

Elmore on his own wrote a piece attacking Chocano and defending democracy. He took it to the newspaper *La Crónica* but they refused to publish the text and covertly passed it to Chocano, who picked up his telephone and proceeded to insult Elmore profusely, including deroga-tory references to Elmore's father. Elmore refused to back down and took his article, expanded to include the recent insults, to the office of another newspaper, *El Comercio*. There he ran into Chocano. The Cantor de América had once been a secretary to Pancho Villa (who had dictated a preface for a chapbook of Chocano's poetry). He had been a speechwriter for the Guatemalan dictator Manuel Estrada Cabrera and had been crowned with golden laurels by the Peruvian strongman Augusto B. Leguía, whom he supported with articles in the pages of *La Crónica* and *El Comercio*. And he always carried a revolver.

It was October 31, 1925. Santos Chocano and Edwin Elmore stopped in their tracks and looked at each other in surprise. Suddenly Elmore grabbed Chocano's lapel and slapped him in the face. Chocano reeled back for the moment, then drew his gun and shot Elmore in the abdo-men. He was rushed to a hospital, where he died two days later.

The apologist for military dictatorships had ended the life of the young democrat and socialist and follower of Vasconcelos, but Elmore's friends did not forget him, or his work. A year later, on the anniversary of Elmore's murder, José Carlos Mariátegui published an essay by him in the third issue of *Amauta*:

Mexico has assumed—with its powerful generation of new men— the glorious responsibilities of today's ideals . . . The voice of

Vasconcelos has filled the vastness of the continent with echoes in less than a decade . . . It is to the present generation of Mexicans that we owe the rebirth of pride and dignity in Latin-American politics. Mexico has vetoed the imperial and corrupting Dollar; she has hurled a resounding NO at the power of England; Mexico has demonstrated to all the countries of our America that they can speak in a masterful and imposing tone to the greatest powers on earth and that the days have arrived in which "the Spirit will speak for our race."

Edwin Elmore, Mariátegui wrote, would have been one of the contributors to *Amauta*. He had died in defense of Vasconcelos. He did not live to see the strange conversion of his hero to the ideas of Chocano. Nor would Mariátegui live to lament it. But the few years of life that remained to him would be enough to write one of the broadest, deepest, and most enduring works of the Latin American century. Because if Vasconcelos (in line with the Hispanic-American nationalism of Rodó) was like a Hegelian fantasist on the destiny of Latin America, Mariátegui brought those ideas down to earth. In a way, he was our necessary leftist, a kind of Marx to Vasconcelos's Hegel, a practical ballast for our sometimes loosely moored republics. But his contributions extended far beyond his politics.

II

José Carlos Mariátegui La Chira was born in the small city of Moquegua, on June 14, 1894; José del Carmen Eliseo was his baptismal name. He himself never learned the truth about the place and exact date of his birth. We know that he changed his name very early and that later he himself would handle the legal process needed to officially become José Carlos. The mystery of his birthplace would nevertheless accompany him for the rest of his life. The secrecy may have been due to a constant fear on the part of his mother, connected with the issue of social prestige in a complex society troubled with old colonial leavings. María Amalia La Chira Ballejos had him believing that he had been born in Lima, the capital of Peru and of course an important place, where his father lived. Francisco Javier Mariátegui Requejo was descended from an eminent creole partisan of independence (it should be remembered that creole—*criollo*—in the Spanish-American world means a Latin American of pure Spanish descent). Especially in the stratified society of Peru, his political and racial ancestry automatically gave Francisco a measure of prestige within *limeña* high society.

Three children were born from the Mariátegui–La Chira marriage: José Carlos, Guillermina, and Julio César. Then his father abandoned the family. It appears that José Carlos never really knew him and the issue of his father's identity became a constant search and a source of shame for him during his infancy and adolescence. María Amalia, his mother, was a descendent of *curacas*, a Quechua appellation for lower Inca nobles. But in Peru, it meant that she was Indian or mestizo and her ancestors were not of a sufficiently high Inca lineage to permit her a possible entrance into higher Peruvian society and the opportunities that such a cachet might have meant for her sons. Some biographers of Mariátegui suggest that María Amalia, a devout Catholic, did not know that the father of her husband had been a liberal excommunicated by the Church for his anticlerical ideas, a realization (if she came to learn the truth) that would have led her into shame and silence. When the father left the family, their economic situation turned precarious. From Lima, where they had gone, they were forced to move again, in 1899, to the provincial city of Huacho, where María's family resided.

The human and family drama was now fully in place, with its ethnic, social, economic, and religious components. In 1901, José Carlos begins school and the following year, only eight years old, he has a serious accident. His left leg is badly injured. It takes him four years to recover, and the injury will leave him lame for life. He has to abandon his formal education but he becomes a voracious and obsessive reader. He absorbs the stories of Moses, Christ, Siegfried, and the Cid and he goes on, precociously, to Anatole France and Francisco García Calderón. He will finally exhaust the small library left by his father. Fueled by his readings, suffused with his mother's Catholic piety, the introspective José Carlos takes his first literary steps, composing poems with a religious and mystical charge.

Solitude and poverty, sadness, religion, and constant pain. Nevertheless, he struggles against his condition, he perseveres and thinks and reads and writes. His entire life will be a struggle against adverse circumstances, waged with an optimistic but never ingenuous or self-deluded spirit. He will live his life of thought and practice bounded by the texturing of his ideas and a will toward precise and effective political action.

III

At the beginning of the twentieth century, Lima was still a city that thoroughly represented "creole superiority." In its central plaza stands the supreme symbol of this hierarchy, the equestrian statue of Pizarro the Conquistador. The monument was erected in 1935, but it shows the lingering feeling of "creole superiority." (In Mexico there is not even a single street named after Cortés.) But Lima, like many other capitals of Latin America, also showed very clear signs of modernity. When José Carlos returned as a young adolescent to Lima, he was fascinated by the electric lights, the streetcars, the cinema. All the technology excited him. And also the culture. He now had a linguistic tool to help him absorb much of what was most current. During his seemingly endless convalescence, he had taught himself French and he always felt proud of his grammar and pronunciation.

As time went on, the economic condition of the family did not improve, and the remote possibility of an encounter with his father vanished for good when Francisco Mariátegui died in 1907. The young José Carlos, only fourteen, had to bring in some income. He went to work at the newspaper *La Prensa*, in a low-level job. Some say he worked as a stockboy for a linotypist, but that would have been difficult work for a slightly built boy handicapped by his bad leg, since it would have required handling heavy boxes full of lead type. However that may be, his personality and intelligence enabled him to move up a notch and he became an assistant to the linotypist Juan Manuel Campos, who was an anarchist and, obviously impressed with José Carlos, would introduce him to the distinguished anarchist intellectual Manuel González Prada.

González Prada was the founder of Peruvian leftist activism and would be remembered as its central figure were it not for the achievements of his disciple, the young boy who now met him for the first time. Years earlier, in 1888, González Prada had delivered his celebrated *Discurso del Politeama* (Address in the Amphitheater), in which he had denounced the incompetence and corruption of the Peruvian ruling class (and its military instrument, the army) and stressed that the lingering effects of ignorance and servitude were underlying factors in the subjection of the peasant masses. And he had even called on the youth of Peru to fight against that situation. His major concern was the unjust condition of the Indian peasants, oppressed by the expansion of the great estates controlled by the *gamonales* (the Andean word for the powerful landowners, whom not even the Peruvian state could control, with the result that they functioned—as Mariátegui would later define them—as feudal lords).

For the young Mariátegui, González Prada seemed the epitome of moral and intellectual commitment. But he, the young José Carlos, was still a worker without a contract, liable to the vagaries of uncertain employment.

One of his duties at the newspaper was to collect the original articles produced by the staff reporters or other contributors and carry them to the layout tables, where the typography was composed and the articles then assembled in the correct order for publication. He had moments of free time en route from the writers to the linotypist. And he made use of them. He inserted an article of his own, signed with the pseudonym of Juan Croniqueur, and passed it along to the typographers. It was published the next day. Who wrote this? asked the director of the newspaper. Mariátegui admitted what he had done. He was reproved but had also gained his opportunity. The article was well written and displayed a sharp and fresh intelligence. As a result he moved up the ladder. From now on he would be an aide, not to the production staff but in the daily work of the newspaper, assisting the contributors and especially attending to the teletype. He was fascinated by this apparatus that supplied information from all over the world. Modernity enchanted him.

From 1914 on, at the age of twenty, he began to publish in *La Prensa*, using his lucky pen name of Juan Chroniqueur. By 1915 he was an assiduous contributor to various journals: *Mundo Limeño* (The World of Lima), *El Turf* (devoted to horse racing and notes on high society), and *Lulú* (where he published poems, social reportage, and short stories). One year later, the young journalist with a growing reputation met one of Peru's most famous writers, Abraham Valdelomar, and together they started a new magazine called *Colónida*. Mariátegui would later describe this period of his life as his "stone age," when he was "an author polluted by turn of the century decadence and Byzantinism." Nonetheless, despite his inclination at the time toward the aestheticism of Gabriele D'Annunzio, he would recognize that he had already absorbed the social teaching of González Prada and learned "to reject the presence of the spirally packaged aristocratic mentality and its academicism."

His major discovery in those years was the impression that the authentic Peru was the indigenous Peru. Valdelomar wanted to raise the Inca past to stylistic heights—not only in literature but in the visual arts and in music. His literary models were Pierre Louÿs (with his polyvalent eroticism) and the more complicated (and greater) writer Gustave Flaubert, whose life work had moved from a "decadent" romanticism into a new, precisely phrased form of realism. The writer Julio Baudouin was one of Valdelomar's circle of literary friends. He had written the libretto, both dialogue and lyrics, for a short operatic piece (the Spanish form is called a *zarzuela*), not at all lighthearted but very serious, about a tragic confrontation between Indian workers in an Andean mine and their Anglo-Saxon managers. The music of *El cóndor pasa* ("The Condor Passes," also known as "Flight of the Condor") was by the composer Daniel Alomía Robles and its final melody, with the same title and based on a Quechua love song, has become an unofficial, internationally known symbol of the people of the Andes. (The Peruvian government in 2004 officially declared it a Cultural Patrimony of the Nation.)

The young Mariátegui, on January 3, 1915, wrote an enthusiastic review in *La Prensa* of *El cóndor pasa* in which he praised "the orientation that it has signaled in the sense of themes specifically national that are, indisputably, those that our writers may treat with greater precision and greater success among the public." And he began to explore the significance of a contemporary figure who had led an uprising of Indians against *gamonalismo* in the highland zone of Puno. The man was Rumi Maqui ("Stone Hand" in Quechua), the combat name adopted by Teodomiro Gutiérrez Cuevas. He was a former sergeant major of cavalry in the Peruvian army and a former provincial official. He had been sent to the Puno region by the government of President Guillermo Billinghurst to investigate massacres of Indians perpetrated in four of its districts. The ex-soldier was so appalled that finally, when he was almost fifty years old, he led a peasant uprising in the Azángaro district of Puno. It was a brief but intense rebellion, and the rebels set out on a march with the goal of seizing and dividing the large estates and the ultimate aim of restoring the empire of the Incas. The rebellion was crushed by the Peruvian army in 1916, shortly after its first major victory. Despite its failure, the rebellion seemed to demonstrate that the Andean Indians were not merely at the margins of what seemed to be the Peruvian nation. In response to the feudal exploitation, the violence and virtual enslavement imposed upon them by the *gamonales*, they were still capable—like Túpac Amaru II in 1780—of confronting their oppressors. Contemplating the figure of Rumi Maqui, Mariátegui had, in his own words, "a revelation." The old could become new; "revolution has vindicated our most ancient tradition."

Mariátegui had finally begun to earn a respectable income and his name was becoming more widely known. He wrote continually: about horses, the Peruvian Congress, literary criticism, poems, theatrical pieces (which were not produced)—a stream of tireless activity. The journal *Colónida* was filled with his literary rebellion, his youthful artistic spirit, but there was barely a hint of the political commitment that would soon become his passion and remain so for the rest of his life. He was more a poet excited about writing, an essayist concerned with metaphysical, even mystical subjects, dissatisfied certainly with the unjust reality of his country and the tired shibboleths of the social and cultural establishments. And he was aware of the political and social conflicts of Europe and would follow, with interest, the course of the Mexican Revolution.

A growing social consciousness led him into a polemic, in the pages of *La Prensa*, with José Mariano de la Riva Agüero, a friend of José Vasconcelos and a distinguished intellectual belonging to one of the more aristocratic groups within the oligarchic coalition that held power in Peru. He was a founder, in 1915, of the National Democratic Party. (Like Vasconcelos, he would become a Hispanicist—exalting the purely Spanish tradition of Latin America—and a pro-Nazi in the 1930s.) In 1917, still only twenty-three years old, Mariátegui would leave *La Prensa* and become chief editor (and congressional reporter) of *El Tiempo*. He continued to be an assistant editor of *El Turf*, where he still would publish pieces on religious themes and daily affairs. But his political journalism in *El Tiempo* was winning out and taking precedence over his many other interests.

In November 1917 two events connected with Russia came to affect his life. One was remote, in Russia itself: the revolution that would later become so important to him. The other occurred in Lima and touched him personally. It was "the scandal of the cemetery." Mariátegui was one of a group of artist friends who persuaded a Russian ballerina named Norka Rouskaya, who was visiting Lima, to dance in a cemetery, among the tombs, to the music of Chopin's *Marche Funèbre*. A violin played the music while Rouskaya danced. That very night, there were angry accusations: "Profanation of the ashes of our venerated dead!" Almost all those involved were arrested. The reaction was not only ridiculous but symptomatic of the rigidities of Peruvian society. As all the witnesses would testify, including Mariátegui, there had never been any intention of sacrilege, only the desire to mount a presentation in praise of art. Nevertheless, the group had now fallen under the watchful eye of the police.

Some of the young writers for *El Tiempo*, including Mariátegui himself, had grown impatient with the moderate line of the newspaper. Along with César Falcón and Félix del Valle, he decided to found a socialist journal, *Nuestra Época*. They would model it after the famous journal *España* (directed by Luis Araquistáin), in which many of the Spanish Generation of '98, including Miguel de Unamuno, had published their work. In the first issue, Mariátegui published an article entitled "Bad Tendencies: The Duty of the Army and the Duty of the State." It led to an incident where a group of angry officers surrounded and jostled him physically, trying to goad him into a duel.

By now he was known as a socialist writer but he was not yet under the influence of orthodox Marxism; rather he was suffused with a general sentiment not necessarily connected with revolution but focused on the working class and trade unionism. He and his friend Falcón agreed to participate in the creation of a Committee for Socialist Organization and Propaganda but refused to support the transformation of the committee into a political party. This reluctance to participate in a struggle for power was a quality Mariátegui always displayed. His way would never be the road to power but rather the moral force of independent criticism.

Mariátegui and Falcón went on to found the first newspaper of the left in Peru. They called it *La Razón* (Reason). In its pages they supported a workers' strike for an eight-hour day and the reduction of prices on basic food supplies. And from those same pages they hailed the student strike in Córdoba, Argentina, with its international ramifications for students throughout Latin America. Always fascinated with events in the broader world, Mariátegui closely followed revolutionary Russia, the politics of Woodrow Wilson, the Great War sweeping Europe.

As might be expected, he and his friends soon had to face the government of the dictator Augusto Leguía. They were given a simple choice: prison or exile (an exile encouraged and even partially financed by the regime). The choice was no choice. Mariátegui had to leave Peru.

IV

He arrived in Paris at the end of 1919 and made contact with the novelist and militant communist Henri Barbusse, the Nobel Prize winner Romain Rolland (whose novels he had read and admired), and the socialist, anti-imperialist group associated with the journal *Clarté*. And in Paris he discovered a real proletariat, numerous and active, a class that barely existed in Peru. "My finest memories," he would write, "are the meetings in Belleville, where I felt the religious warmth of the new multitudes at their highest intensity." The inclination toward religion, evident in his juvenile poems, took a new, definitive direction, channeled into his political enthusiasm. He would never use poetry again to express his deepest thoughts. In one of his essays at the time he quoted Barbusse: "To do politics is to move from dreams to things, from the abstract to the concrete. Politics is the applied work of social thinking; politics is life . . ."

In Europe, Mariátegui gradually experienced an interior and profound transformation. Not only did he stop writing poems but he published much less. It was a time for him to read books and judge facts. He wrote and later published his *Letters from Italy* and very little else. In retrospect, he seemed to be taking a breath, in preparation for his plunge into public life and for works he hoped to write after his return to Peru. And from the moment he set foot in Europe, he understood intuitively that something fundamental had changed in history:

Victory came to those peoples who believed they were fighting because this war would be the last . . . a period has begun of the decadence of war, the decadence of bellicose heroism, at least in the history of thought and art. Ethically and aesthetically, war has lost a lot of ground in recent years. Humanity no longer considers it beautiful . . . Contemporary artists prefer an opposite, antithetical theme: the sufferings and horrors of war.

He left for Italy at the end of the year. One of the attractions may have been a warmer climate but, for a man like Mariátegui, it would have surely been much more important to enter the culture of an Italy that had intrigued Peruvians at least since the turn of the century. In the northern industrial city of Turin, the proletarian culture he had so appreciated in Paris was laid out before him with its most intense contradictions, including the rapid growth of modern industry alongside widespread misery. Here in postwar Italy, all the contemporary political currents were present or in formation: socialism, communism, Catholic trade unionism, the incipient Fascist movement under Benito Mussolini, the background effects of the recent war, the aesthetic influence of modernism, and the dynamic, visual creativity of the futurists, who considered modern technology and the modern city as means toward the material redemption of the world (with a faith in the central importance of energy and vitality that would lead most of them into fascism).

Mariátegui avidly observes it all. He does his first, detailed political analyses and extends his political awareness across the boundaries of Europe, toward the East. He recognizes that Gandhi is a "practical idealist"; notes that in Turkey, Mustafa Kemal (the later Atatürk) is leading a movement of social and political liberation; and notes that at the congress that founds the Third International in 1920, there are delegates from China and Korea.

He is open to evaluating the most divergent thinkers. He reads the liberal Benedetto Croce, the socialist Antonio Gramsci, and the soon to be official "philosopher of Fascism," Giovanni Gentile. He had come to Europe with a feeling that Marxist theory was "confused, heavy, cold" but in Italy he had come "to see its true light and retain its revelation." Much of this new excitement was due, in the words of the scholar Richard Morse, to "the vitalist and voluntarist vision of Marxism" that he

had absorbed under the influence of Croce. The Italian idealist philosopher had only briefly flirted with Marxism as such but he was especially
opposed to any notion of rigid, immutable laws. Mariátegui will agree.
He will become a romantic Marxist, always wary of the reduction of
reality to rigid concepts or the flow of history to some preordained necessity. He is impressed that in postwar Italy, important intellectual figures had their connections as well as their differences. Croce had been
the teacher of both Gramsci, who would become the principal founder
of the Communist Party of Italy, and the Fascist Giovanni Gentile. Such
linkages did not imply a communion, in any sense of the word, but the
possibility of an incessant, open debate, which Mariátegui approved
and celebrated. But he was never blind to the world around him, and
until 1923, when he returned to Peru, the world around him was Italy.
Before the Fascist seizure of power (in October 1922), their *squadristi*
had been in the streets for years with their clubs and daggers and quarts
of castor oil. Mariátegui understood what Gentile's loyalties signified,
and he also knew, well before many others did, what fascism meant to
the future of freedom of thought:

> Now a liberal philosopher like Benedetto Croce—a true philoso-
> pher and a true liberal—has opened up this process [the process,
> Mariátegui meant, of positioning Marx as the philosopher who
> could judge the value of contemporary philosophy] in terms of
> inevitable justice in the face of another philosopher, an idealist
> and a liberal as well, a successor and exegete of Hegelian thought,
> Giovanni Gentile, who would accept a post in the brigades of Fas-
> cism, in promiscuous association with the most dogmatic neo-
> Thomists and the most incandescent anti-intellectuals.

He respects Croce but he cannot agree with him on the value of
the liberal state, put into doubt in many quarters by the debacle of the
Great War, which was the true end of the nineteenth century. With the
Italian example before him, he thought that the liberal democracies of
his time were easy prey for the dictatorial zeal of the right.

He tried to evaluate the phenomenon of Mussolini. The epic-heroic style of Il Duce may have chimed somewhat with his own romantic conception of existence, especially while still under the influence of José Vasconcelos. If so, it was a suspension of judgment that did not last:

"Fascism" is the illegal action of the conservative classes, fearful that the legal actions of the State would insufficiently defend their continued existence. It is the illegal action of the bourgeoisie against the possible socialist illegal action: the revolution.

In the Fascist march on Rome, he saw not only "the capitalist response shattering revolutionary perspectives" but surely heard an echo of the Latin American generals and the boots of their armies.

Europe would expand his perceptions in politics and also his aesthetics. Italian futurism spoke not just for the urbanized present but also for uncontrolled action and he could clearly see the dangerous direction toward which these artists were heading—as was an Italy full of men of violence resentful at how little their country had gained in the Great War. A number of the futurists were veterans of the war but far less weary of it than the "lost generation" of American, French, and some English writers who were drawn to Paris and produced the greatest literature of the 1920s.

He never became a reductive Marxist, judging literature by ideological norms. He would always like D'Annunzio's poetry despite its creator's role (and military adventures) as a poetic inspiration for fascism. But it was a French literary movement that most attracted him, one that spread far beyond France, and he valued it for what he saw as its potential for the liberation of the human mind. Later, in 1928, he would describe his feelings about the broader uses of surrealism: "Super-realism is a preparatory step for true realism . . . One has to release one's fantasy, liberate fiction from its old moorings, so as to discover reality."

And Europe, specifically Italy, gave him even more. Limited by his physical condition (which was already worsening) and the furious pace of his literary activity—first as a means to rise out of poverty and then to take his place in the world of letters—he was not a man with much experience of women. During a trip to Genoa, in a country inn near the city, Mariátegui encountered an Italian intellectual named Anna Chiappe (he would later meet Croce at her home). They became lovers.

He thought they would soon marry. He felt he would need more income and so he began to write a series of *Letters from Italy* for the newspaper *El Tiempo* of Lima. As honest as he always tried his best to be, some of these letters include his thoughts on his "discovery" of woman. In 1921 they married and Sandro, the first of his four sons, was born in Rome.

What he had done in Italy, he wrote, was "wedded woman and some ideas." He depicted (and treated) his wife as an intellectual equal. He cannot be termed a feminist in the modern sense but he was one of the first Latin American intellectuals to recognize and respect the role of the woman in a modern society. And along with woman, he would discover the work of Sigmund Freud; again an intellectual trailblazer for later developments, he would put Freud on a par with Marx and incorporate this discovery into his political vision. In Lima, Anna would bear him three more sons, Sigfrido (after Siegfried, an epic hero of his childhood, bedridden readings), José Carlos, and Javier. He would have a loving family during his few, last, immensely productive years.

As a Marxist, he was already prone to what dogmatic party theoreticians would qualify as "errors." He had chosen communism but he was always an individualistic communist, intolerant of intolerance, which would later lead to tensions between Mariátegui and the Latin American emissaries of the Comintern. He read and admired Antonio Gramsci and was present in 1921 at the Livorno Congress of the Italian Socialist Party, where, led by Gramsci and other socialists of the left, the famous schism occurred that gave birth to the Italian Communist Party. But his appreciation of culture as an instrument of revolution was due above all to the anarchist Georges Sorel, from whom he drew the need for a "new language" and the "perennial value of myth in popular movements," which Sorel characterized as "the creation of a concrete fantasy that works on a scattered and downtrodden people to revive and organize their collective will."

He became a friend of Piero Gobetti, a follower of Croce and a radicalized liberal who nevertheless wrote frequently for the journal *L'Ordine Nuovo*, the communist publication co-edited by Gramsci. This Italian capacity to join distinct and, within limits, opposing positions on the pages of the same publication would later leave its mark on the most important enterprise of his life, the journal *Amauta*. (It was a tendency that would be revived in Italy decades later after the defeat of fascism.)

In 1922, Mariátegui attended an international conference sponsored by the League of Nations. There, in his own small conference, he (together with César Falcón, Carlos Roe, and Palmiro Machiavello) created the first cell of the Peruvian Communist Party. And now it was time to go home.

Before he left Europe, Mariátegui traveled to France, Germany, Austria, Hungary, Czechoslovakia, and Belgium. He spent his days investigating the revolutionary movements that had spread across the continent since the end of the Great War.

Finally the family of three set out for Peru. Europe had granted Mariátegui the experience of observing a Western order created in the previous century that had fallen apart and was now forming into something new, unexpected, dangerous, and also hopeful. In Richard Morse's phrase, Mariátegui had "seen the forging and testing of ideologies in the crucible of action."

And from the vantage point of Europe, he discovered himself anew as a Latin American:

Along the roads of Europe, I met the country of America that I had left and in which I had lived almost as a foreigner and an absentee. Europe showed me how much I belonged to a primitive and chaotic world; and at the same time it set upon me, it clarified for me, the duty of an American task.

v

In April 1923, back in Lima, Mariátegui had to earn a living once again, and for a family of three. Now he would meet another great figure of Peruvian political thought, Víctor Raúl Haya de la Torre. They were of the same age but could not have been physically and socially more different. Haya de la Torre was tall, elegant, of aristocratic lineage, educated in the best schools of Peru, an inspiring orator. He was a friend of the poet César Vallejo, a frequent visitor at the home of Mariátegui's first political mentor González Prada, and frequently corresponded with many leading Hispanic intellectuals, including José Enrique Rodó, Miguel de Unamuno, and José Vasconcelos.

Like Mariátegui he was a Marxist but his rise to prominence, socially and intellectually, had been much more rapid and ostentatious. At the National University of San Marcos he had been president of the Peruvian Student Association, a position that involved him being treated as an advisor (though for the most part symbolically) to the president of Peru, the "moderate" dictator Augusto B. Leguía, who was very much in need of legitimization. But Haya de la Torre would soon leave the presidential fold by supporting a workers' strike and organizing demonstrations in favor of the famous student movement for university reform that had begun in Córdoba, Argentina. When he and Mariátegui met (they had already known of each other) he was already founder and director of the People's Universities that bore the name of González Prada. He could not, nor did he want to, ignore a comrade returning to the fatherland. He gave him work on his magazine (called *Claridad*) and the opportunity to give a series of lectures within the People's Universities on the subject "History of the Worldwide Crisis."

Turmoil over official state support for the Catholic religion,

reminiscent of the nineteenth-century confrontations between Liberals and Conservatives, would send Haya de la Torre into exile and elevate Mariátegui, as his chosen replacement, to the helm of *Claridad*.
President Leguía had announced that a public ceremony would be
held, entrusting the Peruvian nation to the protection of the Sacred
Heart of Jesus. Haya de la Torre saw it as an assault on freedom of
religion and joined in the widespread public protests, which were successful. The ceremony was canceled but the government saw Haya de
la Torre, because of his fame and his incendiary oratory, as the most
prominent figure in the protest movement. Leguía expelled him
from the country. Haya de la Torre would embark on a long journey
of socialist tourism, beginning with Mexico (where José Vasconcelos
would hand him a banner to mark the foundation of the A.P.R.A.,
the Popular Revolutionary American Alliance), a socialist political
program intended to reach all of Latin America. He then went off
to Russia, where he decided that the concept of the proletariat made
no sense for underdeveloped Peru, where the masses were peasants,
and began his movement away from the communists toward a more
nationalist form of moderate socialism.

Back in Peru, entrusted with the journal because of Haya de la
Torre's respect for his abilities, Mariátegui used his lectures at the
People's University to reinforce his developing ideas of socialism and
revolution. From Sorel he drew the idea that violence was legitimate
but could not be bloodthirsty violence. The objective should be a just
victory, supported by a communitarian spirit. And he insisted on the
use of the term "Bolshevik" as a positive adjective. He wanted to justify
the ideas of Lenin but at the same time reserve for himself the liberty
to think freely and independently.

He remained in charge of *Claridad*, now clearly identified as a publication critical of the authoritarian government and strongly socialist. (The fifth issue of the journal dealt almost entirely with Lenin.)
His strong support for the workers' movements earned him, in January
1924, a brief spell in jail. In March of the same year he began a business
venture, the Obrera Claridad Publishing House, but it had barely got

off the ground when an infection triggered gangrene in his good, right leg. It was amputated and he would spend the rest of his life in a wheelchair. But with the courage he had always shown, he rapidly returned to his intellectual labors.

The Mexican Revolution had begun to disappoint him. Later, near the end of the decade, he would sum up his views about the direction it had taken. The Revolution had merit as a "bourgeois democratic movement," but he criticized its acceptance of capitalist principles and the concessions that the victorious *caudillos* had made to North American capital and to the Catholic Church. And perhaps worst of all, the large estates were still intact. The problem of "the Indian and the land" was always near the very center of Mariátegui's thought, and toward the end of his short life, it became his overwhelming preoccupation. Sadly, he would not live to see the agrarian reform of Lázaro Cárdenas, beginning in 1936, which divided the large haciendas and emphasized the *ejido*, the cooperative communal farm with both private and public features. It was a shift in the course of the Mexican Revolution that would have pleased though perhaps not satisfied this sensitive writer and human being who would be most remembered as the prophet of indigenism.

VI

After the amputation, Mariátegui moved back to the front lines of political thought, in articles for the journal *Mundial*. With the series of writings published under the title of *Peruanicemos al Perú* (Let Us Peruvianize Peru), he begins the powerful flow of his mature thinking, not merely as a brilliant commentator but as a theorist of value with his own developing ideas.

To Peruvianize? To make a nation a more authentic nation? The strange thing is that it does not sound strange in Latin America. For one important reason. Since their origin, the nations of "Our America" have lived a double life. The official language, the forms of government, the states themselves, our institutions stem from Western

European culture, while the autochthonous original populations, in many cases the majority and in others a strong ethnic undercurrent, have been relegated to social, economic, and political inferiority. Some of our thinkers have argued that European culture is clearly superior, more rational, more just, and therefore, though it came later in time, a historical improvement. Others (it was the great hope of Martí, Rodó, and the earlier Vasconcelos) predicted a fruitful union in the future between these two cultures. In accord with the idea of progress prevalent in the early twentieth century, this great confluence would happen at the level of race, through racial mixture (*mestizaje*). Mariátegui finds both of these views seriously wanting: "In Peru we have less intellectual nationalism, much more rudimentary and instinctive than how western nationalisms define the Nation." He is uneasy with those intellectual flights that ignore historical reality and presuppose a homogeneity where only division and fragmentation really exist.

At the beginning of the twentieth century, the separation of the races in Peru was endorsed and aggravated by the difficult geography of the country (desert eastward to towering mountains and then to jungle) and, in many areas, by the lack of adequate roads. The Indians were in the mountains (with a small presence of mestizos). Those more Hispanicized, whether creole by blood or culture, were in the lowlands and especially in the cities of the coast. For the cities it was cheaper to import Chinese workers than truck Indians down from the Andes, cheaper to supply the cities with grain on boats from Chile and California. In the mountains the *ayllu* system had decayed and nearly disappeared. *Ayllu*, a Quechua word, was the term dating back to the Incas for an Indian community bound by the ties of extended family, working together on communal land. Each *ayllu* assumed descent from some mythical ancestor. The chief of the ayllu was the *curaca*, and it was not a hereditary position but chosen through a religious ritual or named directly from Cuzco, the Inca capital city.

At the end of the eighteenth century, after the defeat of the uprising led by Túpac Amaru (one of a string of such uprisings across the centuries), the viceregal government had eliminated the designation of *curaca* (Mariátegui's mother came from a former *curaca* family), and the void of local government over the scattered Indian populations was then filled by the feudal landowners, the *gamonales* so despised by Mariátegui and who, answering to no one, neither the national state nor local customs, imposed their arbitrary power.

This was the reality, said Mariátegui, not the hallucinations of intellectuals who, to make things worse, based their politics on an empty ideology:

> Peruvian politics—bourgeois on the coast, feudal in the sierras— has been characterized by ignorance of the value of human capital. Its rectification—on this level as in everything else—begins with the assimilation of a new ideology. The new generation feels and knows that the progress of Peru will be fictitious, or at least it will not be Peruvian, if it does not provide the work, does not signify the well-being of the Peruvian masses, four-fifths of whom are peasant and Indian.

Most Marxists have tended to believe that the subject *belongs* to a specific place and time. Mariátegui wants to believe that *the subject is essentially history*, history that is a process of the will, that we human beings are essentially historical beings, that we live a constant historical process:

> Peru is still a nationality in formation. The sediments of western civilization are constructing it on the inert indigenous strata. The Spanish Conquest annihilated indigenous culture. It destroyed autochthonous Peru. It thwarted the only *peruanidad* ["Peruvianness"] that has existed. A truly national politics cannot omit the Indian, cannot ignore the Indian. The Indian is the foundation of our nationality in formation.

Moreover, without the Indian, the country cannot advance. He is the producer, the true element of progress. There can be no *peruanidad* without him. But Mariátegui is not proposing the folkloric, kitsch indigenism commonly substituted for reality in Latin America and which is really a kind of empty condescension, relegating the Indian to the level of quaint entertainment and permanent tutelage. He wants intellectual, spiritual, and material progress for all:

> Those who say that Peru, and America in general, live at a great distance from the European revolution . . . have no comprehension, even approximate, of history. They are surprised that the most advanced ideals of Europe reach Peru, but they are not surprised that the airplane, the transatlantic steamer, the wireless telegraph, the radio have come to us . . . It would make as much sense to ignore the socialist movement as to dismiss . . . Einstein's theory of relativity.

It will take a few more years for him to fully articulate his ideas and his project. But the structure is already here. The sickly boy, fascinated by electric light and streetcars, has been transformed into a formidable intellectual whose health remains precarious but who retains his excitement over airplanes and streetcars and the radio and now the theory of relativity. (Might he have known that Einstein's critical insight came to him while he was riding in a streetcar?) The heroes of his childhood reading have now changed into the Peruvian Indian and the revolutionary masses. His enthusiasm is totally intact, despite the pain, the adversity, the uncertainty of his life. And in his rehabilitation of the Indian, perhaps a subtle personal theme enters as well: the vindication of his mother, the abandoned *curaca*.

VII
————

The students at the People's University were so moved and illuminated by Mariátegui's lectures that a group of them went to the rector and asked that he be given a professorship. The rector refused. After all, Mariátegui had no academic credentials. From then on he would never have an assured income and would live on the proceeds of his writing. Finding steady employment was not easy and his independence was part of his nature. And within that nature a central idea was production and ownership of the means of production. It was natural then to become a businessman and be master of his own fate. He started Minerva Publishers, with the intention of issuing a series of Peruvian and foreign books, designed to expand the intellectual and psychic ambience of the country. His ultimate aim was to break through the ideological influences of the Peruvian oligarchy that weighed heavily on the new generation of intellectuals and artists. And he looked ahead to publishing a number of books on economics, a subject that had become fundamental in Europe as a basic discipline for making accurate decisions and eliminating financial carelessness vis-à-vis social issues. (With this same idea ten years later Daniel Cosío Villegas would create the Fondo de Cultura Económica, which for decades would disseminate its publications throughout Latin America.)

The first book he published, in 1925, was Mariátegui's own *La escena contemporánea* (The Contemporary Scene), which contained his first formal studies of fascism, the crisis of democracy and of socialism, the Russian Revolution, the relation between revolution and intelligence, essays on the East and (in a striking anticipation of what would later become, through the horrors of Nazism, a pervasive European issue) Jews and anti-Semitism. The authors he discusses, with critical independence and in sober prose that is both spare and precise, are not those admired by an earlier generation but rather a panoply of living men. "Everything human is ours," Mariátegui will say a few months later, as if anticipating the future goal of Octavio Paz for the Mexican people, to be "contemporary with all men."

In February 1926, Minerva Publishing launched a new journal, *Libros y Revistas* (Books and Reviews), with modest format and production values. To fund it, he solicited advertisements. Ads for automobiles, banks, other publishing houses, even millineries appear among the reviews and articles in carefully done, clear, and readable typography. A worthy achievement for someone who had spent so much time in his early adolescence around Linotype machines and their operators. But this editor was only beginning his work of production.

"I came back from Europe with the idea of starting a journal," Mariátegui had once said, And now, in September 1926, the first issue of *Amauta* (Quechua for "teacher" or "sage") appeared. It would become near legendary, in the first (and most immediate) place for the beauty of its production. Its large format, extremely readable typography, photographs, and woodcuts of high quality—all of it made the magazine instantly attractive. In its first editorial, Mariátegui wrote: "This journal, in the intellectual field, does not represent a group. It represents, more precisely, a movement, a spirit," full of differences and disagreements but beyond these, a shared will "to create a new Peru within a new world."

And in effect, everything was there, though suffused with a socialist perspective: avant-garde literature, revolutionary outcries; careful, measured criticism and militant texts of ideology; sweeping cosmopolitan viewpoints and indigenist perspectives (what Mariátegui called *inkaismo*); historical consciousness and the consciousness of making history; the freshness of antiquity and the universality of the local. All of it was elegantly packaged, the typography a pleasure in itself, and as you moved through the variegated writing and illustrations, you might come upon a sudden surprising gem, like a musical partitura or a modernist drawing followed by the woodcut of an Andean face with thick, powerful lines like the work some German artists were doing during the rich and soon-to-be tragic flowering of the Weimar Republic.

There were two sections: one for articles, essays and poems, sometimes translations (for instance the first translations of Freud into Spanish), the second for book reviews. No distinction was made between culture and politics. They followed each other in the natural order of creative thought, which abhors rigid separations. At the time it was a highly innovative decision. Journals were always published with a separate cultural section (sometimes even with a further subdivision of articles only "for young ladies"). This breaking with convention mirrored one of Mariátegui's major assertions. Revolutionary action (and the arguments for it) could not be treated as distinct from art and culture. Nor was one subordinate to the other. Their expression might differ in form but not in spirit. Ever since his book *The Contemporary Scene*, Mariátegui had been explicitly defending the centrality of the imagination as an integral part of politics and even revolution. *Amauta* was the culturally innovative, visually stunning, politically inclusive embodiment of this idea.

For Mariátegui, the journal became his mooring in the world. In large part through the journal, he could support his family, focus his thinking and his action, and be free to further ripen his ideas. And though Mariátegui saw his publishing work, his writing, and his political action as a single, ongoing impulse, there were of course, in practice, different components to his public life. On the one hand, he had begun to diffuse his theories on the union of *inkaismo* (he always preferred the *k*) and communism, both pervaded by a spiritual Marxism. But he was also a left-wing activist, in workers' organizations, in communist cells, and in A.P.R.A.

VIII

The entrance of *Amauta* into the political life of Peru was not welcomed by the Leguía dictatorship. In June 1927, the government denounced the existence of a supposed communist plot and began a crackdown against workers' organizations and intellectuals. Mariátegui was arrested and confined to the Military Hospital of San Bartolomé. *Amauta* was shut down, as was Minerva Publishers. He seriously considered emigrating to Montevideo or Buenos Aires. But he chose to stay in Peru because of his dual but for him unified commitment: to his Indianist philosophy and to Peruvian socialism. The "moderate" Leguía dictatorship would release him. In December, he succeeded in lifting the ban and *Amauta* appeared again.

In 1926, Mariátegui had joined in the necessarily clandestine formation of the first A.P.R.A. cell under the leadership of Haya de la Torre, who had returned from exile. Haya de la Torre, after breaking with the Third Communist International in 1927, had begun designing a plan to convert A.P.R.A. into a political party that would integrate the upper and lower middle classes, abandon revolutionary socialism, and vie for power through the electoral process. His intention was accelerated by a new Peruvian law barring the political activity of any group that was not exclusively national.

Mariátegui was opposed. For him, turning the A.P.R.A. into a political party (to be known as APRA) was to accept the rules of "decadent bourgeois democracy." The two of them argued, not publicly but through an exchange of letters. Later, writing to another friend, Mariátegui would say: "Haya stubbornly insisted on imposing his dominating leadership [*caudillaje*] . . . I had opened up to Haya, accepting his claim to be a revolutionary Marxist—I would later discover that, as far as Marxism went, he had learned nothing. Perhaps I had too much confidence."

They had seemed to share deep convictions. Both felt strongly anti-imperialist. Both had their visions of an archaic Inca communism. "The most advanced primitive communism that history has registered," wrote Mariátegui, and Haya de la Torre would define the Incas as "the civilizing power of the most advanced Communist State of antiquity." But Haya's ideology showed some strange admixtures. His interest in the racial issue was real but complicated with metaphysical rhetoric and the elitist authoritarianism of Vasconcelos, with his "cosmic race" fantasies. And the class difference (and conflicts) between Mariátegui and Haya was now apparent. Irredeemably aristocratic, Haya may well have perceived Mariátegui as ungrateful for the assistance he had received, instead of recognizing the resolute independence of a man who had overcome poverty, physical weakness and pain, the complete lack of a university education, and a working-class origin within Peru's grossly stratified society.

Mariátegui's break with Haya de la Torre over the "bourgeois" and authoritarian future he saw, in large part correctly, for APRA never lessened his dislike for the vulgar applications of Marxism and the rigidities of Soviet-sanctioned orthodoxy. For the defenders of communist purity, he was far too independent, "unscientific," far too concerned with the inspirational power of myth:

> . . . neither Reason nor Science can satisfy all the need for the infinite there is in man. Reason itself accepts the responsibility of showing men that it is not enough. That only the Myth possesses the precious virtue of filling the deep sense of self . . . The strength of revolutionaries is not in their science, it is in their faith, in their passion, in their will. It is a religious force, mystical, spiritual, it is the force of the Myth.

At the heart of his ideas and his conception of reality there beats a strong but in no way conventional religious impulse. The force of it may owe something to the orthodox religion of his childhood and his pious Catholic mother. But it had become far larger and broader for him. When he criticized his mentor González Prada for his antireligious convictions (in line not only with communism but with the anticlerical positions of many nineteenth-century liberals), he would offer his key and concise opinion: "Let the Soviets write on their propaganda posters 'Religion is the opiate of the people.' Communism is essentially religious."

His most influential work, 7 Essays on the Interpretation of Peruvian Reality (*Siete ensayos de interpretación de la realidad peruana*) was his final testament, though published in 1928, when he had two more years to live (and his ideas would still be expounded in later essays). He discounts and attacks conventional prejudices, argues for the preeminent importance of the problem of the land, and expands on his interpretation of socialism, aesthetic and moral, mythically Indianist and economically analytical, practical and spiritual.

He brands as racist and imperialist any idea that the Peruvian Indian must, before anything else, elevate himself morally, and be "educated" into emerging from his subjugated, impoverished condition. The first issue that has to be faced is not education but the ownership of the land. Nor does the Indian, or Latin Americans in general, need the mystifications of "a race destined to triumph. Forget *Ariel*, forget the pontifications like Vasconcelos's 'cosmic race.' " Mariátegui sees the model to follow in his idealized vision of "Inca communism," a return to communal roots. But he does not call for the impossible reconstruction of an ancient agrarian society. We must live in the modern industrialized world. It is more a value he tries to summon from the past, that of communal responsibility and the end of *gamonalista* tyranny.

And as for the giant to the far north, the United States of America, here and elsewhere he insists that the enemy is American imperialism, not the individual American or the American people or the best of American culture: "Roosevelt protected the empire, Thoreau the spirit of Humanity." Worldwide socialism is the absolutely necessary future. Otherwise, for Latin America, the prognosis would be grim: "The destiny of these countries, within the capitalist order, is that of mere colonies." And art and literature, freely explored, are "not a diversion . . . of pure intellectuals" but the assertion of "an historical idea."

IX
___

Mariátegui's mythical duality of indigenism and socialism, with all its immense seductive power, with all its moral beauty, with all its utopian nobility, has been refuted by history, most of all in its first element, indigenism. Luis Alberto Sánchez, in a written debate with Mariátegui, would ask prophetically:

> But, tell me, do you believe that in the opposition between the coast and the sierra, the indigenous community is . . . the solution? Don't you see there a trace of the colonialism that you so condemn? Is the *cholo* [the Andean term for mestizo] not also involved? Couldn't you accept a movement of total and not exclusivist vindication?

Sánchez was rejecting the racism (including indigenist racism) that had divided the ethnic groups of Peru since the Conquest. He spoke for the mestizo and proclaimed himself to be a cholo. But Mariátegui, entranced with his own mythological conceptions, was not prepared to accept the more inclusive, open premise of *mestizaje*. He had called Vasconcelos's mixed-race utopia a "vehement prophecy" that "suppresses and ignores the present," foreign to "the criticism of contemporary reality, in which he exclusively seeks elements favorable to his prophecy."

But Mariátegui perhaps died too young to realize that his thesis was also a "vehement prophecy" as speculative and utopian as that of Vasconcelos. On this point at least, the mestizo affirmation of Vasconcelos—setting aside its absurd detours—has come to seem, in the end, more accurate, not only culturally but also economically and in demographic terms. Mexico, with all its own problems, had attenuated the original ethnic confrontation through a slow, complex process of *mestizaje* that lessened exclusion and ethnic hatred. And the agrarian reform of its president Lázaro Cárdenas in the late 1930s (well after Mariátegui's death) might have seemed a more reasonable solution, even to him, than indigenous communism. And finally, beyond ideas and ideologies, the races would begin to mix more freely in Peru and a process of *mestizaje*—though far less extensive than in Mexico—began to change the ethnic composition of the country. An agrarian reform (though again less intense than the Mexican) did finally come to Peru. This twofold process, not indigenous communism, seemed to point toward a future direction for Peru.

Beyond the problem of the Indian and the land, the second term of the equation, Marxist socialism, would have a melancholy denouement. And yet, thanks in large part to Mariátegui, Latin American intellectuals would offer some of the most intelligent, generous, and elaborated contributions to socialist thought. But long before the collapse of European communism, the closed, self-absorbed minds of the Comintern decided to dispense with the two options offered by Mariátegui and Haya de la Torre. The more middle-class socialism of APRA, committed to the electoral process, had already chosen to sail other waters and would have to confront the problem of corruption, common to the political parties of Latin America. But the silence of orthodox Marxists before the insights of Mariátegui did much more harm to the development of socialism in Latin America. They discarded the most brilliant socialist thinker ever to arise in "Our America" and there is no way to repair the effects of that loss. Even in the 1980s, Latin American writers close to the Soviet Communist Party continued to insult Mariátegui.

Perhaps the worst violence done to his thought and memory was the attempt to make use of his figure and the distortion of his ideas that was perpetrated by the narrowly dogmatic and supremely brutal movement of the *Sendero Luminoso* (the Shining Path) in the Peruvian 1980s and '90s. Myth, for Mariátegui, was a power of the spirit, not a tool for propaganda, which he despised. One of the loftiest intelligences of Latin America meant something far different from rabid cruelty when he wrote that "Marxist-Leninism will open the Shining Path to Revolution."

In 1930, the fate he had evaded since childhood finally completed its vicious circle for Mariátegui. Due to a malignant tumor in his left thigh, he had to enter the Clínica Villarán. He was not spared his final weeks of pain and died on April 16. It is deeply moving to think that this man partially crippled since childhood, who spent his final, intensely creative years in a wheelchair, who had educated himself, who had created enterprises and institutions, produced exceptionally brilliant books and articles, master of a clear and splendid style, generator of theoretical insights of great breadth and an example to us all in his capacity for action despite his lifelong pain, is still waiting for the readers and followers he deserves. But history was preparing a surprise. More than sixty years after his death, his Indo-Marxist myths would take genuine root, not in Peru but in the mestizo country par excellence of Latin America, in faraway Mexico.

PART II

A Man in His Century

5

Octavio Paz

THE POET AND THE REVOLUTION

CANCIÓN MEXICANA

My grandfather, while drinking down his coffee cup
spoke to me about Juarez and Porfirio
the Zouaves and the Silver Gang.
And the tablecloth smelled of gunpowder

My father, while drinking down his shot glass,
spoke to me about Zapata and Villa
Soto y Gama and the Flores Magón.
And the tablecloth smelled of gunpowder.

I kept my silence.
About whom could I speak?

In Paris, midway through the twentieth century, the poet Octavio Paz writes a book about Mexico. He is thirty-five years old and has a long history behind him of poetic achievements and political experience. He has dedicated his Friday nights and his weekends to composing this book, after finishing his workweek as a diplomat. For six years he has lived far from his homeland. Although he misses "the flavor, the smell of Mexican religious festivals, the Indians, the fruit, the sun-soaked patios of the churches, the candles, the street vendors," his motive is not mere nostalgia. He has always known that his own family was a tree with deep roots in the past history of Mexico. And he also knows that in Mexico there is "a past that is underground but alive, a universe of buried images, desires and impulses." He wants to uncover both of these intimately connected past histories, to see them with clarity, to give them expression and to free them for use. Since the early 1940s, like other Mexican writers and philosophers he had intended "to encounter the essential nature of Mexico [*la mexicanidad*], that invisible substance that can be found somewhere. We do not know what it consists of nor through what path we may reach it; we know, obscurely, that it has not yet been revealed . . . it will spring up, spontaneously and naturally, from the depths of our intimacy, when we encounter it in its true authenticity, the key to our existence . . . the truth of ourselves." In Paris he is in the process of encountering this "truth." And for him, this essential key has a name: solitude.

No one in Mexico, except for Octavio Paz, would have fastened on the word "solitude" as anything like a formative, essential characteristic of the country and its people, of its culture and its history. Ever since the Mexican Revolution, the idea of "Mexico" (its history, identity, place in the world, its destiny) has been a national obsession. Mexico as the site of a complex, tragic, yet in its way creative encounter between two radically different civilizations: the Spanish and the indigenous; Mexico as the site of an unfulfilled promise of social justice, progress, and freedom; Mexico as a land condemned by the gods or chosen by the Virgin of Guadalupe; and, finally, Mexico as a country shackled by its various complexes of inferiority. All of this and more but not a people enclosed in a state of "solitude." The very title of Paz's book is truly strange. At first sight, and especially compared with the typical American, the Mexican is a very gregarious being—in every latitude and epoch, including the immigrant living in the United States, the heir to the "pachuco" whom Paz will consider in his book. He or she is a "we" not an "I," not an atom but a constellation: the small village, the community, the neighborhood, the church brotherhood, the structure of obligations between children and their godfathers and godmothers known as *compadrazgo,* and, above all, the Mexican family, partly eroded in modern Mexico but still as solid as the mountainous masses of the Sierra Madre. Nothing is more alien to ordinary Mexicans than the isolated figures in a painting by Edward Hopper. The image of the Mexican, today as for centuries past, is more that of a Sunday family outing in the crowded Chapultepec Park of Mexico City.

But not for Octavio Paz, who had been weighed down since early youth by a piercing and constant feeling of solitude and by doubts about his own identity: "the anguish of not knowing exactly who one is." All of a sudden the thought came to him that his own biography could mesh with the collective history of his country, could serve to present it and be presented within it. And so he had wanted "to tear the veil and to see": "I felt that I was alone and that Mexico too, as a country, was alone, isolated, far from the central flow of history . . . While reflecting on the strange condition of being Mexican, I uncovered an old truth: every man hides an unknown man within him . . . I wanted to penetrate into myself and unearth that unknown person, to speak with him."

As time passed, that book, that revelation of national myths would become a myth in itself, approaching the status of a historical and poetical mirror or a kind of philosopher's stone of Mexican culture. So brilliant were the book's insights on Mexico, on its identity and its history, and so liberating, that they concealed its quality of confession, of a "personal confidence," and for the reader they seemed to bury away Paz's own "unknown person." But this person is the secret presence within El laberinto de la soledad, a tacit autobiography, the labyrinth of Octavio Paz's solitude.

II

The temporal progression that led to El laberinto begins in the 1920s in a large country mansion, located in an ancient (and at that time still suburban) pre-Hispanic and colonial village called Mixcoac, south of Mexico City. The Paz family had taken refuge there in 1914, when the revolutionary factions contending with each other (on one side the followers of Venustiano Carranza, on the other the partisans of Emiliano Zapata and Pancho Villa) began intermittently to occupy the capital. Almost ten years had passed since those events. The Revolution had ended in 1920. Except for Álvaro Obregón, the undefeated caudillo who was president of Mexico between 1920 and 1924, all its great leaders had died by violence: Madero, Zapata, Carranza, Villa. The Revolution, which had cost the country nearly a million dead (by violent death, hunger, or disease), had entered its constructive phase. A generously funded program to expand and improve education had been launched, with the philosopher José Vasconcelos as its creator and director. And the government was taking its first timid steps toward implementing the social reforms outlined in the Constitution of 1917: redistribution of land, stronger laws against the exploitation of workers, greater control over the country's natural resources.

Around the family dining table in Mixcoac, these programs were the subject of intense debate between two Mexicans arguing about the past and future of the country, dramatically linked to the history and destiny of their own lives. A boy around ten years old, the poet-to-be Octavio Paz, was a silent witness to these contending positions. Paz would recall the arguments a half century later in his poem "Canción mexicana," where he remembers these conversations and comments, "The tablecloth smelled of gunpowder." And these were not two men who merely represented positions or served as teachers for the young boy. They were his grandfather Ireneo Paz and his father, Octavio Paz Solórzano. The old Liberal and the revolutionary Zapatista offered him two distinct and atavistic faces of power and authority: "a figure that splits into the duality of patriarch and *macho*. The patriarch protects; he is good, powerful, wise. The macho [the *caudillo*, the 'military leader'] is the frightening man, the hard-ass, the father who has gone off, who has abandoned wife and children."

Ireneo Paz, the patriarch, was born in 1836, in the state of Jalisco. From 1851 to 1876 his life had been an uninterrupted campaign for political liberty, fought with the pen and with the sword. His favorite means of combat was the periodical "in opposition," where he would wield the genre of satire with unparalleled talent. He founded his first publication when he was only fifteen years old and, later, another journal dedicated to defending the liberal Constitution of 1857. In 1863, with a newly acquired law degree, he moved from his native Guadalajara to Colima, where he left his young wife, Rosa Solórzano, and his daughter

Hilda, only three months old, to enlist in the Liberal armies opposing the coalition of French invaders and Mexican Conservatives. His daughter died during his absence. He took advantage of an amnesty in 1865 and started yet another publication in Guadalajara, *El payaso* (The Clown), a daily paper marked by his biting wit directed against the French-backed empire, whose Emperor Maximilian, during his brief reign, was himself actually entertained by its articles. Paz's period of comparative calm was short-lived. He was soon arrested, as he would be at various times in the future, and succeeded in the first of many adventurous escapes that could fill a novel. He would join the Liberal guerrillas and, within the border enclave controlled by the Juaristas, become the interior secretary of the republican government in the state of Sinaloa. And there the news arrived of the execution of Maximilian and the triumphal entry into Mexico City (on July 15, 1867) by the forces under President Benito Juárez. The date marked the restoration of the republican and liberal order opposed by Mexican Conservatives since 1858 (they had been supported by the French invaders since 1862). It seemed like the right moment to finally lower the guns, but for the restless Ireneo Paz, it was only another beginning.

Between 1867 and 1876, Mexico had an opportunity to experiment peacefully with a democratic system, but ten years of war had nurtured a turbulent and adventurous spirit among the young. Ireneo Paz embodied this restlessness. The political problem of the time was essentially a generational struggle. On one side were the men of letters and lawyers who had accompanied Juárez during the long wanderings of his peripatetic government through the years of the War of the Reform (1858–61) and the War of the French Intervention (1862–67); on the other were the young commanders who had defeated Conservative and French troops on the field of battle. The best-known leader of these young soldiers was Porfirio Díaz, who was thirty-seven years old in 1867 and had waged thirty-seven battles. With that kind of record, Díaz was not prepared to patiently await his turn at the presidency. In the rebellion he would then launch, his foremost intellectual lieutenant was Ireneo Paz, who in 1867 founded two periodicals (*La palanca de Occidente* and *El diablillo colorado*) to support Díaz and oppose a third presidential term for Benito Juárez. But Díaz and Paz lost in this first confrontation. Díaz retired to a hacienda in his native Oaxaca and Ireneo Paz started yet another newspaper, one that would make history: *El Padre Cobos* ("Father Cobos"). The government soon arrested him and he had to serve eleven months in the Tlatelolco Prison of Mexico City. From behind bars, he wrote ribald and venomous texts and "prepares his friends in the area of Revolution," because this is the magic word in Mexico for every political movement that takes up arms against a government it considers authoritarian or illegitimate. Not revolt, not rebellion: Revolution.

In 1869, barely out of jail, Ireneo Paz became a relapsed revolutionary. He formulated the plan for another revolt, this time in the state of Zacatecas, and again it was unsuccessful. In 1870 he was imprisoned in Monterrey, under sentence of death, but he escaped disguised as a priest, went into exile in Texas, and then accepted yet another amnesty and returned to Mexico. In 1871 he returned to his old ways and began to reissue *El Padre Cobos*. The country was already on the threshold of new presidential elections (with Juárez once again a candidate) and Ireneo Paz published sonnets like this one, opposing the reelection:

> *Why if, perhaps, you were so patriotic*
> *are you buying up votes with pesetas?*
> *Why do you permit this loathsome fraud,*
> *doling out money to whoever votes for you?*
>
> *Tell me, aren't you disturbed by our bankruptcy,*
> *by the hunger that squeezes your people so tightly?*
> *If you don't mend your ways, though I am no prophet*
> *I am telling you that you will be set out in the stocks.*
>
> *Yes, Saint Benito, now take some other path.*
> *Don't show yourself, my friend, to be such a pirate.*

Notice that the people are no longer so stupid.
Be merciful and set us free, beloved father.

It has already been fourteen years of hemlock.
Set us free, President Old Broken-Down Nag!

After the fourth reelection of Benito Juárez, *El Padre Cobos* became the standard-bearer of a new revolution. In November 1871, Paz articulated the Program of La Noria, on the basis of which Porfirio Díaz rose in arms for the first time against his former mentor Juárez. Yet again, Paz left his family and marched to the north with the intention of closing the pincers of the revolution as Díaz, advancing north from Oaxaca, tried to take control of the center of the country. But Díaz failed and, wearing the disguise of a humble citizen, reached the Sierra de Álica, in western Mexico, where he met with his friend Ireneo Paz. It was a zone controlled by one of the most mysterious personages in Mexican history, the *cacique* ("local strong man") Manuel Losada, who, with his Indian forces, harassed the creole city of Guadalajara. There, as Díaz and Paz were involved in planning conspiracies with Losada, the surprising news arrived of Juárez's sudden death. Paz and Díaz accepted the general amnesty that followed.

In 1873, *El Padre Cobos* began a third epoch of opposition to the government of lawyers and men of letters. It would become the journal's golden epoch, a fiesta of criticism and slander. The political environment then was one of complete freedom of speech, but no freedom was freedom enough for Ireneo Paz. In addition to his merciless satirical pieces and his hilarious dialogues, each issue centered around a scathing sonnet by Ireneo and a cartoon of Father Cobos—Paz's alter ego—squeezing poor President Sebastián Lerdo de Tejada by the scruff of the neck as he thrashes around desperately and even hangs out his tongue. By now Paz owned his own press and had published his first historical novel (on the Conquest), as well as a commercially successful *Álbum de Hidalgo* and plays, short theatrical pieces, and poems. The time for new

elections was approaching and Paz, as was his custom, began to hatch
a new conspiracy. Because of his cartoons, he was briefly jailed again,
"in a dark prison with a glimmer of light entering through a tiny sky-
light at the door, our friend Paz lies, ill due to such harsh treatment."
But he kept firing off his darts. And the revolutionary cycle repeated
itself again, in almost every respect. Once again at the side of his *caudillo* Porfirio Díaz, Paz composed the original version of the Program
of Tuxtepec, announcing Porfirio's renewed revolt against the central government. Early reverses resulted in a fifty-seven-day jail term
for Paz and then exile in Brownsville, Texas, and Havana, Cuba. But
Díaz eventually triumphed, entered the capital near the end of 1876,
and called for new elections, in which of course he won the presidency.
With a brief parenthesis (one of his subordinates was entrusted with
the presidential office from 1880 to 1884) Díaz would stay in power till
1911. His faithful friend Ireneo would finally lay down his arms (he was
by then a colonel) after thirteen continuous years of combat, "in conso-
nance with the times when everything had to be renewed."

Compared with the impending Porfiriato, the "dictatorships" of
Juárez and Lerdo de Tejada had been child's play. As justification for
his loyalty to the regime, Paz would point to the material progress presided over by his good friend Porfirio. Mexico was to leave behind the
era of revolutions, civil wars, and foreign interventions, and enter a
long and energetically sustained period of "Peace, order, and progress":
thousands of miles of railroads, new harbors, increasing exploitation of
mineral mines and oil fields, agricultural and industrial development,
growth in foreign trade, all within the framework of a kind of absolute
monarchy outfitted in republican clothing. Like Mexico itself, Ireneo
Paz settled down and filled his life with "order" and "progress." In 1877
he initiated a new periodical, *La Patria*, with its illustrated supplements
and famous annual almanac. It would appear, issue after issue, until
August 1914. But one element of Porfirio's official ideals would fail to
take firm hold within the life of this highly combative man, the condition expressed by his own family name: peace. Close to the date of the

presidential elections of 1880, Ireneo, as if he still had to pay a debt of violence to his revolutionary past, challenged the young poet Santiago Sierra to a duel. The colonel would kill the poet and this episode of bloodshed would weigh upon him from then on. "You do not know what it's like to carry a corpse on your back through an entire life," he once told some young men who were contemplating a duel.

The killing seemed to weaken every vestige of his physical aggressiveness and he turned definitively to his work in editing and literary creation. Instead of making war, Ireneo Paz devoted himself to *hacer patria,* "creating the fatherland" through writing. His ambition, which he never completely realized, was to become the Benito Pérez Galdós of Mexico, chronicling the story of his country in works of history and fiction as the great Spanish novelist was doing for Spain. After publishing (in 1884) *Algunas campañas* (Some Campaigns), his attractively written revolutionary memoirs, he began a series of Historical Legends (*Leyendas históricas*), which began with the Conquest, then treated important political figures of the nineteenth century (Santa Anna, Juárez, Maximilian, Manuel Losada, Porfirio Díaz) and finally a few twentieth-century revolutionaries. His work ran parallel to that of the authors of the great collection (published in 1884) *México a través de los siglos* (Mexico Across the Centuries). The intention in both cases was to firmly establish a historical consciousness for Mexico by creating a civic pantheon. At one point he was given the federal concession to publish the Diary of Debates held in Porfirio's more than obsequious Congress. The success of his own works and publishing projects was reflected in the life of his family and his material prosperity. Although he had lost his wife and was deeply saddened by the early death of his firstborn son, Carlos, two daughters remained to him (Rosita and the very sensitive Amalia, a lover of literature, who would remain unmarried and be his lifelong companion) and two sons, Arturo and then the youngest born in 1883, Octavio. And Ireneo showed no hesitation in his support for Porfirio, whom he saw as a "ruler who has known how to rescue, almost from the rubble, a nationality to be respected."

But around 1910, the patriarch sensed a return of the deep past, both the country's and his own. His initial reaction was to criticize the "stupid revolution" proclaimed by the anti-reelectionist leader Francisco I. Madero, but then the recollection of his own campaigns with Porfirio Díaz against Juárez and Lerdo and the memory of the years when he had abandoned work and family to launch himself on a political adventure all combined to again awaken the rebel that he had once been. Hadn't he himself coined the phrase: "Valid voting, no reelection" (*Sufragio efectivo, no reelección*), first brandished by Porfirio at the time of the La Noria uprising in 1871 and that had now become Madero's slogan? *La Patria* began to put some distance between itself and the dictator and Ireneo sharpened its attacks on the arrogant political elite that surrounded Díaz, the so-called Científicos. Díaz responded by sending his old comrade, now seventy-five years old, to the Belén prison of Mexico City.

On June 7 1911, Francisco I. Madero entered a Mexico City from which Díaz had fled to France. *La Patria*, under the interim direction of Ireneo's son, Octavio Paz Solórzano, announced in huge front-page headlines, with a photo of the triumphant leader of the Revolution, "ECCE HOMO, he had to win and he won."

But for Ireneo Paz, electoral freedom was one thing and another, very different matter, was the threat of a revolution led by Emiliano Zapata, whose struggle had not ended with the political triumph of Madero. Perhaps Don Ireneo lumped Zapata in with his memories of the "Indian hordes" of Manuel Losada, the "Tiger of Álica," who had fought an ethnic war in western Mexico. Again under the patriarch's direction, *La Patria* lashed out at Zapata, dubbing him "the sadly celebrated Attila of the South" and his soldiers "rabble in revolt," "coarse gangs of fiends" from whom "the soil of the fatherland" had to "purge itself." When Madero was assassinated (February 23, 1913), *La Patria*'s editorial pages drew a skeptical conclusion: "The Mexican people did not understand freedom, nor has it managed to discipline its character." Only liberal education would resolve the political problems of the country and it would take some time. Meanwhile, Ireneo found no problem in supporting the military regime of General Victoriano Huerta, who had led the coup d'état against Madero.

AT THE beginning of the twentieth century, Ireneo Paz's large country home in Mixcoac was a faithful reflection of the "Porfirian peace." It had a jai alai fronton, a bowling alley, a swimming pool, a billiard parlor, pavilions, and even a Japanese garden. His work life was in Mexico City. The Paz publishing house was on Relox Street, very near the Palacio Nacional, and there the young student Octavio Paz Solórzano learned the business while earning his high school diploma and moving on to a degree in law. Díaz, in a famous newspaper interview of 1908, had broached the possibility of not reelecting himself to an eighth term of office and permitting the formation of political parties as well as genuinely free elections. The sympathies of young Octavio (and perhaps also of Ireneo himself) were drawn to the presidential candidacy—then being floated—of the prestigious general Bernardo Reyes, governor of the dynamic northern state of Nuevo León, who in the end disappointed his loyalists by accepting a diplomatic posting to Europe. Octavio praised the political revolution of Madero but there was another revolution that attracted him more, one that would allow him to be more revolutionary than his father.

In the spring of 1911, while the star of Emiliano Zapata was still on the rise, Octavio Paz Solórzano, *El Güero* ("the blond guy," as the Zapatistas later came to call him), had traveled through the Zumpango region of the state of Guerrero to see what exactly was going on. The first stage of Zapata's "Revolution of the South" was over but Paz carefully noted down the events and surroundings and would write down their story many years later. It was the first foreshadowing of his later commitment to the Zapatista cause. After Díaz resigned (on May 25, 1911), Octavio organized a student reception for Madero in Mexico City and an ephemeral Liberal Center for Students, which tried to revive the candidacy of Bernardo Reyes. In August of the same year, in elections far more honest than any that had previously been held in Mexico,

Madero became president. And Paz Solórzano finished his law degree with a thesis on "Liberty of the Press," a subject intimately connected with the life experience of his father.

The triumph of democracy seemed to promise a tranquil life for the young lawyer. In 1911 he published an "Updated Manual for the Voter," established his law office, and married Josefina Lozano ("Pepita," the young and beautiful daughter of an Andalusian wine grower whom he had known in Mixcoac). He moved with his wife to Ensenada, in Baja California, where he filled various posts in the Ministry of Justice, directed by Jesús Flores Magón, the brother of the great anarchist rebel Ricardo Flores Magón. But neither the times nor the character of the young lawyer portended a peaceful life. He had quarreled to the point of combat with the Porfirista prefect in Mixcoac and had the same kind of confrontations with a local *cacique* in Ensenada. Like his father, he was a man always ready for battle.

In 1914, the young couple returned to Mexico City. On March 31, 1914, the office of *La Patria* received a notice for next-day publication. While the federal forces of Victoriano Huerta were locked in fierce combat with Villistas at the city of Torreón and rumors were running through the city about "the almost certain death of the ferocious Emiliano Zapata," Octavio Paz Lozano was born in Mexico City and given the name of his father: "the first delivery by the wife of Licenciado Octavio Paz, the son of our director, who gave birth to a healthy child" welcomed "with great joy." The new Octavio would spend his childhood with his eighty-year-old grandfather because in a few months the elder Octavio, duplicating the destiny of Don Ireneo, would leave his wife and son and "go off to the Revolution." And the child was born among flames: the Great War had begun in Europe and Mexico was undergoing the preliminary stages of a savage civil war between the revolutionaries who had supported Venustiano Carranza and the armies of Villa and Zapata. Three weeks later, soldiers loyal to General Pablo González burst into the Paz publishing house and confiscated everything. The final issue of *La Patria*, number 11767, appeared on August 26, 1914. Since May, Don Ireneo had informed his readers that he was in economic difficulties; and now he suffered the physical blow of a stroke. Cared for by his daughter Amalia, he convalesced in his Mixcoac home. Very soon afterward, he was joined by his daughter-in-law Pepita and his little grandson Octavio.

FROM 1915 on, the Revolution set the country aflame but the violence did not enter Mexico City. Don Ireneo (whom his children called Papa Neo) would live ten more years, organized, athletic, sarcastic, and resigned to the very end. With the sonorous call of a bugle, he would unite his family at the dinner table—his daughter Amalia, his son Arturo with his own wife and children, his daughter-in-law Josefa and the child Octavio. Ireneo spent time in his orchards but, still a restless man, he would also go off elsewhere. His grandson would accompany him on some of these trips: a weekly visit to the mother of the well-known actress Mimí Derba, where he was treated by mother and daughter with great affection, or a trip to collect rents. The grandfather and child would also meet in his library, which held the precious jewels of literature and French history, especially dealing with the French Revolution, and albums with pictures of Ireneo's political and literary heroes: Mirabeau, Danton, Lamartine, Hugo, and Balzac. It was perhaps there in the library—for Ireneo a kind of civic altar, among portraits of Napoléon and Spanish liberals like General Juan Prim and Emilio Castelar—that the grandson first heard him speak of his campaigns in the wars of the Reform and the Intervention and his rebellions against Juárez and Lerdo de Tejada. He was a magnificent conversationalist.

He died peacefully on the night of November 4, 1924. His son Octavio, who by then had a position in the government of Zapata's home state of Morelos, could not return for the funeral. According to the accounts, Ireneo's grandson, Octavio Paz Lozano, a "young man" ten years old, had to preside over the ceremonies of mourning. He would be left with many memories of his grandfather: the walks hand in hand through Mixcoac, his grandfather's "dark silk jackets sumptuously embroidered," his recounting of anecdotes and legends. All of it would

remain firmly fixed in his recollections, like the engravings by Gustave
Doré that Ireneo had shown him:

> *the first death we never forget*
> *though he may die by lightning, that suddenly!*
> *never to reach the bed or the last rites.*

The house in Mixcoac turned ghostly. Living there were the father,
almost always absent; the child's mother, Josefina (a paragon of Catholic piety during a revolutionary era); and his aunt Amalia, who guided
the first literary steps of that child, reserved and timid though also play-
ful, and already extremely sensitive to the sonic resonances of words.
(Why is the word *calcetín*, "stocking," not the name of a small bell—
campanita? he once asked as a small child.) To this solitude of an only
child, abandoned in early infancy by a revolutionary father and now
abandoned forever by the patriarch "who was gone in a few hours /
and nobody knows what silence he entered," the young Octavio would
add the intangible presence of those who had vanished: "the twilight
brotherhoods of the absent": "In my house the dead outnumber the
living." As the years passed, Papa Neo's library became his refuge. Surrounded by portraits, he read Ireneo's collection of novels, poems, and
historical legends, and he preserved his albums, books, manuscripts,
and unpublished works.

Political liberty had been the central concern of Don Ireneo, the
driving force behind his revolutionary campaigns. But his work as a
writer and editor—periodicals, sonnets, and books—had been in the
end his strongest weapon, his way of "constructing the fatherland." He
ended his days believing that "for the dictatorship of one man, the caudillo Díaz, the Revolution had substituted the anarchic dictatorship of
many chiefs and little chieftains." In the obituaries, the press remembered Ireneo Paz as he had really been: "the dean of journalism." He
had lived the nineteenth century over nearly its entire range, from war
to peace, from peace to war. Symbolically, he was the last survivor of
his epoch, the last Liberal.

When the height of the Revolution was over, in those dinner-table discussions in the Mixcoac residence Octavio Paz Solórzano would complain that his father, Ireneo, "did not understand the Revolution." For him, revolution was not a mere political matter or an innocent request for the restoration of political liberty. It was a festive and violent expression risen from deep in the earth of Mexico, an armed demand for justice and equality for Mexico's vast poor majority. And the real revolution was the one to which Octavio Paz Solórzano had devoted the six most important years of his life, the revolution led by Emiliano Zapata.

He had joined the ranks of Zapatismo since September 1914, working as an intermediary between the forces of Zapata and the Villistas. He briefly saw action in the area south of Mexico City, including his own town of Mixcoac. When the forces of the Convention (favored by Zapata and Villa) occupied the capital, he directed a newspaper (which was then taken over by the Villistas). At the beginning of 1915, he left the capital to accompany the wandering government of Eulalio Gutiérrez, which would later, under the leadership of Francisco Lagos Cházaro, establish itself in the cities of Cuernavaca and Jojutla. In the local newspapers Octavio Paz Solórzano floated the idea of a committee to represent Zapatismo in the United States and counteract the negative coverage that the movement was receiving in the international press. The Convention accepted the project. In April 1917, Paz visited "the chieftain Zapata" at his headquarters in Tlaltizapán to finalize his foreign responsibility. Zapata received him while eating a watermelon (which he would cut open with one slice of his machete) and shared anecdotes with Paz, which the young lawyer would remember and include in a later biography of his hero.

Paz had faith in his duties but the truth is that it was already too late for the Zapatista cause. His first, quite long report, written to Zapata from Chautzinca, in the state of Puebla, where he was on the run, shows a mixture of stoicism, enthusiasm, and honesty: "I have gone hungry on various occasions and I have pursued my journey on foot

. . . I have not lost heart for a single moment . . . almost alone, in rags, since the clothes I was wearing are in tatters, and hungry . . ." And he continued:

> As I travelled through the towns, I kept on spreading propaganda in different forms and composed manifestos for many military leaders, so that they could inform their people of the betrayal by the Carrancistas and the reasons why they should help us, also—with every peasant to whom I spoke—I tried to inculcate [a conviction of] their right to the land, and I am deeply pleased to tell you that in Guerrero and Puebla, the land has been redistributed, well even if certainly not in a perfect manner but still many villages have taken possession of the lands that belong to them, in accordance with the sixth article of the Program of Ayala . . .

And as if to convince himself, he adds ingenuously: "the military situation is very favorable to us, since the Carrancistas only hold the railroads, the harbors and the state capitals . . . the word circulates everywhere that Carranza, Obregón and Luis Carrera will flee . . . Wilson doesn't know what he's doing and he is blindly striking out around him . . . the victory we long for is near."

The son would relive the sudden changes, the dangers and the sufferings of his father, Don Ireneo, but he never had his father's good luck. In San Antonio, Texas, he spent a year in useless plotting. His letters reeked of frustration, bewilderment, bitterness, almost of abandonment. Zapatista headquarters was informed of his descent into alcoholism, a weakness that would gravely afflict him right up to his death. All his plans to support the Revolution of the South from Los Angeles failed completely. He formed a conspiracy to attack Baja California but it was discovered and a cargo of weapons was confiscated. Shortly after the assassination of Emiliano Zapata on April 10, 1919, Paz and his friend Ramón Puente (the biographer of Pancho Villa) formed the publishing house of "O. Paz and Company" and started the newspaper *La Semana*, where they published articles by the most noted Mexican exiles, including the philosopher José Vasconcelos. He received, in Los Angeles, a brief visit from his wife and the child Octavio, whom he had abandoned at the age of three months. His work as a publisher excited him but his tone remained somber. "I have been in this country entirely alone and without resources of any kind and sometimes tied hand and foot," he wrote to his former military comrade Jenaro Amezcua. But he nevertheless continued his efforts to unite the various exiles and he tried to secure the freedom of Ricardo Flores Magón, the Mexican anarchist revolutionary who was locked up in an American prison. In May 1920 the money ran out and *La Semana* died. Paz lived immersed in uncertainty. When the rebellion of Agua Prieta, launched by Sonoran generals under the command of Obregón, disowned Carranza, Paz was unable, from his perspective, to sound the bells of victory. Why was there no mention at all of agrarian reform? Why was there no "presence of the south"? How could the Revolution ally itself with generals who had fought against Zapata? "The triumph of the Revolution, the true Revolution," he wrote, "is a long way off." Finally, in June 1920, after six years of "making the Revolution," Octavio Paz Solórzano returned to the family home in Mixcoac.

During the two four-year terms of the "Sonoran dynasty" (Álvaro Obregón from 1920 to 1924 and Plutarco Elías Calles from 1924 to 1928), Paz tried to orchestrate a political career. In April 1922, on the third anniversary of Zapata's assassination, he had written a long biographical essay on his lost leader. As a gesture of loyalty to him, he became a founder of the National Agrarian Party (*Partido Nacional Agrarista*). Elected a member of Congress on that party ticket, he proposed legislation to protect peasants and workers and he put together a list of the abuses that hacienda owners were inflicting on peasants throughout the country. But all his political wagers wound up as losses. In July 1928, Álvaro Obregón, reelected and about to begin another four-year term, was assassinated. His downfall was also the end of the National Agrarian Party, which had been his principal political arm. And with the party, one of its directors, Octavio Paz Solórzano, also lost any chance for a political future.

Between 1929 and 1934, Mexico had three presidents but only one "Foremost Chief" (*Jefe Máximo*), Plutarco Elías Calles, the power behind the scenes. Without any possibility (or any desire) to be re-elected, Calles (who had created the Bank of Mexico and the Bank for Agrarian Credit) would institute a party called the PNR in 1929, a hegemonic political organization that morphed into the PRM (in 1938) and finally the *Partido Revolucionario Institucional* (the PRI), which would govern the country until the end of the twentieth century. Paz Solórzano found no place for himself in this new order. Disappointed in politics, he threw himself into the vocation of journalist and publisher that he had learned from Don Ireneo. In 1929 he published (in daily newspapers, Sunday supplements, and magazines) anecdotes and stories from *his* revolution, the deeds of the Zapatistas. These literary and historic sketches would be a firsthand source for the understanding of Zapatismo, especially in its initial phase before 1915. People, attitudes, significant episodes, and brief narrative insights file vividly through the pages. One listens to dialogues, proverbs, bursts of language, ballads, descriptions of battle. And here and there Zapata himself appears, miraculously close to us:

> Zapata greatly enjoyed inviting highly affected individuals to engage the bulls . . . normally they were sent flying, which Zapata found hilarious. He did it to ridicule them . . . he understood that they did not feel the Revolution.

But Octavio the elder had surely felt the Revolution. And because of it his main preoccupation was not, as with Ireneo, political freedom but social justice. And as the basis of social justice, he envisioned doing historical justice to Indian Mexico: "the basic postulates of the Revolution, especially with the land, date from the first inhabitants of Mexico."

Between 1930 and 1931, Paz Solórzano, with much labor and very little commercial success, compiled an *Álbum de Juárez* (inspired by the work Ireneo had published on Father Hidalgo, leader of the first revolution against the Spaniards) and continued in the tradition of his father by writing a history of journalism in Mexico. He had a passion for being "the lawyer of the people." In his office, recently opened again after two decades of other activities, he committed himself to defending peasants from the villages of Santa Martha Acatitla and Los Reyes, southeast of Mexico City, and he often did the work free of charge. With his clients, he wanted to continue the fiesta, the endless drunken spree of the Revolution, "to face death like a man" and perhaps die among these poor, as if he had died in the Revolution.

THE SIGNATURE of the poet Octavio Paz Lozano resembles that of his father, the same open O without a finishing flourish, the same rhythm, the same sloping inclination. How many times must he have seen this signature among his father's papers? But it is certain that the intermittent presence of his father did not lessen the boy's experience of solitude. The first real meeting between them had been in Los Angeles. A new face for solitude, with the sensation of alienness in a foreign country and surrounded by a foreign language. On his return to Mexico, enrolled in good Catholic and later secular schools in Mixcoac and Mexico City, he experienced another tightening of the screw of solitude. Because of his blue eyes, the other children mistook him for a foreigner. "I felt myself a Mexican but they wouldn't let me be one." Even Antonio Díaz Soto y Gama, a leading protagonist of Zapatismo and a comrade of his father, exclaimed at the sight of the young Octavio: "*Caramba,* you didn't tell me you had a Visigoth for a son!" Everyone laughed at the joke. Except the boy himself.

His mother Josefina, who lived to be very old, would be with Octavio Paz until her death in 1980. A devout Catholic, she often sang him the songs of her native Andalucía. She softened the weight of the abandonment, the emptiness, the need. He had not only his mother but his aunt Amalia, who opened the doors of literature to him (she had been a friend of the greatest writer of the Mexican modernist movement, the poet and chronicler Manuel Gutiérrez Nájera). Years later, the women he came to love, often in a mode that was both intense and tormented, helped to clear the way toward the vocation he early chose for himself: the writing of poetry.

His father, on the other hand, offered no escape but only a wall of silence. The son would have liked to share his father's solitude, to speak with him intimately so as to clarify his own life. "It was almost impossible for me to speak with him," he confessed half a century later, "but I loved him and always sought his company. When he was writing, I would approach him and try to give him my support. I typed up clean, corrected copies of some of his articles, before he took them to the publishing office. He never even took notice of my affection. I turned distant. The flaw in my father, if he had one, is that he didn't notice that affection I showed him. And it's very likely that he took no notice of what I was writing. But in no way do I reproach him."

The articles for which the son typed "clean, correct copies" were specifically Paz Solórzano's articles on Zapatismo. Though he has not been recognized as such by scholars of Zapatismo, Paz Solórzano was the first historian of Zapatismo and the first guardian of its place in history. On that subject, in silence, a permanent bond was nurtured, and the son became a witness of and comrade to his father's life. Paz Solórzano introduced his son to "the real Mexico," the country of the Zapatista peasants, and initiated him into an understanding of the *other* history of Mexico, buried but still living: "When I was a child, many old Zapatista leaders visited my home and also many peasants whom my father defended in their legal troubles and lawsuits over land. I remember some men from an *ejido* [collectively owned farming community] who were claiming some lagoons that are—or were—along the road to Puebla. On my father's saint's day, we ate an extraordinary pre-Columbian meal cooked by the *ejiditarios* . . . it was *pato enlodado* ['mudded duck'] sprinkled with pulque cured with the fruit of prickly pear."

But his father's life outside the house had its shadowy side: "my father had a frenetic social life, women, fiestas; all of it in some way wounded me but not as much as it did my mother." A half century later, peasants whom the lawyer Paz had defended in the village of Santa Martha Acatitla remembered him as a "saintly man." "Of course I remember . . . Octavio Paz! I can almost see him arriving over there! Smiling and with a woman hanging on each arm . . . I can tell you Don Octavio was a real rooster. He adored women and he had many friends." For that "lawyer of the people," a daily visit to Acatitla meant a return to origins, "making the Revolution," touching the truth, the Indian truth of Mexico, eating indigenous foods that dated back many centuries—plovers, lake beetles, fish-egg foam, river shrimp, tadpoles, roasted insect eggs—hanging around with the locals, offering toasts to Emiliano Zapata, and listening to ballads "that everybody sang with enthusiasm and celebratory *gritos*." It meant searching for "a good swallow of rum and very happily drinking down a jug," and it meant hunting ducks on the lagoon and carrying those trophies to his lovers in the village, his "veterans," as he called them. And above all, attending the village fiestas: "Don Octavio loved the village fiestas where the good pulque flowed freely," recalled the son of Cornelio Nava, a friend of Paz Solórzano. "And what good pulque it was! Thick and delicious . . . With Octavio Paz Solórzano, people like Soto y Gama came there . . . and I almost forgot his son, the writer who carries his name. He was a child then but he would be there too."

Buried deep in the poet's memory lay the most horrifying recollection—the events of March 8, 1935. It was of course "a day of fiesta in Los Reyes La Paz," recalled Leopoldo Castañeda, "and the *licenciado* arrived directly there. They say someone was with him when he arrived." He was killed by a train of the Interoceanic Railway. "The body was so frightfully dismembered that the remains . . . carefully collected . . . were carried in a bag to his house" at Licenciado Ireneo Paz Street No. 79 in Mixcoac. The newspaper *El Universal* went on to describe the lawyer Paz's rich historical archive, as well as that of his father, and noted the existence of a valuable historical diary that he kept. His son came to believe that his father had been murdered. The authorities tried to interrogate the man who had arrived with him but he never presented himself. There were people who believed it was an accident but others thought it had been a suicide. It was said that some Indians had found the head fifteen hundred meters from the body. Not long after his father's death, Octavio Paz discovered that he had a sister whose mother lived near the site of the accident.

And so, having "faced up to death," the drunken spree, the Mexican fiesta of Octavio Paz Solórzano was swept into silence, a man "so likable that he even made people laugh who didn't like him," but so somber in his final photos. Paz admitted, half a century later, "I relegated him to oblivion," though he immediately corrected himself and said, "although oblivion is not the right word. In reality he was always present for me but set apart, like a painful recollection." In 1936, a history of the Mexican Revolution was published. The chapters on Zapatismo were by Paz Solórzano, fruit of the great passion of his life. Ten years later, in the poem "Interrupted Elegy," Octavio portrays his father as a lost, wandering soul:

> And someone among us gets up
> and carefully closes the door.
> But he, there on the other side, keeps
> insisting, he lurks in every hollow,
> in the folds, he wanders among the yawns,
> the surroundings, though we may close
> the doors, he keeps on insisting.
> His silence is a mirror of my life.
> His death prolongs itself within my life.
> I am the final error among his errors.

IV

The legacy was there, implicit. If the Liberal patriarch and the Zapatista leader had been revolutionaries, their descendant should be more of a revolutionary than either of them. The adventure began in 1929, when Paz was fifteen years old, as he joined a famous student strike for the autonomy of the National University. The students were also very active in backing the presidential candidacy of José Vasconcelos, who would become one of Octavio's idols. Vasconcelos's term as Secretary of Public Education had been a true educational and cultural crusade. In 1929 Vasconcelos had returned from exile and based his program on a very simple platform: the moral purification of the Mexican Revolution, corroded by militarism and the corruption of the "chiefs and little chieftains" Don Ireneo had observed. Vasconcelos was defeated through the first great electoral fraud perpetrated by the official party near the very beginning of its long history of power. José Alvarado, a friend of Octavio Paz, described the state of mind among the young:

> Mexico was then living through a dramatic time. The Revolution had been halted and betrayed. There was an air of confusion in all areas and the country's youth, defeated through evil maneuvers in the electoral contest of 1929, felt desperate and oppressed. All the best voices had dissipated and the best proposals dissolved. The world seemed gray with the echoes of the American financial crisis, the triumph of fascism in Italy, the winds foreshadowing Hitler, and the disputes among the great powers.

The students moved radically to the left.

In 1930, Octavio Paz Lozano entered the most prestigious public school in Mexico, the Escuela Nacional Preparatoria, where his father had studied. In that noble and highly symbolic building, which had once been the old Jesuit college of San Ildefonso, José Clemente Orozco had painted his celebrated murals on the Mexican Revolution. Friends remember Octavio in heated discussion with his history and philosophy teachers about rural injustice and peasant misfortunes (not long ago he had been typing "clean, correct copies" of his father's pro-Zapatista articles). He became friends with a Catalan student named José Bosch, an anarchist, and the two engineered academic protests, attended anti-imperialist demonstrations, and sometimes were arrested, always to be rescued by Octavio's father, the lawyer Paz Solórzano. Bakunin,

Fourier, and the Spanish anarchists were Octavio's first political mentors, but soon he was "saved," in the jargon of the time, by Marxism. The young Octavio joined the Union of Students for Workers and Peasants, whose objective was to establish educational outreach projects in the city and countryside. (Frida Kahlo also participated in the activities of the *Unión de Estudiantes Pro Obreros y Campesinos*, while Diego Rivera was painting murals adorned with the hammer and sickle in the Ministry of Public Education.) Octavio also became a member of an ephemeral Radical Preparatory ("high school") Party.

In 1931, the best bookstore in Mexico City, Pedro Robredo—one street away from the National Preparatory School—put some twenty new books on sale, almost all of them translations from the Russian: *Anarchism and Socialism* by Plekhanov, Marx and Engels's *Communist Manifesto*, an anthology of writers of revolutionary Russia, *Russia in 1931* by César Vallejo, *The State and the Revolution* by Lenin, and more. Paz and his friends read some of these books and, like almost an entire generation of Latin American students, identified with Sashka Yegulev, the heroic student who gives his life for the revolution in the novel by the Russian novelist Leonidas Andreiev.

They called each other *tovarich* ("comrade") and some of them even dressed like Bolsheviks, in Russian tunics, but very few actually joined the Communist Party. The government of Plutarco Elías Calles, soon to be dubbed the "Foremost Chief," had banned the communists (after his brief romance with the Soviet Union) and membership in the party would put you on the wrong side of the law. Among these boys, one student, the most radical among them, seemed predestined to "make the Revolution": he had been born on November 20, 1914, the official anniversary of the outbreak of the Mexican Revolution. Even his last name, José Revueltas, implied rebellion. Between 1930, when he joined the Mexican Communist Party, and 1935, when he visited Soviet Russia as a delegate to the Seventh Party Congress, Revueltas would willingly suffer two periods of incarceration in the Pacific island prison of the Islas Marías. Much more prison time followed in the course of his life. Revueltas embraced his militancy with religious fervor. His spirit of sacrifice, his willingness to contemplate suffering and accept his own, would later be poured into deeply moving novels. Many times in the future his life would intersect that of his schoolboy friend Paz.

Another friend of Octavio Paz, the poet Efraín Huerta, has evoked the atmosphere of those febrile years: "A light united us, something like a communion."

> *We were like angry stars*
> *full of books, manifestos, heartbreaking loves*
>
> *Afterwards*
> *we gave our veins and arteries*
> *what are called desires*
> *to redeem the world on every warm morning,*
> *We lived through*
> *a cold rain of goodness:*
> *everything winged, musical, everything guitars,*
> *and declarations, whispers at daybreak,*
> *sighs and statues, threadbare clothes, misfortunes*
> *they were all there . . .*

Paz shared the fervor of those times but his road toward Revolution did not, as with Revueltas and Huerta, lead to formal communist militancy. Born among books and printing presses, he very quickly embarked on a life of publishing and of combat in the world of letters. In August 1931 he started the literary journal *Barandal* (Balustrade), which would last for seven issues, till March 1932. There he published his first poems, with a tone that veered from playfulness to desolation. "We all had the dream of having our own magazine," recalls Rafael Solana. "We were thunderstruck with admiration, stupefied, when a friend, Octavio Paz, brought out his [magazine] . . . small, only a few pages, but cleanly produced, young, new."

In December 1931, Paz was only seventeen but in his magazine he published an "Ethics of the Artist," in which he formulated a totally serious prophecy about the future of his vocation. Between the options of "pure art" and "committed art" (an intensely debated topic of the time) he opts for the second, but not in a simple way nor with the arguments of a schoolboy. He had read Nietzsche, ancient Greek theater, the Spanish novel, Russian Marxists and German Romantics, and he believed that literature had to be "mystical and aggressive," elevated and eternal, "possessed by truth." Much more important, he declared himself committed to a cultural mission that would include all of Latin America: "It is indispensable to realize that we form part of a continent whose history we have to construct ourselves. That there is a manifest destiny running through all eras, obliging men to fulfill the will of life and of God." The literary and publishing work of his father and grandfather had made their mark, in various forms and degrees, on the history of Mexico. His own work would unfold on a much larger stage.

For the young Paz, it seemed clear that radical politics had to be fused with cultural modernity. The air was full of radical politics—in the press, political parties, meetings, books, cafés, periodicals, lecture halls—but modernity was not so easy to achieve. The previous generation (born between 1890 and 1905) had set the bar very high. Almost indifferent to politics but closely and actively attentive to the productions of the literary and artistic vanguard, this early generation had clustered—as was usual in Mexico since the middle of the nineteenth century—around a magazine, in this case *Contemporáneos* (which was published from 1928 to 1931). The group included truly outstanding poets and playwrights (Xavier Villaurrutia, Carlos Pellicer, José Gorostiza, Salvador Novo) and the impressive essayist Jorge Cuesta. They were of the same age as the Spanish intellectual Generation of '27 (which included Rafael Alberti, Manuel Altolaguirre, Gerardo Diego, and Federico García Lorca) and they greatly admired the poetry of Juan Ramón Jiménez and Antonio Machado. Their magazine published authors from the *Nouvelle Revue Français* (Gide, Morand, Maurois, Larbaud) and translations of T. S. Eliot's *The Waste-Land*, D. H. Lawrence's *Mornings in Mexico,* and the *Anabasis* by St.-John Perse. And these Contemporáneos cast doubts on the continuing hegemony of the great

Mexican muralist movement, which by that time (at least in the cases of Rivera and Siqueiros) had become repetitive and pedagogic. With *Barandal*, Paz wanted to follow in the steps of the now defunct journal, *Contemporáneos*. He published the modernist French poet Valéry, the Dutch historian and philosopher Johan Huizinga, the Italian futurist Filippo Marinetti. His little magazine was somewhat irreverent in relation to intellectual sacred cows of the academy and did valuable work of recovery and discovery in the visual arts.

But above all Paz was a poet. His teacher Andrés Iduarte remembers him as "timid, or more precisely restrained, capable of explosions that were promptly calmed by much reading of the best writing, a penetrating intelligence that could lead him to doubts and a painful sensibility that could end in despair, spontaneous and revelatory in opening his heart and then tortured and distant to the point of sullenness." His friend José Alvarado has left us another sensitively observed sketch of the young editor of *Barandal*: "Leaning on the balustrade of the top floor" of San Ildefonso, looking at the light above the Valley of Mexico "beyond his bewildered eyes, one already recognized an unbreakable poetic will and a thirst for inventing the world; Octavio . . . did not want to be simply one among many poets, but a true master of poetry; and he did not entrust his identification with the world only to reason, but to every sensation, emotion, all possible judgments . . ."

In 1932, continuing another strand of the family tradition, he entered the law school of the National University. He traveled to Veracruz, one of the most radical states in Mexico, to support peasant groups encouraged by the state governor Adalberto Tejeda. As a member of a Federation of Revolutionary Students, he attended a demonstration in honor of the Cuban communist leader Julio Antonio Mella, assassinated in Mexico in January 1929. The police threw the young demonstrators in jail, from which they were freed one more time by Octavio's father. His anarchist friend Bosch was expelled from the country. Hitler took power in 1933, inspiring Mexican fascists; and the politics (in 1935) of the Popular Front opened political life anew to the Communist Party. Militias were formed, groups like the "Red Shirts" on the left or the

"Golden Shirts" on the right, who would later fight to the death on the streets of the capital city. The philosopher Antonio Caso advised his student Paz to follow the example of Vicente Lombardo Toledano: "he's a socialist but also a Christian." Caso failed to draw Paz to Christianity (he was a liberal Jacobin, like his grandfather) but Lombardo did not convert him to hard-line leftist orthodoxy.

Paz always reserved space for his own creative work. In 1933 he published his first collection of poems, the chapbook *Luna Silvestre* (Wild Moon). But the winds steadily grew more ideological. In September of the same year, the review *Cuadernos del Valle de México* appeared but would only last for two issues. It was directed by a collective that included Paz, and though it published a translation of a section of Joyce's *Ulysses*, it was heavily inclined toward politics. The review printed, for example, Rafael Alberti's poem "Un fantasma recorre Europa," the title obviously drawn from *The Communist Manifesto*: "A specter is haunting Europe." Enrique Ramírez y Ramírez describes the Soviet Union as a "transitory state leading to higher levels." José Alvarado contributes a piece criticizing intellectuals who practice the "invention of novel games and logical enticements" and instead proposes "a higher mission ... The politics of rebellion is the sole creative activity of men, the only work we can do in joy and trembling." Alvarado himself would later describe the torturous Dostoyevskian atmosphere of his generation:

> ... one of these boys, from a Calvinist family, had adopted and abandoned communism to then convert to Catholicism after a long spiritual crisis. Another, a sensitive and intelligent man, was released from prison after an unfortunate homicide which would later lead him to further violence and a mysterious and miserable death. Students and Marxists, a good many of them anarchists ... furious at deception and perversity, had been touched by the lustration of Vasconcelos and his preachings on social justice. Lyricism was political and love, poetry, metaphysics were all political ...

Paz as well would always remember the wasted lives, the suicides, and the abrupt conversions of his generation, infused with its political fervor. His friend Enrique Ramírez y Ramírez had worked in 1930 for *El hombre libre*, a newspaper of the Hispanic right, xenophobic and anti-Semitic. Overnight he had turned to "collectivist rhetoric" and become a communist. And Rubén Salazar Mallén—a somewhat more important writer, who would become one of Paz's permanent adversaries—had veered in the opposite direction. Paz himself was no convert; his path toward radical politics had been naturally rooted in his family saga.

Near the end of 1933, General Lázaro Cárdenas became the next official presidential "candidate," a designation equivalent to election. From the very beginning, he showed his clear intention of actualizing social reforms spelled out in the program of the Mexican Revolution but still unrealized. Like almost all his friends, Paz would welcome the official shift toward the left during Cárdenas's presidency (1934–40) but he never became a party militant. He was a radical in politics but an avant-gardist in culture. As a result, he would form friendships with some of the mostly nonpolitical Contemporáneos and later (in 1935) with Jorge Cuesta, perhaps the clearest thinker of his time. In a polarized world, almost no space had been left for traditional liberal thought. But Cuesta was the most important exception. An essayist whose broad intellectual spectrum and critical passion anticipate the future Paz, Cuesta was a pioneering Mexican critic of Marxism. And from 1933 on, he called attention to what he saw as a central element of Mexican political culture: the persistence of the old dogmatism of the Catholic clergy in the new political and ideological structures of the Mexican state. At the same time he analyzed the contradiction he saw in the controversial government attempt to introduce "Socialist Education" within a capitalist society.

SOMETIME BEFORE the tragedy of his father's death, Octavio Paz had met an eighteen-year-old preparatory student, dancer, and choreographer in the University Theater. She was the beautiful, blond, restless,

difficult, and enigmatic Elena Garro. Her life was a mirror image of
Octavio's life. She was brave and independent, her father was Spanish, the mother Mexican, her grandfather—in tribute to her character—called her "La Generala," and in her family two uncles had fought
and died among the legendary troops of Pancho Villa. An earlier brief
liaison with a woman had left Octavio with a residue of intense jealousy. To heal himself he found no better recourse than a complete reading of Marcel Proust. But in the middle of 1935, Paz began to live his
love life like a character in a D. H. Lawrence novel (always his sacred
scriptures in matters of love). At times his stance was that of Goethe's
young Werther. ("I love you desperately, in anguish. If I didn't love you,
I would die.") His almost daily letters to Elena (whom he rebaptized as
Helena) read like the diary of an inspired and tortured young man, devastated by an elusive love. But perhaps it is not so hard to understand
the roots of this level of desperation. It was likely, in part, a direct product of the grief he felt over his father's terrible death. One of his letters
offers a rare glimpse of his life at the age of twenty-one:

> I am here, in my library, in the midst of my dead, of my beloved
> and bitter tears and solitude, and I feel somewhat separate from
> them, as if their wishes were not mine, as if I were not the blood of
> my father and my grandfather, who bind me to a solitary destiny.
> Because I tell you, Helena, in this house I have felt myself bound
> to a series of dark and decadent things, to a design of death and
> bitterness, as if I were only a depository for rasping words.

So as not to feel himself bound to the fate of his family, and following the violent death of his father, Paz had leaped into a professional
void, abandoning law school with only one course remaining for his
degree. He took a job in the Archivo General de la Nación. He was then
reading *The ABC of Communism* by Bukharin and *The Origin of Family,
Private Property, and the State* by Engels. Late at night he would compose thoroughly Marxist texts on the meaninglessness of work and
the abstraction of money within the decadent capitalist world. And he

sketched in his hopes for a new world, interpreting (in his own way) the aphorism of Engels: "From the reign of necessity to the reign of liberty." He wrote that "tomorrow no one will write poems, nor play music, because our actions, our being, in freedom, will be like poems." Then, all of a sudden, tomorrow would knock on his door; History would fall into line with him and invite him to participate in its unfolding.

It was July 1936. The Spanish Civil War had begun. Alvarado recalls that Paz had defended the agrarian revolution with the same passion he later devoted to exalting the Spanish Republic. Now the republic was in danger. This was clearly his opportunity to participate in history, as Ireneo had done with Porfirio and his father with Zapata. In September 1936, Paz published a long poem titled *No pasarán* ("They will not pass") after the famous cry of the communist firebrand and orator Dolores Ibárruri Gómez (*La Pasionaria*) during the Fascist siege of Madrid in 1936. Suddenly his words are not "rasping" but angry, exalted, and full of hope:

> *Like the dry wait for a revolver*
> *or the silence that precedes childbirths*
> *we hear the cry.*
> *It lives in the guts,*
> *it lingers in the pulse,*
> *ascends from the veins to the lips:*
> *they will not pass.*

> *I see the hands that are fruits*
> *and the fertile wombs,*
> *opposing the bullets*
> *their delicate warmth and their blindness.*
> *I see the necks that are ships*
> *and the breasts that are oceans*
> *being born from the plazas and the fields*
> *in the ebbings of breathed out blood*
> *in powerful exhalations*

crashing before the crosses and destiny
in slow and terrible swells:
They will not pass . . .

Cárdenas's government printed 3,500 copies to be distributed among the Spanish people and Paz gained instant celebrity.

In 1937, as a countercurrent to the rhetoric of commitment, Paz attended to his more personal side and published his first real book of poems, *Raíz de hombre* (Root of Man). The theme is not revolutionary passion but its complement: the passion of human love. It is a passion he had carefully elaborated in his letters to Elena Garro and in the thoughts and late night writings that he would publish some years later. He feels like young Werther but he acts like Goethe: he is omnivorously curious, a philosopher by day and night, in lecture halls and cafés, in the streetcar that he mounts and that takes him from Mixcoac to Mexico City, and above all in his family library. There is not a shadow of frivolity to him—nor apparently of humor—but rather gravity and rigor and intellectual and poetic passion. His friends call him "the Lord Byron of Mixcoac," in joking reference to his vocation, his romanticism, and his physical elegance. But Paz's central dialogue is with himself. And he moves along patiently and firmly: "solitude, you who go on revealing to me the form of my spirit, the slow maturation of my being." Cuesta, in a review of *Raíz de hombre*, recognizes his character: "an intelligence and passion as rare as they are sensitive . . . the most characteristic note of his poetry is desperation, which will soon take on a more precise metaphysical form . . . not the pure psychological idleness of the artist." With this work, Cuesta continues, Paz "in his poetry confirms the domination of destiny over him. Now I am certain that Paz has a future."

His patron deities are Lawrence and Marx. Communism, like physical love, seems to him a kind of "religion" that "seeks the active communion of the desperate as well as the disinherited." Many of his friends became members of LEAR ("The League of Revolutionary Writers and Artists"), formed in Mexico in imitation of its homologous

French organization, presided over by Gide, Barbusse, and Malraux. Paz attended the founding convention in January 1937 and listened to all the anathemas against a culture of "purist" "bourgeois" "foreignizing" art, as well as the defense offered by the Guatemalan poet Luis Cardoza y Aragón, of poetry not as "the servant of the Revolution" but as an expression of "perpetual human subversion." He also heard the more radical speakers reject a lukewarm "revolutionary nationalism" and instead embrace proletarian internationalism, repudiating the Mexican government's offer of asylum to Leon Trotsky, who had just arrived in Mexico. Paz, who by then was friendly with Cuesta and had begun to read him, was aware of all these tensions as well as the polemics in Europe over the repression of dissidents in the Soviet Union and the diatribes of the Third International against anarchists and Trotskyists. Nor was he ignorant of what André Gide had written in his *Retour de l'URSS* (Return from the USSR), which had appeared in translation in Mexico toward the end of 1936: "The dictatorship of the proletariat is the dictatorship of one man over the proletariat." The book unveiled the Stalinist cult of personality, the shortages of food and other necessities, the propaganda manipulations, the terror, the vassalage, the prevalence of informers, and the suffocation of intellectual liberty. The account opened the eyes of many communist true believers. But not for Paz. Cuesta, since 1932, had criticized Gide's conversion to communism and predicted his disenchantment. But he had not been able to convince his young friend, who remained firmly persuaded of the justice of his cause. "I stood with the Communists," Paz would remember. "It was a time when I affirmed with enthusiasm that the revolts throughout the world, including Mexico, would find their fulfillment in communism."

OUTSTRIPPING THE left from the left, the new president Lázaro Cárdenas launched his Agrarian Reform, which would include the whole country and divide 17 million *hectáreas* (about 42 million acres) among three million peasants. On the fourth of August 1937, *El Nacional* would announce, in an eight-column spread, "The Revolution will divide the henequen plantations." It was not so easy nor was it terribly necessary to be a Communist in the Mexico of Cárdenas. It was better to support the president. The natural corollary to this gigantic transfer of property (beginning in 1937) was the expansion of education. And Octavio Paz, full of missionary spirit, left for Yucatán in March 1937 to become director of a federal secondary school.

Paz was now a *narodnik*, an intellectual working with peasants, just like his father in Zapatista territory. Always an enclave for the "Divine Caste" of Yucatecan plantation owners in the midst of an ocean of Maya Indians, the "white city" of Mérida awakened Paz's sensitivity to the hidden depths of Mexican history and his angry, poetic Marxism. He reasoned that "to see things 'as they are' is, in a way, not to see them." And so in Mérida he began to *see* reality, to look underneath it poetically:

> The social subsoil is profoundly suffused with Mayan influence; it crops up at once in all the actions of life; in the delicacy of a costume, in a gesture whose origin you do not recognize, in the predilection for a color or a form . . . the gentleness of behavior, the sensibility, the amiability, the lovely and easy courtesy, it is Mayan.

Everything seems peaceful in the beautiful provincial city but "in an instant the city strips off its mask and, naked, lets you see its living entrails, valiant and silenced . . . the great days of strikes and meetings." The indigenous and mestizo subsoil, and the Revolution—the old emphases of his Zapatista father. But as yet Paz is not an excavator of the Mexican soul. He is a poet with a cause: "Here, as in every capitalist regime, what functions is a process by which man lives through the death of man. At times, at night, you awaken amid rubble and blood. The henequen, invisible but present every day, presides over your awakening."

He composed a long poem on this theme, modeled on Eliot's *The Waste-Land,* and titled it "Between the Stone and the Flower" (*Entre la piedra y la flor*). It was his first attempt to insert poetry into history, to create revolutionary poetry that was not demagogic. Many years later, he would remember, "I wanted to show the relation that, like a real hangman's knot, bound the concrete life of the peasants to the impersonal, abstract structure of the capitalist economy: a community of men and women engaged in the satisfaction of basic material necessities and of rites and traditional precepts but subjected to a remote mechanism. This mechanism was grinding them up but they were ignorant not only of its functioning but of its very existence":

At the dawn of silenced poisons
we wake up as serpents

We wake up as stones,
stubborn roots
fleshless thirst, mineral lips . . .

Under this light of frozen lamentation
the henequen, motionless and furious
in its green forefingers
turns visible that which stirs us
the silenced rage that devours us . . .

Magical money!
It rises up on the bones,
on the bones of men it rises up.

You pass like a flower through this sterile hell,
formed only of shackled time,
mechanical running, empty wheel
that squeezes us out and leaves us empty
and dries up our blood,
and the place of tears is killing us.

Because money is infinite and creates infinite deserts . . .

In Yucatán, Paz taught classes in literature to workers and peasants, published articles, and lectured on the Spanish Civil War. The passion in Latin America for the war was even stronger than in Europe: as in 1898, Latin American intellectuals once again identified themselves with Spain. In '98 they were against American imperialism in Cuba, now (most of them) against fascism in Spain. Paz would live the war as his first great public passion. And in Yucatán he was surprised by an invitation to attend the Second International Congress of Writers for the defense of culture, scheduled to be held in Valencia at the beginning of July 1937. His poem *No pasarán* had made him famous. He had to act very quickly. He had to almost kidnap the reluctant and elusive Elena and marry her (on May 25, 1937) and then mount the gangplank of the boat of History. To write, with words and deeds, the poetry of History. Yet one more romantic poet, "the Lord Byron of Mixcoac," signing on for the salvation of an heroic people.

V
———

The newly married couple arrived in Spain in early July. The Mexican delegation included the poet Carlos Pellicer—Paz's friend and teacher since preparatory school; the novelist Juan de la Cabada; the historian José Mancisidor (both of them active members of LEAR); and the great composer Silvestre Revueltas, elder brother of José.

The Spanish Generation of '98, whose journals, poems, and essays had educated Paz in his craft, was now almost entirely absent. Ortega y Gasset was in exile in Buenos Aires. Unamuno had died after publicly condemning the shouted fascist slogan of "Long live Death!" (*Viva la Muerte!*). Machado kept to his home, languishing there. But the later generations were still active, especially around the review *Hora de España*, which had brought together a number of poets, playwrights, philosophers, and essayists of about the same age and horizons as the Mexican Contemporáneos. Paz sought them out (Manuel Altolaguirre, Luis Cernuda, María Zambrano, Rafael Dieste) as well as the most radical among them: Rafael Alberti and José Bergamín. He met—among a multitude of other writers—some of Latin America's greatest poets (Pablo Neruda, Vicente Huidobro, César Vallejo, Nicolás Guillén); he saw Hemingway, Dos Passos, Silone, and the president of the Congress, André Malraux.

In the meetings, José Bergamín introduced a motion of condemnation against André Gide, who had just published some additions to his polemical *Retour de l'URSS*. The writers connected with *Hora de España*, loyal to their humanist tradition, refused to support the motion. One of them, the Galician poet and dramatist Rafael Dieste, declared that he was "popular front, leftist, liberal, non-sectarian." The Latin American representation voted for the motion, with the exception of Pellicer and Paz. But neither of the two protested publicly. Paz would always reproach himself for that choice of silence. Malraux as chairman bluntly refused to let the motion pass.

In her *Memorias de España 1937*, a humorous and irreverent book but one that also shows her indignation before the ideological and moral confusions she witnessed, Elena Garro writes:

> In Minglamilla, where there was another big banquet in the city hall, women from the village surrounded us, asking us to give them something that was going to be left over from the banquet. I was very moved. There, despite the prohibition of our compatriots against making ourselves public, Stephen Spender and other writers invited us to go out on the balcony of the city hall. From there I saw the women dressed in mourning and the children asking for bread and I burst into tears. I sat down exhausted and . . . during the banquet, I felt like going back to my house. Nordahl Grieg proposed that we give the food set out on the table to the people. With no success . . .

But Octavio Paz had not gone to Spain as a tourist but as a valiant poetic agitator. It was how his Spanish friends would see him. The experience of Spain lasted almost four months and included everything except direct enrollment in the war: revolutionary fraternity, courageous visits to the front, heartbreaking scenes with children and families, rationing, bombardments from the air and from the sea, a "tempest of shells" and mortar fire before which Elena was terrified but Octavio would exclaim: "This is magnificent!" And although he did not take part in battles or return to Mexico with scars (like the painter Siqueiros), he did propose to enlist as a political commissar on the Teruel front. His Spanish friends dissuaded him; he could serve the cause better with the pen than with the rifle. He lived in a state of continuous exaltation: he read and he wrote poems of war, he gave a lecture on Silvestre Revueltas, and in the House of Culture of Valencia he announced the coming of a *new man*: "We yearn for a man who, from his own ashes, in a revolutionary way, would be reborn more alive every time." He continued to believe in "the Revolution" as a new human creation, a fountain of "new life," a "total phenomenon," the advent of a "world of poetry capable of containing that which is born and that which is dying."

In Barcelona, Paz read his "Elegy to a Comrade Dead on the Aragon Front" (*Elegía a un compañero muerto en el frente de Aragón*), a poem he had written in Mexico and that had contributed considerably to his fame:

> You have died, comrade
> in the blazing dawn of the world
>
> And from your death sprout up
> your gaze, your blue uniform
> your face surprised by the gunpowder
> your hands, no longer able to touch anything.
>
> You have died. Irremediably.
> Halted is your voice, your blood in earth.
> What earth will rise and not lift you?
> What blood will run and not name you?
> What word will we speak that does not speak
> your name, your silence,
> the stilled pain of not having you with us? . . .

The comrade was José Bosch, his old anarchist friend from preparatory school, about whose death he had received apparently trustworthy accounts. But Paz was astonished to see Bosch seated right out there in his audience. Later, after the emotions of reunion, he heard Bosch describe a very different war from the one he had been observing: the struggle (often to the death) between the socialists of the primarily Trotskyite POUM and the anarchists of the CNT on the one hand and the communists on the other. "They killed my comrades . . . they did, they did! the communists!"

It had been three months since the POUM and CNT had fought the communists in the streets of Barcelona, a conflict that would be described by the POUM militiaman George Orwell in his soon to be famous *Homage to Catalonia*. Andrés Nin, the most important leader of the POUM, had been arrested and mysteriously disappeared (later to die in the hands of the Soviet NKVD, who were also busily engaged in claiming their rivals had pacted with "fascism," an assertion accepted by much of the Western press but fiercely denied by Orwell, who had survived the Barcelona purge and left Spain in 1937 to begin writing *Homage*). As for Bosch, at that moment, all he wanted was a passport to Mexico. But it was impossible to obtain one. According to Elena Garro, Paz lived through this episode "in great anguish." He was aware of the climate of espionage in Spain, the inquisitorial language of many comrades, the barely disguised presence of spies and of agents of the NKVD, the news of Stalin's recent execution (on January 12, 1937) of Marshal Tukhachevsky, who was a hero of the old-guard communists. But the information supplied by Bosch contrasted with accounts Paz had earlier received and he decided that he had to travel to the Soviet Union to (in Elena's words) "see with his own eyes the country in which the fate of the world was at stake." But he never got there. And in October, the boat in which the couple were returning to Mexico made a stop in Cuba, where the long-established leaders of the Cuban Communist Party, Juan Marinello and the younger Carlos Rafael Rodríguez, introduced him to the exiled Spanish poet Juan Ramón Jiménez.

Traveling with Paz and Garro were the Spanish poet León Felipe and his Mexican wife, Berta Gamboa, "Bertuca." At the age of fifty-three, Felipe had long been an icon in Spain. A pharmacist in his professional training and a wanderer by avocation, he had been a professor in Mexico and the United States, a friend of García Lorca and a translator of Whitman, Eliot, and Blake. His long poems were strangely infused with a sometimes ingenuous, sometimes solemn religious sense. They included prayers, invective, psalms, parables, and allegories. "A furious holy prophet," Rafael Alberti had called him, and Alberti was right. There was always something biblical in Felipe's harsh and sonorous voice, his physical appearance, his moral passion, indignation, and fierce tenderness. When the outbreak of the war caught him by surprise in Panama, he had returned to Spain. On meeting him, Pablo Neruda had found him Nietzschean and charming: "among his attractive traits, the best was an anarchic sense of indiscipline and mocking rebellion . . . He would go to the battlefronts held by the anarchists, where he expounded his thoughts and read his iconoclastic poems. They reflected a vaguely non-conformist ideology, anticlerical, full of invocations and blasphemies."

In Mexico he and Bertuca would live for a while with Octavio and Elena. Octavio truly loved him and once would describe him as "pale, with his hands crossed on the handle of his curved cane and his chin leaning on his hands." Once Elena asked him, "What's going on, León Felipe?" "Spain pains me, my girl," he answered. "Spain pains me." And it would pain Paz as well. In *Oda a España*, a poem of 1937, he had written:

> *It is not love, no, it is not*
> *but rather your outcry, Oh Earth,*
> *hard-working Spain*
> *universal Spanish earth,*
> *it stirs my roots,*
> *the elemental earth that sustains me*
> *and your voice, invading me, penetrates my throat*
> *and your breath hidden deep within my bones . . .*

The Spanish Civil War would leave a lasting mark on his political consciousness. In one of his most famous poems, *Piedra de sol* ("Sunstone," of 1957), in lines that many Mexicans know by heart, he would evoke the double communion that he and his wife had lived in Spain:

> *Madrid, 1937,*
>
> *in the Plaza del Angel, the women*
>
> *were sewing and singing with their children,*
>
> *then the alarm sounded and there were screams*
>
> *houses on their knees in the dust*
>
> *towers split open, housefronts spat out*
>
> *and the hurricane of the motors, unremitting:*
>
> *the two took off their clothes and made love*
>
> *to defend our eternal portion*
>
> *our ration of time and paradise . . .*

In Spain, Paz had seen "creative and revolutionary spontaneity" and "the direct and daily intervention of the people." He had "seen hope" and he would not forget. But he had also seen, seen without seeing, the other, darker side of the Revolution. And as time went on, his silence before this half-glimpsed but rejected reality would torment him.

VI

Back in Mexico at the beginning of 1938, Paz participated in public events where he enthusiastically discussed the culture, the young people, the poetry of the war in Spain. The background of all his emotion was *Hope*, felt as a substitute for the theological Catholic virtue. It was his confidence in an achievable future world of brotherhood, justice, and equality as inscribed for him within the word itself of Revolution. But suddenly his replacement for another Catholic virtue, his new *Faith*, began to weaken. There had been glimpses of doubt for him even in Spain, where he could not escape the atmosphere of spying and persecution that surrounded him. His friend, the painter Juan Soriano, said that "Paz returned from the Civil War very disillusioned with the forces of the left. Something among them didn't work, pure dogmatism, pure fanaticism."

In his published writings of the period, no trace appears of this growing separation from his earlier enthusiasm but in the middle of March, according to Elena Garro, Paz received unexpected news, like a sudden blow: "I saw that Octavio Paz, at breakfast time, cried out with tears, 'Bukharin . . . ! No! Bukharin, no!' Then I read in the newspaper that they had put a bullet in his neck." It was Stalin's third major purge of old communists. The Sunday edition of *El Nacional* (on March 13, 1938) had included Bukharin's "confession" and described the sentence of death. Before these facts, Paz began to shelter and nurture a dissident view of politics, but as yet it still remained unexpressed. And though, years later, he would confess that he had felt admiration for Trotsky, he left no public record of such feelings. Despite his being a voracious reader of texts on the Russian Revolution and authors who, like Bukharin, had been comrades of Trotsky, he never tried to meet that major protagonist of Bolshevism who lived for more than three years in Paz's own city.

When André Breton, the father of literary surrealism (and an outspoken critic of Stalin), arrived in Mexico to visit Trotsky, the young Paz only was present anonymously in the audience at some of his lectures. Escorted by Diego Rivera and Frida Kahlo and a handful of Trotskyist sympathizers, Breton remained in Mexico from April to August 1938. He traveled through the country and signed, together with Trotsky, the "Manifesto in Favor of Independent Art," which was published in *Partisan Review*, but his activities were subjected to harsh criticism not only by hard-line communists but also by some of Octavio Paz's friends. One of them, Alberto Quintero Álvarez, who had been co-editor of *Barandal*, attacked Breton's aesthetics, condemning "the indecipherable obscurity" of the "automatic procedure" of surrealism, whose "experiments" seemed to him "empty of tenderness, heart beat, of all that we wish to bring back to our magic, inexplicable act: our creative act, engaged and secret."

Quintero Álvarez's article appeared in *El Popular*, the newspaper that had just been founded by the foremost leader of the workers of Mexico, Vicente Lombardo Toledano. A Catholic in the 1920s, a convert to Marxism in the 1930s, Lombardo had traveled to the Soviet Union in 1936, published a book called Voyage to the World of the Future (*Viaje al mundo del porvenir*), and founded his newspaper with a group of young disciples. Though Paz was not a member of Lombardo's inner circle, he began to work on the paper as a member of the editorial page staff. He would receive submissions and write editorials, putting his name to some of them and leaving others unsigned. For a writer in that position, it was impossible and unthinkable to seek out Breton, much less Trotsky, because for *El Popular*, which was aligned with the viewpoints of Moscow, Trotsky was an obvious ally of Hitler. The newspaper steadily attacked Trotsky and gave no coverage to the Dewey Commission, formed by American leftist intellectuals, which conducted a thorough investigation of Stalinist charges against Trotsky, including thirteen interviews with Trotsky himself in Mexico, and firmly refuted the collaborationist accusations. Trotsky, for his part, called Lombardo a Stalinist agent. But most of Paz's generation followed Moscow's line on Stalin's great rival.

It was perhaps understandable. The enemy was Adolf Hitler, who day by day was moving toward a confrontation with the world and had no lack of sympathizers in Mexico. The natural battle was with Nazism. And Mexico itself was passing through a period of profound nationalist exaltation. On March 18, 1938, President Lázaro Cárdenas had nationalized the oil fields, expropriating English, Dutch, and American companies. During that same period, the first writers in exile began to arrive from Spain. Paz approved of the nationalization but concentrated his personal and literary energies on welcoming the Spanish exiles. In *El Popular*, he saluted the poet León Felipe as a "great poetic spirit" and continued:

And we wish to draw the true and deep meaning of the revolutionary movement throughout the world from these words of the poet: "Then our tears will have a more illustrious origin." Then, when the human revolution will have eliminated the last villain, the last bourgeois: "our joys, our sorrows will be purer." Through the mouth of the poet we wish to say that we do not renounce our humanity, our sorrow and joy, but we struggle to secure this humanity, completely.

Paz himself was far from living a life of bourgeois comfort. Economically, the Paz family had fallen from its previous status. Octavio supported himself through his newspaper work and continued to receive a small salary from the Ministry of Public Education. To supplement his income, he took a job as an inspector of currency for the National Banking Commission. (His daughter, Laura Elena, "Chatita," would be born in December 1938, and in February 1940, Elena would begin work as a reporter for the magazine *Así*.)

Paz remained a central animator of the Mexican literary scene, especially influential as a bridge between generations and between Mexican writers and the Spanish exiles. His emphasis on Spain continued. (In 1937 he had published Under Your Clear Shadow and Other Poems on Spain (*Bajo tu clara sombra y otros poemas sobre España*) and in 1938 his first Brief Anthology of Contemporary Spanish Poets (*Voces de España*). At the end of 1938, he took an initial solid step toward economic self-sufficiency, founding the magazine *Taller* (Workshop), which issued a thousand copies every two months until February 1941. It was financed primarily by Eduardo Villaseñor, a generous Maecenas, lover of literature and sometime poet, who was undersecretary of the treasury at the time and would later (1940–46) become director of the Bank of Mexico. Yet the finances of the magazine continued to be precarious and, toward the end of 1939, Paz secured a loan of 150 pesos from Alfonso Reyes (one of Mexico's two most important writers in the early twentieth century, along with José Vasconcelos). Paz promised to "repay it at the earliest opportunity."

March 31, 1939, coincidentally Octavio's twenty-fifth birthday, marked the final fall of the Spanish Republic. Paz would continue to defend it and, at least once, not only with words. On April 10, while dining with Elena at a restaurant in the city's center, Paz got into a fistfight with some patrons who shouted "Viva Franco!" According to the newspaper account, "Police took some women from the restaurant who were bleeding and others with their clothes torn." Octavio, his wife, his brother-in-law, and the husband of Elena's sister were taken to the police station. The story is illustrated with a photo that includes a defiant-looking Elena. The caption reads: "two tough women arrested for the same brawl."

In the second issue of *Taller* (April 1938), Paz had published a polite but firm disavowal of the literary stance taken by the generation of the Contemporáneos as well as a program for his own generation. He titled the article "Reason for Being" (*Razón de ser*). Of his masters, the Contemporáneos, he wrote, "their intelligence was their best instrument but they never used it to penetrate the real and construct the ideal, but rather, gently, to escape from everyday living . . . They created beautiful poems, rarely inhabited by poetry." The young generation was in debt to them for creating a formal "instrument," but the young had to apply that tool to nothing less than the salvation of humanity:

> to carry the revolution to its ultimate consequences, giving it . . . lyrical, human and metaphysical coherence . . . to gain, with our anguish, a land that is alive, and a man that is alive . . . to construct a human order, just and our own . . . a space in which we can construct the quality of being Mexican and rescue it from injustice, cultural ignorance, frivolity and death.

But despite this desire to be "revolutionary," *Taller* was no less avant-garde than the magazine *Contemporáneos*, publishing—along with many young Mexican and Spanish writers—translations of T. S. Eliot and of earlier poets central to modernist concerns: Rimbaud, Hölderlin, Baudelaire. And external events also attenuated *Taller*'s revolutionary spirit. For its authors, both Mexican and Spanish, the outbreak of World War II was much less surprising than the signing (on August 23, 1939) of the Hitler-Stalin nonaggression pact, which preceded by seven days the war that began on September 1 with the German invasion of Poland. The treaty would hold till Hitler's blitzkrieg attack on the Soviet Union in June 1941, and the shock of its signing on the worldwide left was deadly. Few Marxists could persuasively defend it. But Lombardo's *El Popular* did, with determination: "A people that does not desire territory, a nation that does not attack weak peoples, the USSR is showing the world that only a socialist, proletarian regime can reject war as a means of life, as a recourse for expansion . . ." But in response, Paz resigned from *El Popular*, perhaps thinking that the warnings of Trotsky may have been partially correct. And then in 1940, there was the armed attack on Trotsky's Mexican home led by the painter Siqueiros and, in August of the same year, Trotsky's assassination. Widely condemned abroad, the killing was not even mentioned in the leading Mexican literary and intellectual magazine *Taller*. Nor did Paz write about it elsewhere.

His silence before the behavior of the Soviet Union (and the Stalinist execution carried out in the heart of his own country) may have been a faithful reflection of his personal dilemma. During the Spanish Civil War, his faith in Russian policies had weakened but not his hopes for the revolution. In what direction should he turn? The route of conventional religion (followed by Eliot and later by W. H. Auden) was impossible for him. Paz had always inclined toward the anticlerical Jacobinism of his father and grandfather, not the pious Catholicism of his mother. The fascist option—chosen by Ezra Pound and José Vasconcelos—would have been equally impossible. Paz detested the fascism that had destroyed the Spanish Republic and he rejected Nazism for its treatment of the Jews and because he considered the movement (seen through his Marxist lens) as the child of capitalism and imperialism: "you can count the various reasons that have made Hitler possible, but they are all included in two words: capitalism and imperialism. Hitler is their final fruit."

And seen from the same viewpoint, neither England nor the other liberal democracies were an option he could support. They were nations that had let Spain die and were marked by "the hypocritical rhetoric of the bourgeois pseudo-democracies." With all these doors closed to him, Paz's feeling of solitude deepened. He did not glimpse the possibility of a democratic anti-Stalinist socialism like that favored by George Orwell or the young American writers associated with *Partisan Review* (a journal that Paz, with his concentration on Spanish and French culture, was not even aware of). In Mexico, almost no one represented that current.

In 1954, Paz would write a defense of *Taller*, which he would come to consider the matrix for the major journals he later directed. The journal had not merely "embraced social causes" but, for most of its writers, "love, poetry and revolution were three ardent synonyms." It can be said that love and poetry, as in Paz's own work, were sumptuously present in the magazine, but the theme of revolution gradually diminished, perhaps lingering only in certain blasphemous pages by León Felipe, whose poems would later inspire Che Guevara.

In 1981, he would carry his retrospective analysis further (or he would encounter it on his personal path, as often happened with Paz). His generation had lived with the hope of a future "revolutionary fraternity." They had believed in the imminence of the "Great Change"; they had wanted to return to the "Great Whole," to "recreate the unity of the beginning from the beginning" and reestablish—like the nineteenth-century Romantics—a fusion of the words "poetry" and "history." And in fact Paz felt that "our defense of the freedom of art and poetry would have been flawless if not for one great moral and political failure that now makes me blush. In *Taller*, one could profess and express any idea except that, due to a prohibition no less rigorous for being unspoken, one could not criticize the Soviet Union."

VII

The beginning of 1941 saw the last issue of *Taller*. Paz was then earning his living at a boring, thankless job. For five years he would spend six full workdays a week with his hands buried in currency, counting

money to be taken out of circulation and then burned. The ironic paradox was startling. In *Taller*, he had once written that "money has no end
or object. It is simply an infinite mechanism that knows no law but that
of the circle . . . It has no earthly flavor. It serves for nothing, since it
aims toward nothing." And in Yucatán he had written his poem against
the money that moved the strings of enslavement on the henequen
plantations. Now the brute presence of money had turned against him
and was moving the strings of his own subsistence.

Mexican culture at the beginning of the 1940s was undergoing
a major change in its practical structure and its orientation. A small
magazine like *Taller* had to compete for funding (now almost always
governmental) with new institutions, with journals and cultural initiatives directly connected with academia. Culture was abandoning
its revolutionary vocation and turning institutional, passing from the
small independent publisher to the university and larger institutional
publishers. Some of them, like the Casa de España or the Fondo de Cultura Económica, were of excellent quality.

This institutionalization of culture corresponded to a broader transformation of Mexican politics and the Mexican economy. The 1930s had
been ideological, polarized, revolutionary, beginning with the collapse
of Wall Street and ending with the Hitler-Stalin Pact and the outbreak
of World War II. Mexico in the early 1940s, still officially neutral, had
become a peaceful and attractive shelter for refugees from Europe
(though it would declare war on the Axis powers in 1942 and send a
small contingent of airmen to fight in the Pacific Theater). Manuel
Ávila Camacho, the new president (1940–46), had been one of Cárdenas's closest subordinates but his attitude was more conciliatory, his
politics more centrist. The "Gentleman President" softened the emphasis on class struggle, declared himself a believing Catholic, halted
the program of land redistribution, and concentrated on building and
strengthening public institutions like social security (Seguro Social)
and the nationalized oil industry (Petróleos Mexicanos). Untouched
directly by the fighting and able to supply goods (and workers) to the
United States, the country benefited economically from World War II,

which gave a powerful boost to Mexico's burgeoning process of industrialization. And then came the heyday of tourism.

Talk of "the end of the Revolution" was in the air, and there were some who had already qualified the era as "Neoporfirismo." Films began to be made showing a highly idealized version of peasant life on the haciendas before the Revolution and nostalgic memories of "the time of Don Porfirio." The Mexican cinema entered its golden age with its movies and songs and actors famous throughout Latin America and even across the ocean in Franco's Spain. Constrained by money pressures, Paz entered the cinematic current in 1943, writing some dialogues and song lyrics for the movie *El Rebelde*, the second film of the superstar Jorge Negrete. The script was a respectful adaptation of a Pushkin novel done by Jean Malaquais, a Trotskyist friend of Paz (and of André Gide). In one scene, Negrete sings a furtive song directed to his beloved, who is listening to him in secret. Neither is able to see the other:

> *I do not see you with my eyes,*
> *when I close them I see you*
> *and I imprison you in my breast*
> *with locks made of sighs.*
> *My lips never name you,*
> *heartbeats are your name*
> *its syllables are the blood*
> *from my heart broken open.*

The style and the almost masochistic lover's anguish bear the mark of Paz's hand.

But Octavio Paz was not the man to accept a new version of Porfirian "peace, order, and progress." The bourgeoisification of Mexico disgusted him. He experienced it as an historic betrayal. He was still sentimentally rooted in the peasant, Zapatista revolution, and ideologically in the world Revolution foretold by Marx, which was due to come to Europe at the end of the war. For Paz, Marxism not only formed part of "our blood and our destiny" but was also an open process of thought for further development. In his personal life, the future remained uncertain and professionally he was now somewhat uprooted. As with his father and grandfather, his life had been inseparable from the printing press and a public life embodied in writing and readers. Editing journals was a mode of expression for him, not in any academic sense but as political and poetic combat. The possibilities for creating a new journal, however, were steadily diminishing.

He continued publishing his poems in Mexican journals and in the most important literary review of the time, *Sur*, under the direction in Buenos Aires of Victoria Ocampo. In 1942 he came out with a new collection *A la orilla del mundo* (On the Shore of the World), which was hailed by José Luis Martínez (then emerging as the most important critic and historian of Mexican literature): " . . . an out-of-the-ordinary poetic richness and a lyrical abundance that can only be compared to some of the great names in Mexican poetry . . . a firm step on a poetic career that will certainly go very far."

But the lack of a journal of his own oppressed Paz. Along with the composition of poetry, it was his way of making the Revolution, of his being in the world. In November 1942 he poured out his resentment in a reminiscence of the "goatherd poet" Miguel Hernández, who had recently died of tuberculosis in one of Franco's prisons, where he had been held in bestial conditions. Paz recalled hearing Hernández sing folk songs in Valencia in 1937 and listening he had shared "true passion." Now he would prefer, as a poetic and impassioned conceit, to leave all that behind: "Let me forget you because to forget that which was pure and true, to forget the best, gives us strength to go on living in this world of compromises and bows, respectful greetings and ceremonies, evil-smelling and rotten."

AT THAT time Paz became friends with the very young painter from Jalisco Juan Soriano. Because of his excesses and eccentricities, his bouts of drunkenness and torment, Soriano was known as "the little Rimbaud" (*el Rimbaudcito*). He was gaining fame as an incisive portraitist and Paz, speculating on the roots of his friend's talent, saw a mirror of his own childhood in Soriano's lonely infancy: "balustrades and corridors where solitary children go running, always on the verge of falling down in the courtyard."

Paz and Soriano spent much time together at the Café Paris in Mexico City and at fiestas and memorable evenings fueled by alcohol. And besides conviviality and a similar childhood, one thing more united them: the parallel lives of their fathers, both of them alcoholics and rakes. Paz had collected the remains of his father at a railroad station but had not even been able to hold a wake for him. The necessary mourning lay there within him, long delayed, oppressive, till the death of his friend's father freed it for expression. "When Octavio saw my father in his sickness," Soriano would remember, "he felt it personally because it revived sad memories and he behaved perfectly." While his friend's father was dying, "he went to see him every day, without fail . . . When my father died, the poet accompanied me and he was a coffin-bearer at the cemetery, because for him, his father and grandfather had been essential."

Soriano experienced the relationship between Paz and Elena from up close. "Few women of that era were more dazzling!" he once noted. Soriano was above all a painter of women, and his idea was to capture the unique soul of each subject on his canvas. Around that time he painted a disturbing portrait of Elena. "The portrait of Elena Garro," he wrote, "seduces whoever comes to know it." And there she is, as she must have been, a beautiful and formidable golden-haired woman, with sensitive yet imperious features, and a bodily stance of elegance and aggressive strength. Behind her is a door, perhaps the same—as Juan Soriano recounts—that she often closed at night, rejecting Octavio Paz. His poem addressing this portrait (A un retrato) flows between images of tenderness and desire and touches of menace, almost of horror:

> . . . The pallid highlights of her hair
> are autumn over a river

Sun turned desolate by a deserted corridor
from whom does she flee? who is she waiting for
undecided, between terror and desire?
Did she see the foul sprouting of her mirror?
Did the serpent coil up between her thighs? . . .

Juan Soriano remembers that she tortured Paz: "By her nature she was very competitive but with him she shot to kill. What a tremendous impression!" Paz, on the other hand, "recognized her intelligence," nourished it and sought ways to help her put it to use.

EARLY IN 1943, Paz convinced Octavio Barreda, editor of the magazine *Letras de México*, to join him in a new publishing venture: a journal "of high quality." It would be called *El hijo pródigo* (The Prodigal Son). Much more than *Taller*, it would be a meeting ground of generations, traditions, and genres. It would publish important essays, translations of contemporary and classical authors, and many theatrical pieces, and from the very beginning it would have a strong emphasis on the visual arts. Paz would later remember *El hijo pródigo* with affection but not with the passion he felt for *Taller*, which had been for him a genuine battlefront. He had tried to stamp "a clearly defined intellectual politics" on the journal, but when he left *El hijo pródigo* in October 1943, his influence would fade away. He later liked to quote an editorial he had written in August 1943: "The writer, the poet, the artist are not instruments nor is their work the blind projectile that many suppose it to be. The only way to defeat Hitler and the universal evil he represents is to save, within the field of culture, a freedom to criticize and denounce . . . Totalitarianism is not the fruit of the inherent wickedness of this or that nation: there where man is simply a *means*, an *instrument* or an object of speculation, there totalitarianism will germinate . . ." The quote is significant because here, at least tacitly, Paz was beginning to see that totalitarianism was not only the province of European fascism.

The small but very quarrelsome literary world of Mexico had recently been rocked by a feud (that would become legendary) between

Paz and the great Chilean poet Pablo Neruda, who had been consul general of Chile in Mexico since 1940. He and Paz were friendly and spent time together. The division between them was sparked by the publication of one of Paz's anthologies of Spanish poetry, *Laurel*, in which Paz did not meet the standards of choice favored by Neruda. The Chilean detested "celestial poets, followers of Gide, intellectual-izers, miserable Rilkeans, surrealist queers." A discussion between Paz and Neruda in a restaurant ended with a physical confrontation. Neruda issued declarations on "the absolute disorientation" and "the lack of civic morality" that, in his view, dominated Mexican poetry. Paz and some of his young friends responded with harsh words. In his "Response to the Consul," Paz wrote:

> Señor Pablo Neruda, Chilean consul and poet, is also a distin-guished political figure, a literary critic and a generous patron of certain lackeys who call themselves his friends. So many different activities cloud his vision and twist his judgments: his literature is contaminated by politics, his politics by literature, and his criti-cism is often a matter of mere complicity with friends. And so, very often, one does not know if the functionary or the poet is speaking, the friend or the politician.

This definitive rupture with Neruda on the plane of aesthetics would distance Paz, by one more step, from the ideological current that identified with the Soviet Union. He continued to embrace Marx-ism and to admire Lenin but, within the new perspectives opening in the world and in his country, it was unclear what this adherence meant concretely.

MEXICAN CULTURE in the 1940s had not only changed its institutional and material structure. It had changed its focus. The shared, general in-terest no longer dwelt on the word "Revolution" but rather on "Mexico." As had been the case in 1915, when World War I isolated Mexico and promoted a time of introspection, Mexican culture during World

War II tilted once again toward itself. The term "autognosis" became fashionable. It had first been used in 1934 by the philosopher Samuel Ramos, who, in his seminal book *El perfil del hombre y la cultura en México* (The Profile of Man and Culture in Mexico), had made the diagnosis (from a social therapeutic standpoint influenced by the thought of Alfred Adler) that Mexican culture was suffering from an "inferiority complex." This intellectual current of introspection was strengthened by the arrival of the Spanish exiles. The philosophers, historians, and creative writers of the Spanish Generation of '98—Unamuno, Ortega, Machado, Azorín—had published famous meditations on the nature of "being Spanish." Now their successors imported and transferred this type of reflection to their new home. Perhaps the first of the exiles to do so was the poet and painter José Moreno Villa, who in 1940 published a small and delightful book called *Cornucopia de México*, detailing the gestures, manner, customs, and idiosyncratic words he had collected while traveling through his new world of Mexico. And José Gaos, former rector of the University of Madrid and a friend of Ortega y Gasset, inspired the first reexaminations of "the history of ideas" in Mexico.

But when Mexican culture was setting out on a search for itself, the young Octavio Paz—despite his feeling of being uprooted or perhaps because of it—had already forged ahead in at least two areas, poetic meditation and art criticism. In his first contribution to the Argentine journal *Sur* (August 1938), Paz interpreted the book *Nostalgia de la muerte* (Nostalgia for Death) by Xavier Villaurrutia as a mirror of "the Mexican spirit," of what is "specifically ours":

> illuminating—or darkening, poetically—all these conquests, I meet with, I touch and explore that which is Mexican [*lo mexicano*]. What is Mexican in him, as in all of us, circulates invisibly and invincibly, like the breath, warm and impalpable, from our lips or the color, lightly sad and dancing, timid, of our words. Of our sweet Mexican words, the same that take rounded form in a Castilian mouth and in ours lose all their body, all their illuminated contours . . .

Another text on the same theme appeared in *El Popular*, on October 28, 1941, titled "On Mexican Literature." The questions Paz raises are not in the least academic. When did the Mexican people encounter and when did they lose their expressiveness (that is to say their feeling, their *being*)? How to regain it? Who will regain it? And then Paz formulates, perhaps for the first time, his vision of the Mexican Revolution as the moment when the Mexican *encounters* himself. The obligation of writers and political leaders had been to keep this encounter alive but all of them had abandoned their people:

> They made the Mexican people hermetic and insensitive, after they had awakened for the first time in their history. Now all of us have turned to solitude and the dialogue is broken, as men are smashed and broken . . . And yet the dialogue will have to be resumed. Because there must be some way, some form that opens the ears and unties the tongues.

It was the poet who had to take on the responsibility of opening the ears and untying the tongues. In that text Paz began to see the possibility of an "ethic of the poet" quite as "mystical and combative" as that which he had laid out in *Barandal*, but now centered not on world revolution but on Mexico, the mysteries of Mexico: "Just as a people nourishes it, poetry nourishes the people. It is an issue of painful interchange. If the people give substance to poetry, poetry gives voice to the people. What to do about a silent people, that neither wishes to hear or wishes to speak? And what to do with a poetry that feeds on air and solitude?" To escape from this labyrinth, the poet could count on the rich instrument of the Spanish language: "a mature idiom . . . which has undergone every contact, all the experiences of the West." Through it one had to express "the most nebulous of things . . . the dawn of a people."

To express a people was to "build" that people: "because our country is in pieces or at least not fully born." The poet literally had to construct Mexico. Because of that responsibility, Mexican literature, always avidly curious about what might be universal, had to look instead "toward ourselves, not so as to find novelty or originality but something more profound: authenticity." This essential quality of being Mexican (*mexicanidad*), sought after by everyone, did not have a nationalist nature "treacherous and preconceived." What was it then? Only the poet, of the same substance as his people, could encounter it. And how? Letting "mystery" do its work, and dreams: "when we dream that we are dreaming, we are close to waking up." *Mexicanidad* was an "invisible substance," located somewhere:

> We do not know what it consists of, nor by what route we can reach it; we know, dimly, that it has not yet been revealed and that up to now its presence, among the best of us has only been as a kind of aroma, a light and bitter taste. Let us be careful that an excess of vigilance does not drive it away; it will sprout up spontaneously and naturally, from the depths of our intimacy when we encounter true authenticity, key to our being. Love is made of dreams and jealousy, of abandonment and requirement. Let us dream while awake.

To BEGIN his search for that "invisible substance," Paz was equipped with superlative tools. His own *mexicanidad* had a number of roots: a well earned and tested connection to the tree of Mexican culture; an impeccable revolutionary genealogy of the Paz family in Mexican wars; a record of lucid, exhaustive, and accurate critical readings of Mexican writers, past and present; and even an indelible and meaningful topography engraved within his memory.

At thirty years of age he had begun to understand the miracle coded in his own biography. His deep Mexican roots extended not only across time but into various sacred spaces. Everything began to seem like a text written in ciphers. The village of Mixcoac (now part of Mexico City) was Mexico in miniature, both the place and the Nahuatl name, a metaphor for the centuries preserved within the present moment; and the small Plaza de San Juan opposite Don Ireneo's sprawling country home was the spiritual center of this miniature. Right beside it was the house of the great nineteenth-century Liberal Valentín Gómez Farías, who was buried in his own garden because the Church had denied him the right to burial in a Christian cemetery. Not far off were six schools for children and the Plaza Jáuregui, seat of the civil government, where each year Mexican independence was commemorated and, directly opposite, a small seventeenth-century church in whose atrium the Day of the Virgin of Guadalupe was celebrated.

And amazingly, in the Mixcoac of the young Paz, not only the colonial but also the indigenous past lingered alive and intact. Paz would remember Ifigenia, the family's Indian cook: "witch and medicine woman, she would tell me stories, she would give me presents of amulets and scapularies, she would have me chant spells against devils and ghosts." Through her he was initiated into the mysteries of the *temascal*, the indigenous steam bath: "it wasn't a bath, but a rebirth." And as if this were not enough, the boy not only shared his existence with living indigenous culture but also had literally unearthed part of the dead or, more precisely, the subterranean Indian culture. On one of his wanderings around the village with his older cousins—among them the future astronomer Guillermo Haro Paz—Octavio had a truly marvelous experience. The boys discovered a pre-Hispanic mound (which now can be seen along the Anillo Periférico, the highway that circles Mexico City). Notified of the discovery, Manuel Gamio—founder of modern Mexican anthropology in the 1920s and a family friend—verified its authenticity. A real discovery! A temple dedicated to Mixcóatl, the Aztec god of hunters, the founding deity of Mixcoac!

That was the order that had been lost, "the unity of the beginning from the beginning," the "Great Whole" to which Paz in the future would have to return poetically. In permanent vigil, in the solitude of his labyrinth, Paz was dreaming while awake, dreaming his own future poem of Mexican history.

BETWEEN APRIL and November 1943, he would publish a series of articles on *lo mexicano*, the quality of being Mexican. They do not contain the sort of revelations to be found in *The Labyrinth of Solitude* but they do anticipate what Paz would write years later in Paris. They are cruel, perspicacious, moving freely through the country and its people. The poet attempts a broad and sweeping psychological examination of his fellow Mexicans. His gaze is above all moral: he tries to probe below the typical attitudes of the Mexican in order to liberate him from them. He investigates the meaning in depth of various popular words like *vacilón* ("fun time") or *ninguneo* ("ostracism" or "total dismissal"). He offers a crude phenomenology of typical personages who pullulate throughout Mexican politics: *el agachado* ("bent over," "a servile man") *el mordelón* ("big-biter," "a bribable policeman or other official"), *el coyote* ("middle-man," "fixer"): *el lambiscón* ("bootlicker"), and other social and political slang words. And as if he were warning against too facile "Mexicanist" analyses, he writes that "Montaigne knew more about the soul of Mexicans than most of the novelists of the Revolution." He would try to find the correct balance that could reveal this soul from a universalist perspective, influenced in style and emotional values by French culture. He would try to become a Mexican Montaigne.

DURING THOSE years of personal crisis and poetic incubation, Octavio Paz developed his exhaustive attention to historical and contemporary Mexican traits and sources. It would become a constant in his work. Fully aware that he had already earned a solid niche within the history of Mexican culture, Paz felt obliged to assemble the components of this history. Collect them in order to properly evaluate the tradition and to establish his own place within it. And in an obituary for his friend Silvestre Revueltas, or a tender and anguished profile on Juan Soriano, or pieces on the poet Carlos Pellicer and the Porfirian landscape painter of the Valley of Mexico, José María Velasco, Paz would leave clues about the kind of art to which he himself aspired. He also, as he wrote about Revueltas, "did not love disorder, nor Bohemia; he was instead an ordered intelligence, precise and exact." With Soriano he shared rebellion and orphanhood. From Pellicer he had learned to hear and see the poetry of nature, a constant presence in his work. And even in the coldness of Velasco, who, like a disdainful eagle gazing down from his Porfirian eyrie, had painted desolate landscapes, empty of humanity, Paz salvaged the importance of "rigor, reflection, architecture . . . [his work] alerts us to the dangers of pure sensibility and a reliance on imagination alone." And he saw his own predilections not only in the mirror of Mexican writers but also in Spaniards whom he admired. On the work of Luis Cernuda, for instance, he commented: "In his pages, we do not encounter displays of cleverness, pseudo-philosophic complications, opulent and empty baroquism . . . Transparency, equilibrium, objectivity, clarity of thought and of words are the external virtues of his prose."

But among all these critical examinations, the most significant is the one he dedicated (in the final issue of *Taller,* January–February 1941) to a recent edition of the Selected Pages (*Páginas escogidas*) of José Vasconcelos. Paz was neither ignorant of nor did he condone Vasconcelos's atrocious ideological turn toward Nazism, directing, since February 1940, the magazine *Timón,* funded by the German embassy in still neutral Mexico. But Paz was deeply attracted by the romantic energy of Vasconcelos and even more by the fierce polemic his work and personality had provoked. It seemed to Paz that Vasconcelos had been "faithful to his era and to his land, even though his passions had torn at his entrails." And above all, Vasconcelos seemed to him a great artist: "a great poet of America, I mean the great creator or recreator of the nature and the men of America." His work, Paz went on, was "the only [project] among his contemporaries, that had ambitions toward greatness and monumentality"; Vasconcelos had wanted "to form, from his life and his work, a great classical monument":

> . . . his best pages on aesthetics are those in which he discusses rhythm and dance: he understands order, proportion . . . there is in his work something like a nostalgia for musical architecture . . . His authenticity, like his greatness, testify to his virile, tender, impassioned nature, and this nature is what we love in him, beyond everything else.

Two years later Paz gave a lecture in Oaxaca, where Vasconcelos was born, and further refined his own perceived vocation for "greatness," implicitly comparing himself to Vasconcelos, as if Paz had been prefigured in an immense mirror—the first pages of Vasconcelos's autobiography *Ulises Criollo* (The Creole Ulysses):

> The destiny of the Mexican poet, between heaven and earth, between the sirens of foreign culture and a soil that he loves without understanding it, meets and defines itself—and this is more than a symbol—in that child Vasconcelos describes in the first pages of his book, lost in a frontier town and pursuing his first studies in a foreign preparatory school. The whole Vasconcelian odyssey is a spiritual odyssey, about the traveler who returns, not to take charge of his home, like the Greek, but to rediscover it . . . It is not important that Vasconcelos . . . stopped halfway through his journey, amid Hispanic forms of nationality; his work is a dawn. What he praises is less important than his direction. And so it is also a lesson. He shows us that it is not necessary to hope for Mexico to arrive at full maturity before daring to speak for the nation.

Now it is Paz's turn to continue on the path, to go beyond the dawn and arrive at high noon, to speak for the nation: "and perhaps it is the poet who will manage to condense and concentrate all the conflicts of our nation into a mythical hero who will not only speak for Mexico, but more important, help to create her."

Vasconcelos had been "a dawn" but then he had lost his way. Now he, Paz, would become Mexico's midday sun. He would further synthesize what he now felt was his mission in a piece called "Poetry of Solitude and Poetry of Communion":

> All poetry moves between these two poles of innocence and awareness, solitude and communion. We modern men, incapable of innocence, born into a society that naturally renders us artificial and that has stripped us of our human substance to convert us

into merchandise, we modern men look in vain for the lost man, the innocent man. All the valiant efforts of our culture, since the end of the 18th century, are directed to recover him, to dream him. Rousseau sought him in the past, like the romantics; some modern poets in primitive man; Karl Marx, the most profound, dedicated his life to constructing him, to remaking him ... Poetry, by giving voice to these dreams, invites us to rebellion, to live our dreams while awake. It points the way to the future golden age and summons us to freedom.

Very few Mexican writers, perhaps only Paz, Vasconcelos, and José Revueltas—despite their great ideological differences—have thought or would think in just this way.

A VISION of this kind would necessarily clash with the neo-Porfirian ambience of the time. Despite his insights, his poetic and personal experience, and his heroic ambition, the years between 1938 and 1943 had been a period of crisis for Octavio Paz. He was beginning to feel he could no longer live in Mexico. He was troubled not only by the ostentatious and rhetorical official culture, the economic orientation of the country, and the considerable weakening of revolutionary politics. He also was drifting professionally. He did not want to become part of the cultural apparatus dependent on the state or on the academy, but unless you were independently wealthy, which Paz was not, there were no other real possibilities for earning a living. Another alternative always open to Mexican writers was the diplomatic corps, but it was perhaps an alternative Paz did not consider at the time.

He saw Mexico as a country becoming blatantly capitalistic. In an "excess of money, cabarets, industry and business deals" Mexico had lost its revolutionary nerve, poetic inspiration, and critical passion. The ambience, he thought, was contaminating culture and literature with a miasma of self-complacency, pretension, mediocrity, and lies. Paz needed to leave the country and he found a means to do so. In November 1943 he received a Guggenheim fellowship to the University of

California at Berkeley and he set out for San Francisco. It was a journey that was supposed to be temporary but—except for a couple of years in the 1950s—Paz would then live abroad for more than thirty years, until 1976. He left for San Francisco alone. His wife and daughter were to join him in a few months. In Mexico two of his friends had committed suicide. One, Rafael Vega Albela, had been a friend since childhood. The other was the essayist (and his sometime mentor) Jorge Cuesta. He would later say to David Huerta, the son of his old friend Efraín, "I left because I didn't want to be trapped either by journalism or by alcoholism."

In San Francisco, almost without willing it, Paz began a diplomatic career that would be his principal support until 1968, becoming part of an old Mexican cultural tradition (similar to France) of artists and intellectuals in diplomacy. At first, his duties, as a "reporter" for the Mexican consulate, were rather imprecise, mostly writing reports as well as articles for the newspapers.

In the streets he once again confronted the strange quality of being Mexican. Seeing the pachucos (young Mexican-Americans whom the age classified as "juvenile delinquents" in their flashy low-slung "zoot suits") and "seeing himself in them," he had the first glimmers of the self-liberating book he would write. "I am them. What has happened to my country, to Mexico in the modern world. Because what is happening to them is happening to us." The essay that he wrote based on these impressions would later become the first chapter of El laberinto. The activity of revolution (in the form he had supported and practiced in his youth) seemed to him steadily more and more distant and nebulous. It was obviously incompatible with a government position. But the energy could be redirected toward the writing of that book about Mexico that would become an essential part of its culture—a prophetic work, visionary and in some sense revolutionary.

In a letter sent to his friend Victor Serge, the Belgian-born Russian writer and former Bolshevik who had fled both Stalin and the Nazis and arrived in Mexico as an exile in 1941, Paz commiserates with Serge about the attacks launched against his reputation by the Mexican

cultural clique closest to the Soviet Union, then comments on the ideological and religious zigzagging of various European artists, which
may have reminded him of a similar pattern in the 1930s in Mexico:

W. H. Auden, the most commanding of the new English poets,
has just published a book that rejects all his former work. Caught
between the betrayed revolution and the "guided" world they are
preparing for us, he has grasped hold of the burning key of the
Anglican Church. His case is not the only one but the most noteworthy because of his talent and his prestige . . .

He declares himself unwilling to "surrender his spirit" to religion,
or to become a militant communist or an ingenuous liberal. There had
to be other options. His residence in San Francisco has given him his
first real access to Anglo-Saxon culture. For the first time, he is reading the democratic socialists who write for the *Partisan Review* and
admires some of the modern American poets, like Karl Shapiro and
Muriel Rukeyser:

The young poets . . . are attempting a more direct, a freer poetry
. . . they dare to use a living, popular language, that does not recoil
before slang, and that seems to me more effective than the language used by our contemporary French and Spanish poets.

It was "stimulating" to live in this country "because the crisis of the
American intelligentsia does not subside into the rhetorical domesticity
of Mexico." He adds that "the Church or the void are preferable to the
Ministry of Public Education." But he continues to feel himself responsible to Mexican literature:

. . . The Catholic ideals, which formed a common faith, are dead
and the liberal revolution has failed or been corrupted. The people
in Latin American countries live a blind and mineral life; their intellectuals, on the other hand, whirl around in the void. Here the

distance between them is not as great, though it exists. It seems to me that cultural forms have never been so isolated as they are now (and especially the political) from the need and dreams of the people. How many things there are to express! And the terrible thing is that we can hardly express our own anguish, our own impotence, our solitude.

Five years later, in Paris, he would finally find a way to express them. His ascent through the world of diplomacy was aided by one of his father's friends. Francisco Castillo Nájera, who had known Paz Solórzano since 1911, secured Octavio's transfer to New York. Another guardian angel who would protect him in the future from the spiderwebs of bureaucracy was the admirable poet (and diplomat) José Gorostiza. Paz taught summer courses at Middlebury College in Vermont and interviewed the New England poet Robert Frost for the magazine *Sur*. Elena worked resentfully for the American Jewish Committee. Paz did some dubbing in a film and even considered joining the merchant marine. But in October 1945, Castillo Nájera, who had providentially become secretary of foreign relations, secured Paz's transfer to an official position at the Mexican embassy in Paris.

VIII

Paris was as much a feast for Octavio Paz as it had once been for Hemingway. There he lived a life composed of various fragmented and difficult lives. An intense diplomatic responsibility, which he fulfilled with substantial and reliable reports to the embassy on French and European politics. A tangled personal life, involving a harsh and tormented relationship with his wife and a close connection with his daughter, to whom he sent (while she was living for a time in Switzerland) installments of a novel he was writing about a group of boys who had gained entrance to the Mayan past through a sacred pool (*cenote*) in Yucatán. A life of Mexican and cosmopolitan friendships including a circle of artists, philosophers, and intellectuals, some of them famous

(Camus, Sartre, Breton), others less well-known but important to him personally and intellectually, like the Greek philosopher Kostas Papaio-annou, with whom he discussed the Russian and Mexican revolutions. Meanwhile his literary career continued, with the publication of a new volume of poetry, *Libertad bajo palabra* (Freedom on Parole) in 1949. In May 1948 he had written to his friend, the writer and deputy editor of *Sur*, José Bianco: "The moments I have spent writing them, correcting them, typing up clear copies and putting them in order, have been the fullest in my life." His activity as an editor of journals was necessarily on hold but Bianco continued to welcome his suggestions so that Paz, though at a distance, functioned as one more advisory editor of *Sur*. His political life was also temporarily suspended, domesticated perhaps by his diplomatic commitments.

His love life was a battlefield. Ever since his time in San Francisco, Paz had had affairs, which he did not hide from his wife; he even suggested that she take lovers, too. In Paris, the two still enjoyed their rich social life and moments of happiness with their daughter, Chatita. But the couple could find no peace or harmony, and even love seemed to be fading. Elena had as yet found no way to direct her talent. She blamed Octavio and was constantly competing with him. Octavio, according to Elena's unpublished diary, could be impatient and irascible. She considered him "controlling" and says she had come to find him "physically repugnant." They often talked about divorce. In mid-1949, while the poet was working on a collection of essays, she would write in her diary: "On that 17th of June [of 1935] Octavio kissed me for the first time . . . This 17th of June of 1949 is a decisive day in my life; Octavio is over with." A "mad love" had possessed her, for the Argentine writer Adolfo Bioy Casares.

But the revolutionary poet, in the middle of 1949, was working on a collection of essays. They dealt with "a theme that is somewhat fashionable," he wrote (apparently giving it little importance) to Alfonso Reyes, another one of his guardian angels looking over him from Mexico: "A small book . . . a minor book on some Mexican subjects." This little book, this minor book (to be published in 1950 by the publishing house of the journal *Cuadernos Americanos*), would become *El laberinto de la soledad*.

Much has been discussed and written about the influences on this book. Paz mentioned his reading of Caillois's *Man and Myth*, Freud's *Moses and Monotheism;* and the effect upon him of D. H. Lawrence, who " . . . was seeking, with greater desperation than anyone else, the secret sources of spontaneity and unity in the darkest, most ancient and ineffable part of man, in what does not admit explication but rather communion and not communication: the blood, the mystery of nature." But the true primordial sources of this primordial book were not external but intimate.

A search for himself in Mexico and for Mexico in himself. An entrance—and simultaneously an exit—from the labyrinth of his own solitude, *El laberinto de la soledad* can be read as the Rosetta stone of Paz's own biography. Who is the man that in the chapter "Mexican Masks" "shuts himself in and preserves himself," who "settled into his surly solitude, prickly and courteous at the same time, jealous of his intimacy, not only does not open himself up, but does not flow outward"? His character involves "distrust . . . the courteous reserve that closes off access for the stranger." This is the Mexican of the high central plateau, or the mestizo tied to duplicity, disguised as a Spaniard but with the brown skin that reveals his suspect origins. But this man is also Octavio Paz.

The fiesta he describes—that which levels all men, the permissive and liberating fiesta, the evanescent burst of joy—is at first sight a universal phenomenon (Antonio Machado, for instance, evokes a similar feeling when he writes about the villages of Andalucía). But if we look more closely, Paz's fiesta shows a key difference: it is a deadly fiesta. The people "whistle, shout, drink and break through boundaries. A communion followed by an explosion, an outburst." What fiestas resound behind his words? The multicolored fiestas of Mixcoac, his own childhood celebrations. But also other fiestas, ferocious fiestas, of pulque and gunfire, those of Santa Martha Acatitla, those of that "total macho," Octavio Paz Solórzano. The fiestas where the sun never rises, the fiestas of death.

Mexico is not the only culture fascinated by death (Spain and Japan, for instance, in their very different ways, share the same obsession). Nor has the Mexican attitude always been one and the same in the face of death. But yet, in *El laberinto*, Paz dwells on an aspect of death that is shared and common to Mexicans. The Mexican, he affirms, "makes fun of death, caresses it, sleeps with it, celebrates it. It is one of his favorite toys and his permanent love." His own death and the death of others. Only a few years earlier, Malcolm Lowry, with his novel *Under the Volcano,* had reconstituted—like Paz in his own flesh and in a memorable book—that infernal paradise of the fiesta, the drunken spree and death in Mexico, and more surprising still, Lowry had written his book in the former territory of Zapata.

"Our indifference toward death," Paz writes, "is the other face of our indifference toward life." *Someone* takes on flesh in this sentence. For *someone*, death is not other than life but really the same. *Someone* "sought it out," someone close to him "sought out for himself the bad death that kills us." And so the poet modifies an old proverb and concludes: "Tell me how you die and I will tell you who you are." Was he thinking of his father as he wrote such passages? Was he masking his own memory? Or was it so glued to his skin that he did not see it, until suddenly, many years later, in an elegy:

> *What was my father*
> *fits into this canvas sack*
> *that a laborer hands to me*
> *as my mother crosses herself . . .*

In *El laberinto*, Paz has pages on the Mexican idiom *chingar* ("to fuck") and *la chingada* (literally the "fucked" or "violated" woman). How many meanings of the verb *chingar* fit into Octavio Paz's life? Is it too much to think that Paz's mother is an incarnation of the woman who has suffered, been violated, *"chingada."* The section "The Sons of Malinche," which includes his thoughts on *chingar,* is—even among the more "anthropological" chapters—perhaps the least autobiographical, the most autonomous, possibly because its subject is language. And yet in no other domain is Paz more skillful, precise, and alert than in that of words.

IN THE second part of *El laberinto,* dedicated to history, the subject is not "the Mexican" or *mexicanidad* but Mexico and its history. In the beginning there were the Aztec people after the Conquest, in an "orphaned" state of radical solitude. Not only had their "idolatries foundered" but also the divine protection earned through the sacrifices. The gods had abandoned them. Fortunately, says Paz, a new order replaces the break in cosmic truth precipitated by the Conquest. It is an order sustained by a new religion and "built to last." And it is not a mere "superimposition" of new historical forms, nor does Paz even qualify it as a form of syncretism. It is a "living organism," a place where "all men and all races were encountering a location, a justification, and a meaning." It was the cultural matrix of Mexico, the Catholic order of the Colony, and it would last for three centuries. "Through the Catholic faith," Paz goes on, "in their state of orphanhood, the connections with their ancient cultures broken, their gods as dead as their cities, the Indians find a place in the world . . . Catholicism restores meaning once again to their presence on the earth, nourishes their hopes and justifies life and death." The poem of Mexican history passes from solitude to communion. In Paz's view, the persistent importance of religion in Mexico is also explained by its pre-Cortesian background: "nothing has disrupted the filial relation of the Mexican to the sacred. Constant force that gives permanence to our nation and depth to the emotive life of those who have been dispossessed." And the man who writes these phrases is not a man narrowly bred in the Hispanicist tradition that automatically foregrounds the inheritance of Spain but is the grandson of Don Ireneo Paz, the Jacobin creator of *El Padre Cobos,* last of the great nineteenth-century Liberals. It has the value of a vision that dares to touch upon the *other* orthodoxy (the Catholic) in order to criticize an official (liberal) orthodoxy in Mexican government and thought.

The orphanhood of the Conquest, the order of the Colony, the rupture at Independence. Paz sees the nineteenth century as the historical site of a detour, almost an aberration. In terms of his own biography (and his idiosyncratic insistence on the "solitude" not only of himself but of all Mexicans), his words at the end of the initial section for the first time project his categories, derived from poetic introspection and personal experience, onto Mexican history:

> The Reform is the great Rupture with the mother. This separation was a fatal and necessary act, because every truly autonomous life begins with a rupture with the family and the past. But this separation still grieves us. Even now we breathe through the wound. And so the feeling of orphanhood is the constant background to our attempts at politics and our internal conflicts. Mexico is alone, like every one of her sons. The Mexican and *mexicanidad* are defined as the living consciousness of solitude, historical and personal.

With the coming of independence, the colonial order had shattered into fragments. Communion, says Paz, is no longer sustainable and dissolves into solitude. Afterward, with the advent of liberalism, "The lie installs itself in our peoples almost constitutionally." Years later, the "triple negation" of the age of Liberal reform (with respect to the indigenous, Catholic, and Spanish worlds) "establishes Mexico." Paz does not deny "grandeur" to this historical process but adds, in decisively judgmental words: "What this negation affirmed—the principles of European liberalism—were beautiful ideas that were precise, sterile and ultimately empty." The age of Don Porfirio would merely be the extreme continuation of this tendency, a mask covering the lack of authenticity, a pretense converted into the automatic second nature of the era. And positivism, the official philosophy of the Porfiriato, "displayed the liberal principles in all their nakedness: beautiful but inapplicable words. We had lost our historical filiation." In these lines, almost inadvertently, Paz turns his back on his grandfather Ireneo. But immediately afterward he rescues someone more fragile and perhaps more beloved: his own father. Because the "filiation" that Mexico had lost in the century of liberalism would be regained in the Revolution, which arose "tearing young men away from their paternal homes: it is the Revolution, the magic word, the word that is going to change everything and that will grant us immense joy and a quick death."

Not only Paz believed that Mexico had encountered its authentic path in the Mexican Revolution. Except for those who remained Porfirians, all of intellectual Mexico thought the same. But it was one thing to encounter the path and another the "filiation" (*filiación*), a key word in *The Labyrinth of Solitude*. For Paz, the authentic revolution would be only one of the Mexican revolutions, the one that had swept away his father: Zapata's revolution.

Perhaps the most intense and impassioned pages of the book are dedicated to the sacred scripture of Zapatismo—the Program of Ayala (*Plan de Ayala*)—with its demands for land and communal rights and for "the most ancient, stable and enduring part of our nation, the indigenous past." Zapata had been the historical hero of his father. And of Octavio Paz as well, though inserted within his personal category of "solitude":

> The traditionalism of Zapata shows the deep historical consciousness of this man, isolated in his village and in his race. His isolation . . . the solitude of the still enclosed seed, gave him the strength and depth to reach the simple truth. For the truth of the Revolution was very simple and consisted of the insurgency of Mexican reality, crushed down by the maneuvers of liberalism as much as by the abuses of conservatives and neo-conservatives.

The final part of this second part is the culmination of the book and of Paz's principal poetic thesis in *The Labyrinth*, in a passage of magnificent Spanish prose but not necessarily valid as a universal and incontrovertible insight:

> The Revolution is the sudden immersion of Mexico in its own being . . . It is an eruption of reality and a communion, a decanting of old dormant substances, many ferocities coming out into the air, many tendernesses and elegances that had been hidden by the fear of existence. And with whom does Mexico commune in this bloody fiesta? With itself, with its own being. The revolutionary explosion is a marvelous fiesta in which the Mexican drunk with himself, finally, in a mortal embrace, comes to know another Mexican.

And with whom does Octavio Paz Lozano commune? Whom does he embrace, in this almost rapturous description? The passage deals with mortal combat but also with love and, from the point of view of love (immersed in violence), Paz communes with Octavio Paz Solórzano, his father, "he who went away for a few hours and nobody knows into what silence he entered." He embraces Octavio Paz, the other and the same. The *fiesta mexicana*, the drunkenness with oneself, the mortal embrace that, for a moment, links them together takes place between two men, father and son, with the same name of Octavio Paz.

IX

Writing *The Labyrinth of Solitude* was an act of liberation for Paz, especially in his more obviously personal work. Once the book was finished, he admitted, in a letter to Alfonso Reyes, that the theme of *mexicanidad* was "beginning to weigh me down":

> . . . this obsession, in a time of peace, displays a twisted nationalism, that will lead to aggression, when it is strong, and to narcissism and masochism, when it is vile, as is happening with us. An intelligence

enamored of particularism . . . begins to lack intelligence . . . I am afraid that, for some, being Mexican consists of something so exclusive that it denies us the possibility of being men.

Nonetheless, his own discovery of *mexicanidad* led him to celebrate it in the few visual artists that he saw as deeply involved with the same theme. For Paz the greatest of them was Rufino Tamayo. Around November 1950, for an Exposition of Mexican Art held in Paris, he wrote an essay in which he tried to settle accounts with the three greatest Mexican muralists and argue for Tamayo, a native of Oaxaca, which is in many ways the most profoundly "Indian" state of Mexico. Paz admires the "materialist" flowering of Diego Rivera but criticizes what he calls the "dialectical" harangue expressed in his work. And if Rivera's problem was "statism," Paz sees in the work of David Alfaro Siqueiros—a painter of movement and dramatic contrasts—another quality to be criticized: "theatrical effectism . . . painted literature." He finds the work of the third major muralist, José Clemente Orozco, closest of the great triad to his own moral sensibility, as a painter who was less ideological, more rebellious, and more solitary. But in opposition to the muralists, he assigns special value to the painters of his own generation (María Izquierdo, Agustín Lazo, Jesús Reyes, Carlos Mérida, and even Frida Kahlo, among others) who, according to Paz, did not try to preach to the people about the epic of their history nor announce an imminent socialist utopia, but were attempting to reach down into their myths, their dreams, their specific modes (in colors, tones, gestures) of ferocity, tenderness, fiesta, and death. Paz saw this kind of painting (and his interpretation of it) as corresponding to the process of self-knowledge (*autognosis*) preached by Paz himself in *El laberinto de la soledad*. Among all these painters, he points to Rufino Tamayo as representing "a place of communion," a consecration carried to its limit— like his own—in contact with the deepest waters of the Mexican past:

Tamayo does not need to reconquer his innocence; for him it is enough to descend to the deepest part of himself where he encounters the ancient sun, the fountain of images . . . if there is antiquity and innocence in the painting of Tamayo, it is because he bases himself on a people: on a present that is in itself a timeless past.

And yet, beyond the "particularism" involved in the search for *mexicanidad*, Paz felt the need for Mexicans to open themselves toward "the possibility of being men" and, in the final phrase of *El laberinto*, "to be contemporary with all men." As part of this impetus, Paz, while in Paris, would come to identify himself completely with the surrealist movement, a linkage he had rejected in his youth but that his work had prefigured since the 1930s. He grew close to André Breton and to another surrealist, Benjamin Péret, with whom he reinvigorated a long-established relationship. Paz came to feel that surrealism, with its emphasis on releasing emotions through access to the unconscious (and its interest in non-European cultures), was an ideal poetic and intellectual medium for confronting the multilayered reality of Mexico. From his explorations among the images and rites of his culture, its desires and popular myths, and later through the poetic freedom of the prose poems of *Aguila o sol?* (Eagle or Sun?), the direct predecessor of Latin American magic realism, his work never became static but continually expanded, with an extraordinary freedom of imagination and experimentation and an interest in a variety of traditions and cultures.

He came to play an important role in the defense of Luis Buñuel's great film *Los Olvidados* (The Forgotten), attacked by nationalist critics for its grim portrayal of Mexican urban poverty. When the film was due for its premiere at the Cannes Festival of April 1951, Paz wrote to Buñuel, who was then working in Mexico as a Republican exile from Franco's Spain: "I am proud to fight for you and your film." He may have remembered the jibes and harsh criticisms his own friends had inflicted on Buñuel's early surrealist film *La Edad de Oro*, on the occasion of André Breton's visit to Mexico in 1938, but also fiercely alive for him were his own memories of the Spanish Civil War. "Thanks to *Los*

Olvidados," he told Buñuel, "in a small way the heroic times return." Paz put considerable effort into creating "an atmosphere of expecta- tion" around the debut of the film, working his connections and seek- ing supporters (he spoke with Prévert, Cocteau, Chagall, Picasso and "mobilized the foot soldiers" of journalists). He wrote a text titled "Buñuel the Poet," which he personally distributed, in loose sheets, twenty-four hours before the premiere. And his dedicated energy may have contributed to Buñuel's winning the prize for Best Director:

> *Los Olvidados* is something more than a realist film. Dream, desire, horror, madness, chance, the nocturnal portion of life also have their part in it. And the weight of reality that it shows us is so atro- cious that it ends up seeming impossible to us, unendurable. And it is. The reality is *unendurable* and therefore, because he cannot endure it, man kills and dies, loves and creates.

The solitude of the major youthful protagonist may have reminded Paz of his own childhood. Perhaps the tragedy of the mother at the film's conclusion, left alone, helpless, abandoned, "fucked over" (*chingada*), consciously or unconsciously evoked the memory of his own pages on the woman (on indigenous Mexico) *chingada* in *El laberinto*. Whatever the case, Paz felt that Buñuel's masterpiece had touched on the essen- tial fabric of Mexican social reality with a lasting moral and aesthetic power.

Midway through the century, in the city of Paris, as a result of early revelations by the French writer David Rousset on the existence of concentration camps in the Soviet Union, Paz began to liberate him- self ideologically. The magazine *Les Lettres Françaises* had slandered Rousset for a supposed falsification of testimonies on the controversial subject (which it was at that time among the French left). Rousset had launched a widely followed suit against the magazine. "The newspa- pers . . . speak of nothing else," Paz wrote to his Argentine friend José Bianco, editor of *Sur*:

Perhaps it would *also be an opportune time* to publish something in *Sur* about this terrible accusation against the country some people still call "the fatherland of the proletariat." Do you know that among the witnesses Rousset presents, one finds *El Campesino* (The Peasant) that general to whom Alberti and other poets of the court of Stalin dedicated poems and homages. Now, one more time, they will have to vomit their canticles.

Valentín González González, El Campesino, had been a communist hero of the Spanish Civil War and received as such when he took refuge in the Soviet Union. (He was the partial inspiration for a character in André Malraux's *L'espoir* and, at another level of art, for the leader of raids into Franco Spain—which he was—in the early 1960s, portrayed by Gregory Peck in Fred Zinnemann's *Behold a Pale Horse* of 1964, though in contrast to the character played by Peck, he would die in his bed in 1983, back in the Madrid of post-Franco Spain.) He was regarded as one of the bravest and most successful Republican commanders but also the man who ordered the mass execution of hundreds of Nationalist prisoners taken in battle in 1937, as retaliation for Fascist atrocities. He had been sent to a concentration camp for showing his impetuous bravery before Stalin himself, criticizing the Stalinist cult of personality, and after his release eventually fled to France. According to the testimony of her daughter, Elena Garro attended the hearing of Rousset's suit against *Les Lettres Françaises*, spoke with El Campesino, and collected information. Relying on Garro's investigation (and the evidence offered by Rousset), Paz wrote his first openly critical piece on Stalinism. No one would publish it in Mexico but José Bianco did in *Sur*. Paz now put himself into an unusual position within Latin America, especially at the outset of the full-blown Cold War—that of an independent socialist. The only other outstanding instance of a similar position was taken by a man of exactly Paz's age, the Argentine Ernesto Sabato, with his book *Hombres y Engranajes* (Men and Gears).

The camps, Paz explained, did not serve a penal or corrective function. They were an essential feature of the bureaucratic Soviet regime, putting into parenthesis its socialist character and its capacity to offer an alternative to capitalism. "The crimes of the bureaucratic regime are theirs, truly theirs," he concluded, "very much theirs and not [the crimes] of socialism." Months later, in a lecture he gave honoring the memory of Antonio Machado on the occasion of the fifteenth anniversary of the Spanish Civil War, he reaffirmed his hope for the "revolutionary and creative" capacity of nations, their capacity to save themselves if only they could "eliminate" the "saviors by profession." His socialist convictions were still solidly held but they did not lead him to follow the opinion of Jean-Paul Sartre (whom his wife Elena Garro used to meet in the Pont Royal Bar). Sartre's recommendation was to ignore the facts presented by Rousset because a public acceptance would play into the hands of imperialism. Paz moved in the opposite direction and his decision brought him close to the Trotskyists. In fact, this first public gesture of criticism coincided with the resignation of Natalia Sedova, Trotsky's widow, from the Fourth International, when she rejected the idea that Soviet Russia was still a workers' state: "whoever loves and defends this oppressive and barbarous regime, no matter what his reasons, abandons the principles of socialism and internationalism." Her statement was published in *Quatriéme Internationale* in May 1951 and Paz had certainly read it.

WITHIN THE Mexican foreign service, Paz continued his career with diplomatic poise and efficiency. He held various postings in India, Japan, and Switzerland. For five years he served within Mexico as director general of international organizations, where he used his position to support the admission of refugees from Hungary after the Russian repression of the 1956 uprising. Following his period in France (between 1959 and 1962) he was named Mexican ambassador to India. On each posting, he sought to immerse himself intellectually in the host culture, whether it was Japanese literature or the versions of Indian thought and writing in translation that he chose to pursue.

In these years of formidable creative liberation and production, his penchant for founding and editing magazines (inherited in a direct line from his father and grandfather) would lie dormant, though much to his regret. José Bianco would receive and often act upon his suggestions and advice on authors, texts, focused points of view: to draw the writers of *Orígenes*, an excellent Cuban periodical, to the pages of *Sur*; to publish Rodolfo Usigli, the Mexican playwright who wrote corrosively about corruption in government; to devote an issue to the new Italian literature. At the beginning of his period of diplomatic service in Mexico, Paz wrote to Bianco:

> I have the sensation that only if I do something concrete will I be able to escape the painful feeling that my presence here is useless. Naturally, nothing better has occurred to me than a magazine. (When writers want to save the world, it always occurs to them to found a magazine.) But I've had no success even in that.

Nevertheless, during his diplomatic tour at home in Mexico, Paz was the hub of literary activity in the capital city. Among other efforts, he was a driving force behind the project *Poesía en Voz Alta* (Poetry in Public Performance), which renovated Mexican theater, and also of the magazine *Revista Mexicana de Literatura*, initially directed by Carlos Fuentes, who as a young writer was very close to Paz and greatly influenced by his personality and his intellectual concerns. Feeling a sense of responsibility for the cultural development of his country, Paz also tried to discover and support new talent. (As part of this search, he made the acquaintance, for instance, of Gabriel Zaid, a young engineering student in Monterrey who wrote poetry and plays.)

With the passing of previous generations (that of Vasconcelos and Reyes and the later generation of the Contemporáneos), Paz's star began to shine more brightly. He was only forty years old but already had a measure of international prestige. Around him gathered a new generation of writers, philosophers, and artists, born in the 1920s and '30s, who shared his critical outlook, his creative freedom, and his receptiveness to experimentation. The poets and novelists, tired of nationalist rhetoric, were drawn to the open and cosmopolitan perspectives of his work. The philosophers, influenced by the phenomenological analyses of Husserl, began to explore the idea of a "Mexican philosophy," following the lines of El Laberinto de la soledad, while the visual artists approved of his rupture with the by now rigidified traditions of the muralists. Although readers of serious works were a narrow segment of Mexican society (books were published in editions of three thousand copies or less and a second edition of El laberinto was not printed until 1959), the country's cultural activity was lively, intense, and in touch with currents of the international avant-garde. Paz had always been most influenced by France. The new novelists were more oriented toward American literature and perhaps the most surprising and impressive among them was Juan Rulfo (who was no less rooted than Paz in a biography heavy with history and violence, though Rulfo's origins were in the Catholic and conservative west of Mexico). Rulfo's book of short stories El llano en llamas (The Plain in Flames) and the novel Pedro Paramo (which dealt, in an original combination of surrealism and expressionism, with the recurrent Latin American theme of the tyrannical patriarch) showed a depth of feeling and perfection of style that, unfortunately, Paz never adequately recognized.

WHILE THE grandson of Ireneo Paz was waiting for the moment to found a new magazine, the son of Octavio Paz Solórzano took advantage of his first opportunity to display, at least symbolically, his revolutionary impulses. The writer José de la Colina recalled the scene:

> It was 1956. A demonstration in support of students protesting an increase in bus fares was marching past the intersection of Paseo de la Reforma and Bucareli . . . I was moving along with great enthusiasm, haranguing [my co-demonstrators] in the tone of a romantic anarchist. Paz came down from his office which was opposite the [monument of] El Caballito and joined that demonstration.

The episode was meaningful but exceptional. Paz's employment in public service prevented him from expressing criticism of Mexican internal politics. Paz would later (in 1978) coin the term the "Philanthropic Ogre" (*El ogro filantrópico*) for the Mexican state, but in 1956, like most Mexican intellectuals, he benefited from the philanthropy of the government. In addition to his salary from the Department of Foreign Relations, literary friends (Alfonso Reyes as president of the Colegio de México; José Luis Martínez, who was an official in the nationally owned Mexican Railways) helped the poet with scholarships that freed him for his creative work.

During this period, he would publish a philosophical volume, *El arco y la lira* (The Bow and the Lyre), that would be highly praised by the leading Mexican philosopher José Gaos; *Sendas de Oku* (Paths of Oku), the first translation of the Japanese poet Basho into a Western language; and *Las peras del olmo* (The Pears of the Elm—a Spanish metaphor for demanding the impossible), a collection of essays on artists, writers, and classical and contemporary literatures. But if he never expressed his criticism in prose, he did so in poetry.

In his memorable poem of 1955 *El cántaro roto* (The Broken Pitcher), which would have fascinating repercussions more than a decade later, he expressed his feelings of distress and of hope.

During a time when Mexico seemed (at least to many) an island of peace, order, and prosperity under the paternal command of the President and the PRI, *El cántaro roto* disturbed the conscience of many Mexicans and was also attacked for its supposedly communist content. It was inspired by a journey of readings and lectures across the northern states of San Luis Potosí and Nuevo León. It is not a political or sociological interpretation of contemporary Mexico. Like *The Labyrinth of Solitude*, it is a mythical analysis and judgment. Paz (from the standpoint of a later, sparer style) would condemn what he termed the "verbal excesses" of the poem but never its substance.

El cántaro roto begins with a reverie of the poet on the vanished Aztec past:

wind! The gallop of water between the interminable walls of a throat of jet,
horse, comet, rocket that strikes true at the heart of the night, feathers, fountains
feathers, sudden flowering of torches, candles, wings, invasion of the white man
birds of the islands singing under the forehead of the man who is dreaming

But the poet opens his eyes to a different landscape, the *other* Mexico, a wasteland depicted in images from the northern desert:

Only the plain: cactus, desert acacia, enormous stones that crack open under the
                                                                    / sun
The cricket was not singing,
there was a vague smell of lime and burnt seeds,
the streets of the village were dry gulleys
and the air would have broken into a thousand pieces if someone had shouted
                                              / "Who goes there?"

The poet's bewilderment spills into a cascade of painful questions, some of it in the style of Nahuatl lamentations:

The maize-god, the flower-god, the water-god, the blood-god, the Virgin,
have they all died? Have they all gone away? Broken pitchers at the rim of the
                                              / stopped-up fountain?
Is only the toad alive,
only the greenish toad glittering and glistening in the night of Mexico,
is only the fat chieftain of Cempoala immortal?

This wasteland is the creation of the present, or rather of the past weighing upon the present. It is the work of those who command and continue to command, of power personified in the historic figure of the "fat chieftain of Cempoala," ally of Cortés but reincarnated across history as the Catholic bishop or inquisitor, the nineteenth-century military dictator, the revolutionary general or the banker:

Stretched out at the base of the divine tree of jade watered with blood, while two
/ young slaves fan him
before the people on the days of great processions, leaning on the cross: weapon
/ and walking stick,
in battle dress, the sculptured face of flint inhaling, like a precious incense, the
/ smoke of executions by gunfire,
weekends in his armored house near the sea, beside his beloved covered with
/ neon jewels,
is only the toad immortal?

But the poet still hopes that there will "finally surge the spark, the shout, the word." He puts his faith in poetry:

we must disinter the lost word, dream inward and also out to the world
decipher the tattoos of the night and stare face to face at midday and tear
/ away its mask,
bathe in solar light and eat the nocturnal fruits, interpret the writing of the
/ star and that of the river,
remember what the blood says and the tide, the earth and the body, return
/ to the point of departure.

Two years later he would publish one of his most famous works, *Piedra de sol* (Sun Stone), which Paz saw as the end of a cycle begun in 1935. The wasteland now was not only Mexico. It was the world, a prisoner of history and of myth. And as in *El cántaro roto*, his hopes for the future rest on words, dreams, fraternity, and love.

x

Despite this somber vision, during the four presidential terms in which he served the government, from Miguel Alemán (who took office in 1946) until 1968, when he made his great renunciation during the presidency of Gustavo Díaz Ordaz, Paz believed that, in general, his country had kept moving in an ever more positive direction, despite great social inequalities, the subordination of labor organizations to the state, poverty in the countryside, and a growing dependence on American capital. In 1959 he added to the second edition of *El laberinto* his comment that "our evolution is one of the most rapid and continuous in [Latin] America," due to the nationalist inheritance of the Revolution and state intervention in the economy. Paz was not the only accomplished intellectual to herald the progress of the country in those optimistic times. Even the historian, editor, and essayist Daniel Cosío Villegas—the most critically incisive heir to the nineteenth-century Liberal tradition—thought so and came to moderate the harsher judgments he had poured into his celebrated essay, written in 1947, *La crisis de México*. Trained as an economist in American universities, founder and director of the government-funded publishing house Fondo de Cultura Económica, a scholar of nineteenth-century liberalism, Cosío Villegas had always believed, like Octavio Paz, that the Mexican Revolution had been a valid and justified historical movement and that its modest and nationalist social agenda (achieved to a degree under President Lázaro Cárdenas) had been diverted during the 1940s toward a predominantly capitalist model, foreign to the original social commitment of the Revolution and its primary focus on the agricultural countryside. But also like Paz, Cosío could not ignore the obvious economic and institutional progress in the country.

Nonetheless, there were important differences between the views of Cosío Villegas and Paz. Cosío, in his own words, was "a museum quality Liberal," Paz a moderate Trotskyist in transition toward a perspective of independent socialism with anarchistic tendencies. The "major wound" of Mexico, for Cosío Villegas, was the concentration of power in the hands of the president and other factors that impeded the development of a true electoral democracy. Paz, on the other hand, continued (and would long continue) the use of Marxist tools of analysis. As late as 1967, in his book *Corriente alterna* (Alternating Current), he would write that "Marxism is barely a point of view but it is our point of view. We cannot abandon it, because we have no other." He would continue to apply class analysis and discount "free enterprise" as a "relic," would remain for many years disdainful of the inheritance of nineteenth-century liberalism, and would never lose faith in the possibility of an egalitarian community of men (the Golden Age of Zapatismo). Disenchanted with the Soviet Union, he came to regard the Chinese Cultural Revolution with a measure of sympathy (based on inadequate knowledge). He would praise the Yugoslav attempts at self-sufficiency and above all put his trust in the prospect of nationalist revolution among the nations at the periphery of the Western world.

Why then did he become a critic of the Cuban Revolution? The young intellectuals and university students of Mexico—including such friends of his as Carlos Fuentes—had no doubts. For them the Mexican Revolution had died, and almost all of them displayed immense enthusiasm for the "true" Cuban Revolution. Cosío Villegas, who had laid the major responsibility for the "lamentable" turn of Cuba to communism upon the United States, would maintain, from the very beginning, a definite distance toward the events in Cuba. Paz was less of a skeptic. In a letter to Roberto Fernández Retamar, he expressed his "great desire to go to Cuba to see its new face as well as its old one, its ocean and its people, its poets and its trees." But he soon lost this desire, as shown by his words in a letter to José Bianco (whose support for the Cuban Revolution would lead to his leaving *Sur*) dated May 26, 1961, after the failed CIA-sponsored invasion at the Bay of Pigs:

> Although I understand your enthusiasm (and I almost envy it) I do not entirely share it. I do not like the language used by the enemies of Castro, nor their actions, nor their morality, nor what they represent and are. But neither does the Cuban Revolution please me. It is not what I wanted (and want) for our countries. Our countries, like those of Africa and Asia, will choose the way of Castro. No other recourse (they are permitted no other) is left to them. Aside from the wars and calamities that [this situation] will unleash, the results can only be dictatorships of the right if the popular movements are destroyed or, if they triumph, totalitarian

dictatorships like that of Castro . . . I think that our century will see the triumph of "Marxist ideology"; what it will not see, at least in our generation, is the triumph of socialism.

Three times he was invited to visit Cuba as a member of the panel of judges for the Cuban Casa de las Américas literary prize. He never accepted. In 1964 he would refuse to participate in an homage to surrealism sponsored by the Casa de las Américas and he would write to Retamar:

> I rapidly recognized that a radical dichotomy existed between the regimes of Eastern Europe (now including those who govern China and elsewhere) and the liberating intentions of poetry. This dichotomy is due not only to the nightmare that Stalinism was for my generation (in Latin America for some of my generation) but that it forms part of the nature of things. I won't say more, I don't want to say more. I love Cuba too much . . . and Latin America, to ignite a new polemic now.

He would still describe himself, in another letter of 1967 to Retamar, as a "a friend of the Cuban Revolution in what stems from Martí, not Lenin." It would still be a few years before he would openly break with Cuba.

XI

In the early sixties, Paz was almost universally beloved, followed, read, and respected not only in Mexico but also, to a growing degree, in France (where he had long been publishing in magazines and translations of his books of poetry were beginning to appear). But still he was not happy. On the one hand, his professional situation was unstable. He was stationed in Mexico but would the Foreign Service send him to France, where he wished to go? Or to UNESCO? Or should he consider accepting a professorship? To make things worse, there was no market for his articles in Latin America and he even thought he might move to Argentina or Venezuela. He was forty-five years old when, in March 1959, he wrote to Bianco:

I have passed the last fifteen years doing something I do not like, putting off or killing off my desires (even the most legitimate like writing or doing nothing or falling in love) and hoping that, one fine day, things would change. The only thing that has changed is me: my life goes on in the same way (I work many hours in a ridiculous office, with the pompous title of Director General of International Organizations). I am poorly paid and subjected to the capriciously administered rules of distant bureaucrats.

He had survived due to a "salutary innate stupidity—formed of confidence in life, resignation (of an Andalusian peasant, for sure) and being permanently available." But then, finally, he was transferred to Paris, where he remained for two years and published *Salamandra*, a new collection of poems. The appointment as ambassador to India followed. Jaime Torres Bodet had recommended that he remain in the foreign service where "you will have 60% of your time free to write."

To write but also to reach some resolution in his intimate life. "Why did Octavio Paz and Elena Garro separate?" wrote the philosopher María Zambrano, who had lived with them in Paris. "They had achieved the most difficult thing: hell on earth." For years, Paz and Garro had lived apart, in an "open marriage." He had frequently considered divorce but kept putting it off. In 1959 he would tell Bianco that the situation had become unendurable. He would soon be divorced and he let slip one weighty reason: "I think that I am—I have been, I will be—in love. It makes me more miserable but gives me vitality. Or at least it nourishes my plans, my hunger for the future." The woman he alluded to (without mentioning her name) was the beautiful Italian painter Bona Tibertelli de Pisis, the wife of the French writer André Pieyre de Mandiargues. Octavio and Elena had been friends, since Paris, with the partners in that other "open marriage." The French edition of *Águila o sol?* (published in 1957) included five etchings by Bona. And in 1958, André and Bona had traveled in Mexico, visiting the coasts and colonial cities and attending ancient festivals accompanied by one of the best guides possible: the author of *El laberinto de la soledad*.

The tormented relationship between Octavio and Elena was finally broken, after twenty-two years. "Helena," he confessed to Bianco (still using the name he had once given her), "is a wound that will never close, a sore, a vice, an illness, a fixed idea." But despite his animosity, Paz would retain the intellectual admiration he felt for Garro. Encouraged by Octavio, she had achieved literary success in the 1950s with works of the theater and short stories of a style similar to the oneiric and spiritual universe of Juan Rulfo. But with her novel *Recuerdos del porvenir* (Memories of the Future), her prestige was firmly established. Paz would write to Bianco, his great respect for her writing coupled with an undertone of intimate hostility:

> Did you get Helena's book? What do you think of it? I'm surprised and amazed by it. How much life! How much poetry! Everything seems like a pirouette, a rocket, a magical flower! Helena is a *magician*! She is a sorceress (and also a witch: Artemisa, the huntress, the perpetual Virgin, mistress of the knife, enemy of man). Now I can judge her with objectivity.

The quality of Garro's novel had astonished him. Later, after Bianco had responded with his own words of admiration, Paz would write: "About this, at least, I was not mistaken." He had always believed "in her sensibility and spiritual insight, in her gaze of a true creator, of a poet and never, not even in the worst moments and most sordid situations, have I renounced her." And he concluded: "To have known, loved and lived with her for so many years and to finish it now with a eulogy of her as a writer! Does only what they call 'the work' remain of us?" And he added a surprising coda: "I say to myself: you can sleep in peace: you came to know a really marvelous being."

In 1960, the affair with Bona had advanced to the point that

Paz—after securing a divorce by proxy from Elena—announced his imminent wedding in another letter to Bianco. "Bona is the niece of De Pisis, that Italian painter of Chirico's generation, whom perhaps you may know. Ungaretti, Ponge, Mandiargues and others have written about her painting. She will soon be my wife. We are going to marry." But in 1962, when he was already in India, the relationship fell apart.

There seemed to be a fatal pattern: all the blessings of life (creativity, recognition, security) except that of love. In 1963, his faithful and generous friend José Luis Martínez proposed him for an International Poetry Prize at the Biennial of Knokke-le-Zoute, in Belgium. Against potent rivals—Vicente Aleixandre and Henri Michaux—Paz was awarded the prize. The Mexican press showered him with praise. The philosopher José Gaos predicted that "the next Nobel Prize for the Spanish language will be yours." The articles he published in the journal of the National University (collected in the book *Corriente alterna*) were received with reverence. But Paz, now fifty years old, had returned to his state of solitude. When he invited Martínez and his wife, Lydia, to visit him in New Delhi, Paz described "a very pleasant house, with a marvelous garden of 3000 meters. The only thing that troubles me is to live in it alone."

Writing from Paris in 1964, he reviewed the broad picture of his emotional life:

Elena was an illness . . . if I had stayed with her, I would have died, I would have gone mad. But I haven't encountered "health." Maybe now . . . Will it not be too late? In recent years, after some blows and brutal surprises (not the slow and exasperating psychic splintering that was my amorous illness with Elena but the blow of a hatchet, the treacherous dagger, the thunderbolt [of his breakup with Bona], I aspire to a degree of wisdom. Not resignation but tranquil desperation—not death but learning to see death and woman face to face. Eroticism bores me and frightens me (it's like religion: either one is a devotee or a saint—I am neither Casanova nor Sade . . .) I believe in what is deepest, in love . . .

BUT IN the very year he wrote this letter, the skies had cleared for him in a miraculous and lasting way. In India at the age of fifty he had come to know a young woman—in one poem he calls her a girl (*muchacha*)—who would accompany him for the rest of his life, in a full and vigorous love. She was extraordinarily beautiful and talented. And cheerful, respectful, and faithful to him. She was Corsican and her name was Marie-José Tramini. When they met, in India, she was married to a French diplomat and so their mutual attraction had to be treated with reserve. In the subcontinent, their paths crossed briefly and then they went their own ways. By chance they traveled separately to Paris and met there, again by chance, on the street. And suddenly (the expression "suddenly"—*de pronto*—is frequent in Paz's poetry as a marker of chance) one of those moments of "objective chance" changed their lives, as Paz had once foreshadowed it in a lecture on surrealism delivered in 1954: "this encounter, major, decisive, destined to mark us forever with its golden talon, is called love, person beloved." Marie-Jo would recall, "I met him then and I never left him." Together they returned to India and were married in Delhi on January 20, 1966. "Meeting her was the best thing that happened to me after being born," Paz would say.

The years in India with Marie-Jo were a period of unalloyed happiness for Octavio Paz, perhaps for the first time in his life. "It must be very delightful to be so much in love," the wife of the writer Agustín Yáñez commented when seeing them together. It was a period of great productivity for Paz, including the poems published in *Ladera este* (Eastern Slope) and *Hacia el comienzo* (Toward the Beginning). Scattered through the poems are moments of his rapt middle-aged love in the heated air of India:

> *Space spins*
> *the world tears up its roots*
> *Weighing no more than the dawn are our bodies*
> *   stretched out*
>
> (*from* Viento Entero)

You are dressed in red

         you are

the seal of the burned-up year

the carnal firebrand

         the fruit-bearing star

In you I eat sun

(from "Cima y gravedad")

Or in the long poem *Maithuna* (a technical Sanskrit word for the sacralized act of love), Paz moves across his beloved's body:

To sleep to sleep in you

Or better to wake up

         to open my eyes

at your center

         black white black

white

    To be sleepless sun

that your memory sets on fire

         (and

the memory of me within your memory . . .

For Paz, who was so often a poet of desire, "woman is the gate of reconciliation with the world." After decades of loves marked in part by anguish and uncertainty, pain and drought, fleeting and insubstantial affairs, Marie-Jo opened this "gate of reconciliation." She lessened his sense of emptiness, his feelings of need. She saved him from his personal labyrinth of solitude and was his constant inspiration.

SINCE THE days of *Barandal*, Paz had felt that something was missing in his life, his ancestral avocation of founding and editing journals. He began to explore the possibility of publishing a literary and critical magazine that could speak to all of Latin America. For now he had no luck, even with a proposal he and Carlos Fuentes made to the government of France, whose minister of culture was then André Malraux.

And something even deeper within him had failed to come to pass: the greatest public event, the Revolution. Paz remained obsessed by the idea of the Revolution, but he encountered and reworked it in only one area of experience, the incessant subversion and free experimentation of his poetry. Since his youth, with less luck but with nobility and enthusiasm, he had sought the Revolution also in action: working for a time in Yucatán, writing for revolutionary Mexican newspapers, going to Spain during the Civil War and seeing there the unforgettable visage of hope, of possible fraternity, the "creative spontaneity and direct and daily participation of the people." And perhaps, above all, he had gone looking for the Revolution in the world of thought, among the great "possessed" writers of Russia, in the canonic texts of Marxism, the heretical texts of Trotsky, and later, in the polemics of Camus and Sartre.

He could not renounce his hopes for it. In the essays of *Corriente alterna*, he devotes his most inspired and poetic prose to the central myth of his time, to the Revolution:

> Revolution designates the new virtue: justice. All the others—fraternity, equality, liberty—are based on it . . . As universal as reason, it admits no exceptions and is equally ignorant of arbitrariness and of pity . . . Revolution: word for the just and for those who deal out justice. For revolutionaries, evil does not reside in the excesses of the established order but in that order itself.

And among the India-centered poems of *Ladera este* comes "An Interruption from the West, a Mexican Song," which succinctly sketches his revolutionary pedigree and the dilemma of his political life, a poem that recalls, with nostalgia, his grandfather and his father and how Paz felt himself to be history's orphan, an orphan of Revolution. Drinking their coffee or their alcohol they spoke to him of great national events, of true heroes "and the tablecloth smelled of gunpowder":

I kept my silence:

About whom could I speak?

XII

And "suddenly" (*de pronto*) the winds from the West brought the smell of gunpowder to Octavio Paz in India. While he and Marie-Jo were at a hotel in the Himalayas in the summer of 1968, Paz received with "incredible emotion" news of the rebellion of students in Paris and saw, in the possible fusion of the student movement with the French working class, the long-awaited fulfillment of Marx's prophecy, the beginning of revolution in the Western world. Finally, thought Paz, the Revolution was being born in the "splendid attitude" of the young generation of the West, the new nomads of the industrial age, reinventors of neolithic values, scornful of the future, worshippers of the instant, and in the no less hopeful attitude of the young people of Eastern Europe, not only disillusioned but disgusted with Marxism. On June 6, Paz wrote to José Luis Martínez: "The revolt of young people is one of the surest signs of change in our society—at times it seems to me that I'm returning to the thirties." Six days later, he wrote an impassioned letter to the English poet Charles Tomlinson in which he reaffirmed his feeling of returning to his origins, to his conversations with his anarchist friend Bosch, his readings before he became a convinced Marxist, a return that was also a new beginning and a change of direction:

> The mediocre order of the "developed" world is teetering. The reappearance of my old masters thrills and exalts me: Bakunin, Fourier, the Spanish anarchists. And with them the return of the poet seers: Blake, Rimbaud etc. The great tradition which runs from German and English romanticism to surrealism. It is my tradition. Charles, *poetry is turning into action.* I think that we are on the point of exit from the tunnel, this tunnel that began with the

fall of Spain, the Moscow trials, the ascent of Hitler, the tunnel dug by Stalin and that the Eisenhowers, the Johnsons and the capitalist and communist technocrats told us was the road to progress and well-being. Whatever may be the immediate result of the French crisis, I am certain that something has begun in Paris that will decisively change the history of Europe and, perhaps, of the world. The true socialist revolution—Marx was right about this— can only happen in the developed countries. What he did not say (although at the end of his life, after the Paris Commune, he partly accepted it) was that the revolution should be socialist and *libertarian*. What is now beginning is not only the crisis of capitalism and the gloomy caricatures of socialism that are the Soviet Union and its satellites and rivals (the delirious China of Mao)—it is the crisis of the oldest and most solid instrument of oppression that men have known since the end of the neolithic age: the State.

On July 28, 1968, the Mexican student movement erupted. A minor incident among students provoked police repression in Mexico City, and from there the movement escalated until it reached national dimensions. The army, in a senseless act of exaggerated aggression, used a bazooka to shatter the centuries-old door of the National Preparatory School. Some high school students were wounded, and the authorities of the National Autonomous University (to which the preparatory was formally connected), precisely in defense of their autonomy, led the first of a number of marches in which thousands of people (for the first time in decades) took part in street demonstrations against the government, which they saw as stagnant, corrupt, demagogic, and authoritarian. Certainly the Mexican political system had no concentration camps. Nor did it propagate the ideology of a Supreme State free to enter into all areas of experience. But it did wield almost absolute power based on the convergence of a party (the PRI, which functioned as a centralized agency for employment, corruption, and perquisites while at the national level it always triumphed in the regularly held, thoroughly manipulated elections) and a monarchical president, selected every six years by the outgoing president and party elders and endowed with all-embracing powers over the treasury, national resources, state-owned enterprises, the army, Congress, the courts, governors, mayors, and the major means of communications. His only limit was temporal—a president could not serve more than one term.

Mexican intellectuals (like Paz himself) were traditionally integrated into the structure of the state and were expected to collaborate in "the building of the nation." For those who instead chose to oppose the regime—trying to form opposition parties or criticize government actions—the machinery of the Partido Revolucionario Institucional would usually find ways—sometimes violent—to crush their efforts. But in reaction to the student movement, one of Mexico's most respected intellectuals, the historian, editor, and essayist Daniel Cosío Villegas, now seventy years old, ended his career in public service and began to contribute—in the newspaper *Excélsior*—weekly articles in which he renewed a critical attitude that had remained dormant since the publication, back in 1947, of his famous essay on "The Crisis of Mexico." Like Paz, Cosío Villegas had participated in a succession of PRIista governments, as both diplomat and financial advisor. He recognized that, despite all its faults, Mexico had achieved a significant degree of material development: a sustained growth of 7 percent a year with a stable currency and no appreciable inflation. Recognizing its long period of stability and development, the international community had honored Mexico with the forthcoming (in October 1968) Summer Olympics. But for Cosío Villegas, the intolerant treatment of students by the government was unacceptable, and he saw the responsibility of the intellectual as "to make public life truly public." His present duty was not to integrate himself into the workings of power but to criticize it, an activity that also made more sense now that the Mexican reading public had grown considerably. Paz had quarreled with Cosío Villegas over the cancellation of a scholarship Paz had been receiving from the Colegio de México but their paths now would converge around the issue of critical freedom.

From New Delhi, Ambassador Paz was following the events with a growing sense of unease and seriously considered resigning his post. On August 3, he wrote to Tomlinson:

> It seems that the repression in Mexico is severe, brutal . . . I am afraid these disturbances will strengthen the right. The inheritance of the revolution is dissipating . . . For quite some time I have been planning on resigning my post and what has been happening now contributes to or dissipates my last hesitations. I will go to Mexico in November and there definitely settle my situation. Maybe I can obtain something at the University or the Colegio de México.

One month later, after the "March of Silence," when four hundred thousand demonstrators paraded through the streets with kerchiefs or shawls over their mouths to protest government brutality, and after the presidential "state of the country" address (the yearly *informe*), in which President Díaz Ordaz clearly threatened the use of force to stifle the protests, Paz wrote to Secretary of Foreign Relations Antonio Carrillo Flores:

> Although at times the phraseology of the students . . . recalls that of other young [protesters], French, North-American and German, the problem is absolutely distinct. The issue is not social revolution—though many of the leaders are radical revolutionaries—but of accomplishing a *reform* in our political system. If we do not begin now, the next decade in Mexico will be violent.

On September 18, the army violently occupied the National Autonomous University of Mexico. In that period when the Cold War was still at its height, Díaz Ordaz was convinced that the country could fall into the hands of the communists. On September 27, in another letter to Tomlinson, Paz confessed his feeling of acute remorse for not having already acted:

My remaining in the Mexican foreign service is incongruous—
from a moral point of view as much as an emotional one. Specifically I have now initiated the process to secure my retirement.
What is going on now reveals to me that I should have done this
earlier. All of it keeps me anguished, ashamed and furious—with
others and, above all, with myself.

On October 2, 1968, the government massacred hundreds of students in the ancient Plaza of Tlatelolco. Their crime had been to raise
the banner of political liberty. On the very next day, Paz wrote a
poem of shame and fury about the collective crime: "Mexico, Olym-
piad of 1968." And after "examining my conscience" on October 4, he
wrote Carrillo Flores a long letter attacking the violent policies of the
government and submitting his resignation: "I am absolutely not in
agreement with the methods used to resolve (in reality to repress) the
demands and problems that our youth has presented." It was his first
firmly political act since the Spanish Civil War. But this time it was
his rebellion. This public step was also the completion of an intimate
cycle, the promise inscribed in his lineage—to go off to the Revolution.
In communion with the student revolt, Paz went off to *his* revolution
by breaking with a petrified revolution. He began to convert himself
into the third protagonist of his "Mexican Song." "About whom could
I speak?" he had written about his father's and grandfather's heroes
and now the answer was himself. His gesture had made him a hero to
young Mexico. Even the delay in his resignation, about which he had
felt "ashamed," fell "suddenly" into place, because it would by chance
permit him to resign as a Mexican ambassador in direct response to
the worst, most murderous crime of the Díaz Ordaz regime. It was
his finest hour, an unheard-of gesture in the history of Mexico. And it
would change not only his own life but the intellectual life of Mexico
and, to a considerable degree, of Latin America.

To explain the atrocity to himself, Paz searched for a myth or an
episode of the historic past that could illuminate it. *Behind and below*

the facts, he felt a mythic reality moving the strings. What had happened, he decided, in poetic and in actual terms, was nothing less
than an act of human sacrifice. He sketches it as such when writing to
Tomlinson on October 6, alluding to his vision of archaic power in *El
cántaro roto*: "The old gods are unleashed again, and our president has
become the Grand Priest of Huitzilopochtli [the Aztec god of war],"
and he adds, "I chose not to continue as a representative of the Great
Moctezuma (the First, famous for the number of victims he sacrificed
on the Teocalli)."

Octavio and Marie-Jo Paz spent the rest of Díaz Ordaz's presidential
term in voluntary exile at the University of Cambridge in England, and
later, in the United States, at the University of Texas. Paz was writing his book of political essays, *Posdata* (Postscript), clearly meant as a
sequel to *El laberinto*. In it, surprisingly, he affirms that Mexico does not
have "an essence but rather a history." Nevertheless, he will continue
probing for the essence of history within myths that are still alive in the
culture. He explores the pros and cons of the student movement, giving
special weight to its call for democratizing the government. But in a
long and controversial chapter, he turns to the Aztec worldview to reaf-
firm and expand on his vision of the slaughter as an atavistic act, almost
as if it were prescribed, magically and fatally, by the ancient gods. The
conceit also leads him to a more convincing assertion. He sees the PRI
as a *pyramid*—both "tangible reality and subconscious premise." At its
apex stood the President of Mexico (Díaz Ordaz or his predecessors),
who is not the typical, charismatic nineteenth-century *caudillo* but a
figure whose legitimacy stems not from his personal qualities but from
another source. The President was an *institutional* figure, with almost
theocratic powers, like the Aztec emperor, the Tlatoani. The country
was subordinated pyramidally to him—in its political structure and
the paths available for social advancement. This political invention, Paz
affirmed, had until then freed the country of anarchy and blatant dictatorship, but by 1968 the system had become oppressive and asphyxiat-
ing. Paz believed that he saw, in the bureaucratic petrification of the
PRI, a parallel with the Soviet Union. His conclusion: "In Mexico there

is no greater dictatorship than that of the PRI and no greater danger of anarchy than that provoked by the unnatural prolongation of the PRI's political monopoly . . . Whatever correction or transformation may be attempted will require, first of all and as a necessary precondition, the democratic reform of the regime."

WHILE PAZ was writing his book, an old comrade of his was serving a sentence (yet one more time) for sedition in Mexico City's notorious Lecumberri prison. He was José Revueltas, who had been one of the intellectual leaders of the student movement. He was now fifty-five years old and had retained the faith and force to still believe in the Revolution but also the courage to denounce the crimes of Stalinism and oppose the Soviet invasion of Czechoslovakia. He was the eldest among Díaz Ordaz's political prisoners. He had been jailed for nine months and there was no way for him to know when, if ever, he would be freed. Imprisoned with him were many young men from the student movement. He was sharing his cell with a young teacher named Martín Dozal. In August 1969, in a message sent to his friend and comrade Paz, Revueltas described a poetic connection between the prisoners and the poet who had resigned a distinguished position in solidarity with their suffering.

Revueltas wrote: "Martín Dozal reads your poems, Octavio, your essays, he reads them, he goes over them again and then he meditates at length, he loves you at length, he reflects upon you, here in prison we all think of Octavio Paz, all these young men of Mexico think of you, Octavio . . ." And who is Martín Dozal, a young man whose destiny was inscribed in El cántaro roto? "He is twenty-four years old . . . he was a teacher of poetry or mathematics and he moved from one place to another, with his angry mane, with his arms, between the dry stones of this country, among the denuded bones which crush other bones, among the drums of human skin, in the country occupied by the sinister chieftain of Cempoala." And who were the young prisoners who read Octavio Paz? "These are not the young men already solemn and obese there on the outside . . . the future chieftains of Cempoala, the immortal toad." They are "the other face of Mexico, the true Mexico, and you, Octavio, see them! Look at the prisoners, look at our country imprisoned with them." The mere fact that Dozal and other young prisoners were reading Octavio Paz filled Revueltas with "profound hope."

But Mexico, in 1969, was passing through a long night. Not only power but public opinion seemed to have forgotten these political prisoners. The final months of the Díaz Ordaz government were, in effect, a night of silence, complicity, fear, lies, and death. It was the darkness Paz had laid out in *El cántaro roto*, a poem that these young people read and reread, like an implacable prophecy, come to fulfillment in their own lives:

> Ay, the night of Mexico, the night of Cempoala, the night of Tlatelolco, the sculptured face of flint that inhales the smoke of executions by gunfire. That magnificent poem of yours, that lightning bolt, Octavio, and the hypocritical respect, the false consternation, and the vile repentance of those who were accused, of the newspapers, the priests, the publishing houses, the poet-counselors, well-off, soiled, tranquil, who shouted "thief, thief!" and rapidly hid their money, their excrement, to conjure away what had been said, to forget it, so as to feign ignorance while Martín Dozal— who was then fifteen years old, or eighteen, I don't remember— was reading it and weeping with rage and we asked ourselves all the same questions as the poem: "Is only the toad immortal?"

Not even during the Spanish Civil War had Paz's poetry realized his revolutionary aspirations so fully as in the reading of *El cántaro roto* in Lecumberri prison.

Gustavo Díaz Ordaz, in a television interview, had denigrated Paz as a poet. Revueltas alludes to this assault in his concluding paragraph:

> There came the night that you made your announcement, there came the dogs, the knives, "the broken pitcher fallen in the dust."

And . . . now that you take your place in the plaza with yourself
and with us, for the trembling chieftain of Cempoala you have
stopped being a poet. Now, at my side, in the same cell of Lecumberri, Martín Dozal is reading your poetry.

Poetry had turned into action.

ON DECEMBER I, 1970, a new president took office, Luis Echeverría
Álvarez. Although Díaz Ordaz had taken personal responsibility for
Tlatelolco, few doubted that Echeverría—Díaz Ordaz's right-hand man
and the anointed to succeed him—shared that responsibility. Months
before, during the presidential "campaign," Echeverría had expressed
his intention to impose a drastic shift in Mexican politics. He had
begun to speak of "autocriticism" and coined the term "democratic
opening." University students who had sympathized with the movement of '68 were invited to accompany him on his campaign tours. The
composition of his cabinet marked a change of generations and a turn
to the left, while Salvador Allende and his Unidad Popular were rising
to elected power in Chile. Echeverría wanted to be a "new Cárdenas"
(Lázaro Cárdenas himself had died a few months earlier, in October
1970) and preached a return to the Mexican Revolution: the division of
large estates, support for an independent labor movement, confrontation with the "big business right," a sharpened tone of anti-imperialist
rhetoric, an increase in support for education and in university budgets
(especially the National University) and, to complete the circle, establishing a direct and positive contact with Mexican intellectuals, notably
those of his own generation, but also with others of great public influence, like Daniel Cosío Villegas and Octavio Paz.

For some months things seemed to be working out well. Paz returned to Mexico (he had briefly visited in 1967, to give his acceptance
speech on being inducted into the Colegio Nacional, the highest Mexican cultural honor). He praised the proposals for self-criticism by the
new government as well as the decision to liberate the prisoners of '68
still in custody, including his friend Revueltas, with whom he began

discussions about founding a political party. Within the cultural and political world, mostly concentrated around three publications (the weekly supplement "Culture in Mexico" to the journal *Siempre!*, the Sunday supplement to the newspaper *Excélsior*, and the *Revista de la Universidad*). Paz was expected to become editor of "Culture in Mexico" and so take his place as the high priest of literature.

But an unexpected happening dimmed the prospects for reconciliation. On June 10, 1971, the political prisoners of '68, recently released by the government, organized a demonstration and were brutally repressed. Their attackers were a mysterious paramilitary group known as "The Falcons" (*los halcones*), who, it was later discovered, were acting for the government. It was a small-scale but very bloody encore to the Tlatelolco massacre. The Falcons entered hospitals and Red Cross aid stations and riddled wounded students with gunfire. Dozens were killed. That very night Echeverría appeared on television and spoke to the press, promising a rapid investigation to find and punish those responsible. On the following day, Paz came out in support of the president, affirming that Echeverría had "restored transparency to words." But in part as a direct result of this new mortal insult to the young people of Mexico, it was one of Paz's earlier, private statements, in a letter to Charles Tomlinson, that would prove truer to the moment: his fear that the next decade in Mexico could be "violent." Many angry and impatient university students of the Generation of '68 (men and women born between the years of 1935 and 1950) opted for more radical positions, a good number of them for urban and rural guerrilla warfare in emulation of Che Guevara and to accelerate the social revolution "here and now." On the other hand, the most representative figures of the preceding generation (the Mid-Century—Medio Siglo—Generation) decided to support the Echeverría government, declaring themselves convinced that "obscure forces of the right" had orchestrated the repression in order to intimidate a progressive administration. One slogan, coined by the influential journalist and editor Fernando Benítez, became famous: "Not to support Echeverría is a major historic crime." Carlos Fuentes produced another, no less memorable formulation: "Echeverría or fascism."

The investigation Echeverría had promised never happened, though the appointed Regent of Mexico City, accused of overseeing the slaughter, was removed from office. Years later he would testify that he was acting on orders from superiors. The generational divisions were now supremely clear. The young left—in the halls of the universities, in cafés and newspapers and publishing houses and often in guerrilla actions—had become revolutionary while the older intellectuals (of Echeverría's own generation) closed ranks with the regime, supported it unconditionally, and eventually were incorporated into it. An elder among Mexican intellectuals, Daniel Cosío Villegas, accepted the National Prize for Literature in the autumn of 1971 from the hands of the president, but soon put distance between himself and the government, criticizing it for inflationary politics, ill-conceived populist gestures, and what he called "the personal style of Echeverría." His books would sell in the tens of thousands, a very high number for Mexico. What would Octavio Paz do?

XIII
———

Still of great importance to Paz was his desire to start another journal for intellectuals, to continue the family vocation and add one more masthead to the sequence of *Barandal*, *Taller*, and *El hijo pródigo*. The prospects were difficult. No literary journal could support itself in Mexico through sales alone and advertisers were—to say the least—diffident toward culture. There came an invitation from the highly respected journalist Julio Scherer—director of *Excélsior*—to accommodate and finance, within his newspaper, a journal that would reach subscribers and be sold at newspaper kiosks. Paz accepted the offer with enthusiasm. *Excélsior* was run as a cooperative and its workers were not particularly pleased with the prospect of what they saw as an elitist journal, but Scherer persuaded them. He promised

Paz complete freedom of expression and never wavered in his commitment.

Reflecting the mind-set Paz was now calling for in the public and intellectual life of Mexico, he chose a simple but inspired name for the journal: *Plural*. It would appear monthly from October 1971 to July 1976. It would publish numerous important American, European, and Latin American writers, mostly very well-established figures. The majority of contributors were of course Mexican. And the writers of the Mid-Century Generation (a long list that included Carlos Fuentes, Alejandro Rossi, Ramón Xirau, Luis Villoro, Julieta Campos, and Elena Poniatowska) would be given great prominence in *Plural*. The voices of the angry young—the Generation of '68—were almost entirely absent from its pages.

The journal ranged over a spectrum of literary genres, social sciences, and criticism of the visual arts. Paz sought to make *Plural* not an intellectual monopoly, nor an organ aspiring to hegemony, but rather a voice of dissidence. Dissidence, of course, toward the orthodoxies of the PRI (its bureaucratic culture, its ideological lies, its exalted vision of itself, and its official History) but also dissidence toward the predominant Mexican culture of the left. Paz considered himself a man of the left and felt that his journal spoke for the left, but he also insisted that the history of socialism (and most especially the effects of Stalinism) in the twentieth century called for an intellectual and moral reform of the left. Other Mexican journals, literary supplements, and various publications disagreed. *Plural* had the merit of breaking with a long tradition of cultural unanimity in Mexico.

PAZ'S WRITINGS in *Plural* (and the viewpoint of the journal) form an important step in the progressive transformation of his political ideas. This movement can clearly be discerned in his "Letter to Adolfo Gilly," published in the February 1972 issue of *Plural* in response to Gilly's book *La Revolución traicionada* (The Revolution Betrayed). Gilly, an Argentine Trotskyist who had participated in the student movement of 1968, was still imprisoned in a Mexican jail. Paz wrote that he was in accord with Gilly on more issues than not: on the need for socialism, on the necessary return to the programs of Cárdenas, on preserving the system of the *ejido* (communally owned agricultural communities), and the need to form an independent popular movement including workers, peasants, sectors of the middle class, and dissident intellectuals. Where he and Gilly differed, wrote Paz, was on the theme of political freedom.

Paz could not call the Soviet Union and its satellites "workers' states" and he invites Gilly to consider alternative approaches, which might well be found in traditions critical of capitalist society but anterior to Marx. In this instance, Paz meant the utopian thinker Fourier, whose life straddled the eighteenth and nineteenth centuries. Fourier was a predecessor of the ecological movement, supported women's rights, and gave considerable value to love and pleasure as well as calling for a more organic connection between production and consumption. They were qualities that appealed to Paz's poetic vision of himself and the world. He would write in an issue of *Plural* dedicated to Fourier:

> The tradition of "utopian socialism" is immediately contemporary because it sees in man not only the producer and the worker but also the being who desires and dreams: passion is one of the axes of every society because it is a force of attraction and repulsion. Starting from this conception of man as a passional being we can conceive of societies directed by a sort of rationality that is not the merely technological form reigning in the 20th Century.

Paz in general was writing for readers on the left. They were the only ones that mattered to him and, intellectually at least, he saw them as almost the only audience that existed. "The right has no ideas, only interests," he repeated more than once. He almost never wrote about the Church but he showed his disdain for the National Action Party (Partido Acción Nacional), which had been formed by conservative Catholic intellectuals—most of whom had favored Franco in the Spanish Civil War—but, since its founding in 1939, had struggled to democratize the Mexican electoral process. Paz would not even give them credit for these democratic aspirations. And he continued to criticize the "national bourgeoisie," whom he considered capable of conniving with the army and paramilitaries in order to take full power (not merely dominate) within the PRI. Toward the United States he showed a tendency toward acceptance of the turn-of-the-century ideas of Rodó and Darío about the essential incompatibility between "us," modest but "spiritual," and them, powerful but empty. His notion of New York or any other great American city, expressed in June 1971, was derived from the opinions of a somewhat outmoded American cultural elite: "[the cities] demonstrate that this development ends in vast social infernos."

His dialogue then was with the Mexican left, and above all with the young left. The Generation of '68 had grown up reading *El laberinto de la soledad* and may have accompanied their first loves by reading or reciting lines like these from Paz's poem "Sun Stone":

> to love is to do battle, when two people kiss
> the world changes, desires take on flesh
> thought takes on flesh, wings sprout
> on the shoulders of the slave, the world
> is real and tangible, wine is wine
> the bread tastes good again, water is water . . .

But in August 1972, something unexpected happened. A group of young writers who had collected around the prestigious critic Carlos Monsiváis at the Culture in Mexico supplement of *Siempre!* joined together to produce an issue critical of Paz and *Plural*. Their curious commitment was to *darle en la madre a Paz*, an idiom that might be translated as "hit Paz damn hard!" What disturbed these writers? On the one hand, Paz's cadenza in the final chapter of *Posdata*, where he brought in the old gods and myths to explain the slaughter of Tlatelolco. The group considered the connection to be false as well as politically irresponsible, attenuating the guilt of the assassins. Why hadn't

Paz written a poem instead of an essay? The young critics were beginning to perceive, in Paz's prose, an aestheticization of history and a tendency toward abstraction and generalization. They were also bothered by his political "reformism," his sudden and to them inexplicable abandonment of the revolutionary path. None of them were armed revolutionaries but they looked, with hope and sympathy, on the guerrilla action in the southern state of Guerrero and they were trying to document, in strikes and other demonstrations of discontent, the signs of an imminent popular insurrection. The periodical's "anti-Paz" issue was titled "About Mexican liberalism in the '70s." (By "liberalism" they were drawing on the Latin American use of the word, closer in part to the European historical meaning: non-Marxist, linked to nineteenth-century values of anticlericalism and a free market, stressing constitutional and republican principles and gradual social progress; while in Mexico, certainly when connected with the historical figures of Juárez and Madero, liberalism also involved a strong emphasis on electoral democracy and complete freedom of expression.)

Headed by the older Monsiváis, these young men (David Huerta, Héctor Manjarrez, Héctor Aguilar Camín, Carlos Pereyra, and myself) applied the word "liberal" to Paz's new political positions as, to them, an obvious stigma and they spoke pejoratively of formal liberties, rule of law, freedom of expression, and democracy. They were convinced that, in the revolutionary Mexico of the 1970s, these anachronistic emphases had no place. It was a matter of almost literally "expelling liberals from the discussion."

In an unsigned article in *Plural*, "The Criticism of the Parrots," Paz responded with a pair of strong "counterpunches." He reminded his critics that even the great theoreticians of Marxism (from Marx and Engels themselves to Kolakowski and Kosik and including Rosa Luxemburg) never insulted the ideas of freedom of expression and democracy. And he reminded them that their ability to freely publish opinions contradicted their denigration of "freedom of expression." Their anger against the system led them into careless assertions. Their "point of view was Marxism"—as had been Paz's in the 1960s, and they wanted radical change. Paz, on the other hand, had turned away from many of his illusions. This duel on the printed page was the first clear indication of a rupture between Octavio Paz and the Generation of '68.

IT WAS true that Paz had become "reformist" but he was not really a "liberal." He would never lose a measure of respect for the political system he had served. To deny that history was to deny the Mexican Revolution. He was, in both a cultural and biological sense, a son of the Mexican Revolution. The "system," he affirmed, had produced economic achievements, educational progress, and "very important" cultural and social advances. And in the political sphere, given the chronic oscillation between anarchy and authoritarian militarism in Latin America, it was no small thing to have reached "a compromise between dictatorship and *caudillismo.*" Such a compromise was the essence of the PRI, which, with all its defects, was "not an appendix of imperialism and the bourgeoisies." Nevertheless, if the objective was to construct "a democratic socialism based on our history," it had to be sought outside the PRI. His motto was "a popular movement along with democratization."

The word *democratización* but not "democracy" frequently appears in his writings of that time. What did he mean by it? Most of all he meant full freedom for public demonstrations, uncensored expression, political participation and criticism, liberties that the PRI had violated (or corrupted with payoffs) for decades and crushed in the repression of 1968. "Democratization" for Paz meant, above all, creating a space for words. Significantly, he never used the term "vote," he never referred to elections, nor did he criticize the control of the PRI over their so-called elections. He did not believe in Western democracy.

But he did believe that, for any debate on ideas to be honest and fruitful, writers had to maintain "their distance from the prince," by which he meant the government. Paz understood (as did Cosío Villegas) that his personal dependence on governmental philanthropy had inhibited his ability to criticize. Power had to be criticized in Mexico, in Latin America. It was the theme of our time. In May 1971, denouncing the false "confessions" attributed to the poet Heberto Padilla by the Cuban government, he had written:

> Our time is marked by a plague of authoritarianism. If Marx criticized capitalism, we have to criticize the state and the great contemporary bureaucracies, those of the East as well as those of the West. A criticism that we Latin Americans should complete with another of an historical and political nature: the criticism of an exceptional government by an exceptional man, that is to say, criticism of the *caudillo*, that Hispano-Arab inheritance.

Paz saw the task as immense. It was not enough for the writer to resist the seduction of power. (Paz preferred the term "writer" [*escritor*] to the word "intellectual" [*intelectual*]. There was another, more incisive power: "the fascination of orthodoxy." And, starting from this assertion, Paz, for the first time (in the October 1972 issue of *Plural*) hints at a direct criticism of the central myth of his century and his life, the Revolution:

> The history of modern literature, from the German and English romantics till our own day, is the story of a long unfortunate passion for politics. From Coleridge to Mayakowski, the Revolution has been the great Goddess, the eternal Beloved and the great Whore of poets and novelists.

The criticism poured into the poetry of *El cántaro roto* has become movement and action. Paz had criticized power as personified, each avatar filling the role in turn of the "fat chieftain": the Tlatoani, the Spanish priest, the viceroy, the *caudillo*, the president, the banker, the corrupt political leader. Now he would begin to exercise a dissident form of criticism, of ideologies and orthodoxy, of the Revolution itself.

WHILE A sector of Mexican and Latin American intellectuals dreamed of resorting to (or would actually conduct) the "criticism of arms"

or else entrust "the weapons of criticism" to the comandante of the
Cuban Revolution, Gabriel Zaid—who had published a poem against
Díaz Ordaz—was a solitary dissident. After the "mini-Tlatelolco" of
June 10, 1971, however, even the director of *Siempre!* did not dare to
publish Zaid's assertion that "the only historic criminal is Luis Echeverría." Zaid resigned in protest and some months later became a
member of the editorial board of *Plural.* Octavio Paz had called for
criticism of the Mexican political pyramid and the need for finding an
alternative model of development. A poet and essayist of considerable
and original talent, Zaid (in his monthly column, "Moebius Strip") addressed both issues. His articles, elegant as theorems—later collected
in his book *El progreso improductivo* (Improductive Progress)—asserted
that the continued existence of poverty in Mexico demonstrated the
failure of the statist model of modernization.

A new project had to be designed (as Paz had insisted) and Zaid offered
various possibilities meant to affect Mexico's huge population of rural and
urban poor. Among them were ideas like support for microbusinesses,
the establishment of a bank for the impoverished (a direct foreshadowing
of the Grameen Bank of Bangladesh, which would earn its founder, Mu-
hammad Yunus, the Nobel Peace Prize in 2006), and the direct payment
of cash to members of the poorest part of the population, with most of
it going directly to women (an idea accepted in the 1990s by the government, to become a social program acclaimed both nationally and abroad).
Once adopted, these ideas of Zaid seemed totally natural measures.

ANOTHER SORT of political criticism demanded by Paz was the criticism of dogma. Aggrieved by the twofold assault of 1968 and 1971,
attracted by the images and the ideas of Che Guevara, a portion of Mexican youth was growing more and more impatient and moving toward
armed insurrection. Paz saw in these young people the very image of
his high school comrades in the 1930s—"boys of the middle class who
transform their obsessions and personal fantasies into ideological fantasies in which 'the end of the world' assumes the paradoxical form of
a proletarian revolution . . . without the proletariat."

Paz used Marxist categories to criticize the Latin American guerrilla movements. He considered them an anachronistic version of the "Blanquism" repudiated by Marx and Engels. (Louis Blanqui was a nineteenth-century French revolutionary who championed—and devoted his life to—violent uprisings against established power.)

> Perhaps it is not completely correct to call these Latin-American extremists "blanquistas." Luis Blanqui was a romantic revolutionary who belongs to the prehistory of revolution (though some of his theses show a disturbing resemblance to Leninism). In any case, the ideology of the Latin-Americans is a "blanquism" that does not recognize itself. Perhaps more precisely it is a terrorist reading of Marxism.

The new Mexican left, unlike in the 1930s, was not made up of union members, the Communist Party, progressive groups within the regime (of whom there were many under President Lázaro Cárdenas), and, in lesser number, by artists and intellectuals, The new Mexican left was formed, above all, of middle-class, university-trained young people (and this was its great novelty). Paz would characterize them (and in some sense address them) with these words written in 1973:

> The left is the natural heir of the movement of 1968 but, in recent years, it has not been committed to democratic organization but to the representation—drama and farce—of the revolution, using the universities as their theaters. Perverted by many years of Stalinism, influenced by Castroist *caudillismo* and Guevarist blanquism, the Mexican left has not been able to recover its original democratic vocation. Moreover, in recent years, it has not been distinguished for its political imagination: what is its concrete program and what does it propose now—not in some improbable future—to Mexicans? . . . Incapable of elaborating a program of viable reforms, they struggle between nihilism and millenarianism, activism and utopianism. The spasmodic and the

contemplative modes: two ways to escape from reality. The road to reality passes through democratic organization. The public plaza—not the cloister or the catacombs—is the site for politics.

IN OCTOBER 1973, Paz published a protest against the CIA-sponsored military coup in Chile. His rejection of Latin American militarism is explicit, continuous, and total. He includes a sentence on the "bloody hands of Nixon and Kissinger" and fully supports the (demolished) democratic regime in Chile but he also gives more space to a criticism of leftist extremism, which he accuses of contributing to the fall of Allende by alienating the middle class and small businessmen. The panorama of politics in Latin America he sees as growing darker and more radical. On the one hand are the "reactionary military dictatorship" in Chile, populist militarism in Peru, techno-military dictatorship in Brazil, and, at the other extreme, the growth of the Guevarist guerrilla movements. "Latin America is a continent of rhetorical and violent men." Despite the tragedy of Chile—or due to it—he is convinced that "socialism without democracy is not socialism."

In the winter of 1973, in the home of Harvard professor Harry Levin, Paz met the Russian poet in exile Joseph Brodsky (who had been expelled from Russia a year earlier for his dissident opinions). It was an encounter that catalyzed Paz's own political reorientation. His disenchantment with the Soviet Union—which perhaps began in 1937—had been gradual but steadily growing stronger. Now he met with the reality of a writer who had been persecuted in the Soviet Union. Their conversation turned to a discussion of Marxist authoritarianism. Paz brought up Hegel, and Brodsky said that he thought the problem dated back to Descartes, "who divided man in two and substituted the soul for the ego." To the Americans, Paz remembered, the use of the word "soul" seemed odd. Paz commented to Brodsky, "All that you've said reminds me of Chestov, the Christian philosopher of the absurd, Berdyaev's maestro." Brodsky was very moved: "What a pleasure to meet someone *here* who remembers Chestov! Here, at the heart of scientism, empiricism and logical positivism . . . This could only happen with a Latin-American poet!"

Brodsky's living testimony on the fate of writers in Russia greatly disturbed Paz. Soon after he would read Solzhenitsyn's *The Gulag Archipelago*. The reading closed the cycle of change for him and began a complementary cycle of contrition. On March 31 he would be sixty years old. During four nights in February he wrote a series of short poems titled *Aunque es de noche* (Although It Is Night), an anti-Stalinist suite. "Stalin had no soul: he had history / An uninhabited Marshal with no face, servant of the void." The reading of Solzhenitsyn had freed him: "Solzhenitsyn writes. Our dawn is moral: writing in flames, flower of conflagration, flower of truth." But he, Paz, blames himself: "Coward, I never saw evil right in front of me."

The poems appeared in the March issue of *Plural*, accompanied by an essay central to his later work: "Powder of That Mud" (both words are plural in the Spanish: *Polvos de aquellos lodos*). More than an essay, it is a trial and a judgment on Bolshevism and Marxism, on his former "point of view," and a severe judgment on himself. "That mud" is his, his youthful reading, his fixed beliefs, the truths not seen, the truths never spoken. The text begins with an epigram from Montaigne: "J'ai souvent ouy dire que la couardise est mere de cruauté." ("I have often heard it said that cowardice is the mother of cruelty."). With obsessive exactitude, he remembers—as if to redeem himself before himself and the tribunal of history—that he had denounced Stalin's camps in 1951 and that he had been subjected to accusations by orthodox Stalinists since the 1940s (when he had criticized the socialist aesthetic and quarreled with Neruda). They had dubbed him a cosmopolite, a formalist, a Trotskyist, and then there had been the more recent accusations: CIA agent, "liberal intellectual," "structuralist at the service of the bourgeoisie." But the recounting alone did not console him. As a result of his intense conversation with Brodsky, and in order to situate Solzhenitsyn intellectually in a tradition of dissidence (as well as, more modestly, himself), Paz reviews the tradition of "Russian spirituality" relating

Solzhenitsyn (and Brodsky) to Chestov, Nikolai Berdyaev, Dostoyevsky, and Soloviev, all Christian critics of the modern era. He is moved by the moral force of that tradition but also stresses his own "tradition" (Blake, Thoreau, Nietzsche) and especially "those who were irreducible and incorruptible—Breton, Russell, and Camus and some few others, some dead and some living who did not yield nor have they yielded to the totalitarian seduction of communism and fascism or the comfort of the consumer society." Did Paz consider himself to be among "those few others"? He will, by the end of the essay.

It was perhaps the first time that Paz quoted Bertrand Russell. He also referred for the first time and at length to a book by the dissident Soviet physicist Andrei Sakharov (published in France in 1968) and Hannah Arendt's *Origins of Totalitarianism* (first published in 1951) and two more recent authors who dealt with the aftermath of the revolutionary passion in Russia (James Billington) and the atrocities under Bolshevism (Robert Conquest). The work of Solzhenitsyn especially seemed to Paz a matchless testimony, in the religious sense of the term, "in the century of false testimonies, a writer became a witness for man." (He would repeatedly defend Solzhenitsyn for his devastating exposure of the gulag system, against Mexican critics who considered Solzhenitsyn "pro-imperialist." But he also mentioned the archaic and racist Slavic nationalism of the great Russian dissident.)

In the essay, Paz continues the trial. In the dock of the accused he places some of the classics he had so admired, especially Lenin's *The State and the Revolution*, his former bedtime reading. He is still moved by its "enflamed semi-anarchism" but cannot close his eyes to the role of Lenin as the founder of the Cheka and the innovator (at least for the Bolshevik regime) of terror. Trotsky and Bukharin are filtered through the same sieve: "eminent men though tragically mistaken" yet in no way comparable to "a monster like Stalin." Could Marx and Engels themselves be saved? Partially, for Paz. He recognizes the "germs of authoritarianism" in the mature thought of both writers but he considers the case less severe than with Lenin and Trotsky. Toward the end, the argument leads, unexpectedly, to Bertrand Russell, whose

essential objection to Marx was his disastrous abandonment of democracy. Here was another innovation. For the first time—though
within a quote from Russell—he writes the word "democracy." Not
"democratization" but democracy. And he points to the double standard with which the Latin American left treated "formal freedoms,"
protesting their suppression in Chile while tolerating their repression
in Russia or Czechoslovakia (Paz does not mention Cuba). Certainly
one had to oppose American imperialism, its racism and its unjust
capitalist system, and one had to denounce "caesarism" (the imprisonment of the Uruguayan writer Onetti, Pinochet's slaughter in
Chile, torture in Brazil), and the existence of *"ciudad Netzahualcóyotl*
with its million human beings living a sub-human life at the very
gates of Mexico City forbids us any hypocritical complacency." But
"formal freedoms" had to be defended. Without freedom "of opinion
and expression, of association and movement, the right to say *no* to
power—there is no fraternity, or justice, or hope of equality." The
encounter with Brodsky and the reading of Solzhenitsyn had made
him return, for the first time, to one of his own traditions, even older
than his high school anarchist readings, the liberal tradition of his
grandfather, the same historical strain that, invited by Paz, Daniel
Cosío Villegas defended in the pages of *Plural*.

But the time had not yet come for Paz to affirm and identify himself with that tradition. On the verge of his sixtieth year, he was now
immersed in a process of self-analysis and contrition. He thought of
Aragon, Éluard, Neruda, and other famous poets and writers who had
written in favor of Stalin and he compared "the shudder I feel when I
read certain passages of Dante's *Inferno*." He justified the generous impulse of his youth in supporting the victims and opposing imperialism.
But he warned that "unknowingly, from compromise to compromise,
men find themselves entangled in a net of lies, falsehoods, deceptions
and perjuries until they lose their souls."

One more defendant had to stand trial: Octavio Paz. Could he be
"saved"? No, at least not completely. And he would apply the notion
with an unexpected Christian overtone:

I will add that our political opinions on this subject have not been mere errors or failings in our capacity of judgment. They were a sin, in the ancient religious sense of the word: something that affects the entire being. Very few of us would be able to look a Solzhenitsyn or a Nadezdha Mandelstam in the eyes. This sin has stained us and has also fatally stained our writings. I say this with sadness and humility.

PAZ AT the same time was writing one of his most famous poems: Nocturne of San Ildefonso (*Nocturno de San Ildefonso*—the building that housed his preparatory school), a long poem about returning to the sites of his youth in Mexico City:

> *We were carried along*
> *by the wind of thought*
> *the verbal wind . . .*
>
> *The good, we wanted the good:*
> *to straighten out the world*

But Paz's outlook is not, as in '68, festive and hopeful. He finds no joy in his return to the '30s because he has confronted the reality that resulted from that revolutionary passion. He has seen history, *his* history:

> *Circular scenario:*
> *we all have been*
> *in the Great Theater of Filth.*
> *judges, executioners, victims, witnesses*
> *all*
> *have given false testimony*
> *against the others*
> *and against ourselves.*
> *And the vilest thing: we were*
> *the public that applauded or yawned in their armchairs.*

The guilt that did not know its guilt,

innocence

was the greatest guilt.

Each year was a mountain of bones.

Conversions, retractions, excommunications,

reconciliations, apostasies, retractions,

zig-zag of the demonolatries and the androlatries,

the bewitchments and the deviations:

my history . . .

Each line, each word seems to refer to a fact, a person, a concrete episode. With those who "yawned in their armchairs," is he remembering the Congress of Writers in Valencia during the Spanish Civil War, dealing with the proposed condemnation of Gide for his criticism of the Soviet Union? Was Paz innocent because he did not know, because he half knew, because he did not wish to know, because he felt himself innocent? Was he guilty of innocence? "Now we know," he would write, "that the splendor, which seemed to us the coming of the dawn, was a blood-soaked, burning pyre." He had believed in that splendor, in that dawn, believed in it too long. His faith in Marxism had lasted to the end of the 1960s. He would dedicate the final three decades of his life to purging that "sin." And in dealing with the subject, his words would always display the weight of a profound religious conflict, lived at a depth Paz had previously left almost unexplored, the Christianity inculcated by his mother that had formed the very foundation of Mexican identity.

XIV

Plural had remained faithful to Paz's resolutions. He had kept the magazine at a distance from the government. His first objective (a serious criticism of the PRI) was furthered in the pages of *Plural* by Paz himself and, most especially, three other contributors. Daniel Cosío Villegas

systematically analyzed the antidemocratic usages of the PRI and denounced the "personal style" (rhetorical, wasteful, often rife with meg-
alomania) of the successive oligarchs in the Presidential Chair. Richard
Morse published a piece in which he sustained that Mexico still lived
under the cultural paradigm of neo-Thomistic thinking produced by
Spain in the seventeenth century and represented chiefly by Francisco
Suárez. Gabriel Zaid concentrated on the serious consequences (in the
1970s) of economic policy controlled by a single man: severe currency
devaluation (which would reach 100 percent), a sixfold increase in foreign debt, double-digit inflation, the loss of stability and of potential
growth. And by publishing writers like Brodsky, Aron, Kolakowski,
and Djilas, Paz opposed the dominant ideological current in Mexico,
which he vilified as "worthless people defending their Dogma, who
dress like bearded guerrillas and are revolutionary a la Guevara." But
he also complained that "except for two or three isolated figures,"
almost all the Mexicans who wrote for *Plural* showed no interest in
political and ideological criticism.

Meanwhile, young thinkers on the left continued their verbal attacks against him: he had abandoned the left, he was now on the right,
he was doing the work of the government, he was "a liberal" (which,
strictly speaking, he was not, least of all in his economic preferences).
Paz responded with language that grew more and more bitter, qualify-
ing intellectual life in Mexico as "mean-spirited" and "heinous [*infame*]."
His personal solution was the same as always:

> One has to write, to write—black on white—while the presidents,
> the executives, the bankers, the dogmatics and the swine, laid out
> on immense mountains of three-colored [referring to the Mexican
> flag] garbage or just entirely red, talk, listen to each other, digest,
> defecate and go back to talking.

Plural was swimming against the current even within its own host
newspaper, *Excélsior*, where Julio Scherer had to continually defend Paz
against those who considered him an elitist and no longer of practical

worth to the newspaper. Even his most recent book of essays published in Spain, *Los hijos del limo* (The Sons of the Slime, published in translation as *Children of the Mire*), an ambitious meditation on romantic poetry and its relation to the modern avant-garde, only received two reviews in Mexico, described by Paz as "one of them incompetent and the other distracted, inexact and with its embellishments of ill will." Earlier he had vented his dissatisfaction with the Mexican intellectual climate to his friend Tomlinson:

> Mexico makes me suffer but I make the Mexicans suffer. At times I think they don't like me but I am exaggerating: I don't exist, I don't belong, I'm not one of them. The same happened to Reyes, the same is happening to Tamayo. Their painter is Siqueiros—they adore him. And their true poet should have been Neruda . . . What bad luck they have had with me—and I with them.

Life in Mexico seemed almost unbearable for him, but he knew that, sometime soon, he would have to return physically and live in his native country. Except for five years (1954–59) the parenthesis of his exile had lasted twenty-five years. Soon he would have to find his way back.

XV

His poetry had begun that return, veering away from the avant-garde and its emphasis on experimentation, returning to a more classical (though still free verse style), returning to the examination of his fundamental beliefs, returning to his origins. In 1975 Paz wrote (in the vein of *Nocturno de San Ildefonso*) one of his longest and most celebrated poems, *Pasado en claro* (Clean Copy, or The Past Turned Clear and Clean, though it has been previously translated into English, by Eliot Weinberger, as A Draft of Shadows). The poem is no longer the site of memory, the revelation and consecration of the past, but rather the magic corridor that leads the poet "to the encounter with himself." And here appear—with the wonder of the past suddenly renewed—the "big house" in Mixcoac "foundered in time," "the patio, the wall, the ash tree, the well," the garden and the trees, the (tastes, colors, stalls) of the plaza and its swarming humanity. There appears "the fig tree, its fallacies and its wisdom"—and for the first time in this remembered setting, Octavio Paz himself appears, reading at night in the library:

> By the light of the lamp—the night
> now mistress of the house and the ghost
> of my grandfather now master of the night—
> I would penetrate into the silence,
> body without body, time
> without hours. Each night,
> transparent machines of delirium
> within me the books were building
> architectures raised upon a chasm.
> A breath of the spirit raises them,
> a blink of the eye undoes them.

It is the child within the first circle of his solitary labyrinth:

> Child among taciturn adults
> and their terrible childishness,
> child along the corridors with high doors
> rooms with portraits
> crepuscular brotherhoods of the missing
> child survivor
> of the mirrors with no memory . . .

"In my house the dead were more than the living." And the poet sketches in some of them. His mother, Josefina, "a child a thousand years old, mother of the world, my orphan," and his aunt Amalia, "a virgin talking in her sleep" who "taught [him] to see with eyes closed, to see within and through the wall." The memory of his grandfather Ireneo is soft and sweet, but that of his father, Octavio, is sorrowful:

> *Between vomiting and thirst,*
> *lashed to the colt of alcohol,*
> *my father passed back and forth in flames.*
> *Among the rails and the crossties*
> *of a fly-blown, dusty railroad station,*
> *one evening, we picked up the pieces of him.*

In life, there was silence. In death, there is a dialogue, where the two never confront the horror of the elder Octavio's death:

> *I could never speak with him*
> *I meet him now in dreams,*
> *that blurry fatherland of the dead.*
> *We always talk about other things.*

The theme of the father appears again, ennobled by politics, in a long interview Paz gave in November 1975, titled "Return to The Labyrinth of Solitude." He reveals some previously unknown details of his own personal and historical genealogy. When the questions turn to Zapatismo, the tone of his responses intensifies and he hammers home the filial connection, historical and personal, with his father. "From that time on my father thought that Zapatismo was the truth about Mexico. I think that he was right." The subject leads him to evoke the friendship of his father with the Indian peasants to the south of Mexico City, the defense of their lands and even the delights of the pre-Columbian delicacy, "mudded duck," that he ate with his father in the villages. The conjunction of tradition and revolution, a mark of Zapatismo, had "impassioned" him. "Zapatismo was a revelation, the coming to the surface of certain hidden and repressed realities." More than a revolution or a rebellion, it was a revolt (*revuelta*), a turn and return (*vuelta*) of deepest Mexico and a movement toward that profundity. "Zapata," he concluded, "was beyond the controversy between liberals and conservatives, Marxists and neocapitalists. Zapata exists *before*—and, perhaps, if Mexico does not extinguish itself—he will exist *afterwards*."

Poems, interviews, the recuperation of historic and family origins, of the landscape of infancy and juvenile geography, acts of contrition, examinations of conscience, confessions—all ways for the past to turn clear and clean—foreshadowings of his return to Mexico.

XVI

On March 10, 1976, when Daniel Cosío Villegas died, Paz was already back in Mexico. Since the 1950s they had frequently been in disagreement and had never really been friends. Cosío Villegas had stood neither with the government nor with the left. He was, by his own definition, "a museum quality Liberal" and a moderate nationalist. He enjoyed immense public prestige. Paz attended his funeral, alone, with a serious and thoughtful demeanor, keeping himself toward the rear of the mourners. He would dedicate the April issue (number 55) of *Plural* to Cosío's memory. His own deeply felt contribution was an article titled "Illusions and Convictions." It was a dialogue with the historical vision of Cosío Villegas, who had considered the political liberalism of the nineteenth century, as expressed in the federal Constitution of 1857, to be the cornerstone of modern Mexico. He had also contended that both the long dictatorship of Don Porfirio and the governments of the Revolution had abandoned this project of constitutional liberalism to replace it with a centralized state, monopolizing power. This movement had led—at least until 1970—to a notable material modernization of the country but had seriously limited political progress. Cosío had felt that the social aims of the Revolution (such as the agrarian reform, labor legislation, and universal education) were not incompatible with democracy and freedom. The central problem of Mexico was the need for political reform—limiting the concentration of power in the hands of the president and developing a system of government that would be more open, free, and responsible. Strangely, though, he never really treated the theme of electoral democracy.

Paz experienced Mexican history with autobiographical passion but his emphasis (and really his knowledge) were not those of an historian but of a philosopher and poet of history. Like Cosío, he was a son of the Mexican Revolution and shared his ideas on the positive "constructive" aspect of the governments that succeeded it, but he still considered the constitutional liberalism of the nineteenth century as an "abject" period, a historical *fall*, the imposition of a European doctrine upon a reality alien to it, a tragic negation of the indigenous and Spanish roots of Mexico. Paz was not advocating an impossible return to those roots but calling for a creative synthesis of the three "Mexicos": the Indian, the Spanish/Catholic, and the modern. (He never spoke of the most striking synthesis in Mexican cultural history, *mestizaje*, the "mixing" of races physically and culturally.) In his historical judgment, the three Mexicos should have carried on a fruitful interchange but the political suppression of the Conservatives in the nineteenth century, accomplished by the Liberal reform of Benito Juárez, had driven a part of Mexico's profound reality (which the Conservatives represented) underground. But it had proceeded to insinuate itself surreptitiously into the political life of the country, enthroning "the Lie." Through this striking, almost Freudian explication, Paz would explain, for example, the conservatism of the PRI, the formal heir to liberalism but, in his view, the actual descendant of the centralist and even monarchical thought of the nineteenth-century Conservatives.

Though Paz and Cosío differed significantly in their historical overviews, they agreed on one premise: the need for free discussion of problems, causes, projects. Cosío Villegas, the liberal nationalist, would have wanted the PRI itself to lead a political and moral renovation. Paz, as an "anti-authoritarian" socialist, had trusted in the rise of a party and project of the left but he now considered his hopes to be vain illusions. He recognized the public trajectory of Cosío Villegas—a half century of service as an editor, essayist, historian, diplomat, and critic—to have been marked by clarity and bravery. "Cosío Villegas, with a smile, passed through the funereal dance of disguises that is our public life and emerged clean, undamaged . . . upright, ironic and incorruptible." As an epigraph to the article, Paz used a quotation from W. B. Yeats: "He served human liberty."

In July 1976, freedom of expression in Mexico suffered a blow that confirmed Cosío Villegas's contention that Mexico needed to impose a legal and institutional limit on the power of the president. Tired of the criticisms directed at his policies in the pages of *Excélsior*, President Echeverría orchestrated a coup against Julio Scherer within the *Excélsior* cooperative. Scherer left the newspaper and a few months later founded *Proceso*, a magazine of news and analysis that would become Mexico's most respected weekly magazine right up to the present day. Paz and the writers of *Plural* resigned in solidarity with Scherer. They soon decided to start a new, independent intellectual journal.

To assemble the small amount of initial capital needed, a raffle was held to which 763 people gave donations. The prize was a painting donated by Rufino Tamayo and the winner was a young and promising Oxford-educated philosopher, Hugo Margáin Charles.

The collaborators met to decide on a proper name for the new journal. Paz was about to publish a new collection of poems, with the same introspective tilt as in *Pasado en claro*. It would be entitled *Vuelta* and in its keynote poem with the same title, Paz had raised the question:

> *I have returned where I began*
> Have I won or lost?
> (Questions
> What laws determine "success" and "failure"?
> The songs of the fishermen float by
> before the motionless shore.

The last four lines are Paz's rendering from an English translation of a poem by the great Chinese poet and painter Wang Wei (699–759 A.D.) who, in the autumn of his life, now without "eagerness to return," distances himself "from the world and its struggles" to "forget his learning among the trees." Paz, in the autumn of his life, chooses a different path, which, within the poem, closes the above parenthesis:

> *But I do not want*
> *an intellectual hermitage*
> *in San Angel or Coyoacán)* [districts of Mexico City where many intellectuals then lived].

And the new review would not be intended as an intellectual hermitage but more precisely a fortress. Alejandro Rossi suggested the name. Paz had his doubts but then agreed. It would be called *Vuelta*, a word with the double meaning of "return" and "change of direction."

XVII

The magazine set up its offices very near the "big house" of Don Ireneo, in the same quarter of Mixcoac where Paz had grown up. It was a small building with two floors, the first very small but large enough for meetings, the second with offices for the deputy editor and the proofreader. The street adjoined an old market and a pulque bar.

The first issue came out in November 1976. It seemed as if the mechanics of publication did not require Paz to live in Mexico. When he was out of the country, the magazine was administered by its assistant director, Alejandro Rossi, assisted by José de la Colina as literary editor. Paz seemed happy with his partial return and with the journal. At the beginning of 1977, he completed an authorized compendium of the work he wished to preserve, his *Obra poética*. A poem written in 1977 is interesting for its attitude toward Mixcoac and the ambiguity he felt about returning to Mexico. It was called *Epitafio sobre ninguna piedra* (Epitaph Upon No Stone), in the style of a memorial poem from *The Greek Anthology*:

> *Mixcoac was my village. Three nocturnal syllables:*
> *a mask of shadow over a face of sun.*

Our Lady came, the Dustcloud Mother.
Came and ate it up. I went off through the world.
My words were my house, my tomb the air.

Things quickly became more complicated for Paz. He returned to Cambridge, England, but in March a cancer was discovered. He underwent a successful operation, but it left its traces. Meanwhile, Rossi and Gabriel Zaid (who had articulated a plan for the business aspect of the journal) recommended me to Paz. I was to become Deputy Editor and general administrator of the magazine. After his operation, the Editor in Chief, Octavio Paz, returned in good spirits to Mexico. From then on, though he would often leave the country, he would never spend long periods attached to foreign universities. He now, for the first time, had a journal that was really his own, modest, with a limited number of pages, without the color supplements of *Plural*, but much more independently *his* than *Barandal, Taller, El hijo pródigo,* and even *Plural* had ever been.

He would write: "We abandoned *Plural* so as not to lose our independence, we publish *Vuelta* to continue being independent." That independence had, first of all, to be financial. Depending entirely on the government (the traditional mode in Mexico) would force him to negotiate the journal's editorial line. It would be desirable but impossible to depend entirely on buyers and subscribers (who would never number more than ten thousand). Paz and his collaborators opted for a balance, accepting a degree of government sponsorship but looking for funds in a direction formerly unthinkable (for an intellectual journal): the private sector. *Plural* had been completely financed by the newspaper *Excélsior. Vuelta* had no such luxury. After much effort, various national and foreign companies were persuaded to purchase advertisements in the journal. Subscriptions began to arrive, from Mexico and abroad. The journal showed a modest profit. It was a viable enterprise.

For the next twenty-two years, *Vuelta* would be Paz's fortress but also his literary workshop. In his apartment on the historic avenue of the Paseo de la Reforma he set up his library, a replica of his first library in Mixcoac, with his grandfather's books all included. He would phone the journal daily and discuss articles, reviews, translations, stories, poems, which he had previously sent to them by messenger. He kept up with dozens of European, American, and Latin American publications, and he maintained contact with hundreds of authors and publishing houses. He never hired a literary agent. Alfonso Reyes, the prolific man of letters who had preceded Octavio Paz as the presiding eminence of Mexican literature, had once complained that "Latin America is a late arrival at the feast of world culture." Since his early youth, Paz had decided to join that feast, and *Vuelta* would set out places for the earliest companions of his intellectual life: Ortega y Gasset, Sartre, Camus, Breton, Buñuel, Vasconcelos. But *Vuelta* would also create a banquet of its own, with the literary presence of hundreds of writers from various continents and generations.

Literature was the center of Paz's life. His library was his intellectual hermitage and he never maintained an office in the *Vuelta* building. (He had spent too many years of his life working in offices.) He taught no classes at Mexican universities. Conversation with him in person or by telephone was a constant exploration. Although he admitted having the "irritable nature" that Horace ascribes to poets (especially in the morning), he was invariably serious about all issues. But he could also show an almost childlike enthusiasm in the breadth and degree of his intellectual curiosity. Large themes fascinated him and he wrote about them at length: reflections on poetic creation and language; articles on the course of Western poetry from the enthusiasms of Romanticism to the ironic vision of the modern avant-garde, in which he compared not only works in different languages but placed them against the background of other, non-Western poetics; his thoughts on modern culture, politics, and society, always emphasizing the need for a careful, critical outlook on the world. And he was excited by new scientific discoveries or intellectual inquiries: the latest theory on the Big Bang, debates about the nature of the mind or the decipherment of the Mayan script. Then unexpectedly signaled by a sudden change of gesture or of manner, his conversation would swerve toward unpredictable subjects:

French erotic literature of the eighteenth century, medieval theories on love or melancholy.

Now, at the age of sixty-three, Paz seemed to have, on the personal level, everything he could wish for: romantic love, the affection of new and old friends, material stability, independence. In Europe especially, his books sold well. Some of them, especially *El laberinto* itself and *Libertad bajo palabra*, had become classics in Mexico. And he would have the time and enough concentration to write a major work centering around the poetess he saw as his poetic counterpart in certain essential ways: Sor Juana Inés de la Cruz, of the seventeenth century.

He would return to the 1930s in a polemic and guilt-ridden mode, fighting with his abandoned faith and an earlier version of himself. He published a new version of his Yucatán poem *Entre la piedra y la flor*, intense in its own way but stripped of what he now considered ideology and rhetoric. And the political stance of the magazine was strongly anti-Marxist and anti-Soviet, supporting the dissident writers of Eastern Europe (such as Kundera and Michnik) and contemporaries who, like himself, had turned against their Marxist past, though in varying degrees (Kolakowski, Furet, Besançon, Bell, Howe, Jean Daniel, Castoriadis, Enzensberger) as well as similar critics in the Spanish-speaking countries. Perhaps most offensive to Mexican leftist intellectuals was his promotion of the "new philosophers" of France (particularly Bernard-Henri Lévy and André Glucksmann) who had rejected Sartre and championed Camus, coupled with invitations—some of which were accepted—to speak on Mexican television.

PAZ WAS a man who lived in a constant state of exaltation. He looked like a lion with a full mane and that was how he behaved in his ideological quarrels. In his polemical persona, there was an echo of those dinner-table discussions in his Mixcoac childhood between his grandfather Ireneo and his father, Octavio. But now the positions had changed. He was sitting in his grandfather's chair and the young Mexicans, angry or idealist, who opposed his views assumed the role of his father or even, it might be said, his own role as a young pro-Bolshevik who had dreamed of being a hero or a martyr. He had returned to Mexico to rid himself of ambiguities but he encountered the greatest ambiguity of them all: the Revolution—in its avatar of the 1970s and '80s—had entranced the Generation of '68 and (perhaps even more) the succeeding generation. And it was neither liberal nor anarchist but strongly suffused with orthodox Marxism.

Paz would insist that his intense disagreements with the Mexican left stemmed from the fact that he was still a socialist: "perhaps the only rational solution to the crisis of the West." His resignation as ambassador to India in 1968 had been an act of solidarity with rebellious youth and had been warmly received and recognized as such. But, as his present views became clearer, his claims were rejected. The young left especially did not believe him. Paz, not them, had changed.

And Paz had changed, but not to the extent of favoring capitalist values or even liberal democracy. His basic disillusionment was with the communist faith of his youth, and at least in Europe, many thinkers and writers and activists were moving in the same direction. There was the growing, active dissidence in Russia and the countries of the communist bloc, which Milan Kundera described as "kidnapped Europe." In Western Europe, the various currents of "Eurocommunism" (which were not completely anti-Marxist), the transitions to democracy in Spain and Portugal, the positions of some thinkers in Germany and France (eventually even including Sartre) signaled the decline of Marxism. Dissident movements in the east involved more danger to participants' lives and freedom than the revolts in Berkeley or Paris. Young people opposing the Vietnamese War or capitalism in general had been killed or maimed by police in the United States or in Europe but the numbers were small (though not overseas in Vietnam) compared to an event like the Russian repression of the Czech uprising. But in Latin America—and even in Mexico—the dead were by no means few. The students and professors in Mexico could not ignore the fact that protest in Mexico had been met in 1968 with the mass slaughter of Tlatelolco and then the "mini-slaughter" of June 10, 1971. In 1973, the university students (and much of the world) were shocked by the military coup in

Chile and the death of Salvador Allende. It was a death (and the obliteration of socialism in Chile followed by the Pinochet regime of torture and murder) that many young people felt as a personal assault. Here was threefold evidence for them that social revolution was the only viable path.

Paz's writings and public statements at the time showed an impatient quality. He was exasperated by what he considered the romanticized ignorance and blindness about the real conditions within the Russian and Chinese spheres (an ignorance and blindness that to a sensibility like Paz's was made all the worse because he himself had once shared them). He feared that the countries of Latin America were plunging downward, in a landslide of revolutionary violence that could lead either to consummately brutal military dictatorships or a totalitarianism of the left such as he saw developing in Cuba. The first alternative had already swept away political freedom in Chile, Uruguay, and Argentina. Aside from Cuba, the second possibility was vested in guerrilla uprisings and was strongly present in Colombia, several countries of Central America, and partially in Venezuela. Neither result seemed impossible for Mexico. If the 1930s had not created a democratic space between the two extremes, the '70s should attempt it. Paz saw this revision of the scenario of the '30s as his dissident mission.

His young critics wanted exactly the opposite: to renew, revivify, and accomplish that scenario. Their largest contingent consisted of university students who—with the increased opportunities for education offered by the Echeverría government—had greatly increased in number and were becoming more and more radical. Echeverría was obsessed with washing away his considerable complicity in the slaughter of '68 and spent much effort in reaching out to academics and students (including a huge increment in subsidies to the public universities). Not without reason, he saw student discontent as a danger, a potential spark of revolution. And notwithstanding these efforts, a segment of students decided to emulate Che Guevara and joined guerrilla foci in the mountains of the state of Guerrero or turned to urban terrorism. Against them the government launched Mexico's own "dirty war," much smaller in scope (and body count) than the repressions in Central America or the Southern Cone but still ferocious. Another segment of the young left joined numerous militant groups that supported workers' strikes, organized in factories, or established connections designed to assist the Guatemalan guerrillas, who were fighting perhaps the most savage among the savage armies of the region. Most of them eventually became affiliated with public universities or preparatory schools, a number of them created in the 1970s.

The influence of the Mexican Communist Party (the PCM) was also growing on the campuses, not only among professors and students but also the workers in the powerful university union. Like other parties and sects of the left more or less connected with Moscow or with Trotskyism, the PCM had been a marginal organization for decades, with some presence in public sector unions like the railwaymen and the teachers. But the public universities of the 1970s provided the PCM with an ideal growth environment.

While Marxism was going out of fashion among many European intellectuals, its influence was growing exponentially in Mexican universities. In Mexico it had been a doctrine favored by labor leaders (Vicente Lombardo Toledano), visual artists (Rivera, Kahlo, Siqueiros), romantic revolutionaries (like José Revueltas), and a few offbeat millionaires (such as Víctor Manuel Villaseñor and Ricardo J. Zevada). But its academic and intellectual legitimacy was recent, dating primarily from the 1960s, and owed much to the influence of Sartre and the immense and continuing prestige of the Cuban Revolution. The journals and cultural supplements that preceded *Plural*—the *Revista de la Universidad* and *La cultura en México,* among others—were supporters of the Cuban Revolution and continued to be so even after a case like the falsified "Confessions" of Heberto Padilla. Any criticism paled before the educational and social achievements of the Cuban Revolution and its gallant defiance of the U.S "Empire."

New courses in Marxism appeared in many fields of study. The UAM, a new public university, included Marxism even in its curriculum for graphic design. A brilliant student in this field wrote his thesis on the Marxist philosopher Louis Althusser. His name was Rafael Sebastián Guillén Vicente, and like many other young Mexicans, he would go to Cuba and Nicaragua to learn the techniques of guerrilla warfare. In 1983 he would disappear into the jungles of Chiapas, taking a guerrilla alias that many years later would become legendary: Subcomandante Marcos.

A publishing house was needed to supply the rising interest in Marxist literature. Siglo XXI Editores, under its director Arnaldo Orfila Reynal (originally an Argentine *arielista* who had directed, with great taste and discernment, the Fondo de Cultura Económica between 1947 and 1965) fulfilled that requirement, establishing a close connection in 1965 with the Casa de las Américas of Cuba. Mutually they intended to publish a systematic edition of all the fundamental Marxist works. Hundreds of thousands of copies were sold of the works of Che Guevara or the writings of the Chilean Marta Harnecker, who had fled for her life to Cuba after the Pinochet-led coup.

Refugees from the Southern Cone were another factor contributing to the process of radicalization. Persecuted by the newly installed governments of Uruguay, Chile, and Argentina erected on the pillars of torture and extermination, profoundly angered at the United States for its patronage of the coup against Allende, many distinguished professors and other intellectuals entered the universities of Mexico. They were the new refugees, welcomed by Mexico as others had been. Finally, the new attitude of the Catholic Church after the Second Vatican Council created its own leftward-moving current. Many students who had studied with the Jesuits were especially impressed and moved by the decision of the order to move from its traditional role in educating the elite toward helping the Mexican poor.

For this Marxist universe, Octavio Paz was the great heretic. It was a status that deeply offended him and maintained him in a state of exaltation and constant readiness for combat. From the time he returned to Mexico, he would live with a drawn sword.

———

HIS MOST frequent accusation against the left was that of "intellectual sterility." He lamented what he termed its "strange idealism: reality at the service of the idea and the idea at the service of History." He accused the left of a moral double standard, justifiably indignant and saddened by the crimes of Latin American right-wing dictatorships in Brazil, Argentina, and Chile but inexplicably silent before conditions and events in Czechoslovakia, Bulgaria, Cuba, or Albania. "The silence and docility of the factional writers," he proclaimed, "is one of the causes of the intellectual stagnation and moral insensibility of the Latin-American left."

Toward the end of 1977, one of the most distinguished representatives of the intellectual left felt himself slurred by Paz and published an article against the "new" Octavio Paz. He was the writer Carlos Monsiváis, a man of great learning, sharp-witted irony, and formidable influence among the young. He reproached Paz especially for a tendency toward "generalization and pontification." In terms of specific content, he criticized Paz for being too soft on the PRI, the right, and imperialism and for disdaining the labor and popular movements of the left. And, he felt, Paz had a suspiciously favorable attitude toward Mexican religious traditionalism, and was trying to substitute the concept of class struggle for what Monsiváis considered the real Mexican issue of a struggle between "developed and underdeveloped" Mexico. Paz was asking Monsiváis for an inadmissible disconnection from ideology, Paz was obsessed with criticism of the state, and Paz refused to recognize "the epic force it took to build the People's Republic of China, the heroism that created the identity of the Vietnamese people, the sum of significances that the Cuban Revolution accumulated and is accumulating in Latin America— Criticism of the deformations of socialism must be accompanied by a combative defense of the conquests that cannot be abandoned."

Paz replied with ferocity. "Monsiváis is not a man of ideas but of witticisms . . . his prose is marked by the three fatal 'fu's': confused, profuse, and diffuse." Paz claimed that Monsiváis had distorted and truncated his arguments, the better to hang the label of "rightist" upon

him. It was Monsiváis who was "abstract." Paz was calling upon the
Mexican left to follow the model of the socialists in Spain or the *Movimiento al Socialismo* (the MAS) in Venezuela, who had renounced the
dogma of the "dictatorship of the proletariat." To note the devotion
of the Mexican people to the Virgin of Guadalupe did not mean that
he, Paz himself, was a traditionalist. Wasn't Monsiváis aware of the
various criticisms, published in *Plural* and *Vuelta*, against private sector
bureaucracies, against the unions and other political and economic
monopolies? Why hadn't he mentioned them? Obviously because his
objective was to downgrade him, Paz:

> He accuses me of being an authoritarian in the same paragraph
> in which he dares to impose upon me (as a condition for criticiz-
> ing bureaucratic socialism) "the recognition of its great achieve-
> ments." Has he asked himself whether these "great achievements"
> are inscribed in the history of human liberation or that of op-
> pression? . . . The analysis and denunciation of new forms of
> domination—in capitalist countries as well as "socialist" and the
> underdeveloped world—is the most urgent task of contemporary
> thought, not the defense of the "great achievements" of totalitar-
> ian empires.

Did these positions make Paz a "rightist"? Those who, like him, were
turning away from Marxism as well as many social democrats would say
that he was not. But for many left-wing academics—and their intellectual
spokesmen—his words were all they needed to present him as a man of
the right. The historian and essayist Héctor Aguilar Camín published an
article titled "The Apocalypse of Octavio Paz" in which he merely reproduced a number of Paz's statements as if they refuted each other. Paz's
problem, he went on to argue, was that he was "aging badly":

> from the bohemian of his twenties and thirties to—in his sixties—
> the disconsolate clarifier of his past, from the healthy, foundational

nationalist of *El laberinto de la soledad* to the buffoon with socially
vacuous myths and circular images of *Posdata*, from the indisput-
able, captivating intellectual of barely a decade ago—school and
emblem of a generation—to the Jeremiah of recent years. Paz is
substantially inferior to his past and is, politically, to the right of
Octavio Paz.

It should be noted that, with the passage of years, Monsiváis came to
share many of Paz's opinions and Aguilar Camín, in a gradual process,
even more.

BUT AMONG those who disliked Paz's politics, there were also more
dangerous individuals, in an epoch of sporadic but active urban guerrilla warfare. On August 29, 1978, the battle of the generations reached
into the inner circle of *Vuelta*, not with words but with lacerating violence. A frequent contributor to the journal, Hugo Margáin Charles
(the young philosopher who had won the Tamayo painting in the raffle
organized to benefit *Vuelta*), was kidnapped by a guerrilla commando
and later found dead, bled dry, with a bullet in his knee. (The author
or authors of the crime would never be caught.) A few days later, an
envelope with no return address arrived at the offices of *Vuelta*. In it
was a piece of writing signed by "J.D.A., Poetry in Arms" that included
a threat: "you will hear from us again." The text was titled "Epistle on
the Death of Hugo Margáin Charles." It condemned the public outrage of *Vuelta* over the murder. Every day, it affirmed, peasants in Latin
America and Mexico were dying "machine-gunned in their fields or on
their way home" and workers were "cut to pieces in a drainage ditch
with twenty stab wounds." And then it proceeded to justify the killing:
Margáin was the dog who had to be killed so as to continue the process
of eliminating rabies.

Octavio Paz thought that his last hour had come. And he faced it
with courage. He wrote a poem in which he challenged the author
of the anonymous letter and almost seemed to be calling for his own

immolation. The editorial board, and especially Gabriel Zaid, dissuaded him. The poem was never published but in the November issue
an editorial from the board appeared with the title "The Motives of the
Wolf." It quoted a substantial portion of the letter and went on to note:

> Beyond the threats and the cowardice of cloaking yourself in the
> shadows to spit on a corpse, the message is pathetic for its circular
> and necrophilic logic. It preaches the murder of innocent people
> because if "capitalism and not the dog engenders purulent rabies"
> then "to finish off the dogs will result in the long run in rabies
> having no defense." The wolf is thus concerned with the purity
> of the flock. It kills to finish off death . . . We are not supposed to
> condemn the assassination but rather understand the motives of
> the assassin.

In relation to the murderers' complaint that *Vuelta* had no right to
complain, the board simply stated that it would have been a monstrous
thing if his friends did not proclaim their grief over the murder of a
man of worth. *Vuelta* was accusing no one specifically because it had no
proof against anyone. But yes, it condemned the assassination, wher-
ever it may have stemmed from, whatever the source: terrorists or authorities, left or right, stupid adventurism or cold calculation:

> The nihilist Nechaev [a nineteenth-century Russian revolutionary
> committed to violence] is repugnant to us just like . . . all those in-
> tellectuals—philosophers, professors, writers, theologians—who
> tacitly justify murder. In the end, however condemnable may be
> the motives of the exterminating angels (whether it be Somoza
> or Pinochet or the Red Brigades) they are to be condemned in the
> first place for their actions.

IN THE end it was not the army that ended the guerrilla war in Mexico.
It was the Political Reform conceived and implemented in 1978 by a
prominent political liberal, Jesús Reyes Heroles, who was secretary of

the interior during the first years of the José López Portillo administration (1976–82). The Communist Party was legalized and, together with other leftist groups, entered Congress and the field of public politics. From that moment, the left began to take on a new strength, although its true consolidation in the realm of electoral politics would wait till 1988, when a dissident group within the PRI—headed by Cuauhtémoc Cárdenas, the son of Mexico's most socially progressive president—left the party that his father had helped to found. Cuauhtémoc would run for president and after losing to Carlos Salinas de Gortari, in an election heavily marred by suspicious manipulations, formed a party that Don Lázaro might have wished for but never dared to establish, a party that would unify the left under the banner of the Mexican Revolution but with no connection to the communists.

Though the Political Reform corresponded to the democratic ideas Paz had been proposing to both the left and the government since the essays of *Posdata*, the ideological war did not let up. In 1979, *Vuelta* welcomed the Sandinista Revolution in Nicaragua against what had seemed the endless family tyranny of the Somozas. The magazine continued to publish articles analyzing and criticizing the military regimes of Chile, Argentina, and Uruguay. From 1980 until the reestablishment of democracy in Argentina, *Vuelta* was banned by the generals in power. But in 1984, to give its own small welcome to democracy, *Vuelta* initiated a South American edition published in Buenos Aires. Nevertheless, the insults, the constant accusations of "rightist," continued against Octavio Paz. Toward the close of the 1970s (and after the murder of Margáin), Paz, feeling himself harassed and isolated, broadened his presence in the media. He would publish not only in *Vuelta* but also in the pages of the newspaper *El Universal,* where two of his friends—José de la Colina and Eduardo Lizalde—were in charge of a weekly literary supplement "The Letter and the Image" (*La letra y la imagen*). Soon after, Paz also began to appear on television, on the dominant private network Televisa, providing commentaries on international affairs for its major evening news broadcast, Jacobo Zabludovsky's *24 horas.* He had decided not to permit people to "take him lightly." The decision (to appear on a network that many Mexicans regarded as far too closely linked to the PRI) drew new verbal attacks. But Paz recognized, earlier than most Mexican intellectuals who later followed his path, the power to spread the influence of his ideas and his persona afforded by the medium of television.

XVIII

For several years, Paz had been working on his book about the poetess Sor Juana Inés de la Cruz. It was his definitive return to a study of the order imposed by Catholicism, which he had viewed (in *El laberinto*) positively, as an essentially benevolent force that had mitigated the "orphanhood" of the conquered Indians and, according to *El laberinto*, given them a sense of protection and relevance. But he was no longer the same man who had written *The Labyrinth* of *Solitude* more than twenty years before. His criticism of the order imposed by twentieth-century communism had awakened a new, less positive opinion: the lingering presence of the colonial and Catholic form of order through the nineteenth and into the twentieth century had impeded the modernization of the country to a degree that perhaps he had not sufficiently considered, even if he had, in *The Labyrinth of Solitude*, referred to the petrified scholasticism, "the relative infecundity of colonial Catholicism." In Paz's vision of the colonial centuries, there was an inescapable duality (based on a real enough historical duality). But now he was dealing with it directly, in the biography of a great poet and a woman who had suffered grievously from the antifeminine atmosphere of the Church, especially during the Counter-Reformation (an environment opposed as well to her considerable secular learning and surely jealous of her beauty and her talent). She had chosen a monastic life at least in part because, in a context that denied educational equality to women, it promised her more freedom to study and to write. She had been driven into expressions of unwarranted contrition, like her famous statement that she was "the worst of all" (*la peor de todas*), and later a forced renunciation of writing.

Paz had been interested in Sor Juana since the 1940s. He would now produce his *Sor Juana Inés de la Cruz o las trampas de la fe* (Sor Juana Inés de la Cruz or the Traps of Faith), published in 1982. Clearly he felt her to be a sister soul. They both saw themselves as solitary individuals and both, separated by three centuries, were seekers. Their trajectories had been parallel but inverse. Since his youth, in a world at war but in a country free of it, he had sought for order and reconciliation, which were qualities of her world under the aegis of a dominating religion. Sor Juana, within her closed and ecstatic personal universe, had sought an opening outward, the capacity for liberty, which was his environment and his chosen world. He had written in *El laberinto*, "The solitary figure of Sor Juana becomes more isolated within this world formed of affirmations and negations, which ignores the value of uncertainty and of inquiry . . . Her renunciation, which ended in silence, was not a commitment to God but a negation of herself."

Negation of herself or affirmation of herself? Paz would not admit (as some angry Catholic critics insisted he should) that Sor Juana had denied her creative life for another, truer commitment. He saw the two rigid orthodoxies, of Marxism and Catholicism, as convergent. Both felt they were "owners of the truth." He poured his own feelings of contrition about the past into his portrait of Sor Juana. Why had she obeyed the orders of her confessor and burned her extensive library? Why had she sacrificed her intellectual curiosity (which had nourished her since childhood) on the altar of faith? Why, after rising to the literary, philosophical, and intellectual summit of her age, had she completed the sacrifice of her liberty and her genius, and died not long after (from an illness contracted while tending to grievously ill nuns)? Sor Juana, thought Paz, must have incorporated the same kind of baseless guilt expressed by the victims of Stalin's party purges in the 1930s. But he would not renounce his freedom nor stop testifying to what he saw as the truth in confrontation with both orthodoxies. Before the guardians of the Catholic faith, he had written a book that claimed the nun as a martyr to liberty. Before the new "clergy" of the left, he would continue pointing to political crimes. He would not fall into "the traps of faith."

FREEDOM WAS incompatible with rigid Catholic orthodoxy, but was it incompatible with Christianity? In 1979 Paz had addressed the issue in a brief and striking essay on the death of his friend, the leftist José Revueltas. He described Revueltas (a totally convinced atheist) as a Christian Marxist, disillusioned with his original faith but nevertheless impregnated with the deep Catholicism of his parents, his infancy, and the Mexican people. He had transformed his original faith into Marxism and lived his revolutionary passion as a *via crucis*. In his journey through the stations of his suffering (prison terms, countless deprivations) Revueltas had often come up against the dictates of orthodoxy. Confronted with dogmas, precepts, party discipline, he had shown not obedience but doubts when he truly felt them. But "there is something distinctive about the doubts and criticisms of Revueltas, the tone, the religious passion . . . The questions that Revueltas raised on different occasions make no sense nor can they be deciphered except within a religious perspective . . . and precisely that of Christianity." Paz sees him as a primitive Christian confronting the evil of the world (capitalism, poverty, oppression, injustice) and also, sometimes, the power of his own secular church.

> Revueltas, intuitively and passionately, resorted to a return toward the most ancient part of himself, to the religious answers, mingled with the millenarist ideas and hopes of the revolutionary movement. His religious temperament led him to communism, which he lived like a road of sacrifice and communion. This same temperament, inseparable from the love of truth and the good, led him at the end of his life to a critique of bureaucratic socialism and Marxist clericalism.

Within the Catholic Church, Paz concluded, "Revueltas would have been a heretic, as he was within communist orthodoxy."

His depiction of Revueltas was an indirect self-portrait. Their lives could not have been more disparate. Paz's personal and existential suffering cannot be compared to the sufferings of Revueltas in the flesh. But both in a way had been Christians without a church, Christian Marxists opposed to the dogmas of Catholicism or the Comintern. Each was possessed by the absolute. Both born in 1914, they had at first embraced the same faith, moved away (though differently) from their fixed convictions, and continued believing in the possibility of hope. Revueltas had died "lashed to the colt of alcohol" like Paz's own revolutionary father. It was now up to Paz to continue on the path of heresy, because—like some of the Russian writers he so loved—his dissidence was not merely political but a heterodoxy based on his strong feelings of guilt over previous silences, previous blindnesses, conscious or not, in the 1930s and much later. A very Christian heresy, the product of sin and contrition.

PAZ RARELY mentioned God. Toward religion, he was closer to his Liberal, antireligious grandfather than to his mother, the pious Doña Josefina. He saw in the three major monotheistic religions a legacy of intolerance incompatible with his commitment to plurality. He liked to tell the story of a fervent Muslim he and Marie-Jo had met in the Himalayas and who had said to them, partly in sign language, "Moses, *kaput!* Jesus, *kaput!* Only Mohammed lives!" Paz believed that even this most recent prophet was *kaput!* and that the only religion that made any sense about the process of living and dying was Buddhism. Paz was drawn to the wisdom of Socrates, not Solomon; he read and reread Lucretius, not the Bible; he admired not the emperor Constantine, but Julian the Apostate for his attempt to revive worship of the pagan gods. (Paz devoted a poem, as had the great Greek modernist Cavafy, to Julian.) In his universal curiosity about art, thought, and science, Paz was a man of the Renaissance. In his free spirit and his touch of libertinism, he was an eighteenth-century philosopher. His creative verve and his political and poetic passion were those of a revolutionary romantic of the nineteenth and of the twentieth centuries.

And yet he wrote his greatest book about a nun and, in 1979, he treated the life of his friend Revueltas as an atheist *Imitation of Christ.*

When Paz's mother died in 1980, Gabriel Zaid, a practicing Catholic, arranged for a *novenario*, nine days of prayer for the dead. Paz was deeply moved by the gesture.

X I X
———

In 1981, Gabriel Zaid published a long piece in *Vuelta* (it appeared simultaneously in *Dissent* and *Esprit*) on the civil war in El Salvador, titled "Enemy Colleagues, a Reading of the Salvadorean Tragedy," and another, three years later, in 1984, on the sequel to the Sandinista Revolution: "Nicaragua, the Enigma of the Elections." According to Zaid, both were conflicts between university-educated people of the left and the right, to the cost of the general population. In both cases, Zaid argued for the solution of democracy: clean elections in El Salvador, and submitting the Sandinista government to a popular vote in Nicaragua.

His arguments were given respectful, even enthusiastic attention (especially abroad, for instance by Murray Kempton in the *New York Review of Books*) but were strongly attacked by many Mexican publications. Octavio Paz had defended Zaid's positions and in 1984, on a stage in Frankfurt while accepting the Prize of the Association of German Editors and Booksellers, Paz—without mentioning Zaid directly—alluded to his younger colleague's position on Nicaragua. He traced the history of the Somoza "hereditary dictatorship," which "had been born and had grown under the protection of Washington," and the factors that had led to the Sandinista uprising and the fall of the regime. He would add:

> Shortly after the triumph, the case of Cuba was repeated: the revolution was confiscated by an elite of revolutionary leaders . . . Almost all of them came from a native oligarchy and had passed from Catholicism to Marxist-Leninism or formed a curious mixture of both doctrines. From the beginning the Sandinista leaders sought inspiration in Cuba. They have received military and technical aid from the Soviet Union and its allies. The actions of the

Sandinista regime show its will to install a bureaucratic-military dictatorship in Nicaragua according to the model of Havana. They have thus denaturalized the original meaning of the revolutionary movement.

Paz then mentioned that the anti-Sandinista groups had various components (he specifically mentioned the Miskito Indians) and noted that the technical and military aid supplied to the anti-Sandinista Contras was encountering growing criticism from the U.S. Senate and American opinion. He then pointed to the recent elections in El Salvador as a model to follow.

In Mexico, the reaction to Paz's speech was ferocious. A large crowd marched in front of the American embassy on Paseo de la Reforma (a short distance from Paz's apartment) carrying effigies of President Ronald Reagan and Octavio Paz. Some of them chanted "Rapacious Reagan, your friend is Octavio Paz" ("Reagan rapaz, tu amigo es Octavio Paz"). Someone lit a match and the effigy of Paz went up in flames. On the following day, the great cartoonist Abel Quezada published a cartoon titled "The Traps of Faith," in which Paz appeared hanging from a rope, devoured by fire as if in an auto-da-fe of the Holy Inquisition and repeating a sentence from his Frankfurt speech: "The defeat of democracy signifies the perpetuation of injustice and physical and moral misery, whoever may win, the coronel or the commissar." Quezada himself added, "The communists burned the effigy of Octavio Paz . . . If they did this to the best writer in Mexico now that they are in opposition [to the ruling government], they won't let anybody speak if they rise to power."

The episode was the culmination of the long and often sordid onslaught against Paz. He himself would later write, in a letter to his Catalan editor Pere Gimferrer:

My first reaction was an incredulous laugh. How was it possible that a rather moderate speech unleashed such violence? Then a certain melancholy satisfaction. If they attack me, it's because [what I said] hurts them. But—I confess to you—it also hurt me. I felt (and I still feel it, though not the emotional hurt) that I was the victim of an injustice and of a misunderstanding. In the first place . . . it was an action conceived and directed by a group with the intention of intimidating me and intimidating all those who think as I do and dare to say it . . . In the second place, the national combustible: envy, resentment. It is the passion that rules the class of intellectuals in our era, especially in our [Latin American] countries. In Mexico, it is a chronic illness and its effects have been terrible. To it I attribute—in large part—the sterility of our literati. It is a deaf and dumb anger that surfaces at times in certain glances—a furtive, yellowish, metallic light . . . In my case, that passion has attained a seldom seen virulence through the union of resentment with ideological fanaticism.

IN 1979 Paz had collected his polemical essays against Dogma and the Lie, against Catholic and Marxist orthodoxy, in *El ogro filantrópico* (The Philanthropic Ogre). The title essay revealed another aspect of Paz's duality, this time in relation to the political system he had served from 1945 to 1968. He recognized the corruption of the PRI and pointed to certain unpardonable crimes, especially the events of 1968, but he felt that neither the left nor the right (represented by the National Action Party, the PAN) had formulated a realistic and responsible project for the country. The PRI had the advantage of having launched the Political Reform and this, he felt, would shape democracy in Mexico. Toward the system in power, his attitude was almost optimistic. By dissolving its own duality (a process he saw as under way), the hegemony of the PRI could lose its quality of "ogre" and retain its "philanthropy" but within a context of political freedom.

The book was published during a period of the greatest oil boom (and euphoria) of the century in Mexico. OPEC (the Organization of the Petroleum Exporting Countries) had utilized the occasion of the Yom Kippur War (between Israel and Egypt, supported by Syria) to impose a boycott on shipments to pro-Israeli countries and enormously increase the worldwide price of oil. Mexico was not an OPEC member but benefited all the same.

The "pharaonic" president López Portillo applied the oil revenue to numerous and extremely expensive projects. Two men trained as engineers, Gabriel Zaid and, to his left, Heberto Castillo, pointed out (in the face of general support for the president's policies) that the enormous overspending was based on a very fragile foundation, the price of a barrel of oil. If the price fell, everything would collapse. And it did, in September 1982, driving Mexico to bankruptcy.

The political system was thrown into crisis. López Portillo, in his farewell address to the country, broke into tears and nationalized the banks. The general opinion on the left was that this had been a brave and revolutionary action. Writers in *Vuelta* criticized the nationalization as a distracting populist gesture and suggested that the only reasonable alternative for the country was to fully establish democracy. In January 1984, I published an essay in the journal, which was entitled "For a Democracy without Adjectives." The article argued for an immediate transition to a democratic system and against the assignment of the usual Marxist adjectives appended to the word "democracy," words like "formal" and "bourgeois." What was needed was simply an electoral democracy.

A sector of the intellectual and political left responded positively to the idea. The Trotskyite activist Adolfo Gilly called it a prospect for "a modest utopia," and Heberto Castillo, respected head of the Mexican Workers' Party (who had been Lázaro Cárdenas's friend and a mentor to his son Cuauhtémoc), also publicly supported an immediate transition. In those years, Porfirio Muñoz Ledo and other members of the PRI began to form a Democratic Current, which would lead to the postulation of Cuauhtémoc Cárdenas as a presidential candidate and the final unification, after 1989, of most of the Mexican left under the banner of the Party of the Democratic Revolution, the PRD (*Partido de la Revolución Democrática*).

Paz himself was in a bind. The system had not fulfilled his hopes and expectations. What direction should he take?

PAZ CONSIDERED himself liberal by descent, and also through his distance from the Church, his knowledge of the French Revolution, and his impassioned reading of the *Episodios nacionales* (by the Spanish novelist Benito Pérez Galdós), with whose protagonist, Salvador Monsalud, he strongly identified. But for him the word "liberal"—Spanish in its origin as a noun—alluded to a mood, an attitude, an adjective. His liberalism was literary rather than historical, juridical, and political. There was a duality in his vision of liberalism, as in his view of Catholicism, the same kind of duality but seen from the opposite extreme, since it began with a rejection rather than an acceptance (of what he had seen as the benefits of colonial Catholicism for the "orphaned" Indians). In *El laberinto*, he had conceded "grandeur" to the nineteenth-century Liberals but considered their movement a historical "fall." With independence and then, most especially, the Reform under Benito Juárez, Mexico according to Paz had lost its "filiation" with its Catholic (and presumably Indian) past. But in confronting the closed and oppressive political structures of the twentieth century, Paz (as he had applied his new views in a different way to Sor Juana) came to reevaluate the liberal tradition he had disdained in his classic study. To the nineteenth-century Liberals and their heir, the assassinated president and initial leader of the Revolution, Francisco I. Madero, Mexico owed the possibility of a democratic and constitutional government just barely on the horizon in 1984. Before the cameras of Televisa, Paz would declare: "the salvation of Mexico rests on the possibility of realizing the revolution of Juárez and Madero."

But liberal democracy could not satisfy Octavio Paz. It was too insipid and formal a concept. It had no "transcendental" content. And so Paz would try to combine his new commitment with his historical-poetical vision of the Mexican Revolution as a return to origins and a revelation of the hidden face of his people. He wanted to maintain the validity of the Revolution as he had imbibed it from his father:

I think that in Mexico, the Zapatista inheritance is still alive, above
all morally. In three aspects . . . First of all, it was an anti-authoritarian revolution: Zapata had a true aversion to the Presidential
Chair . . . Secondly, it was an anti-centralist revolt . . . Zapatismo
affirms the original nature not only of states and regions but even
of each locality . . . And finally, Zapatismo is a traditionalist revolt.
It does not affirm modernity, it does not affirm the future. It affirms that there are profound, ancient, permanent values.

One had to vindicate the liberals Juárez and Madero, but also to
"correct Liberalism with Zapatismo." This was his formula for national
redemption.

"We Mexicans must reconcile ourselves with our past," Paz had insisted. In *The Labyrinth of Solitude*, he had reconciled himself with his
father, seeing in the Zapatista revolution "a communion of Mexico
with itself," with its Indian and Spanish roots. But in the 1980s another
character began to sit down at his table—his grandfather Ireneo Paz.
Confronted with the corrupt, inefficient, paternalistic, and authoritarian Mexican state, it seemed right to recover liberal and democratic
values. By embracing them, Paz began to close the cycle of his life.
Now it was possible for the three Pazes—Ireneo the grandfather, Octavio the father, and Octavio the son—to sit together, equals, at the same
table. The tablecloth smelled of gunpowder, but also of the prospect of
political freedom.

In 1985, Paz published an article in *Vuelta*, titled "PRI. Hora cumplida"
(The PRI. The Time Has Come). It was his final appeal to the system,
asking that the party allow free and competitive elections. Paz did not
foresee the PRI losing power (and even less did he wish for it to do so).
But he did conceive of a gradual transition in which the ruling party
would yield more space to the opposition both in Congress and the
individual states.

At that time the PAN (*Partido Acción Nacional*) was gaining strength
in the northern states of the country. Since its foundation in 1939, it
had become (though at first as a very small party) the opposition force

on the center right. Paz had not conceded even a minimal instinct for democracy to the PAN. He considered them a retrograde, Catholic, nationalist party, heirs to the conservative, antiliberal forces of the nineteenth century, and especially to the nineteenth-century ideologue Lucas Alamán. Certainly, in the area of social morality, the PAN had always maintained a conservative attitude, close to the upper hierarchy of the Church. And it was true that many of its members had been pro-Franco in the 1930s and, even after the formation of the party, some of its leaders had shown sympathy for the Axis in World War II. But the political behavior of the PAN in its legislative proposals and its internal workings had been democratic and its economic ideology was liberal rather than following the statist and protectionist principles of Alamán. Paz would always keep his distance from the PAN and would frequently criticize the party, but when an especially egregious voting fraud deprived the PAN of its victory in the Chihuahua governmental elections, Paz agreed to join a group of Mexico's most prominent intellectuals (including some of his longtime critics) in signing a petition asking that the rigged election be annulled. This event was an important catalyst for Mexico's democratic transition. Now not only the PAN but the parties of the left would commit themselves to democracy rather than revolution.

XX

In 1987, Paz returned to Valencia, in eastern Spain, to a conference attended by many writers as well as some survivors of the Spanish Civil War. It was a conference to commemorate that Second International Conference of Writers, held half a century before in the midst of the Spanish War. Paz delivered the inaugural address. He titled it "Place for Testing" (*Lugar de prueba*): "History is not only the dominion of contingency; it is the place for testing." In his poem *Nocturno de San Ildefonso*, he had written "History is error." Here in Valencia he says, "We are condemned to make mistakes." Like the most severe of judges, he recounts what he considers his own mistakes. He saw a serious collapse of the revolutionary ideas he had once shared, the mortal blows received not so much from its adversaries but from the revolutionaries themselves: "where they have conquered power, they have muzzled the people." But very quickly his theme and tone take on a religious quality:

> We wanted to be the brothers of the victims and we discovered that we were accomplices of the executioners; our victories became defeats and our great defeat is perhaps the seed of a great victory we will not see with our own eyes. Our condemnation is the mark of modernity. And more: the stigma of the modern intellectual. Stigma in the double sense of the word: the mark of sainthood and the mark of infamy.

Condemnation, stigma, sainthood, and infamy. The confession—which the speech really was—recorded the moral grandeur of that distant conference: the love, the loyalty, the valor, and the sacrifice that had been its living environment. But he also remembered his own weakness: "the perversion of the revolutionary spirit." And speaking of the proposal for the condemnation of André Gide, who had written of his disillusion with Stalin's Russia, he felt a need to expiate his own personal sin of silence: "Although many of us were convinced of the injustice of those attacks and we admired Gide, we kept silent. We justified our silence with . . . specious arguments . . . And so we contributed to the petrification of the revolution." (Of course, not everyone had kept their silence, and the chairman of the conference, André Malraux, had refused to let the condemnation be approved. But it was his own personal sense of sin—not the upshot of the specific event—that preoccupied Paz.)

But the value that remained was "criticism": to "examine our actions and cleanse them of the fatal propension of conversion into absolutes . . . to insert others into our perspective." And he devoted the final paragraphs of his address to those *others* he had come to know in the

Civil War. They were the faces of the Spanish people: soldiers, workers, peasants, journalists he had met. "With them I learned that the word 'fraternity' is no less precious than the word 'freedom': it is the bread of men, bread that is shared." He was referring to an actual episode: the peasant who, during a bombardment, "cut a melon from his orchard and, with a piece of bread and a jug of wine, shared it with us." Way back in Spain, in 1937, Paz had encountered, in human fraternity, in the common people of Spain, the bread and wine of his Communion.

BUT OCTAVIO Paz had to confront, in the present and not in the sins of the past, a "place for testing" the strength of his democratic convictions after the "results" of the 1988 presidential election were announced. Cuauhtémoc Cárdenas, the candidate of an improvised coalition of the left (before the postelection formation of the PRD), was gaining an overwhelming quantity of votes when the government (at that time still in total control of the vote count) announced an unexpected "crash of the computers," reportedly (by some who were present) when the crushing Cárdenas majorities in Mexico City had begun rolling across the screens. A sizable sector of public opinion immediately suspected that a fraud was under way, a fear they felt was completely confirmed when the computers miraculously revived in the morning to give the PRI candidate, Carlos Salinas de Gortari, a highly unlikely 50.48 percent of the vote (an unprecedentedly low claim, by the way, compared to the usual confections of a PRI-managed electoral count). The candidate of the PAN, Manuel Clouthier, launched a hunger strike to protest the fraud, even though it was clear to him that he himself had not won the election. There were many other demonstrations and protests in the street. Cárdenas was trapped for some months within a real dilemma. Should he call for an insurrection against what he considered a usurpation or should he accept it and turn to the formation of a new unified party of the left? After various months of tension, he chose the second alternative.

Paz, in contrast to most informed Mexican opinion (including some of *Vuelta*'s own writers), refused to recognize the election as fraudulent.

There had only been "irregularities" and after all, this was the first election "of this sort," one with strong opposition candidates on the left and center right. One might partially review the process but under no circumstances should the election be annulled, as the Mexican left was demanding. Paz favored a "transition," not a brusque change. The allegations were unjustified and the "agitation" was not only "noxious but suicidal."

A sector of the Mexican public believed that Paz's arguments were in direct conflict with his stated defense of democracy. Paz never agreed. He did not believe that there had been a fraud. Perhaps he had convinced himself, as Don Ireneo had done at the beginning of the Porfiriato, that the project of Carlos Salinas de Gortari (who had once been his student at Harvard and had written for *Plural*) to open up and modernize the economy was what the country needed in terms of change.

IN 1989, on the occasion of the bicentennial of the French Revolution, the government of France awarded Paz the Tocqueville Prize. In his acceptance speech Paz declared the mythical cycle of the Revolution to be over and done with: "We are present at the twilight of the idea of Revolution in its final and unfortunate incarnation, the Bolshevik version."

After the fall of the Berlin Wall in 1989 and—no less a miracle—after Latin America began a generalized move toward democracy, Paz felt that history had justified his convictions. A number of his former adversaries had already abandoned their commitment to Soviet-style socialism. And some of the publications that had attacked *Vuelta* with the greatest virulence now paid a silent homage to the journal by accepting many of its positions.

In 1990, *Vuelta* organized a conference, listed as an "Encounter" and titled "The Experience of Freedom," during which, without any emphasis on triumphalism, an international and varied group of intellectuals analyzed the light and the shadows of that watershed of history, the collapse of Eastern European communism. Among the most outstanding participants were Czesław Miłosz, Norman Manea, Leszek

Kołakowski, Adam Michnik, Irving Howe, Daniel Bell, Mario Vargas Llosa, and many other prominent writers and thinkers. *Vuelta* made a special effort to invite representative writers of the left, and about ten of them attended, including the old Marxist Adolfo Sánchez Vázquez and Carlos Monsiváis. The sessions were transmitted on television and financed by contributions from the Mexican private sector. Books were published that included the many subjects of discussion.

The Encounter drew considerable public attention though voices from the die-hard left castigated the participants as "fascists," an accusation that especially angered some older participants who had been survivors of the Nazi concentration camps. Paz once again delivered his criticisms of Eastern European socialism, on the verge of its total demise, and referred in detail to what he termed the complicity of Mexican intellectuals across six decades. But he also castigated "private monopolies," the "blind mechanism of the market," and "the domination of money and commerce in the world of art and literature." At one juncture, when the Peruvian Vargas Llosa described the Mexican political system as "the perfect dictatorship," Paz charged to its defense: "what we have endured is the hegemonic domination of a party. This is a fundamental and essential distinction [from a dictatorship]." He was speaking, yet one more time, as a son of the Mexican Revolution.

During the same year, Paz was awarded the Nobel Prize for Literature. After that, in the Spanish-speaking world, he held a place that had only been matched earlier by Ortega y Gasset. Paz had emerged from his personal labyrinth and had, to a considerable degree, brought Mexico out of its tangential position and into the full light of Western culture.

Once, at a dinner, Paz was talking about the Revolution. Without the least intention of offending him, his old friend José Luis Martínez dared to say to him quietly, as a friendly jibe, "But Octavio, you were never really a revolutionary." Paz rose to his feet and responded in a loud, almost angry tone: "What are you saying? That *I* was not a revolutionary!" Martínez of course was referring to revolutionary action, whether the violent action of a revolutionary soldier or guerrilla, or the considerable dangers accepted by a militant, like José Revueltas. Paz had practiced the Revolution essentially with his poetry and thought, but considered himself nonetheless a revolutionary. And he had paid his own dues, in sorrow and guilt, for having been one.

Clearly there was a living flame of Revolution still present in the aging Paz. And on January 1, 1994, Octavio Paz—and all of Mexico— would awaken to the incredible news of an indigenous insurrection in the southeast of Mexico. Its leader was a certain Subcomandante Marcos and the group called itself "Zapatista."

For Paz this turn (and return) of history was deeply confusing. At first he deplored the "relapse of the intellectuals" who immediately showed their enthusiasm for the movement and he criticized the turn toward violence. But as time passed, his articles began to show a subtle sympathy for what was happening in Chiapas. How, after all, could he condemn a movement that brandished the image of Zapata? And he was genuinely impressed with the literary skills of Marcos: "The invention of the beetle Durito, as a knight errant, is memorable; on the other hand his tirades only win me over half way." But to win Paz over, even "only half way" was a great victory. Christopher Domínguez, one of the young literary critics who wrote for *Vuelta*, once reproved him: "Why have you written more about Marcos than about any one of us?" to which Paz answered, "Because you haven't risen in arms."

These were distant echoes of his youth. Nevertheless, he had no doubt that "Liberal Democracy is a civilized way of living together. For me it is the best among those [systems] that political philosophy has conceived." And then he formulated what was, for him, the simple and final synthesis of his long passion for history and politics:

> We must rethink our tradition, renew it, and seek the reconcilia-
> tion of the two great political traditions of modernity: liberalism
> and socialism. I dare to say that this is "the theme of our time."

TOWARD THE end, even his face began to look more and more like that of his grandfather. He said he wanted a quick and serene death, like Don Ireneo, but that final blessing was not granted to him. He had been born during the historic conflagration of 1914, and the final stage of his life would be marked by a tragic fire, which in 1996 destroyed much of his apartment and library. Shortly afterward, he was diagnosed as having spinal cancer (a metastasis of the cancer that had been suppressed by the operation of 1977). And toward the end, just like his grandfather, he became concerned about the shadow of anarchy that seemed to be spreading over Mexico. He finally appeared to have lost faith in the autogenerative capacities of the system. "What will occur in Chiapas? What will happen with Mexico?" he would ask. He died on April 19, 1998. Two years later, Mexico would make a definitive transition to democracy.

During a public ceremony of farewell, in the open air, he had turned once again to the image of Don Ireneo, the protective, wise patriarch. He repeated his favorite metaphor of Mexico as "a country of the sun" but then immediately reminded the audience about the darkness of our history, our "luminous and cruel" duality that already reigned within the cosmogony of the Aztec gods and had been an obsession for him since childhood. He wished that some Socrates might appear who could free his people of the darker side, of all the destructive passions. Unusual for him, he was actually preaching "like my grandfather," he said, "who loved to preach after a meal." And suddenly he looked up toward the cloudy sky, as if he wanted to touch it with his hand. "Up there," he said, "there are clouds and sun. Clouds and sun are related words. Let us be worthy of the clouds of the Valley of Mexico. Let us be worthy of the sun of the Valley of Mexico." For an instant the sky cleared, leaving only the sun, and then Octavio Paz said, " 'The Valley of Mexico,' that phrase lit up my childhood, my maturity, and my old age."

In the following weeks, both his Revolutionary father and Liberal grandfather dropped out of his consciousness. He was left with only the memory of his mother and the presence of his wife. And one day, unexpectedly, she heard him whisper to her, "You are my Valley of Mexico."

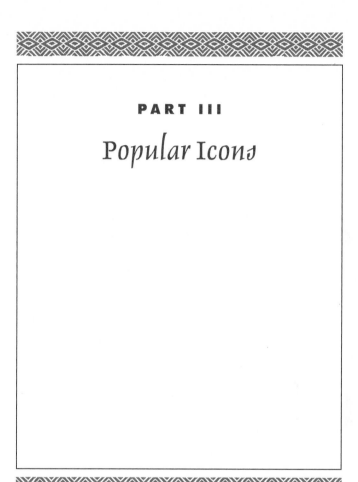

PART III
Popular Icons

6

Eva Perón

THE MADONNA OF THE SHIRTLESS ONES

Thinkers and politicians through the ages have long been aware that politics is a kind of theater, but after the public opinion polls gave Ronald Reagan a victory in the televised presidential debates of 1980 against Jimmy Carter, the Cuban writer Guillermo Cabrera Infante was moved to consider the parallels between political power and the movies. Exiled from his own country by Fidel Castro, whom he considered a consummate actor, a maestro of monologue, Cabrera had personally suffered from the impact of a politician with the skills of an actor. Now the performance of Reagan, "that Errol Flynn of B movies," convinced the Cuban writer that, while being an actor was not a sufficient qualification for becoming a politician, it surely did help a great deal. On that critical night for his campaign, Reagan spoke with ease, projecting calmness, security, even benevolence: the forthright American who within the *High Noon* of the Cold War would save what could be saved of the American century. "It was the best performance of his career," wrote Cabrera Infante, "worth an Oscar, but they only gave him, as consolation prize, the presidency of the United States."

Politicians with the skills of actors filed in a long stream across the stage of the twentieth century. Some of them were admirable, most of them contemptible. There were fewer actors turned politicians but they played equally imperious and disturbing roles in government. Jiang Qing, a minor and unsuccessful actress in low-budget films, made use of her acting gifts and experience to successfully represent a whole series of historic roles: fervent follower of the leader of Hunan, a protagonist of the Long March, and finally—a happy though not final ending—omnipotent wife of the omnipotent Mao Tse-tung. During the same period, at the other end of the world, another famous dictator, General Juan Domingo Perón, had once declared that "the Argentine who can perform on the speaker's platform the way Gardel does on the screen will hold Argentina in the palm of his hand." Carlos Gardel, legendary actor and singer of tangos, had died in an airplane accident in 1935. And so the stage was empty and ready but it was not Perón who would take Argentina into the palm of his hand. It would be his consort: another minor actress and veteran of low-budget films, Eva Duarte.

IT ALL really began with the impact of Hollywood on a young girl living in poverty in Junín, a small provincial city of Argentina. There she read the magazine *Sintonía* and clipped photographs of Norma Shearer. The girl had seen Shearer play the role of Marie Antoinette. She would dream of being the American film star, acting the same part and listening from her prison cell to the drumrolls at the guillotine. The girl had no resources, no education, not even any particular physical gifts other than a very smooth skin, translucent, like alabaster. Although she industriously practiced a kind of schoolgirl recitation of poetry, her pronunciation was painfully poor. But nothing would hold her back. She had decided that she would become an actress and that her hometown was far too small for her. On New Year's Day of 1935, when she was fifteen years old, she left Junín for Buenos Aires, the capital of the country.

For almost ten years she would work at her chosen vocation with very little luck: nonspeaking parts in plays, minor roles in movies, photographs for entertainment magazines or advertising posters. Every step was due to the patronage of one or another impresario who sometimes would favor and protect her, but more often merely exercise, at her expense, his droit de seigneur. A woman who worked with her during that period remembers:

Eva was a slight little thing, delicate, thin, with black hair and a long little face . . . She was so skinny that you couldn't tell if she was going or coming. Due to hunger and poverty and somewhat because of negligence, her hands were always wet and cold. And she was also cold in her acting work: a piece of ice. She was no girl to awaken passions. She was very submissive and very timid.

"I was bad at theater; in the movies I knew how to get by but if I was good at anything, it was radio," she would confess years later. And to a degree she was right. The genre of radio plays stirred a sentimental fever of emotions throughout Latin America. Every evening, from Mexico to Patagonia, women of all social classes would pass their time listening to the umpteenth version of *Cinderella*. (The same is true now with telenovelas.) The fragile Eva began to be recognized as a heroine of these radio plays, where the only thing that counted was the melodramatic tone communicated by her voice: high-pitched, quivering, honest, suffering. Nevertheless, the first six months of 1943 were a nightmare for her: she was then an unemployed and faded Cinderella. Suddenly, the military coup of June 1943 (the first in Argentina since 1930, and the preamble to a long though varied military hegemony) rescued her from her despair. Through the patronage of a certain Colonel Aníbal Imbert, she signed a contract with Radio Belgrano to star in a series dedicated to eighteen celebrated women, all of whom were to be either artists, like Sarah Bernhardt and Isadora Duncan, or, preferably, empresses: Elizabeth of England, Eugenia de Montijo (the wife of Napoléon III), Carlota of Mexico, Anna of Austria, Catherine the Great of Russia. The weekly magazine *Antena* would now even describe her as "the famous actress Eva Duarte."

Her meeting with her Prince Charming, Juan Domingo Perón, on January 22, 1944, instantly changed her own life and that of her country. "Thank you for existing," she said to him. It was the conventional happy ending of a radio play become vivid reality. Once established as the lover of the powerful General Perón, who was then minister of labor, Eva continued to do radio programs and to climb the rungs of the movie business. Her last role on the big screen was as the star of the film *The Prodigal Woman* (*La pródiga*), a typical Spanish drama of religious conversion: a woman sinner atones for a licentious life through works of charity. The poor make her into a saint, calling her "the Señora," "mother of the poor," "sister to the afflicted." Once she had risen to power, Eva would have all the copies of *La pródiga* destroyed, not really because of an impulse toward self-criticism but rather for a deeper and more revelatory reason—her radio embodiments of those actresses and empresses together with the story of *The Prodigal Woman* had provided her with the libretto for her future. It would be an occasion when a movie was not inspired by reality but exactly the reverse: a film would leap from the screen to seize power over the real.

With her role now clear to her, a physical transformation was needed. Years before, she had told her hairdresser, "Cut my hair, Julito, like Bette Davis." Later he had begun to do her hair like Olivia de Havilland in *Gone with the Wind* but now her new part—not for a movie but within history—called for something more than just a change of style. It was then that she decided to abandon her past life as a *morocha* (the Argentine term for a dark-haired, lower-class woman) and dye her hair. She was reborn as a blond Madonna. "It was a theatrical and symbolic gold," writes Alicia Dujovne Ortiz, author of the biography *Eva Perón*, "which served the same function as the halos and gilded backgrounds in the religious painting of the Middle Ages: to isolate sacred figures."

Evita herself would say, "The poor like to see me lovely, they don't want to be championed by some lady who doesn't dress well. They dream of me and I cannot disappoint them." And so that she would not disappoint them, she asked for advice on elegant clothes from women of high society, and in Europe bought Dior dresses and Rochas perfumes. Jewels drove her wild—or, more precisely, they nourished and calmed her—but she did not, in any way, disdain hard cash. When she died, she would own 1,200 gold and silver brooches, three ingots of platinum, 756 pieces of silver and gold work, 144 ivory brooches, a 48-karat emerald, 1,653 diamonds, 120 wristwatches, and a hundred clocks made of gold, as well as other unnumbered precious gems, necklaces, platinum brooches, and of course stocks and property, all of it worth tens of millions of dollars.

One could leaf through any copy of *People* or *Paris Match* or endless fan magazines without encountering an actual or cinematic fate that can be remotely compared to Eva Duarte's. Not only did she truly embody Cinderella but also the good and miraculous fairy godmother and the former sinner to whom Providence had done justice by filling her to overflowing with fame, power, and many millions. But she was not just any millionairess. She was a new "prodigal woman," "the Lady of hope," "the foremost Argentine samaritan." It took only a few months for her to utterly fascinate her country, but she felt Argentina was too small for her. In 1947 she tried to add Europe to her conquests. The reporters christened her triumphal journey of that year "the Rainbow Tour" (*la travesía del Arco Iris*). Glittering at the head of her royal procession, she conquered Spain, had less success in Italy and some other countries, but in Paris, Cardinal Roncalli—the future John XXIII—would exclaim, when he saw her about to enter Notre Dame: "The Empress Eugenie has returned!" When she felt that she had won the heart of Europe, her ambition increased considerably: "What I want is to pass into History." Her sudden illness would swell the limits of that dream into a wish for immortality. And to achieve it, she herself ordered (specifying every detail) that her body be embalmed. (A darker version of this decision claims that Perón himself decided on the embalming, and ordered that Evita begin to be injected months before her death with "chemical preparations" that would retard the visual deterioration of her body; he also, according to this story, forbade the use of painkillers, which could have interfered with the cosmetic chemicals.) She would die of cancer of the uterus, at the age of thirty-three. Half a million people attended the monumental funeral, showering her with 1.5 million yellow roses, alhelís, and chrysanthemums. But afterward the body would find no rest. As if animated by a life of its own and casting a spell over anyone who took charge of it, the angelic object would endure an incredible nomadic journey of almost twenty years across Argentina and Europe. It was hidden, buried, and dug up various times; once it was mutilated and it wound up eventually accompanying Perón into exile. This necrophilic process of wandering is the central theme of the dark and fascinating novel *Santa Evita*, by Tomás Eloy Martínez. And in the end, after the no less incredible triumphal return of Perón to Argentina in 1973, pressure grew to repatriate Evita's remains. After the *caudillo*'s death, his widow Isabelita—who, it is said, tried to absorb the soul of the dead Evita—brought the body to Argentina and gave it a Christian burial in the cemetery of La Recoleta, where Eva Perón now rests. But is she really at rest?

II

If the history of the embalmed body belongs more to the literature of the macabre (with overtones of Dracula himself), the ongoing obsession with remembering Evita has two sides to it: the religious and the mythological. Long before her death, Eva Perón had attracted a level of devotion in Argentina comparable to the adoration normally accorded to the various representations of the Virgin Mary. It was an idolatry that reached extremes of hysteria. People sent her letters so that they might "have a place in your thoughts." "It is like being in the mind of God," wrote a victim of polio. Many Argentines decided that the best way to demonstrate love for their saint was to establish new records: for unremitting work, for fasting, for dancing the tango, for linked sequences of shots on a pool table. Tomás Eloy Martínez offers a lively re-creation of scenes that surpass the *Guinness Book of World Records*. To ask God that He heal Evita's illness, a harness maker makes a thousand-kilometer pilgrimage on foot to a statue of Cristo Redentor in the Andes. He is accompanied by his wife and three children, one of them a babe in arms. Questioned about his intentions, he answers, "If Evita dies, thousands will be abandoned. You can find people like us anywhere, but there's only one saint like Evita." For many months after her death, the radio stations of Argentina would interrupt their broadcasts at 8:25 every evening to inform their listeners that, exactly at that moment, "Eva had entered immortality." The Vatican received forty thousand letters asking that she be canonized. (The Holy See refused to consider it.) The fetishism that accrued to her person and to objects that she had touched would reach the extreme of treating as "sacred" the banknotes she had lavishly distributed. It was a collective fervor not easy to explain. Jorge Luis Borges has observed that "no one is Catholic in Argentina but every one has to pretend to be . . . the Catechism has been replaced by Argentine history." Perhaps Evita, for this very reason, would, for a while, come to fill the void of faith in Argentine piety.

The "religious" devotion to Evita—her life viewed as hagiography—would diminish with time but not the mythology that had collected around her. Endless articles, newspaper stories, factual revelations, and books would be written. Documentaries and fiction films would be produced. She would be both venerated and despised: the Great Saint, the Great Whore.

III

What were the wellsprings of her oceanic ambition? The first ingredient was certainly her position as not only an illegitimate child but (culturally even worse) the product of an adulterous relationship. Juan Duarte, Evita's father, was a man of the Argentine middle class, who administered haciendas. While Evita was growing up, her father was supporting his legitimate family in the town of Chivilcoy. Years before, he had abandoned Eva's mother, Juana Ibarguren, leaving her with five children: his son Juan and his four daughters. Doña Juana was an illegitimate child herself and in bringing up her offspring, she suffered real need. She lived with all her children in a single room of the inn that she managed and she had to take in other people's sewing, working in the same room on her Singer machine. The elusive Juan Duarte did not even attend the baptism of his youngest illegitimate daughter, Evita, "a daughter not of love but of habit," in his own words to Juana as reported by Martínez. Juana remembered, "He saw Evita so rarely that if he had run across her in the middle of the fields, he would not have recognized her." Eva came to know her father only in his coffin on the day of his burial, when his legitimate family brutally expelled Juana Ibarguren and her children from the graveside funeral.

Fueled by the weight of his illegitimate birth—a particular badge of shame within Catholic societies—a president of Mexico, General Plutarco Elías Calles, would unleash a war with the Catholic Church that cost seventy thousand lives during the 1920s. As for Eva, she retained her rancor and resentment across the long years. Before formally marrying Perón, she returned to the town of Los Toldos, her actual birthplace, where she removed the original record of her birth (as Eva Ibarguren) and then had a new certificate deposited in Junín under the name of Duarte, which her father had denied her. During her time in power, she was obsessed with finding fiancés for women who had been prostitutes and marrying off couples living out of wedlock with their children. In 1951 she was the godmother at 804 weddings.

Another source of resentment was her sexual history. Many jokes and insults would be heaped upon her and her memory, based on the assumption that she had been a prostitute. Borges, who hated her, told me a story of this kind, involving a pun in Spanish. A proposal is made to change the name of the city of La Plata to Evita Perón. But Perón himself has doubts about it. A member of Congress comes up with the ideal solution: "Let's call the city La Pluta," a fusion in Spanish of the words *plata* (silver, money) and *puta* (whore). What is nevertheless certain is that the role of seductress hardly suited her. "Those who knew her," Martínez says, "considered her the least sexual woman in the world." The male lead in one of her movies later said about her, "You couldn't get yourself excited about her even if the two of you were alone on a desert island." Dujovne presents Evita's amours—except for the Chilean Emilio Karstulovic, editor of her favorite magazine, *Sintonía*, and of course Perón himself—as transient, unhappy, and often humiliating. In *Santa Evita*, Martínez reconstructs from the statements of two friends a picture of her in those first six months of 1943: "a weak little creature, sick, insipid . . . she had small breasts and a complex about them . . . she was like one of those street cats that have survived cold, hunger, the harshness of human beings."

Martínez was able to establish that between February and May 1943, she spent time in the Otamendi y Miroli clinic of Buenos Aires under the name of María Eva Ibarguren:

She was pregnant . . . Neither she nor the father wanted the child . . . The problem was that the abortion ended badly. They tore the base of her uterus, the ligaments, the fallopian tube. A half hour afterwards, she collapsed covered with blood, and with peritonitis . . . In those months she would have rather been dead . . . she could have put a bullet into her head.

The episode was only one chapter in a long catalogue of insults and injuries that Eva retained in her memory, with the hope of eventual revenge. "If Eva managed to become somebody," said one informant to Martínez, "it's because of her intention never to forgive." Someone told the actress and singer Madonna (who played Eva Perón in Alan Parker's overly facile and trivializing musical film, *Evita*) that "Evita had the sweetness of revenge running through her veins."

Her liaison with Perón redeemed her. He would raise her to a position from which she could reverse her fate and avenge every affront. But Perón needed her as much as she needed him. Based on his recent experience as a military observer in Mussolini's Italy—a leader whom he venerated and for whom he would have "raised a monument at every corner"—Perón had learned what he saw as the key to seizing hold of Argentina: "managing men is a technique . . . an art of military precision. I learned it in Italy in 1940. Those people really knew how to command." He was also an assiduous reader of *Mein Kampf* and had visited Berlin during the war. Taking Goebbels as a guide, he would emphasize the importance of oratory and especially the medium of radio in the political manipulation of the masses. And here was where Evita and the sociological circumstances of the time met in perfect union. Buenos Aires, like other Latin American capitals, was filled with a new body of urban workers, uneducated people who had swarmed from the country to the city—like Evita herself—near the beginning of World

War II. They were *los descamisados*, "those without shirts," uprooted masses hungry for a savior. They were Evita's people and she was Perón's perfect partner in the enterprise of power, the orator who could hypnotize the *descamisados*, the *caudilla* of the *Justicialista* movement.

Perón himself was a complex and cleverly manipulative man. The old wolf was twenty-five years older than his consort. A distinguished athlete, an idiosyncratic author of texts on military history and the place-names of the Mapuche Indians of Chile, he was more a charismatic and astute politician than a soldier. Years later, he would assert, from his comfortable exile in Madrid, that "I created Eva." And in a sense he was right.

Did he and Evita love each other? Perhaps they did. In some way. Or so we can gather from their exchanges of letters, although figures at their level of power are always thinking of an additional anonymous recipient: the later generations.

Eva's true stardom began October 17, 1945, when Perón was acclaimed by a crowd of three hundred thousand in the Plaza de Mayo. Now as the wife of the president of the republic, she moved with him to the Palacio Unzué, a modest residence of 283 rooms, barely enough to accommodate Eva's wardrobe. From the heights of her new position, she could remold her own history from its roots. It was like reviewing the film of her life and doing it over as she wished it might have been. She began by altering the paper trail to legitimize her birth. And then she would accumulate the fortune that she felt she deserved. Nothing could ever be enough because her social rancor was so intense. Displaying wealth and power was her way of emulating and defying the stratified and rigid society that had treated her with disdain. (Also, in effect, a scandalously racist society where the light-skinned upper class—who considered themselves quite "English"— rained down their contempt on the lower classes, the *cabecitas negras*, with their often darker skin colors.) Eva as a child had an additional burden. She had grown up with a calcium deficiency that made her painfully conscious of her vulnerability. The young girl saw her own image in a mutilated doll that her mother gave her for Christmas. It is hardly surprising that after reversing the course of her own destiny, she tried to do the same for all the poor of her country.

During Christmas of 1947, she gave away five million toys. Year after year she distributed tens of thousands of shoes, pants, dresses, jars, dolls, tricycles, soccer balls, baby bottles, food products, dentures, sewing machines. "You have the right to ask!" she would shout to the ecstatic beneficiaries of her charity, while not only the free bread mounted up but also a flood of social work as hallucinatory as it was tangible and often effective: small cities for students and others specifically for children (they were in some sense pre-Disneylands), polyclinic institutes, residences for the aged, hospital trains moving through the country. Who paid the price? Not Eva herself, certainly, but the treasury reserves Argentina had accumulated over the decades, or the workers themselves with their "voluntary" donations, and, of course, the future generations impoverished, thrown into debt, devoured by inflation. The couple found a country that was economically among the fifteen richest in the world (with a huge budget surplus after World War II) and left a nation divided and very far from the levels of production and efficiency that Argentina had shown through the 1940s.

Within the history of populism, Eva Perón broke all records. She would receive twenty delegations a day. She would frenetically visit factories, schools, hospitals, union centers, sporting clubs, neighborhoods, and small towns. With equal devotion she would inaugurate bridges, new stretches of roads, rural schools, and soccer tournaments. When she had nothing else to give away, she distributed banknotes or advice. And she was also, in some real sense, a feminist who gave the women of Argentina the right to vote and be elected to office.

Everything she did, she would supervise personally. (Fairy godmothers, as is well-known, rarely delegate authority.) She would question people on their individual situations: "How many children do you have? Do they sleep in beds?" Her confessor, the Jesuit Father Benítez, wrote: "I have seen her kiss lepers, people with tuberculosis and cancer . . . embrace the poor in their rags and be inundated with their fleas." Although an element of theater was always clearly present in these manifestations of charity, there is no doubt that she was moved by a genuine compassion for human suffering. By a kind of mission.

IV
———

Juan and Evita Perón had their opponents (dissident journalists, leftists, independent critics) jailed, sometimes killed, often tortured. According to Dujovne, in at least one instance, involving the electric torture of women employees of the Telephone Company who had refused to join the Peronist Party, Evita herself was rumored to have given the order for the prods to be applied. The facts remain no less incriminating even if it must be added that the Peróns' use of torture and murder cannot be compared to the orgy of sadism unleashed by the military government and its paramilitary allies during the Argentine "Dirty War" of the late 1970s and early '80s. But toward the end of Perón's first period in power, his torturers would learn more sophisticated techniques from some of the century's greatest experts at the trade: the Nazi war criminals who flooded to sanctuary in Argentina.

The admiration of the Argentine army for their German counterparts (proverbial during the final decades of the nineteenth century) had grown even stronger with the crisis of 1929—a humiliating time for Argentina, with its export economy dependent on England—and it would become even more firm and solid with the rise of Hitler. Perón was a member of the military group that in 1943 left no doubt about their sympathies in a secretly composed manifesto: "Today Germany is giving life a heroic meaning. It is an example to follow . . . The struggle of Hitler, in peace as in war, should lead us on." The Argentine government placed its bets on the Axis, literally until the last minute. When Argentina declared war (nominally taking the side of the Allies) on March 27, 1945, the real reason—according to the cynical account of Perón himself—was to provide a way to save Nazi lives. And he was successful. According to Dujovne, by 1947 ninety thousand Nazis were living securely in Juan and Evita's Argentina.

Not long after meeting Perón, Evita had moved to a sumptuous mansion: the considerate gift of one of Perón's friends, the German millionaire (and Nazi agent) Rudolf Ludwig Freude. This individual, along with three of his countrymen named Dörge, Von Leute, and Staudt, would figure in a still obscure episode. (Dujovne notes that the facts have never been fully established but the evidence she offers, based on dozens of sources and investigations, is overwhelming.) The issue was nothing less than the delivery of the treasure of the Nazis to safekeeping in Argentina. The action took place around the time of the collapse of Nazi Germany in 1945. Two German submarines deposited their cargo on the docks of La Plata. There are at least two precise documentations of the contents. The lists coincide: tens of millions of dollars in various currencies, 2,511 kilograms of gold, 4,638 karats of diamonds, and a river of jewels, works of art, and precious objects stolen from the Jews of Europe and formerly deposited in the Reichsbank of Berlin. Vice Führer Martin Bormann is supposed to have entrusted the operation to Otto Skorzeny, chief of Hitler's commando forces. According to Dujovne, the operation also was supported by members of the Vatican hierarchy. Whether that is true or not, it is certain that Croatian priests were central figures in the operation of what Allied intelligence called "the rat line," which funneled Nazis and Nazi "property" to sympathetic Latin American countries and most especially Argentina.

It is said that Bormann himself was scheduled to arrive in Argentina and oversee the treasure. According to various sources—among them Skorzeny, who led the commando raid that freed Mussolini in 1943 and would, in 1948, find a comfortable postwar refuge in Argentina—the real overseers were none other than Juan and Evita Perón. Certainly Perón had been a key element in the operation, and he would never hide his great sympathy for the Nazis. Among other direct actions, he is supposed to have provided the military attaché of the German embassy with eight thousand Argentine passports and 1,100 identity cards; and he would refer to the refugees of the Luftwaffe as *"Justicialistas* of the air." In recompense for his services, the Nazis opened an account for him in Switzerland and gave him a mansion in Cairo where, in 1960, he would live for a time.

Perhaps, up to this point, Evita was playing a nonspeaking role: serving coffee, accepting gifts. But later, during her "Rainbow Tour" across Europe, odd events began to multiply. In Rapallo, Italy, she met with an important figure in the Vatican hierarchy. Almost at the same time, a shipment of Argentine wheat docked at Genoa. Was she only discussing the wheat? And her itinerary seemed to lack rhyme or reason: Lisbon to Paris to the Côte d'Azur to Switzerland to Lisbon to Dakar. She spent five days in Switzerland and in Lisbon had a long meeting with the deposed king Umberto of Italy. Various clues collected by Dujovne, derived from monographs on the subject, as well as testimony from Skorzeny himself suggest that Eva, with the aid of someone in the Vatican hierarchy and the mediation of King Umberto, deposited in Switzerland at least some part of the treasure of the Nazis. The death of her brother Juan, less than a year after hers, under circumstances that have never been clarified (it was said to be suicide but he was probably murdered) may support the hypothesis that he was the guardian of the secret bank deposit. The four Germans supposedly involved—Dörge, Von Leute, Staudt, and the millionaire Freude himself—all died between 1948 and 1952, perhaps executed by order of the Nazi hierarchy "in exile," which could thereby claim full use of the treasure for their own purposes. Perón is also supposed to have returned part of the hoard to Skorzeny. The real story continues to be veiled in mystery. Dujovne even speculates that the 1994 bombing of the Jewish Community Center in Buenos Aires had some connection with the documentation being developed there on Nazi networks and dealings in Argentina.

There is no mystery at all about the direct aid given by Evita to the mass murderers of Croatia, one of Hitler's most savage satellites. In 1954, *Izbor*, the magazine of the Argentine Croatian community, would write: "We wandered through Europe from country to country until the day on which our suffering knocked on the doors of the noblest heart then beating in the world, that of Eva Perón, who was then in Rome." Among the war criminals who, thanks to Evita Perón, obtained visas or passports through the International Red Cross was Ante

Pavelic, the Croatian führer himself, who had presided over the mur-
ders—by direct, hands-on methods—of many hundreds of thousands
of Serbs, Jews, and Gypsies in the concentration camps of fascist Croatia. He reached Buenos Aires under a false name and wearing the robe
of a priest, together with his compatriots Vjekoslav Vrancic (decorated
by Hitler in honor of his planning skills at the work of mass deporta-
tion) and Branko Benzon, who became Juan Perón's personal physi-
cian. With them came a band of Ustashe (Croatian fascist) refugees,
some of whom, says Dujovne, contributed their more developed skills
at torture to the repertoire of the Peronista police.

In 1955, the Revolución Libertadora (which overthrew Perón) put
some personal belongings of Juan and Evita on exhibit. Among the objects was a sumptuous storage box adorned with inlay and containing
a set of silver plates. On the lid was a Star of David in mother-of-pearl.
Obviously a part of the Nazi plunder, its significance could not have
passed unnoticed even by the most uninformed of fairy godmothers.

v

The critics of Eva Perón used to say that she had done "good very badly
and evil very well." Perhaps they were somewhat off in the first half
of the statement. Eva came from the disinherited and she was able to
genuinely communicate with a significant number of them and, fleet-
ingly at least, they thought and felt that she helped them. The second
part of the assertion, however, is surely no mistake. The political conduct of Peronism is a stunning example of what Latin American nations concerned with the creation of a responsible future are trying to
overcome.

Peronism was a veritable manual of antidemocratic practices. The
liberal opposition (the *Partido Radical*), the socialists and the communists, opposition labor leaders and factions were all systematically
persecuted. The official, nationalist newspapers—among them the
Nazi *Deutsche La Plata Zeitung*—could count on generous tax exemp-
tions. The free press almost disappeared, with the government (falsely

claiming a scarcity) rationing their supply of newsprint and then forc-
ing sales to government loyalists or directly expropriating newspapers
or else shutting them down with strong-arm actions. The grounds of
the National University were violated on various occasions and the
institution was progressively stripped of its autonomy. "The martial
figure of Perón and the angelic figure of his spouse, wrapped in delicately pinkish clouds," recalls the historian Tulio Halperín Donghi,
"began to decorate the readers for primary schools." Raúl Apold, a
disciple of Joseph Goebbels, was given the job of creating the apparatus of Peronista propaganda. His office produced the slogan "Perón
accomplishes, Eva dignifies." Public competitions were organized and
mass-participation games invented in which the villains were always
the anti-Peronistas.

In the best fascist style, a committee was created to investigate "anti-
Argentine activities" (a synonym of course for anti-Peronista actions
of any kind). The committee censured books and jailed authors. They
imprisoned the writer Victoria Ocampo, editor of the internationally
acclaimed magazine *Sur*, which had for decades published the best literature of the Hispanic world. Jorge Luis Borges's mother was put under
house arrest, his sister was sent to jail, and Borges himself fired from
his job in the National Library and given the position of chicken inspector for the markets of Buenos Aires (which he obviously refused). Radio
stations could not broadcast even the slightest criticism of the government. Radio Belgrano, for which Eva had portrayed famous women,
became her personal property. Any musician or dancer or singer who
failed to demonstrate attachment to the regime suffered for it, while
court poets flourished as never before.

Punctiliously observing the old Spanish tradition of patrimonial
power, Juan and Evita behaved like a single and only legitimate lord
and master of Argentina. The entire Duarte family would prosper
under the shade of Evita. Her brother Juan became Perón's corrupt and
influential secretary, one of her brothers-in-law was a senator, another
director of the customs agency, another one a prominent judge. Congress functioned as a simple adjunct to the Peróns, who eliminated the

protections of congressional immunity. Once when Evita visited the Supreme Court, the chief justice asked her politely to sit down in the public area—next to his own wife—rather than on the bench by his side. Evita had him fired from the court. She would later, by fiat, fire many judges throughout the legal system. Toward the end of her career, she proposed herself for the vice presidency of the republic. But this time Juan Perón, under pressure from the military, refused to support her wishes. Had she lived, perhaps she might even have considered trying to overthrow him. She had already played, and well remembered, the role of Catherine the Great.

POPULISM IN itself is a neutral term that can be applied to any political program that claims to be overwhelmingly concerned with improving the economic condition of the majority of a country's population and that speaks and appeals directly to them. Peronism was really the first great populist movement in Latin America, and was strongly stamped and branded by three features: the vertical mobilization of the masses, the tendency to privilege demand rather than productive energy (with its serious economic consequences), and its cult of the leader, the *caudillo*, in this case two of them, Perón and Evita. Peronism ushered the lower economic classes into the citadel of the State. This acceptance of them was not in itself so different from some other Latin American countries, including Mexico. Where it radically differed was in the fact that the "organized workers' movement" was the first of its kind not to embrace the doctrines or traditional programs and demands of the political left. Embodied (almost incarnated) in the figure of Evita, Peronism was (in a mode very different from, for instance, the Mexican PRI) a program of distribution from on high, propagandistically fueled by the engine of social resentment.

Caudillismo, the oldest of the continent's social ills—a distant echo both of Moorish sheiks and Christian warlords during the war of the Reconquista in medieval Spain—means the concentration of power into the hands of a single man, and, in this exceptional case, of power (though shared with Perón himself) into the grasp of a single woman, a *caudilla* richly endowed with charisma. When the *caudillo* takes over, the strictly *personal* passions of a leader (traumas, obsessions, whims) are transferred to the history of the nation, converting history into a kind of "biography of power." Almost all our countries have experienced this phenomenon, but in Peronist Argentina, it acquired a special emphasis of its own, since the personal power of Juan and Evita Perón had no institutional limits at all except eventually for the veto of the army. Eva could and did convert Argentina into a stage for the movie of her own life.

But why, since the collapse of the dictatorship, has the prestige of Perón still continued to influence national politics so that a party of moderately left Peronistas now holds (and was freely elected) to power? The answer likely lies in the fact that Evita forced the elite to recognize the existence of the poor and because the Peronista programs, however unbalanced and financially spendthrift, are remembered as an age when the needs of the *cabecitas negras* took center stage in Argentina. And we have the curious phenomenon of these social programs (as well as a hand strong enough to carry them through) appealing to the "left Peronists" while a ruthless authoritarianism (often linked to the parochial interests of morally corrupted unions) spoke to the "Peronists of the right."

Across the rainbow of ideology, Evita moved from being the goddess of right-wing populism to the icon of many (especially the terrorist Montoneros) among the Marxist revolutionaries who were the first target (to be followed by many others) of the exterminationist military regime of 1976–83. "If Eva were alive, she would be a Montonera," said these Argentine urban guerrillas. Were they right? The question is not answerable but history did provide an ambiguous and horrifying response. During one of the most murderous military dictatorships in the history of Latin America, many of these "left-Peronist" guerrillas (as well as thousands of men, women, and children who had never lifted a finger in violence) would die (often thrown, still barely alive, from airplanes into the Atlantic Ocean) after long weeks and months of unspeakable torture at the hands of—among others—"Peronists of the right."

Peronism involved a formidable machinery of repression but it was not, strictly speaking, an essentially militarist dictatorship. Perón was not a traditional Argentine soldier. He permitted elections and his social policies were intensely disliked by most of the traditional military elite, who when they seized power also did ever-increasing economic damage to the country. But in the government of Juan and Evita, another gross weakness (as through much of the history of Argentina and other Latin American countries) was a commitment to intense chauvinism. Chauvinism is in essence an overvaluation, careless and ultimately erroneous, of the situation and destiny of one's own country among the nations of the world. Argentina, gifted with an immense and wealthy territory, a relatively literate and homogenous population, might have concentrated its energies into a process of balanced development, without wasting its accumulated wealth. But Argentina lost its way and almost the entire century, victimized by a false dream of total self-sufficiency and an unhealthy obsession with opposing the Anglo-Saxon world.

As for Eva Perón, she was certainly the greatest female demagogue of the twentieth century. Perhaps she represents a little of the best in the Spanish Christian heritage of Latin America, an echo of the old sense of distributive justice, a footnote to the universal history of charity. But it should not be forgotten that she and her husband also represented some of the worst of this tradition (and of the troubled twentieth century) and that their history places them within the range of human action well described by the title of one of Jorge Luis Borges's books: *The Universal History of Infamy.*

7

Che Guevara

THE SAINT ENRAGED

"Do not forget this minor condottiere of the twentieth century," wrote Che Guevara to his parents in March of 1965, as he was about to embark on the final stage of his adventurous voyage through life. The revolution to which he made a decisive contribution; the communist utopia he wanted to build (and could not construct) through the power of his will; the two, three, many Vietnams that he dreamed about and could not ignite; the thousands of young men and women who took to the mountains in emulation of him, to create the "new man" or meet death as martyrs; the sequel of desolation and slaughter left by the guerrilla wars and their suppression from Mexico to Argentina—all of it was vaguely predicted within the course of history long before November 25, 1956, the day that Che and Fidel Castro and a handful of comrades set off from the coast of Mexico in a barely seaworthy boat headed for Cuba. The history of Latin America foreshadowed—almost in the religious sense of the term—a figure like Che Guevara. And he duly arrived, at the right time and place. From then on, not only Latin America but the entire world would have ample reason to remember this "condottiere of the twentieth century."

Those years of revolution cannot be understood without considering the growth of anti-Americanism in Latin American history. It was not the same throughout the continent. In the Southern Cone, it was an ideology presented as a conflict of cultures: Hispanic America against the Anglo-Saxons, Ariel against Caliban. In Central America and the Caribbean, the confrontation was far more direct and practical. The military, political, and commercial presence of the United States had been growing, especially since 1898, and was sometimes overwhelming. For these countries, the problem was never abstract or vaguely ideological. How to struggle with this great power, how to channel it, how to limit it, and eventually, how to fight it. And perhaps no other country would experience this drama with the same intensity as Cuba.

From the beginning of the century and into the 1950s, the collective memory of many Cubans would develop a backlog of searing historical facts (like the continued presence of American troops after the Spanish-American War, only remedied by Cuban agreement to the Platt Amendment, which established American interference in Cuban domestic and foreign affairs and ceded Guantanamo to the American navy). But the greatest insult was the total identification of American national and private commercial interests. Theodore Roosevelt's cabinet included three secretaries with direct financial interests in Cuba. In 1922, a Cuban journalist would predict, "Hatred of the Yankees will become the religion of Cubans." In 1947, the liberal Mexican historian Daniel Cosío Villegas would write prophetically:

> . . . in Latin America, there lies sleeping, quiet as stagnant water, a
> thick layer of distrust, of rancor against the United States. On the
> day when, under the protection of governmental tolerance, four
> or five agitators in each one of the principal Latin American coun-
> tries launch themselves into a campaign of defamation, of hatred
> toward the United States, on that day all of Latin America will
> seethe with restlessness and will be ready for anything

By the end of World War II, Latin American liberals like Cosío Villegas were a species on their way to extinction. They were being replaced by the extremes of right and left, which were equally contemptuous of what they termed "Anglo-Saxon democracy." The brief episode of Franklin Delano Roosevelt's Good Neighbor policy and the heyday of Pan-Americanism was quickly followed by the proxy politics of the Cold War. In various countries of Latin America, the right, formerly pro-German but with its model defeated in war, would find some common ground with the growing left in anti-American nationalism. The United States—as José Martí had warned, incessantly—did not have the vision to understand (let alone respect) its neighbors and so they did not notice (or noticed too late, after 1959) that they had valuable allies in the democratic leaders of the region.

Among them, the most outstanding was the Venezuelan Rómulo Betancourt, who had been fighting since 1929 for democracy in his country. Venezuela, since the days of the Liberator Bolívar, had never had a single free election before 1947. As an appointed interim president of Venezuela from 1945 to 1948, Betancourt supported the 1947 campaign of the writer Rómulo Gallegos, who won the election. Shortly afterward, a military coup removed him and democracy from Venezuela. Predictably, the United States supported the new dictator, Marcos Pérez Jiménez. President Eisenhower, in 1958, invited him to Washington and honored him for his service to democracy, while the democrat Betancourt was stigmatized as a "communist." And this sort of abuse was not limited to politicians. Cosío Villegas, an impeccable liberal, reaffirmed the imminent danger in Latin America of a "belated nationalist revolution." He was invited to give a paper at Johns Hopkins University, but it had to be read by an American surrogate, because Cosío was denied a visa. The American academic read Cosío's observation that, in Latin America, communist militancy could proceed "in ideal conditions."

The Americans would not become aware quickly enough of this swelling tide of hatred. Or when they did take note of it, they would act to feed it, as in Guatemala in 1954. Colonel Carlos Castillo Armas, openly supported by the CIA, violently overthrew the duly elected nationalist and reformist government of Jacobo Arbenz. The spark that would later flame into the Cuban Revolution was truly struck in the streets of Guatemala, among its labor unions and its students. And it was there that a twenty-six-year-old Argentine doctor, Ernesto Guevara, closely observing the sequence of events, mourned the fact that Arbenz had not armed the people and that his government had fallen "betrayed within and beyond its borders . . . like the Spanish Republic" and then added: "it is time that the bludgeon be answered with the bludgeon. If one has to die, better that it be like Sandino" (the leader of the guerrilla resistance to the American invasion of Nicaragua in 1927–33, who was assassinated by Anastasio Somoza, founder of a pro-American family tyranny that lasted forty years) "than like [Manuel] Azaña" (the last president of the Spanish Republic, who died an exile, in Nazi-occupied France, after resigning his presidency).

The Argentine doctor was in Guatemala on one of his wanderings through Latin America. He had become convinced that "someday the dark forces that oppress the subjugated, colonial world will be defeated"; and he was filled with "growing indignation" in response to "the way in which the *gringos* have been treating Latin America." In the cultural microcosm of the city of Córdoba, where he had grown up, the young doctor had encountered an ambience that stimulated his initial and fundamental anti-Americanism, involving an intense cultural contempt for the "Yankees" (though Guevara would always prefer the much more negatively charged word *gringos*). Ernesto would have also imbibed feelings of anger at injustice within the atmosphere of his own family when, as a boy of ten, he met refugees from the Spanish Republic who were welcomed into his home. And the husband of his maternal aunt was a newspaper correspondent during the Spanish Civil War. He would have heard a firsthand version of the Spanish agony.

II

Ernesto Guevara de la Serna was said to be born on June 14, 1928 (actually one month earlier, the later date meant to mask his mother's premarital pregnancy). Both his mother and father came from families of high status in Argentine society. His mother, Celia de la Serna, whom Che would adore all his life long, could trace her ancestry back to a royal viceroy of colonial Peru and she received a substantial inheritance at the age of twenty-one. Ernesto Guevara Lynch, his father, was a great-grandson of one of Argentina's richest men, and his genealogy was studded with noble Irish and Spanish names, though his family was no longer all that wealthy. But the couple tended toward a lifestyle that was more extravagant than their means really afforded them and they displayed the characteristic insouciance toward money of aristocrats by birth but no longer by income. They were left-wing and egalitarian in their values. The presiding political eminence for Ernesto's mother was Alfredo Palacios, the first socialist ever elected to the Argentine parliament and the author of a law requiring employers to allow their workers one day off a week, to enjoy their Sunday rest, as well as prescribing other required free time especially for women and children. It was Argentina's first venture into labor legislation.

The family traveled from place to place as Ernesto's father pursued business prospects that never quite jelled for him, and at one point he became the owner of a five-hundred-acre yerba maté farm in the jungle, where he would be remembered many years later by the local Guarani Indian laborers as a "good man." But both the farm and Celia's income from a family estate in Córdoba province were seriously reduced in the 1930s by the effects of the Great Depression and a severe drought. Times became difficult for them, and even more seriously complicated by expenses and anxiety due to the illness of their eldest son, Ernesto. Their moves were often driven by the effort to find a place where young Ernesto could gain some relief from the condition that was his lifelong curse and stimulus—the asthma that he developed as a child. The attacks would almost strip the boy of his breath, force him to rest motionless, to lie against his mother's breast or sleep pressed close against the chest of his father. In the city of Córdoba, the family found a climate less harmful to Ernesto, and there he went to school. His attendance was irregular, punctuated by asthmatic attacks, by injections and inhalations. During his enforced days of rest, he would try to free himself from his confinement with novels by Robert Louis Stevenson or Jack London, or all twenty-three books by Jules Verne.

But the adolescent Ernesto was not about to accept the limitations imposed by his asthma, no more than he would tolerate other limitations in the future. He chose to escape from his precarious physical condition through sheer will. He took up rugby, a favorite sport of the

Anglophile upper classes of Argentina. He would edit the first Argentine magazine, called *Tackle*, dedicated completely to rugby. And he would sign his articles *Chang-cho*, a would-be orientalized version of one of his nicknames, Chancho (Pig), which he adopted proudly, based on his careless way of dressing and his asthma-inspired aversion to cold water. When he grew older, into a handsome and voluble young man, this "Bohemian" look, amid upper-class adolescents totally committed to neatness and the latest styles, helped rather than hindered his attractiveness to women.

His fellow rugby players called him "Furibundo Serna," or "Raging Serna," for the intensity of his game. Rugby is surely one of the most grueling physical ordeals an asthmatic could face. It combines the continuous running necessary in soccer with harsh physical contact.

The ideal physique for a rugby player is the kind of solid, even massive but relatively supple musculature that Ernesto lacked. It requires great endurance, since the action never stops, nor do the physical encounters. And it is a team game, where the player has to hold his position, no matter what, partly to protect other players. A hole in the formation can leave a teammate more liable to injury. And though the hitting is not as fierce as in American football, it is constant and wearying. A rugby player has to tolerate pain and exhaustion—and transcend them both, ideally, to keep on playing even with broken fingers or cracked ribs. Though it was a favorite game of English public school boys, its origins are more plebeian. (And its international championship teams are ultra-macho.) The sport requires toughness, discipline, obedience, and comradeship.

For a slightly built asthmatic like the young Ernesto, its challenges were enormous. Sometimes, very much against his will, he would have to go to the sidelines because he was unable to breathe, and he would spend minutes drawing on his inhaler, painfully gasping for breath, and then insist on returning, to hurl his body against larger and stronger men, rolling in the dirt and mud of the playing field. In a sense, rugby was a training school for his physical and political future. And he did succeed in greatly strengthening his body, though to his dying day, the threat of crippling attacks of asthma would always be with him.

Mastering problems through the force of his will would be one of the leitmotifs of Guevara's life. The constant shadow of his own illness and the beginning of his beloved mother's twenty-year struggle with cancer probably contributed to his eventual choice of medicine as a career. He did well enough in school, though he never seemed to study, but Ernesto could not be just an ordinary student. He borrowed books from his friend Gustavo Roca, the son of Deodoro Roca, who had been the intellectual leader of the 1918 reforms at the University of Córdoba, a major impulse in moving the conservative, Catholic ambience of that city toward the much more progressive atmosphere in which Ernesto's mother was raised. The elder Roca (Ernesto's friendship with the son would last a lifetime) centered his ideas around a theory of "the integral man." Ernesto's girlfriend Tita Infante gave him a copy of *Bourgeois Humanism and Proletarian Humanism: From Erasmus to Romain Rolland,* by Aníbal Ponce, one of the major influences on Guevara's later thought. Ponce insisted that it was the responsibility of socialism "to construct a new sensibility" and he preached the need to envision socialism and communism as the permanent and continual creation of "a new culture and a complete man, unified, not torn or mutilated, a man absolutely new."

For the young Ernesto, these seemed to be fresh and exhilarating ideas and they would combine with a more physically appealing impulse, the will to learn more and to expand his horizons by a direct experience of "our America." The young man who would pass into history as *El Che* would soon begin to move from his Argentine identity toward a larger fatherland, a broader loyalty, becoming a "citizen" of what he would call (broadening out the phrase of José Martí) "our America with a capital A."

With his newly forged strength and endurance, he would set off on voyages, at first relatively local and then traveling rough through much of Argentina by himself in 1950 (stopping off to visit friends) on a motorbike trip of more than 2,500 miles. Two years later, with a friend and a motorcycle, he would journey across the body of Latin America. The urge to "move on" became another constant in his life. He kept a travel journal and steadily wrote to his family and his girlfriends. Women entered his life when he was quite young, yet he tended to move on from them as well. In the beginning it was a search for adventure without direction, but then his roaming—and his studies—came to be charged with a purpose, to confront and diminish human pain. He worked in leper hospitals on his travels; he thought he might become a celebrated allergist; but it was the discovery of America, the southern continent, the vast land and its miseries and its relation to the Colossus of the North, that finally possessed him.

On the motorcycle trip of 1952 (he also took various forms of ground travel, as the bike broke down) Guevara noted the "absurd sense of caste" in Bolivia (a country that at the time was actually undergoing its first agrarian reform—including some distribution of land—under President Paz Estenssoro). His sense of egalitarianism was deeply offended, as later he would be disturbed during his first voyage to Russia by the fact that there was a special elevator in a government building for party officials only. On his way to Machu Picchu he commented in his journal that "Peru hasn't yet emerged from the feudal condition of the colony. It's still waiting for the blood of a liberating revolution." As usual, he took on his asthma like an enemy to be faced down, swimming two and a half miles in the Amazon. He would later write that "America will be the theater of my adventures in a way much more important than I would have believed. I really think I have come to understand America and I feel myself American, different from any other people on the earth."

While he was in Peru, he met Doctor Hugo Pesce, director of Peru's leper treatment program, who had been a militant companion of José Carlos Mariátegui. (They had been co-founders of the Peruvian Socialist Party. Pesce wrote for Mariátegui's journal *Amauta* and was one of the delegates sent by Mariátegui to the 1929 Congress of the Comintern in Argentina.) Pesce gave him some of Mariátegui's writings and, long after, when he had already become *El Che*, Guevara would send

Pesce a copy of his book *Guerrilla Warfare* inscribed "To Doctor Hugo Pesce, who aroused, perhaps without knowing it, a great change in my attitude toward life and society. With the adventurous enthusiasm of always but now directed toward aims more in harmony with the needs of America."

In retrospect, Ernesto's time in Peru during his first great geographic adventure would be a critical turning point in his progress toward the near mythical persona of *El Che.* The young Argentine doctor had apparently begun the trip with his intention still intact of a future (hopefully outstanding) career as an allergist, the choice of a specialty clearly influenced by his own great physical problem. And he would speak with medical people and spend time (which he later described) working in a leprosarium. But in his personal diaries there is almost nothing about medicine. He does write about his asthma, briefly mentions his encounter with lepers, and raises questions that are not clinical but political. Sometimes he refers to his conversations with Pesce, but the points of interest are overwhelmingly political and social. It is already the picture of a young man on his way to becoming a revolutionary.

At the end of his trip, Guevara spent a brief and unhappy time in Miami. Back in Argentina, he quickly finished his medical studies. Then he left for good, for "America." With the fall of the Arbenz government to the CIA-sponsored coup in Guatemala (the beginning of almost four decades of guerrilla warfare and army genocide in that country), Guevara moved toward a more conscious Marxism, a strongly pro-Soviet position based on emotion rather than knowledge (he would cling to it for years and then in large part abandon it), and an ever stronger sense of the social illness that he felt was stripping the breath away from Latin America. He had a very specific idea about the cause of all this: "the blond and efficient administrators, the Yankee masters." In the *bananera* zone of southern Costa Rica, he would write:

I had the opportunity to pass through the dominions of United Fruit, convincing me yet one more time of how terrible those capitalist octopuses are. I have taken an oath before a picture of the old and lamented comrade Stalin not to rest until [I see them] destroyed.

When, by chance, he came to meet Rómulo Betancourt, the Venezuelan democratic politician, Guevara raised the question many felt to be necessary during the Cold War: "If war breaks out between the United States and Russia, who would you support?" Betancourt inclined toward Washington and Ernesto on the spot branded him as a traitor. Of course, at the time, the American government had decided that Betancourt was a communist.

Among the young radicals attracted to the Guatemala of Jacobo Arbenz was a young Peruvian exile, three years older than Ernesto, named Hilda Gadea. She had more political experience than him but less committed passion. In April 1954 he wrote to his mother: "I'm carrying on interminable discussions with Comrade Hilda Gadea, an Aprista girl. With my characteristic tact, I've been trying to convince her to abandon that shit-eating party." Hilda would become his first wife. It was a relation of intellectual and political comradeship between the radical reader of Mariátegui and the adherent of Haya de la Torre. True to its tradition of welcoming political exiles, Mexico gave shelter to the young couple and other refugees from the Guatemalan military coup.

"In those days, Guevara had a Bohemian quality, a pedantic sense of humor that was provocative and Argentine, he went around shirtless, was somewhat of a narcissist, olive-skinned, of medium height and strongly built, with his pipe and his *mate*, somewhere between an athlete and an asthmatic, he would alternate Stalin with Baudelaire, poetry with Marxism." This perfect description of Ernesto is that of Carlos Franqui, a journalist at that time, who would later play an important part in the cultural life of Cuba during the first years of the Revolution. He had been sent to Mexico by the Cuban anti-Batista movement *26 de Julio* to make contact with their leader, Fidel Castro, who was living in exile after his already legendary and unsuccessful attack on the Moncada Barracks.

Guevara had arrived in Mexico in 1954. He would remain there till the end of 1956, when the *Granma* cast off from the port of Tuxpan, on the coast of Veracruz. He had worked for a time as a sports photographer and practiced his originally projected profession of allergist at the Centro Médico of Mexico City. (The doctors who worked with him remember him as limited in his knowledge but full of medical passion.) His patients adored him. In Mexico he and Hilda married, a daughter was born, and he traveled incessantly across Mexico and through the landscapes of his own imagination. One hundred and sixty-one times in his letters, he writes about traveling. He climbs volcanoes, visits the Maya country, dreams about Paris, where he intends to go "swimming, if need be." He is a "knight errant," a "pilgrim," "an anarchic spirit," "a total vagrant," a man "ambitious for horizons." Suddenly he meets someone who stops him in his tracks. For almost ten straight hours, they talk.

Fidel Castro, writes Che, "impressed me as an extraordinary man. The most impossible things were just what he would confront and resolve. He had an exceptional faith in the fact that once he set out for Cuba he would get there. That once there he would fight. That once he began fighting, he would win." By the time Guevara embarked on the voyage that would finally define his life, Che's ideas had taken on a sharply ideological cast. He was reading Marx; he supported the Russian intervention in Hungary; he took classes in Russian (though he would never be any good at languages); he established a friendship with Nikolai Leonov, a Russian "student" who later came out as a full-fledged KGB agent attached to the Russian embassy in Mexico. And he not only devoured Lenin and Marx, he tried to turn them into poetry:

> and in the bugle call of new countries
> I receive head-on the spreading impact
> of the song of Marx and Engels.

Setting aside the literary worth of his writing, it is in his poems that he expresses his most intimate feelings. He had once thought he might write a book on Latin American "social medicine." He would now raise medicine into the sphere of revolutionary practice. He stood by the bed of an old woman, an asthmatic, who was dying, and, stretching his hands out over her, he swore, with the "low and virile voice of expectations / the most red and virile vengeances / so that your grandsons will experience the dawn." It would seem that, for him, asthma was a metaphor for the suffering of Latin America, the United States its cause, the Revolution its cure. And one night, Che makes his decision—to enlist as a doctor in Castro's band of future expeditionaries. Symbolically, it was a meeting of the two great strains of Latin anti-Americanism—the abstract ideological disdain of the Southern Cone and the grievance-fueled resentments of the Caribbean.

The rebels trained in secret. They practiced rowing, wrestling, gymnastics, mountain climbing, and hiking. They rented a ranch near Mexico City, where they could fire their weapons undisturbed. Among them was the asthmatic Dr. Guevara, who, as in the rugby days of "Raging Serna," excelled at his commitment. He was the best marksman among the trainees.

They were arrested by the Mexican police and about to be extradited to Cuba directly from their cells. Former president Lázaro Cárdenas, the social and nationalist reformer of the 1930s, interceded for them before President Adolfo Ruiz Cortines and in favor of Fidel Castro, whom he described as "that young intellectual with a vehement temperament and the blood of a warrior." Che would write a poem that, as is usual with his verse, is far more interesting emotionally than poetically. He called it "Canto to Fidel":

> Let us go,
> blazing prophet of the dawn
> along remote, paths without boundary wire
> to free the green caiman that you so love.

(The "green caiman" is a metaphor for Cuba from the poetry of Nicolás Guillén.)

With a few exceptions, such as Che himself and Fidel's brother Raúl, the expeditionaries on the *Granma*—most of whom, on landing, were killed in battle or summarily executed—did not consider themselves Marxists. They were "guerrillas," like the first idealistic adventurers to have been so designated, the irregular Spanish soldiers who harassed Napoléon's invading army in 1808. Guevara, as a non-Cuban volunteer, would add an important chapter to the history of this romantic impulse—like Francisco Xavier Mina, the Spaniard who crossed the Atlantic in 1816 to fight against his own country for the independence of Mexico, or like Byron on his way to support the Greeks against the Turks. Che had chosen war as a higher form of poetry.

III

Che's campaign in the Sierra Maestra established his reputation as a skilled, egalitarian, and courageous leader of men. As a military commander, he was a stern disciplinarian who demanded much of his men but no more than he did of himself. He was "parsimonious and ascetic," says the historian Hugh Thomas. "Guevara was regarded as first in the fight, first to help a wounded man, first to make sacrifices." And Carlos Franqui remembers:

> . . . Che did it alone. With his skill, his force of will and his bravery. Che converted sick men, with broken weapons, into the second strongest guerrilla force in the Sierra. He made the first forays down into the lowlands. He created the first liberated territory in El Hombrito . . . [Although] he wasn't sentimental, he didn't forget that a soldier was a human being.

But he also could be merciless. Rapists, traitors, and deserters among Che's troops were shot. Che in his diaries describes some of these executions almost clinically, with the cold eye of a surgeon. In Jon Lee Anderson's biography, a much more balanced picture of Che than the often idealized figure in the biography by Paco Ignacio Taibo II, Che describes the killing of an informer:

The situation was uncomfortable for the people and for him. So I ended the problem giving him a shot with a .32 caliber pistol in the right side of the brain, with exit orifice in the right temporal lobe. He gasped a little while and was dead.

And Anderson comments in general: "Che's march across the Sierra Maestra was littered with bodies of informers, deserters and criminals, men whose deaths he had ordered and sometimes executed himself."

In Paco Ignacio Taibo's book, we witness Che's gradual discovery of the *guajiros*, the Cuban mountain peasants, and the "magic aura" that they conferred upon him. It was from this genuine connection that Guevara—always disposed to devise general theories out of his personal experience—came to develop his notion of the central role of the peasantry in a revolution. In the Sierra Maestra, as new recruits swelled the guerrilla ranks, the importance of peasant adhesion seemed, for Guevara, an unquestionable fact. Nevertheless, the peasant population of the Sierra Maestra was sparse. (It was the least fertile territory in Cuba.) The guerrilla force never amounted to more than two or three thousand soldiers at its highest point, most of them combatants from the cities recruited by the clandestine urban movements. The idea that the triumph of the guerrillas was due to peasant fighters would later, at least in part, cost Che Guevara his life.

The chroniclers of the Cuban Revolution all stress Che's recurrent struggle during his time in the Sierra Maestra with severe attacks of asthma. An old peasant woman describes one of them: "He didn't move, he was breathing deep . . . it was painful to see a man that way who was so strong, so young, but he didn't like pity." It was action he wanted, the discharge of adrenaline that would compensate for his condition. Raging Serna on the rugby fields became the comandante in the Sierra Maestra, putting himself boldly in the way of death (or dealing it out): "I have discovered that gunpowder is the only thing that relieves my asthma." He would always have something of the adolescent about him—as did the ideals of the 1960s. He was always, in the phrase used by Jorge Castañeda, "escaping toward what lay ahead." And he was always ill at ease (like the spirit of his age) with doubts and ambiguities, with the essentially uncertain nature of reality.

The Cuban victors believed that their moment of glory would last forever. They would build a just Cuba, autonomous, prosperous, proud, free, egalitarian. And in the abstract formulation of these ideas, Che went beyond his comrades—beyond Castro himself, who always maintained a far sharper and more harshly pragmatic sense of political reality. Victory transfigured Guevara, indelibly impressing the features of a personal (and incurable) dogmatism immune to any refutation by reality: an absolute conviction of the superiority of the socialist world—especially (at first) the Soviet Union—as opposed to the West; an almost theological hatred of Yankee imperialism, of "bourgeois democracy, houses of parliament"; a belief that the Cuban revolutionary experience could be exported to Latin America and the Third World in general; a total faith in the power of his will; an intolerance for complexity or ambivalence in action and ideas.

Raging Serna would try to create a utopia by implementing, in total purity, the principles in which he believed: immediate and total agrarian reform, nationalization of the economy, bureaucratic centralization, the eventual abolition of monetary transactions, moral rather than material incentives to increased production, and so on. He felt absolutely convinced that Cuba could attract unqualified and unconditional support from the countries of the communist bloc, in order to build a great industrial power in the Caribbean.

From the early days of the revolutionary victory, Guevara began to show a harsher side of the new man forged in war. The Cuban Revolution, freshly in power, officially executed hundreds of people accused of being war criminals during the Batista regime. And in the prison of La Cabaña, Che figured as the "supreme prosecutor." Reports differ on the degree of his personal ferocity and the fairness of his decisions, not as a trial judge (a role he did not fill) but as a final voice on the verdicts. Anderson notes: "There was little overt public opposition to the workings of revolutionary justice. On the contrary. Batista's thugs had committed some sickening crimes and the Cuban public was in a lynching mood." But in responding to this tide of opinion, the Revolution disappointed some of its sincere partisans, who felt that the victors should be more magnanimous than the murderous regime that it had overthrown. Guevara soon became involved with unquestionably dark aspects of the Cuban revolutionary state: the efficient apparatus of its security system (which had to face genuine exterior threats but moved steadily in a more and more authoritarian direction) and the repression of freedom of thought in the press and in university life. In Guanahacabibes, he would create Cuba's first labor camp, for the internment of those who, as described in his own words, "have committed transgressions of revolutionary morality to a greater or lesser degree . . . as a kind of reeducation through work . . . hard work not bestial work." But among those sent then and later to the camps were homosexuals, Jehovah's Witnesses (whose religion forbade them to serve in the army or swear allegiance to the state), beggars, dissidents—all those who seemed to diminish the image of a healthy, strong, and popular revolution.

IV

Che Guevara liked to tell a joke about himself that, with variations, ran as follows: Fidel has already decided who would be minister of defense. Clearly it should be his brother Raúl. But there is the question of the economy. Who should take charge of the economy? He calls the leaders of his movement to a meeting and asks, "Is anybody here an economist?" A hand goes up. It's El Che. He is immediately put at the head of the Cuban economy. Once in office, someone asks him about the specifics of his economic knowledge. "Economist?" Che answers. "I thought Fidel said communist!"

Most of Che's biographers (and reports from some of those who worked with him) agree that he was not prepared for the responsibility he was given over the economy. Che did a stint as the director of the National Bank of Cuba and flamboyantly signed its banknotes with a mere "Che." He ran the bank in a military style and drove off almost the entire administrative corps (and some kept going all the way out of the country). An anecdote, this one not a joke, comes from the former president of the National Bank of Cuba, Salvador Vilaseca:

> When he was named President of the Bank, he called a friend to ask him to work with him on a matter of importance to that institution. The friend, afraid of the responsibility, indicated to him that he did not believe he had the qualifications to take on that responsibility, since he knew nothing of banking, to which Che answered, "I don't know anything about it either and I'm the President."

The biographers contend that El Che—though he was an avid reader—did not understand what he had gotten himself into, and that his knowledge of economics consisted of only a few (often confused) ideas. Jorge Castañeda, in *Compañero: The Life and Death of Che Guevara,* details the disasters of Cuban economic policy as it was managed (to a considerable degree) by Guevara. He stresses the general economic inexperience of the revolutionaries, the loss of technical expertise as the middle classes fled into exile, the scarcity of resources due to the American embargo, the "administrative chaos" that every revolution brings in its wake.

Later, as minister of industry at the head of 287 enterprises of every sort (sugar, telephones, electricity producers, construction companies, publishing houses, even chocolate factories), Guevara put into practice methods that had proved disastrous during the period of "war communism" in the Soviet Union (1918–21). Of course some of the atmosphere (for Cuba the continuing American military threat) and the objectives (developing the means needed to resist foreign aggression) were similar. But so were the results. Che tried to create heavy industry and to implement methods that would "organize and micromanage everything," says Castañeda, "regardless of the damage done by similar efforts in the USSR and socialist countries." Guevara did not know the basic history of the Soviet Union, the nation that he so ardently admired. His economic policies contributed to driving the Cuban economy into an unsustainable deficit, into chronic scarcities and the rationing of essential supplies. But for years to come, the Russian subsidies would mask at least some of these structural flaws.

The Czechoslovakian economist Valtr Komárek (he would later become the first vice president of postcommunist Czechoslovakia) worked directly with Guevara as an economic advisor during intensely active periods of 1964 and 1965. In his memoirs, he says that Guevara's outlook was Marxist but "he knew a great deal about the American economy" and that (at least by then) he could not convince himself that the efforts of the communist bloc could ever compete with the market economy of the capitalist countries: "Look, Komárek, the socialist economy is garbage, not an economy." And Komárek goes on from there to report on the conclusion Che drew from his opinion: "Look, the only chance for socialism rests on its moral values, we have to talk about moral incentives, about human life." The statement is pure Che. In a conversation with French agronomist René Dumont, mentioned by Thomas, Che said that his aim was to give workers "a sense of responsibility," not of property, and he was also already critical of the Soviet Union's new emphasis on material encouragement for hard work. He refused to participate in the creation of a "second North American society."

The United States was the primary customer for Cuba's sugar, its main agricultural product. "I just hope to Christ the United States doesn't cut the sugar quota . . . it would make Cuba a gift to the Russians," said Hemingway shortly before Eisenhower cut Cuba's sugar quota. But the truth is that the Cuban connection with the communist bloc was by then irreversible. When the tensions between Cuba and the United States began to sharpen in the spring of 1960, the revolutionary government had already signed a series of agreements with the Soviet Union, East Germany, Czechoslovakia, and other communist countries, at the suggestion of (among others) Che Guevara. And the Cuban state had begun to absorb large businesses and the means of communication, without paying any indemnities. It was in the summer of 1960 that the Eisenhower government sharply reduced the sugar quota, convinced that the Cubans were forming an alliance with Russia, heralded by a trade agreement already reached with the Soviets on the sale of sugar. Fidel Castro then demanded that the Cuban-based American refineries process sugar for delivery to Russia. They naturally refused. In response, on July 6, 1960, the Cuban government issued Law No. 851, authorizing the expropriation of assets and enterprises belonging to American citizens without any payment of indemnities. Anastas Mikoyan, deputy premier of the Soviet Union, brought his country to the rescue of the Cuban sugar industry. The agreement would send 425,000 tons to Russia in 1960, then a million per year until 1965, as well as providing technical assistance for the projected industrial transformation and credit for a billion dollars. The die was cast. The country was now locked into monoculture to sweeten the teacups of another giant patron.

The most surprising thing about this decision was that the revolutionary government, from the beginning, had been aware that Cuba needed to reduce its dependence on the sugar industry, because other sugar-producing countries, like Brazil and Australia, were now in a position to compete for a share of the lucrative American market. And American internal production was also increasing. Che was correct when he said that the American quota was "an instrument of imperialist oppression," but the solution was not monoculture at the service of another empire. What the country required was a rational diversification responsive to the market. Carlos Franqui was the chief editor of the government newspaper *Revolución* and would later become one of the most respected Cuban dissidents. In his Family Portrait with Fidel (*Retrato de familia con Fidel*) of 1981, he writes:

> The Cuban cattle industry . . . supplied milk and meat for national consumption. Cuba imports forty million dollars worth of fats, when her soil can produce peanuts, castor, sunflowers. It can

produce grains, potatoes, bananas . . . fruits and vegetables. It can increase its rice and cotton production. Export coffee and tobacco.

It never happened, because the government merely substituted one buyer for another and became utterly dependent on the high prices (above market value) offered by the Russians. The subsidies were very generous but they were artificial, since the world price of sugar had begun to steadily decline. The movement in Cuba toward centralization and Soviet-style measures was obviously furthered by the continually growing economic, protective, and even physical importance of the Russians. Between 1961 and 1962, foreign aid from the communist countries for Cuba was worth $570 million, clear evidence that the Cuban economic project was running poorly on its own. The country would increase its sugar production, to 8 million tons per year, a huge portion of it sent off to the Soviet market. In 1990, just before the collapse of the Soviet Union, 90 percent of Cuban exports consisted of sugar. Along with the Soviet Union, the Cuban sugar industry crumbled. And it has never been able to recover.

v

Under American influence (and the heritage of a slave economy), Cuba had been a racist society. A major source of loyalty for the revolutionary regime was the promise (and substantial achievement) of ethnic liberation, raising the status of the *guajiros* and Cuba's large black underclass. On May 7, 1959, an economic step was taken, long championed by Guevara, for the benefit of the entire peasantry. Agrarian reform decreed the expropriation of large estates (many of them American owned) to be divided and distributed among the peasants. "Today," said Che, "the death certificate has been signed for the great estates. Never did I think I would be able to place my name with such pride and satisfaction on the necrological document of a patient I had tried to heal." Agro-industrial enterprises were exempted from the law and former landowners were to receive payment (including interest). The law was almost universally applauded and not rejected even by the American government. The Eisenhower administration, in a formal response from the State Department on June 11, recognized the Cuban right to expropriate large estates, including those owned by American companies like United Fruit. But it demanded that the indemnities should not merely be promised but paid. The first new deeds of ownership were distributed to peasants, beginning on December 9, in public ceremonies where names were read out and greeted with shouts of joy. But almost immediately, under communist inspiration, pressure mounted for collectivization—the creation of cooperative farms. The Second Reform Law and Second Declaration of Havana in 1961 instituted forced collectivization of the land, though in contrast to almost all other aspects of the economy, it was never complete. Anderson notes:

> Despite the large-scale expropriations, much of Cuba's cultivated land remained in the hands of small farmers, who continued to till their plots without hindrance from the state. In 1963, a new bill reduced the size of private landholdings still further, but the revolution never completely eradicated its fiercely independent *guajiro* farmers.

Che from the first favored total state ownership of the land. In Franqui's words, "He wanted to unleash the class struggle, the conflict with the United States and creole capitalism . . . [and] end the distribution of the land in favor of statist nationalization." In the end, it was this project that overwhelmingly prevailed. For Che, says Franqui, "They were all enemies, large landowners, overseers, managers, inspectors, technicians, cows, bulls, canefields, rice paddies, haciendas, houses, machinery. A cyclone lashing left and right." And remaining after the cyclone was the State.

From then on the country lived in the context of confrontation with the United States, opposition within the island, and a growing resort to exile, amounting (at the beginning of 1961) to sixty thousand people.

VI

In January 1961, John F. Kennedy succeeded Dwight D. Eisenhower and came into office with a flock of young, bright (and aggressive) new faces. On his desk was a plan for the invasion of Cuba, which he approved. On April 17, a CIA-trained force of Cuban exiles came ashore at Playa Girón on the Bay of Pigs. The militia was ready for them and, led by Fidel himself, demolished the invading force in three days. The result was a powerful reinforcement for the Cuban government and its prestige, within the island and throughout the world.

The menace of an imminent war had diminished. The problems of the economy remained. Che Guevara launched himself against them. But productivity continued to fall dramatically and Che's moral exhortations could not halt the decline. Some later figures (of 1963) are significant for the countryside. Absenteeism was increasing and workers on the cooperative farms were spending an average of four and a half to five hours on the job (of the eight for which they were being paid). By then the private sector of agriculture was twice as productive, while Che, then minister of industry, was reorganizing Cuban industrial enterprises according to their respective products, without taking into account the need for efficiency.

Che's performance at one meeting of ministers was both impressive theater and a sad commentary on the problems of mass production without adequate training and technology, and, most thoroughly, on his total opposition to a market economy. Guevara is described as

clearly angry and he begins to drag things out and put them on the table: dolls so misshapen they look like little old ladies, a tricycle that's a piece of crap, a shoe losing its heel because it's held together by only two nails instead of the eight or ten it needed, a defective zipper (and there are 20,000 more) for the fly of a pair of pants that keeps opening and that the people humorously call "Camilo" (because of Comandante Camilo Cienfuegos's reputation as a Don Juan), a bed whose feet are falling off, a shampoo that doesn't clean hair, some face powders that have no color, ammonia that you have to strain so as to make it usable. The conclusion is tragic: production in the factories is getting steadily worse . . .

But the underlying cause was the decision that Che had adopted as an absolute dogma, the abolition of private initiative and investment, the total disappearance of commerce, down to the most minimal level.

Guevara himself continued to maintain a high level of personal austerity, rejecting any special privileges for himself or his family. What really mattered to him was the transfiguration of the individual through moral incentives. A powerful egalitarian spirit infuses the official descriptions of "the Sundays of solidarity in voluntary labor," with Che himself taking enthusiastic part—cutting cane, building schools, loading sacks of rice, exhausted but happy, working "to the sound of revolutionary songs." But voluntary labor was no remedy for economic failure nor was it a realistic incentive for human labor. Fidel Castro himself was critical of it. According to Hugh Thomas, in the summer of 1965, the year that Che disappeared from the Cuban political scene, Castro said to some sugarcane workers: "we cannot choose idealistic methods that conceive all men to be guided by duty because in actual life that is not so . . . it would be absurd to expect that the great masses of men who earn their living cutting cane will make a maximum effort just by being told that it is their duty, whether they earn more or less. That would be idealistic."

The Soviets, who were hardly the pure and generous Bolsheviks of Che's imagination, were thoroughly aware of Cuba's problems, and they began to recoil from the incessant stream of requests and demands. And so did Che from the Russians. The Cuban Missile Crisis of October 1962 deepened his disappointment with the Soviet Union. The Russians had pressed the missiles on the Cubans and then taken them away without consultation. It was clear that the real confrontation was between the Soviet Union and the United States, that the Cuban government had no say and no control over the use of the missiles. But the Cubans were outraged by the Russian capitulation (which was later shown to have been not quite a capitulation, since the Americans secretly agreed to withdraw their own missiles from Turkey); and the Cuban rhetoric was hostile toward the Soviets, and verbally reckless. Che certainly considered the Russians guilty of a kind of historical ingratitude. As reported by Castañeda, Che would later say to a British communist newspaper (in an interview not fully published at the time) that "if they attack we shall fight to the end. If the rockets had remained, we would have used them all and directed them against the heart of the United States, including New York, in our fight against aggression." He was obviously aware of what the consequences would have been but they did not frighten him: "[It would be] the chilling example of a people prepared to be immolated atomically so that its ashes might serve for the foundation of a new society." Clearly he was not disturbed by the image of a devastated New York, nor did he propose consulting the Cuban people about their own possible obliteration.

And Castañeda also gives Anastas Mikoyan's response to Che's expressed willingness to fight the Americans to the end: "We see your readiness to die beautifully, but we believe that it isn't worth dying beautifully."

In those frenetic years, Che's youthful inclination toward poetry would reappear, connected with the themes of redemption and martyrdom. He wrote about his feelings to one of his favorite poets, the Spanish Republican León Felipe, who had escaped from Spain in 1938:

> Maestro: Some years ago, when the Revolution took power, I received your most recent book, with your signed dedication. I have never thanked you . . . but perhaps it may interest you to know that among the two or three books I keep at my bedside is *El ciervo* [The Deer]; I can rarely read it because in Cuba it is still quite simply a sin (a flaw in leadership) to sleep, to let time go by without filling it with something, or to relax . . .

Che loved León Felipe's poetry and one of his favorites, from his bedside book *El ciervo*, was the poem "To Christ":

Christ!

I love you

not because you came from a star

but because you showed me

that man has blood

tears

anguishes

keys

tools

to open your doors closed to the light.

Yes . . . You taught us that man is God.

A poor God crucified like You.

And that one who is on your left

on Golgotha

the bad thief

He too is a God!

VII

The four walls of an office could not hold Che Guevara. However much time he had to spend shuffling papers, he still had the soul of the would-be romantic poet and the fierce dedication of the guerrilla fighter whose "only cure for asthma was gunpowder." Economic and political failures had not undermined Che's essential faith, but they had certainly increased his sense of impotence and unease. He would turn his attention to "dreaming of horizons"; he would travel the world, to great effect, as an ambassador of the Revolution. He supported Cuban aid to various Latin American revolutionary groups, and he participated in planning and inspiring an abortive attempt to establish a guerrilla movement in his own Argentina, led by an old friend he had personally chosen, Jorge Ricardo Masetti, a well-known journalist (founder of *Prensa Latina*) but emotionally unstable and not at all suited for his role. The small group was soon wiped out and Masetti, following Che's orders and inspiration, went to his death.

The guerrilla venture in Argentina was doomed to failure, both in its strategic planning and in its very conception. Argentina was predominantly a middle-class country, prosperous and with a democratic system in place. The Argentines in general were not disposed to support Che's war. But there was a broader failure of conception. Che always believed that the Cuban Revolution had triumphed through the guerrilla actions in the Sierra Maestra, his own great adventure, and not through the union of many forces against a steadily more repressive dictator like Batista. The conviction led him to repeat the same error, over and over, risking the lives of others and his own. Franqui remembers a conversation between him and Che at an official celebration. He describes Che as "sober, ironic, somewhat withdrawn, in an old worn uniform, with his pipe, his Baudelarian air." He remembers saying to Che, "Your problem, Che, is that you lived through a single experience, the Sierra," and Che answering, "Yes, but if it wasn't for the guerrillas you would have ended up dead . . . Franqui, and don't you forget it . . . You overestimate the role of the city. You underestimate the importance of the guerrilla struggle, the source and motor of the Revolution."

In a message resigning his bureaucratic responsibilities, Che would write to Fidel: "Other lands call for the contribution of my modest forces," and in secret (at first in disguise) but with Castro's knowledge and support, he set out, in April 1965, to spread the Revolution himself by force of arms. Guevara's final ports of call were really the stages of his martyrdom: the Congo and Bolivia. Both adventures were so poorly conceived and so disastrously executed that one begins to wonder whether Che was not unconsciously seeking a kind of immolation as the supreme act of revolutionary creativity. His clandestine arrival in the Congo in 1965—leading a group of Afro-Caribbean Cubans—was designed to support the political heirs of the murdered Congolese leader Patrice Lumumba; but he found himself confronted with Congolese allies, the undisciplined troops of Laurent Kabila, who were unable and unwilling to fight at anything near the level required to defeat the European mercenaries on the other side. Che and the

Cubans who survived just barely escaped with their lives. And when the remnant of the Cuban forces were about to mount a launch that would take them to safety across a lake, Che was consumed with guilt because he only had room in the boat for a small number of Congolese troops and also of course because the forces under his command had been forced to flee. He actually considered staying. Just himself. Perhaps he could find some way to fight on, making contact with a friendly force that was hundreds of miles away through the jungle, which he would have had to cross almost on his own. It would have been suicide and he did not choose that option.

In Bolivia two years later, Guevara would launch his guerrilla movement at the wrong location with inadequate information and, though his men won a few early victories, they never really had a chance to establish or to expand their movement. The choice of Bolivia could not have been more unfortunate. The country was going through a period of agrarian reform and, more critically, the two groups that might have aided him, the miners and the Communist Party, had clearly indicated that they would not join a guerrilla war. Only a few Bolivians ever fought beside or even aided Che. Some analysts of the Cuban Revolution feel that the heroic and useless sacrifice of Che in Bolivia was a great relief for Castro. Che would not be around to impose his moral consciousness on Castro's pragmatic decisions, nor to rival his charisma. And Che's image would remain, available for manipulation.

Simon Reid-Henry argues differently in his meticulous study *Fidel and Che: A Revolutionary Friendship*: "Temperament and not ideology lay behind these gradually sharpening differences. 'Fidel would agree in principle with anything' [a quote from Carlos Franqui's *Family Portrait with Fidel*] but Che did nothing except out of principle." Reid-Henry details Castro's commitment to the Bolivian venture from the very start, with Bolivia chosen as the possible site for a revolutionary beachhead in Latin America because of its geographical centrality and the drawback, in other potentially approachable Latin American countries, of intense left-wing factionalism. But disunity on the left in Bolivia (and the lack of support for an armed struggle on the part of the Soviet-centered

Communist Party as well as the local campesinos) would deal the final blow to Che's Bolivian enterprise. According to Reid-Henry, Fidel kept in touch with the events as much as he could. He remained hopeful of success almost to the end but could provide no help to Che as the Bolivian army (with American tactical help) closed in and hunted him down.

Che had always faced the prospect of death bravely. In Bolivia, "moving on" to the next horizon without checking the lay of the land, Raging Serna charged into a fatal corner. The description of his final hours in a remote village, where the Bolivian high command ordered his death, leaves no doubt that he was not a deliberate suicide. The execution was initially opposed by the CIA, who apparently wanted him for further questioning, but it was also not countermanded by the Americans. And a CIA agent, Félix Rodríguez, was there on the spot, spoke with Guevara, and was photographed with the haggard captive. In Rodríguez's autobiography, *Shadow Warrior*, he states that it was he who received the radioed order for Guevara's execution and passed it on to the Bolivian commanding officer. He also claims that he and Guevara embraced as fellow warriors while other accounts state that Guevara thought of him as a "worm" (*gusano*, the Fidelista term for antirevolutionary Cubans) and basically exchanged insults with Rodríguez.

It was only when the drunken Bolivian sergeant assigned to kill him entered the hut that Che was sure of his coming death. And whatever the exact details of Che's last moments may be, even his archenemy Rodríguez affirms that Che "conducted himself with respect to the very end." As he had written to his mother, during one of his first trips abroad after the victory of the Cuban revolution, "I feel . . . an absolute fatalistic sense of my mission, which frees me of all fear." Perhaps, when the bullets ended Raging Serna's final charge, he may have felt, at least for an instant, that he was embodying a line of the Cuban national anthem: to die (beautifully) for the (universal socialist) fatherland is to live.

And Che would live on. Trivially, as a widely marketed image in objects that range from the vulgar to the devotional: cups, T-shirts, posters, tattoos (on Mike Tyson's abdomen, on the right arm of Diego Maradona), and, more seriously, as a visual icon for decades of rebellious (and revolutionary) young men and women in Latin America and many other areas.

But deeper resonances and reasons exist for the continuing afterlife of Che Guevara. There is an aspect to his life—the wanderings, the abandonments, the final, unexpected martyrdom, the almost insensate commitment to personal courage—that appeals to a wider range of people than those who fully share his politics or his cultural background. In a balanced and wide-ranging book, *Che's Afterlife*, Michael Casey interviews Che's illegitimate son (though not accepted as such by most of the Guevaras), the well-regarded Cuban poet Omar Pérez, apparently born of Che's brief affair with a beautiful twenty-year-old woman immediately before his departure for Africa and eventually Bolivia and death. It was a pregnancy Che would never even know about. Pérez resembles his presumptive father physically and in his personal independence, which earned him a year in a Cuban labor camp picking tomatoes as the government's response to a display of artistic and intellectual dissidence. He was twenty-five when his mother revealed his real father to him and among his preoccupations have come a search for psychological linkage with Guevara and a strong personal interest in Buddhism. In his interview with Casey, Omar Pérez comments on a major feature of Che's life and lingering image, seen from two different but complementary angles:

Why do people always leave? We all leave at a certain time. We leave our wives; we leave our children; we leave our job for a better job or a worse job . . . We abandon everything for something new. We trade religions, beliefs—political, ideological—so it is not something that you can say is a characteristic of a person or persons or a historical trait. This is a human trait, to abandon things for something else.

Himself abandoned by Che Guevara (though, in his case, Che never knew of Omar's impending existence), the Cuban poet recognizes and accepts this "human trait," which of course, at the personal level, often inflicts emotional and material pain on those who have been left behind, but he also tries to place Che's continual moving on in a broader and deeper context, the idea of nonattachment (present in Christian tradition but far more emphasized and explored in Buddhism and other forms of Indian religion and speculation):

> What in fact is the ultimate point of attachment? . . . when you go through life . . . and you have already said good-bye to your family a few times, like my father did . . . maybe then, when you are in the middle of nowhere, like in the middle of the Congo, or Bolivia, maybe then you discover some other kind of attachment. And that attachment is far more resilient, far more resistant than love for women or for drink or success or whatever. What is this thing? . . . It has to do with the real essence of ourselves, because what we are trying to attach to there is that which we think we really are. It's nothing less than that.

The freedom to move on, to search for the ultimate (as seen by the individual), to disdain mere material achievement and pleasure (though he was no conventional ascetic) is a feature of Che's life that attracts and likely will continue to attract the sympathies of those who are or would like to be "seekers after truth." Certainly with Che Guevara it was a freedom enchained within his willed and abstractly accepted principles, and his goal was a utopian Marxist revolution accompanied by a moral "transfiguration" of human beings that, to him, was an ultimate and (in his belief) achievable condition. And yet the final, clumsily misbegotten chapter of his life was not only an extended Calvary but, in the eyes of many, progress on a "path," the search of a spiritual (but armed) warrior for his portion of enlightenment.

It was not long before the story of Guevara's final hours became a kind of sacred history for people of various inclinations on the left who in some measure agreed with his revolutionary ideas, and especially for those who shared the same temptation toward the absolute in hatred and in faith, the same almost religious devotion to violence and death. And throughout the 1970s and into the '80s, the long-standing quarrel raged again between two shadows from the past: the oppressive and omnipresent giant to the north and the self-protective and proud culture to the south. In the fiercely fought and ferociously repressed guerrilla war against "imperialism and its allies" in the countries of Latin America, Guevara was the patron saint of the movement, the armed prophet, the model of these modern revolutionaries.

Jorge Castañeda was one of those many thousands: a militant radical who trained in Cuba. In *Utopia Unarmed: The Latin American Left after the Cold War* (published in 1994), he wrote:

> Che represents the heroism and nobility of myriad middle-class Latin Americans who rose up in the best way they could find, against a status quo they eventually discovered to be unlivable . . . He will endure as a symbol, not of revolution or guerrilla warfare, but of the extreme difficulty, if not the impossibility, of indifference.

Three years later, in his analytical biography of Che (1997), Castañeda said:

> Che endowed two generations of young people with the tools of that faith, and the fervor of that conviction. But he must also be held responsible for the wasted blood and lives that decimated those generations . . . His death allowed him to sidestep a question he could never have answered: why so many university students from the region's emerging middle classes sallied forth so innocently to their slaughter.

How to explain the shift in Castañeda's perspective? His dilemma was shared by many young men (and some women) of the Latin American middle class who believed in good faith that the solution of the problems of Latin America was to be found in redemption through arms, not by way of politics. Many, like Castañeda, contemplating in memory all the death and destruction, would turn again to the electoral process. The paradox of the guerrilla movement was that it was not a rebellion of oppressed peasants but of the educated middle class. It was a guerrilla movement born in the universities and led by the educated. (The writer Gabriel Zaid, in his article about El Salvador, was the first to note this fundamental characteristic of the Central American guerrilla movements, which he dubbed a *guerrilla universitaria*.) Che himself was one of these university-trained revolutionaries but he was also far more, both in his life and in his afterlife.

IX

The Christian path to Calvary is another route toward understanding the guerrilla fighter who died at thirty-nine, helpless in the hands of his enemies. Five centuries of faith and iconography in Catholic Latin America have contributed to the martyrology of Che Guevara. Che was an atheist, but he was formed in a mental world constructed on the basis of the Christian vision of good, evil, salvation, and eternal condemnation. Régis Debray, who spent time with Che's guerrillas in Bolivia, wrote that "Che liked to compare himself to a Christian of the catacombs confronting the Roman Empire that is the USA," images of course issuing from the deep substratum of Latin American life: the culture of Catholicism.

Immolation as the route to purification and redemption strikes a deep Christian (most especially Catholic) chord. And the association of Che's death with Christian martyrdom was intensified by a public relations error of the Bolivian military. Che's body was cleaned, shaved, and barbered (with the intention of masking the summary execution, since the official statement claimed he had died in battle). The result was the now famous photograph of a visibly still handsome Che, stripped to the waist, whose dead body resembled a Renaissance painting of the Lamentation over Christ, especially that of Andrea Mantegna. In the long and continuing afterlife of Che Guevara and his variously interpreted image, the aura of revolutionary martyrdom would combine with ancient and profound echoes of Christian sacrifice.

Within the Catholic faith, Che as icon functions for many like the effigy of a saint (whether the photo of his body after death or the serious face of the young comandante with tousled hair and a star on his beret, taken by the Cuban photographer Alberto Korda). If a saint dies as a martyr, his sacrifice recasts his entire life. It can offer salvation to others. The saint is depicted on a medal or as a picture small enough to be worn or carried in a purse or wallet. And he begins an afterlife different from what he actually lived, not Ernesto de la Serna but simply El Che. To die in pain and as a witness to one's faith is in itself an expiation of sin. For those who honor him, Che died for his belief in a just society, for human equality and the end of oppression. The objective facts in many ways refute that myth, but many would swear it is the truth.

In the spiritual life of Latin American Catholics, the iconography of the sacred is not part of a history course, nor is it a matter of specific reality but rather of transcendent *truth*, which does not require (and is perhaps contradicted by) any verifiable reality. In these countries, saints are not only moral examples. They intercede for you, they redeem you. The list of saints (the *santoral*) honored among the people includes figures never considered by the Vatican. Down the length and breadth of Latin America, one can meet with altars to actresses who died young, assassinated politicians, even figures like the Mexican Holy Death (la Santa Muerte), a skeletal figure who is the patron saint of drug dealers but also of many humble people in a country where a cult of death (often quite innocent) dates back to pre-Hispanic beliefs.

And even some of the guerrillas who followed the path of Che Guevara saw him explicitly as a saint and even as Christ. The poet Roque

Dalton, who died at the hands of another guerrilla (Comandante Joaquín Villalobos) in the internecine quarrels within the Salvadoran Civil War, would write in his "Credo of El Che":

> *El Che Jesus Christ*
> *was taken prisoner*
> *after finishing his Sermon on the Mount*
> *(with a background of the rattling of machine guns)* . . .
> > *. . . there was no road left for Che*
> *than being reborn*
> *and keeping his place to the left of men*
> *demanding that they quicken their pace*
> *forever and ever*
> *Amen.*

The exemplary life of the new "El Che Jesus Christ" leads to his resurrection where he stands "to the left of men" and goads them into action, or (as in the poem of the Uruguayan Mario Benedetti, who was driven into exile by the Uruguayan military government of the 1970s and '80s) to feel shame at not being "like Che":

> *comfort makes you ashamed*
> *and the asthma of shame*
> *when your commander is falling*
> *machine-gunned*
> *fabled*
> *pure . . .*
> *they say that they incinerated*
> *all your vocation*
> *less one finger*
> *enough to point us the way*
> *enough to accuse the monster and his burning embers*
>
> *to squeeze the triggers again.*

Emanating from the nature of his death, the intensity of his devotion to his personal faith (and the impact of two iconic photographs), the "Christ-like" afterlife of Che has moved peasants to prayer and (especially in the 1970s and '80s) the university-educated to revolutionary commitment. But a secular "Imitation of Christ" was not only a chosen route for many who tried to follow his example but also, in part, a feature of Che's own emotional-political life (and of the era in which he lived). He interpreted the experience of Cuban socialism as an act of sacrifice, both personal and national, on a journey toward Redemption:

> In our country the individual knows that the glorious epoch in which he has come to live is one of sacrifice; he understands sacrifice. The first to understand this were those in the Sierra Maestra and wherever the struggle was being waged. Later we have understood it throughout Cuba. Cuba is the vanguard of America and must make sacrifices because it occupies the frontlines, because it points out the road to liberty for the Latin-American masses.

And then there are the notions of conversion and sacramental devotion. Che was convinced that the Cuban Revolution was a kind of "exemplary story," which would inspire a conversion to revolution across the world, while he saw his own commitment to socialism as, in a sense, a revolutionary offering that had led him to abandon or totally subordinate personal and family attachments.

Even his emphasis on creating the "new man" connects with the Christian tradition, dating back at least to St. Paul. (Various formulations of this idea were central to the thought of the early twentieth-century Argentine thinkers Deodoro Roca and José Ingenieros, but they too were touched by the Catholic culture that surrounded them.) For St. Paul, the faith in Christ ultimately involved a radical change in human nature. In the society of the future, Che affirmed, "Men will have different characteristics." Selfishness would be suppressed and the human being would achieve "the complete awareness of his social being, which is the same as his full realization as a human being, with all the chains of alienation shattered."

Moreover, like the first Christians who expected this world to end in their lifetimes and a new, radiant, and eternal world to become their possession forever, Che was certain that he lived in a time of apocalypse. Like the dwellers in the catacombs, he would come into the light and see the new world with his own eyes.

One additional element of his feelings perhaps completes the Christian picture, or at least suggests it: the call for love. But it is not the Christian concept of universal love. In his *Socialism and Man in Cuba*, in a passage that would become widely quoted, he wrote: "the true revolutionary is guided by great feelings of love . . . Our vanguard of revolutionaries should idealize this love for the peoples, for the most sacred causes and make it entire, indivisible." It is not of course universal love, but love for "the people" and for the comrades fighting beside you. And the rite is not Communion but battle, violence, and, when necessary, death. And the injunction certainly does not include loving your enemies.

Aside from his emphasis on revolutionary love, Che's life had been filled with fury and with hatred. In a sense, he kept playing the rugby of redemption, filled with a sense of certainty beyond any doubts. Perhaps the moment when he acquired it appears in his travel diaries of 1952. He may have incubated the idea in Miami, as an effect upon him of his journey across Latin America. He wrote it down in Buenos Aires and called it "Note on the Margin." It is a passage totally different from the rest of his journal. He sets his words within an imagined (or remembered) scene in which he receives a political illumination from a mysterious unnamed figure, described as a European exile who has fled his native country. Che had not yet become a dedicated Marxist, let alone a revolutionary, yet the violent words were a premonitory vision of action. In the rambling, melodramatic paragraphs, the young man of twenty-five seems to be experiencing a conversion to revolutionary rage:

Now I knew . . . I knew that when the great ruling spirit deals the enormous stroke that divides all humanity into only two opposing factions, I will stand with the people and I know, because I see it printed on the night, that I, the eclectic dissector of doctrines and psychoanalyst of dogmas, howling like a man possessed, will charge against barricades and trenches, I will stain my weapons with blood . . . I already feel my nostrils flaring, savoring the acrid odor of gunpowder and blood, of enemy death.

It is a dialogue, an encounter of Che with himself, one voice and another voice of his imaginary universe, as if a firmly united self were born from the experience, without hesitations, a kind of surrender without questions, without doubts, almost without thought: a form of faith.

At one point in his life, he had written, "[I have] no house, no wife, no children [though by then he had them all], no parents, no brothers, my friends are those who think as I do and so long as they do . . . and yet, nevertheless, I am happy, I feel that I am something in life. I feel not only a powerful inner force, which I have always felt, but also the capacity to inject it into others." He is like the violent incarnation of a Christian apostle, guided by his confidence in being able to communicate "the good news" and conversion to others. But only those who think like him are his good neighbors.

Che held to his beliefs as a Catholic might cling to the dogmas of his faith. Hatred for him was a creative emotion. In his well-known "Message to the Tricontinental" in 1967, before going to Bolivia, he praises "hate as a factor of the struggle, which drives a man beyond the natural limitations of the human condition and converts him into an effective, selective, cold killing machine. That is how our soldiers have to be." He was not incoherent, nor cowardly, nor weak. If his captors in Bolivia had left him alive, what would he have done? He was never willing to compromise on his principles, or to accept negotiation. Redeemers do not negotiate.

Did he win or lose? After his death, one, two, three thousand Ches set out to emulate him. Did they win or lose? In practice, the option chosen by Che ended, for the most part, with the defeat of the guerrillas by repressive armies. Trapped between those violent extremes the people of their countries endured hunger and illness and often chose the road of emigration. They were the beloved objects of redemption but had not been consulted on the best route to achieve it. When the guns went quiet, those who were left would prefer the ballot box to the whir of bullets.

PART IV

Politics and the Novel

8

Gabriel García Márquez

IN THE SHADOW OF THE PATRIARCH

All dictators, from Creon onwards, are victims.
— GABRIEL GARCÍA MÁRQUEZ

In the course of writing his memoirs, Gabriel García Márquez was to remember—many years after the event—that distant afternoon in Aracataca, Colombia, when his grandfather set a dictionary in his lap and said, "Not only does this book know everything, it's the only one that's never wrong." The boy asked, "How many words are in it?" "All of them," his grandfather replied.

Anywhere in the world, if a grandfather presents his young grandson with a dictionary, he is giving him an instrument of knowledge; but Colombia was not just anywhere. It was a republic of grammarians. During the youth of García Márquez's grandfather, Colonel Nicolás Márquez Mejía, who was born in 1864 and died in 1936, a number of presidents and government ministers—almost all of them lawyers and partisans of the Conservative faction—published dictionaries, language textbooks, and treatises (in prose and verse) on orthography, philology, lexicography, meter, prosody, and Castilian grammar. Malcolm Deas, a scholar of Colombian history who has studied this phenomenon, claims that the obsession with language expressed by the cultivation of these sciences—their practitioners, Deas notes, insisted on calling them "sciences"—had its origin in an urge for continuity with the cultural heritage of Spain. By claiming "Spain's eternal presence in the language," Colombians sought to take possession of its traditions, its history, its classic authors, its Latin roots. This appropriation, preceded by the foundation in 1871 of the Colombian Academy of Language, the first offshoot in America of the Royal Spanish Academy, was one of the keys to the long period of conservative hegemony—it lasted from 1886 to 1930—in Colombian political history.

García Márquez's grandfather is a prominent figure in the writer's early novels, and he was no stranger to this politico-grammatical history. Colonel Nicolás Márquez Mejía fought in the ranks of the legendary Liberal general Rafael Uribe Uribe (1859–1914), one of the few genuine military autocrats (*caudillos*) in Colombian history. His story in turn inspired the character of Colonel Aureliano Buendía in *One Hundred Years of Solitude*. A tireless and hapless combatant in three civil wars, a soldier in the civic battles between Conservatives and Liberals, Uribe Uribe was also a diligent grammarian. During one of his stays in prison he translated Herbert Spencer, and in 1887 he wrote the *Diccionario abreviado de galicismos, provincialismos y correcciones de lenguaje* (Abbreviated Dictionary of Gallicisms Provincialisms, and Proper Usage), which seems to have had moderate commercial success.

In 1896 the general stood alone in Parliament against sixty Conservative senators. Finally the crushing majority left him no choice but, in his own words, to "give the floor to the cannons." Uribe Uribe was the central protagonist of the bloody Thousand Days War in 1899–1902, which ended with the signing of the Peace of Neerlandia. The signing was witnessed by Colonel Márquez, who years later would receive his former general at the family home in Aracataca, near the scene of the events. Uribe Uribe was assassinated in 1914. Two decades later, his lieutenant presented his eldest grandson not with a sword or a pistol, but with a dictionary.

This tome that anywhere else would be an instrument of knowledge was, in Colombia, an instrument of power. Influence and power would eventually come to this grandson, Gabriel García Márquez, though not in his wildest tropical dreams could Colonel Márquez have imagined the prodigious *ars combinatoria* that his grandson—whom he called "my little Napoléon"—would apply to that dictionary, the "almost two thousand big, crowded pages, beautifully illustrated," which "Gabito" set out to read "in alphabetical order, with little understanding." García Márquez won the Nobel Prize for Literature in 1982, and his most important novels have been translated into many languages. With their extraordinary force of storytelling, their poetic intensity, their prose so flexible and rich that at moments it actually seems to include all the words in the dictionary, these books are read everywhere. And rightly so. His hometown is the site of literary pilgrimages. In Cartagena de Indias, the walled port city where the young reporter García Márquez endured years of hardship, the taxi drivers point out the "Prize House," one of several that "Gabo" owns in cities around the world. The fond nickname reflects the popular sympathy that he inspires.

In 1996, García Márquez settled an old score in Colombian history by heading a small revolution against the dictatorship of dictionaries. To the horror of the Royal Spanish Academy and its American counterparts gathered in Zacatecas, Mexico, the celebrated author—lord and master of "Spain's eternal presence in the language"—declared himself in favor of the abolition of formal spelling criteria. The snub was the final victory of liberal Colombian radicalism over conservative grammatical hegemony. The ghosts of General Uribe Uribe and Colonel Márquez would have smiled in satisfaction. And Fidel Castro too, who had once said that he shared "the scandalous theory, probably sacrilegious for the academies and doctors in literature, about the relativity of the words in a language." But when García Márquez gave him a gift for his seventieth birthday, Fidel praised it as the "most fascinating" of his gifts, a "real jewel." It was a dictionary of the Spanish language.

"I write so my friends will love me," García Márquez has said repeatedly. One of those friends is the dictator of Cuba. In Latin American history, no bond between pen and scepter has been as strong, as intimate, as enduring, as mutually beneficial, as the alliance between Fidel and Gabo. In 1915, when the great Nicaraguan poet Rubén Darío (an important influence on García Márquez) was old, ailing, and in need of assistance, he accepted the support of the Guatemalan dictator Manuel Estrada Cabrera and even dedicated some laudatory poems to him. Castro's political motives for his public association with the great writer are not hard to understand, and they are as clear as those of Estrada Cabrera: for him the possible dividend is an increase in legitimacy. But what motivates García Márquez, who, unlike Rubén Dario, is certainly, at this stage of his life, under no economic pressure at all? Through a voluminous biographical study by the English scholar Gerald Martin (*Gabriel García Márquez: A Life*), the psychological origins of this extraordinary relationship come into clearer focus. They can be traced back to the family house in Aracataca, and especially to the bond between the young Gabo and his personal patriarch, Colonel Márquez. There lies the seed of his fascination with power: coded, elusive, but magically real, like the story of the dictionary, symbolically passed from the Colombian colonel to the Cuban *caudillo* through the hands of the writer.

"LIFE IS not what one lived but what one remembers and how one remembers it in order to recount it," writes García Márquez in the epigraph to his memoirs. This is how he has remembered, reworked, and in various ways recounted a tragic incident in his grandfather's life. It took place in 1908, in the city of Barrancas. García Márquez mentions it in *Living to Tell the Tale* as a "duel," an "affair of honor" in which the colonel had no choice but to confront an old friend and former lieutenant. The man was "a giant sixteen years younger than he was," married and the father of two children, and his name was Medardo Pacheco. The quarrel—in this version—began with "a base remark" about Medardo's mother that was "attributed" to García Márquez's grandfather. The public explanations for this insult failed to calm Medardo's rage, and the colonel, his "honor wounded," challenged him to a duel to the death. There was no fixed date for the encounter, and it took the colonel six months to settle his affairs and ensure his family's future before he went off to meet his destiny. "Both men were armed," García Márquez notes. The mortally wounded Medardo collapsed into "the underbrush with a wordless sob."

A previous version of this story, told in an interview with Mario Vargas Llosa, omits the duel: "At some point he had to kill a man, when he was very young . . . it seems there was someone who kept hounding him and challenging him, but he took no notice until the situation became so difficult that he simply put a bullet in him." According to García Márquez, the town was on his grandfather's side, so much so that one of the dead man's brothers slept "at the door to the house, in front of my grandfather's door, to prevent the family from coming to avenge his death."

"You don't know how a dead man weighs on you," his grandfather repeated more than once, unburdening himself to Gabito, who listened raptly to his war stories, and who has emphasized the importance of this episode in his life: "It was the first incident from real life that stirred my writer's instincts and I still have not been able to exorcise it." Precisely in order to conjure it away, he chose to re-create it not as it really happened but as "one remembers it in order to recount it."

Perhaps the first literary reworking of the incident came in 1965, in his script for the film *Time to Die*, by the Mexican filmmaker Arturo Ripstein: After languishing for years in prison, Juan Sáyago returns to the town where he killed another man, Raúl Trueba, due to an incident at a horse race. Sáyago wants to rebuild his house and win back the woman he left behind, but the dead man's sons, convinced that their father was killed in a sneak attack, have been waiting for him all this time and they aim to exact their revenge. The script absolves the protagonist: "Sáyago didn't kill an unarmed man"; he didn't kill "dishonorably"; "he killed him face-to-face, the way men kill." In the end Sáyago has no choice but to kill one of Trueba's sons, face-to-face, and later he is shot—in the back, dishonorably, while unarmed—by the other.

The same scene recurs in *One Hundred Years of Solitude*, transformed into a cockfight, after which Aureliano Buendía orders the insolent Prudencio Aguilar to find a weapon so that they may confront each other on an equal footing. Only then can he kill Aguilar with a sure thrust of his spear. Like Colonel Márquez in real life, the first Aureliano embarks on an exodus with his family that leads him to found a new town: the real Aracataca, the magical Macondo. But new horizons do not dissipate the shame. Both characters, real and imaginary, live in the grip of "terrible remorse." Both refuse to repent, and both insist: "I'd do it all over again."

After interviewing the descendants of eyewitnesses, Gerald Martin reconstructs a diametrically different version. "There was nothing remotely heroic about it," he concludes. Medardo's mother was the spurned lover of the boastful colonel; the offended son wanted to cleanse his honor. Colonel Márquez (who was forty-four years old at the time) chose "the time, the place, and the manner of the final show-down." He killed Medardo dishonorably: Medardo was unarmed. In the *Departmental Gazette* in the town of Magdalena for that November, the colonel's imprisonment for "homicide" is mentioned. After a stay in jail, like his literary avatars, he did not return to Barrancas (where he may well have received the same treatment as Juan Sáyago), but instead set out on the momentous journey to Aracataca, in the hope that the new banana bonanza would bring him prosperity and conjure away the past.

The bond between grandfather and grandson explains Gabi-to's need to create that original fiction and to cling to it. "We were always together," remembers García Márquez in his memoirs. They even dressed alike. At home "the only men were my grandfather and me." Separated in early childhood from his parents and surrounded by a herd of "evangelical women"—his grandmother, his aunts, Indian maids—"for me, grandfather was complete security. Only with him did my doubts disappear and did I feel my feet firmly on the ground and myself firmly established in real life." "Beached in the nostalgia" of that stout and half-blind old man with his black-rimmed spectacles, the grandfather who celebrated his grandson's "birthday" each month and praised his precocious talent as a storyteller and made him retell the plots of movies when he came home from the theater, García Márquez viewed his grandfather with a worshipful and indulgent sentimental-ism, as the incarnation of love and power. "I was eight when he died . . . something of me died with him . . . since then nothing important has happened to me." In Martin's opinion, this was no exaggeration: "One of the strongest impulses in García Márquez's later life was the desire to reinsert himself into his grandfather's world," which meant inheriting "the old man's memories, his philosophy of life and political morality," a political morality that fit into a single phrase: "I'd do it all over again."

A CENTRAL element in the political consciousness of García Márquez is his anti-imperialism. It is expressed (and originally formed) with genuine facts and literary elaborations around the subject of the United Fruit Company. In *One Hundred Years of Solitude*, as in *Living to Tell the Tale*, Aracataca is not just a company town (with its plantations, railroads, telegraph offices, ports, hospitals, and fleets), but also the scene of the "Biblical curse" of Yankee imperialism, a sweeping historical force whose "messianic inspiration" stirred the hopes of thousands (among them García Márquez's grandparents) only to befoul the waters of the original paradise, disturb its peace, and exploit its people. In its wake, this "plague" left behind only the "leaf-trash," the "scraps of the scraps it had brought us." At the start of his memoirs, recalling his return to the place of his birth with his mother at mid-century, García Márquez portrays his childhood surroundings as Caribbean apartheid: the "private . . . forbidden city" of the gringos, with their "slow blue lawns with peacocks and quail, the houses with red roofs and screens on the windows and little round tables with folding chairs for eating, among palm trees and dusty rose bushes . . . These were fleeting visions of a remote and unlikely world that was off limits to us mortals." Are these historical facts, or good stories? Lived reality, or reality reworked in order to be recounted?

One important point is that the main driving force behind the company was none other than General Uribe Uribe, who was a former agent of the New York Life Insurance Company and a professor of economics who devoutly believed in the market economy and in agriculture for export. The legendary soldier also owned one of the biggest coffee plantations in Antioquia. Martin does not mention these facts, but notes that Uribe Uribe's comrade Colonel Márquez, the writer's grandfather, was in fact one of the first beneficiaries of this foreign investment. His comfortable house in Aracataca may not have had a pool or a tennis court, but it had cement floors, and it was one of the largest houses in town. Since he was the municipal tax collector, "the Colonel's own income depended heavily on the financial well-being, physical intoxication and resultant sexual promiscuity of the much despised 'leaf-trash.' How conscientiously Nicolás carried out his duties we cannot know but the system was not one which left much freedom for personal probity." The colonel oversaw establishments called *academias*, "where both liquor and sex were freely available" and through which must have passed the "unlikely whores" who would serve as inspiration for his grandson's stories and novels all the way through to his last novel, *Memories of My Melancholy Whores*.

Swept up by the force of the "remembered" version in *One Hundred Years of Solitude*, Martin overlooks the family's ambiguous relationship with the United Fruit Company—a love-hate relationship, typical of Caribbean attitudes toward the Yankees. The company was condemned for its abandonment of the townspeople, but not for its existence. In his memoirs García Márquez notes that his mother, Luisa Santiaga (the real-life version of Ursula in the famous novel), "yearned for the golden age of the banana company"—that is, for her days as a "rich girl," her clavichord classes, dance classes, English classes. And he himself confessed that he missed his pretty teacher at the Montessori school and his shopping trips with his grandfather. The truth is that the banana company brought with it much more than leaf-trash. As the historian Catherine C. LeGrand explains, the enclave was a melting pot of cosmopolitanism and localism, of "green gold" and witchcraft, of Parker pens, Vicks VapoRub, Quaker Oats, Colgate toothpaste, of Chevrolets and Fords, of magic potions and homeopathic medicine (like that practiced by Eligio, Gabito's erratic, impecunious, and absent father), of Rosicrucian books and Catholic missals, of Masons and Theosophists, of demonic tales and modern inventions, of craftsmen and professionals, of residents with centuries-long roots on the coast and immigrants from Italy, Spain, Syria, and Lebanon. García Márquez's mother would have liked that "false splendor" to last forever. Which is why, in the memoirs, when she sees the square where a massacre took place, she says to her son: "That's where the world ended." The world she meant was *her* world. Paradise did not predate the company. Paradise, for that family, was the world created with the arrival of the company—a tropical alchemy that García Márquez would re-create in his first novels, and, most admirably, in *One Hundred Years of Solitude*.

And after the memory of apartheid came that of apocalypse. One that was very real. In 1928, at the request of the United Fruit Company, federal troops opened fire on a gathering of workers on strike at the railroad station in Ciénaga, very near Aracataca, where Gabriel García Márquez, who was born the previous year, lived with his grandparents. Hundreds were killed. The slaughter—re-created with expressionistic hyperbole in *One Hundred Years of Solitude*—sullied the reputation of the Conservative regime and paved the way after 1930 for a series of Liberal governments. Their important social reforms would meet with opposition from Conservatives, who adopted ever more reactionary positions. For the elections of 1946, the dominant Liberal Party split into two factions, one moderate, in support of Gabriel Turbay, and the other radical, behind their charismatic leader Jorge Eliécer Gaitán. In his popular anti-imperialist harangues, Gaitán constantly referred to the massacre of 1928, which he had investigated and denounced as a member of Parliament. Then, against the backdrop of the ninth Pan-American Conference held in Bogotá on April 9, 1948, Gaitán was assassinated and massive riots broke out in the streets of the capital.

The episode, known as El Bogotazo, was the starting point for a decade of ferocious social and political violence to which the Colombians refer with the highly understated term, *La violencia*. The young law student Gabriel García Márquez lived the tragedy up close. It was his political turning point—as it was for Fidel Castro, who was also in Bogotá at the time. It fueled his hatred of American imperialism and awakened his sympathy for communism. In addition to the glorification of the colonel and the demonization of the banana company, the young writer began to develop a mistrust of representative democracy and republican values. Martin succinctly supports this viewpoint in an assertion like: "Colombia is a curious country in which the two major parties have ostensibly been bitter enemies for almost two centuries yet have tacitly united to ensure that the people never receive genuine representation." But this idea of Colombia as a sham republic does not fully correspond to reality. According to the historian Malcolm Deas, from the earliest decades of the nineteenth century, people in the remotest places in Colombia have been exercised by national politics, taking part in mostly clean and competitive elections, with a real separation of powers, and enjoying—at least in the twentieth century—significant liberties. Except for the fleeting episode of General Gustavo Rojas Pinilla in the 1950s, Colombians have not countenanced coups or dictatorships. It is probably not an exaggeration to say that no other country in the region in the second half of the twentieth century has experimented more tenaciously with democracy (not even Chile, until the military coup of 1973, or Uruguay, until the brutal repression of the 1970s against the militant Montonero revolutionaries, or Costa Rica, or Venezuela from 1959 until the arrival of Chávez).

And yet violence seems second nature in Colombia. The main reason for this violence was the discord between liberals and conservatives—a quarrel of political, economic, social, and religious values dating back to the nineteenth century in Latin America. Despite its democratic and republican tendencies, Colombia failed to find a formula for stability and dragged its internecine political and cultural conflict out to the point of exhaustion. In Colombia, the legalist and formal traditions of the reigning grammarians were overturned time and again by the call to arms. "In Colombia," declared President Rafael Núñez at the end of the nineteenth century, "we have institutionalized anarchy." This incapacity for peace was manifested once more in the Bogotazo of 1948, planting in the young García Márquez an iron sense of the futility of liberal and conservative ideologies. Like Colonel Aureliano Buendía, he came to believe that "the only real difference between liberals and conservatives is that liberals attend the five o'clock mass and conservatives attend the eight o'clock mass." He forever after agreed with Simon Bolívar's famous statement that "I am convinced to the marrow of my bones that only an able despotism can rule in America." An able despot, a *good* patriarch, a new and anti-imperialist Uribe Uribe would become Gabito's ideal. To find such a figure, he would embark on a long and difficult path. And instead of cannons, his tools would be words, just as his grandfather had wanted.

I I
———

Gerald Martin's *Gabriel García Márquez: A Life* is an authorized biography, the official version of the writer's literary and political saga. The book is divided into three sections. The first, centered on Colombia from 1899 to 1955, overlaps to a certain degree with Gabo's own *Living to Tell the Tale*, but it freshens up the family history with new information, sketches each member of the extended family in the house of Aracataca, and provides a detailed reconstruction of student life at the prestigious school of San José. It touches on the few joys and the many sorrows of García Márquez's family, enriched and impoverished each year by the arrival of a new sibling. And above all, it describes the vicissitudes of a penniless young man in a succession of cities (Cartagena, Barranquilla, Bogotá), surrounded by journalist friends and literary mentors, passionately committed to pursuing a life as a writer, and willing to earn his living by selling encyclopedias or adapting radio soap operas.

Curiously, Martin almost entirely bypasses the cultural context in which García Márquez grew up—the open and lighthearted atmosphere of the Caribbean, with its extraordinary liberality, its carnivalesque sensuality, its worship of poetry, its musicality, its propensity for outrageous jokes, black magic, and easy death. He somewhat exaggerates the richness and the complexity of García Márquez's literary education, which seems to have been limited to Darío and the Spanish Golden Age, quite a bit of Faulkner and Hemingway, some Kafka, a touch of Freud, and even less of Mann.

Although very few letters or primary documents from private or public archives are cited in his book, Martin—known to the García Márquez clan as Tío Jeral ("Uncle Jeral")—spent seventeen years interviewing more than five hundred people: family members, friends, colleagues, editors, biographers, hagiographers, and academics (most of them inclined to speak favorably of the writer). These testimonies are vivid and sometimes dubious. Irrefutable firsthand accounts, like that of García Márquez's longtime friend the intellectual and diplomat Plinio Apuleyo Mendoza, confirm the young writer's crushing poverty—but did he really live in a room of only ten square feet? Did he really accustom himself to a "virtual disregard of his own bodily needs"? And elsewhere, did he really sleep with the wife of a military man who, upon discovering him in the act, forgave him out of gratitude to his homeopath father? Did he write *Leaf Storm*, his first novel about Macondo, inspired by the trip with his mother to Aracataca? And did this trip—so strikingly similar, as Martin suggests in a note, to the journey at the start of *Pedro Páramo*, the novel by Juan Rulfo that was crucial in setting the tone for *One Hundred Years of Solitude*—really take place in 1950, and was it as fundamental to his experience and creativity as his memoirs indicate? A letter not mentioned by Martin, dated March 1952 and published in *Textos costeños* (García Márquez's first volume of journalism), seems to suggest otherwise:

> I've just returned from Aracataca. It's still a dusty village, full of silence and the dead. Unsettling; almost overwhelmingly so, with its old colonels dying in their yards, under the last banana trees, and an impressive number of sixty-year-old virgins, rusty, sweating out the last vestiges of sex at the drowsy hour of two in the afternoon. This time I chanced it, but I don't think I'll go back alone, especially after *Leaf Storm* comes out and the old colonels decide to get out their guns and fight a personal and exclusive civil war against me.

Martin's second section follows Gabo from his European wanderings and his time in Paris in 1955–57 through his marriage in 1958 to Mercedes Barcha—the astute and patient sweetheart of his adolescence—and his adventures in New York as a reporter for *Prensa Latina*, the Cuban news agency created after Castro's triumph, up to the year

1961, when he settled for good in Mexico, a hospitable country (happily authoritarian, anti-imperialist, and orderly, at least in that era). There his two sons, Rodrigo and Gonzalo, were born, and there for the first time he made a decent and reliable living at a couple of American advertising agencies (J. Walter Thompson and McCann-Erickson) and successfully directed two commercial magazines (*La familia* and *Sucesos para todos*). He also tried his luck in the film business and published *No One Writes to the Colonel*. In Mexico he renewed old friendships (especially with Álvaro Mutis) and started many new ones, no less fecund and long-lasting (for example, with Carlos Fuentes), bought his own house and car, enrolled his sons in the American School, was menaced by writer's block, feared being a victim of a "good situation," and finally, in 1967, at the age of forty, surprised generations of readers with the appearance of *One Hundred Years of Solitude*.

"Everyone has three lives, a public life, a private life, a secret life," García Márquez warned his biographer. Beyond the notable revelation about the writer's grandfather, Martin's book unravels only a single episode in García Márquez's "secret life": his relationship in Paris—before his marriage—with an aspiring Spanish actress. Stormy and ill-fated, this affair was important not only in itself but as inspiration for *No One Writes to the Colonel* and the disturbing short story "The Trail of Your Blood in the Snow." But other aspects of his "secret life" remain in the shadows. Why did he suddenly break off his relationship with *Prensa Latina*? Only the Cuban archives, if they are ever opened, can shed light on that. What was the arc of his long epistolary engagement to Mercedes Barcha? Impossible to know. Both claim to have burned their letters. How did his ties to his fellow writers evolve? Except for the letters exchanged with Plinio Apuleyo Mendoza and a few others, the available literary archives were not consulted by Martin.

The account of the European "private life" of the bohemian writer, who loved to sing and dance, contains some moving anecdotes. Is it true that he "collected bottles and old newspapers and one day had to beg in the Metro"? As Plinio Apuleyo Mendoza points out, a deeper truth is that García Márquez seemed totally uninterested in the experience of Europe. He lived in an insular mode, immersed in his own projects. According to Martin, "it is striking how much of Europe East and West he managed to see," but García Márquez himself says, "I just drifted for two years, I just attended to my emotions, my inner world."

Where public life is concerned, Martin follows the journalist García Márquez—in those days a star reporter for the Colombian newspaper *El Espectador*—as he makes his way through East Germany, Poland, Hungary, and the Soviet Union. He notes, for example, the writer's strange fascination with Stalin's embalmed corpse: "nothing impressed me so much as the delicacy of his hands, with their thin transparent nails. They are the hands of a woman." In no way, says Gabito, did he resemble "the heartless character whom Nikita Khrushchev denounced in an implacable diatribe." Martin also records García Márquez's "intoxication" at the physical proximity of János Kádár, the man who suppressed the Hungarian uprising and whose actions he tries to justify. Upon learning of the execution of the rebel leader Imre Nagy, García Márquez criticizes the act not in moral terms, but as a "political mistake." "It should perhaps not surprise us," says Martin, in one of his few moments of critical boldness, "that the man who wrote it, who at the time clearly believes that there are 'right' and 'wrong' men for particular situations and who quite cold-bloodedly puts politics before morality, should eventually support an 'irreplaceable' leader like Castro through thick and thin."

The pages dedicated to the writing of *One Hundred Years of Solitude* are genuinely exciting, but Martin's conclusion seems excessive. He calls the novel a work—a mirror—in which the continent at last recognizes itself, and establishes a tradition. If it was Borges who sketched in the frame, it is García Márquez who provides the first truly great collective portrait. So that Latin Americans would not only recognize themselves but would now be recognized everywhere, universally.

The enthusiasm with which we all read that extraordinary novel did in fact lead to it being seen as a kind of bible (which is what Carlos Fuentes maintained), or at least an "American Amadis" (this was Vargas Llosa's phrase); but the truth is that García Márquez's world was not a complete reflection of Latin America. At least two essential elements were missing from his fictional account: the Indians and the Catholic faith.

Still, it was an hallucinatory mirror of the Caribbean, which is no small thing. Yet the opinions were not unanimously glowing. Two great Latin American writers did not like the book, both committed to aesthetic perspectives very different from Gabo's.

Jorge Luis Borges commented that *"One Hundred Years of Solitude* is all right, but it would be better if it was twenty or thirty years shorter."* And Octavio Paz's verdict was also harsh: "García Márquez's prose is essentially academic, a compromise between journalism and fantasy. Watered-down poetry. He is the continuation of two currents in Latin America: the rural epic and the fantastic novel. He is not untalented, but he is a dilutor."

III

In the beginning was the representation of power: in the short novels, then in *One Hundred Years of Solitude* (with its powerful colonels, but always old and lonely, despondent, "beyond glory and the nostalgia for glory") and finally, in 1975, in *The Autumn of the Patriarch*, García Márquez's own favorite among his books. In 1981, he told the critic Plinio Apuleyo Mendoza that this novel was "a poem about the solitude of power." It was a theme that aroused his emotions: "I have always believed that absolute power is the highest and most complete realization of being human." But he also claimed that there was a hidden dimension to the novel: "the book is a confession." Martin accepts this idea and asserts that the book has the moral zeal of an "autocriticism." The ambitious, lascivious, repugnant, cruel, and solitary—above all, solitary—patriarch would be García Márquez himself: "a very famous writer who feels terribly uncomfortable with his fame" and tries to free himself through an autobiographical confession.

The Autumn of the Patriarch was not the first novel about a tropical dictator written in Spanish in the twentieth century. Already in 1926, the

Spanish writer Ramón del Valle-Inclán published *The Tyrant Banderas* (about an imaginary Caribbean dictator). *Mr. President*, based on the life of Guatemalan dictator Manuel Estrada Cabrera, came out in 1946, a novel by the Guatemalan Miguel Ángel Asturias, who won the Nobel Prize for Literature in 1967. According to the Guatemalan novelist Augusto Monterroso, a number of Latin American writers in early 1968— Monterroso mentions Fuentes, Vargas Llosa, Cortázar, Donoso, Roa Bastos, Alejo Carpentier, but not Gabriel García Márquez—agreed on a plan to publish books about the dictators of their respective countries. The project was never carried out. "I was afraid I would end up 'understanding' and 'feeling pity' for him," said Monterroso, who would have had the grim task of portraying Somoza. Against this background, it would seem that García Márquez undertook the eventual writing of his dictator novel more in a spirit of competition than contrition.

He had spent years turning it over in his head, and he had produced extensive drafts. He would "teach" Asturias and the others "how to write a real dictator novel." And if *The Autumn of the Patriarch* proved anything, it is that the subject of tyranny makes a good fit with the expressive demands of magic realism.

The abruptness and the arbitrariness of the dictator, his use of power as a form of personal expression, his Dionysian intoxication with his own strength, are natural fodder for the fusion of reality and fantasy. The patriarch "only knew how to express his most intimate yearnings through the visible symbols of his colossal power." He aspired to be a historical and even cosmic thaumaturge, to alter the forces of nature and the course of time and distort reality. In a way García Márquez's patriarch is reminiscent of Camus's Caligula: "Behold the only free being in all of the Roman Empire. Rejoice: at last an emperor has come to teach them freedom . . . I live, kill, wield the rapturous power of the destroyer, next to which the power of the creator seems a caricature."

These excesses form part of the experience, and the memory, of many countries. The esteemed Venezuelan writer Alejandro Rossi knew something about this "inherited iconography." Writing in 1975, and not inclined toward magic realism in its most "adolescent and elemental" form (as it manifests itself occasionally in *The Autumn of the Patriarch*), Rossi praised the "intense and beautifully crafted images," the "intricacies and art" of the prose, and the "often perfect rhythms" of the work—but he objected to its substance:

> The incorporation of so many familiar elements turns the book into an elaborate and brilliant exercise that nevertheless does not change our historical and psychological view of dictatorship. *The Autumn of the Patriarch* aesthetically explores a worn-out and exhausted vision of ourselves. García Márquez's skill and unquestionable stylistic accomplishments almost never transform the underlying substance, which remains buried in the novel's cellar, untouched by any literary spark. In that sense it is a Baroque book . . . a sealed literary net that sometimes—though with perfect manners—suffocates its narrative subject matter.

Setting aside the issue (however important) of language, the narrative of the novel is a continuous recording of the tyrant's subjectivity: his nostalgias, his fears, his sentiments. And the simplicity of his inner world is morally offensive: only rarely does the reader encounter reflections on the obligations and the dilemmas of power, or ruminations on evil, debasement, or cynicism, much less a hint of any crisis of conscience. The top tier of the dictator's consciousness is reserved for his private anguish: the sacrifices that he made for his mother, the chronicle of his lusts and his "unrequited loves." It would almost seem as if the dictator has no public life, only private passions. The historical figure is curiously exempted from history. Conversely, the characters who surround him have no space of their own: everything they think, say, and do is a part of public life, because it revolves around the dictator. In a story in which the central axis is a despot's lyrical and emotional "I," everything else is reduced to a stage on which that "I" unfolds. The victims are props.

When García Márquez centers on the despot, it is not to expose or analyze the inner complexity of a man of state, but to inspire compassion for a sad, solitary old man. The dictator is a victim of the Church, the United States, a lack of love, his enemies, his collaborators, his orphanhood, natural disasters, poor health, ancient ignorance, bad luck. After he rapes a woman, she consoles him. There is also the fantastic conceit of the retirement home for dictators who have fallen into disgrace, where they spend their afternoons in exile playing dominoes. Their nostalgia assures them immunity. By blurring the reality of power and turning dictatorship into a melodrama, the novel dehumanizes the victims and rehumanizes the dictator.

The Autumn of the Patriarch's prose is an overwhelming and uncontainable torrent that sweeps through eras, continents, and characters; the narrative itself becomes autocratic. The book opens with an eighty-seven-page paragraph, a torment (at times delightful) for the reader, which García Márquez justified by saying that "it is a luxury that the author of *One Hundred Years of Solitude* can permit himself." In this book, there is room only for the consciousness of the dictator. Everything happens through, for, and in the perception of the patriarch. He is the omniscient narrator, the author of a country. Other consciousnesses are secondary, derivative, or nonexistent. "Devoted to the messianic pleasure of thinking for us . . . he was the only one who knew the true dimensions of our fate," García Márquez writes. And "in the end, we could no longer imagine what we would be without him." "He alone was the nation"—and the novel.

The book differs in many ways from *Mr. President*, which is more of a surrealist novel—poetic, political, and revolutionary—but perhaps the main difference is that in Asturias's book it is not only the voice of the tyrant that is heard. Street beggars speak, as do civilians and military men, in anger and in self-criticism, people with evolving lives of their own, who grow angry, who are capable of criticizing themselves. In Asturias's novel their voices are honored, and experiences of prison and torture are described. When depicting abuse, corruption, and the whims of power, the tone is not just unequivocally critical, it is contemptuous. There is no immunity. In *The Autumn of the Patriarch*, by contrast, the victims are part of the scenery, never active participants in the story.

"The political aspect of the book is a great deal more complex than it seems and I am not prepared to explain it," García Márquez declared when he finished his novel. And he would proceed to put his fame at the service of a cause—the Cuban Revolution—headed by a man who, paradoxically and more and more over the years, would come to resemble the patriarch of the novel. "In this absolutely ruthless cynicism about human beings, power and effect," writes Martin, "we find ourselves forced to consider that power is there to be used and that 'someone has to do this.' " Based on this "Machiavellian" view of history—the adjective is Martin's—the biographer believes that he understands why García Márquez "would go straight . . . to seek a relationship with Fidel Castro, a socialist liberator who was, as it turned out, the Latin American politician with the potential to become the most durable and the most beloved of all the continent's authoritarian figures."

Perhaps *The Autumn of the Patriarch* represented the final literary exorcism of the "duel" involving the writer's grandfather, in which the word "tyrant" softens gently into "patriarch." The patriarch dictates the whole novel, with no breaks, periods, commas, or air for anyone to breathe, except him. It is the novel in which the ghost of Medardo Pacheco would disappear for all eternity. His voice is silenced, to be heard no more. And after depicting the patriarch in literature, it was time to seek him out in real life. Martin confirms this: it was "Fidel Castro, the only man, his own grandfather figure, against whom he could not, would not dare, would not even wish, to win."

From Macondo to Havana: a miracle of magic realism.

ALTHOUGH ONE of García Márquez's bits of reporterly advice was to "poison the reader with credibility and rhythm," in his vast body of journalism he did not practice magic realism so much as socialist realism. In Spanish his articles fill no fewer than eight fat volumes, the pieces dating from 1948 to 1991. They have not been translated into English, and Martin barely skims them.

The first series of García Márquez's journalism is important because it gives a glimpse into the secrets of his "basic exercises," his "literary carpentry." The second (1955–57), which covers his reporting from Europe and America, has more political content but nowhere near as much as his key political articles, written between 1974 and 1995 and gathered in *Por la libre* and *Notas de prensa*—one thousand pages in all.

In three pieces of reportage, written after a long stay in Cuba in 1975 and titled "Cuba de cabo a rabo" (Cuba from One End to the Other), published in August/September of that year by the magazine *Alternativa* (founded by García Márquez in Bogotá in 1974), Gabo expressed an absolute faith in the Revolution as it was incarnated in the heroic figure of the Comandante (whom García Márquez had not yet met): "Every Cuban seems to think that if one day no one else were left in Cuba, he alone, under the leadership of Fidel Castro, could carry on the Revolution, bringing it to its happy conclusion. For me, frankly speaking, this realization was the most exciting and important experience I have ever had."

It likely was—and to such a degree that in thirty-five turbulent years García Márquez has never publicly detached himself from that vision. What did he see that anyone else could see? Tangible achievements in health care and education, though he did not ask himself whether the maintenance of a totalitarian regime was required in order to attain these social objectives. And what didn't he see? The presence of the Soviet Union, except as a generous purveyor of oil. And what did he say he hadn't seen? "Individual privileges" (although Castro and the top echelon of his government certainly enjoyed such privileges) and "police repression or discrimination of any kind," although harshly administered detention camps had existed, at least since 1965, for homosexuals, religious believers, and dissidents—they were euphemistically called Military Units to Aid Production, or UMAP.

What he saw, in sum, was what he wanted to see: five million Cubans who belonged to the Committees for the Defense of the Revolution, not as the spies and enforcers of the Revolution but as its spontaneous, multitudinous "true force," or, more plainly—in the chilling words of Castro himself, admiringly quoted by García Márquez—"a system of collective revolutionary vigilance that ensures that everybody knows who the man next door is and what he does." He saw many "alimentary and industrial items freely sold in stores" and he prophesied that "in 1980 Cuba will be the most developed country of Latin America." He saw "schools for all," and restaurants "as good as the best in Europe." He saw the "establishment of popular power through universal suffrage by secret ballot from the age of sixteen." He saw a ninety-four-year-old man immersed in his reading, "cursing capitalism for all the books he hadn't read."

Most of all, he saw Fidel. He saw "the almost telepathic system of communication" that he had established with people. "His gaze revealed the hidden softness of his childlike heart . . . he has survived unscathed the harsh and insidious corrosion of daily power, his secret sorrows . . . He has set up a whole system of defense against the cult of personality." Owing to all that, and to his "political intelligence, his instincts and his decency, his almost inhuman capacity for work, his deep identification with and absolute confidence in the wisdom of the masses," Castro had managed to achieve the "coveted and elusive" dream of all rulers: "affection."

These virtues were solidly supported, in García Márquez's view, by Fidel's "fundamental and most underappreciated skill": his "genius as a reporter." All the great achievements of the Revolution, its origins, its details, its significance, were "chronicled in the speeches of Fidel Castro. Thanks to those spoken reports, the Cuban people are some of the best informed in the world about their own reality." García Márquez admitted that these discourses "have not solved the problems of freedom of expression and revolutionary democracy," and the law that prohibited all creative works opposed to the principles of the Revolution struck him as "alarming"—but not because of its limitations

on freedom. What troubled him about the repressive law was its futility: "any writer rash enough to write a book against the Revolution
shouldn't need to stumble over a constitutional stone . . . the Revolution will be mature enough to digest it." In his view, the Cuban press
was still somewhat deficient in information and critical judgment, but
one could "foresee" that it would become "democratic, lively, and original," because it would be built on "a new real democracy . . . popular
power conceived as a pyramidal structure that guarantees, to the base,
constant and immediate control of its leaders." (Years later, in an interview with the *New York Times*, he was asked by Alan Riding why he did
not move to Havana, since he traveled there so often. "It would be too
difficult to arrive now and adapt to the conditions. I'd miss too many
things, I couldn't live with the lack of information.")

Another paradigmatic piece of his political journalism is *Vietnam por
dentro* (Vietnam from the Inside). A year before it was published, in December 1978, García Márquez had founded an organization called the
Habeas Foundation for Human Rights in the Americas, with the aim of
"advocating the freeing of prisoners. Rather than taking tyrants to task,
it will strive as far as possible to uncover the fate of the disappeared and
smooth the way home for exiles. In sum—and unlike other equally
vital organizations—Habeas will take a greater immediate interest
in helping the oppressed than in condemning the oppressors." In this
spirit, it was to be expected that the tragedy of the boat people who fled
in desperation from Vietnam would attract his attention, as it attracted
that of Sartre and other sympathizers with the Vietnamese regime.

But on his trip to Vietnam the founder of Habeas attended only to
the official story. In García Márquez's dispatch we are given a mag-
istrate of Ho Chi Minh's people's court, a "top official," the Communist Party's minister of external relations, the mayor of Cholon, the
minister of foreign affairs, and, of course, Prime Minister Pham Van
Dong, who with "quiet lucidity . . . received me and my family at an
hour when most heads of state are still in bed: at six in the morning."
During a stay of almost a month, García Márquez's group had occasion to attend "cultural festivities" at which "lovely damsels played the

sixteen-string lute and sang doleful airs in memory of the battle dead," but he said they had no time to consider the plight of the refugees. "Their story," García Márquez wrote candidly, "took second place to the grim reality of the country." This "grim reality," of course, was the history of the war against Yankee imperialism and the danger of a new war with China.

What seemed truly momentous to García Márquez in Vietnam was that it "had lost the war of information." For the founder of Habeas, the tragedy was not the hundreds of thousands of fugitives, starving and ill, huge numbers of them drowned or else stripped of their few possessions or raped or murdered by Thai pirates and other predators. The calamity was that the world knew about all this. García Márquez regretted that the Vietnamese (the ones he had interviewed, not the refugees in their distant internment camps) did not possess the "foresight to calculate the vast scale of the international effort on behalf of the refugees."

All these dispatches adhered to the model of García Márquez's earlier pieces on Hungary, and revealed the pattern of all his political journalism, then and now: to listen only to the voices of the powerful, and to counteract—to withhold, downplay, distort, falsify, and omit—any information that could "play into the hands of imperialism."

IV

Despite those dispatches of 1975, Fidel Castro remarked to the journalist Régis Debray that he was not yet convinced of the Colombian writer's "revolutionary firmness." He knew that García Márquez had refused to support the Cuban poet Heberto Padilla in the famous affair of his forced "confessions," that tropical echo of the Moscow Trials that led many Latin American intellectuals to turn away from the Cuban regime. Castro noted this, but still was not convinced of his loyalty, and so Gabo was not granted an interview in 1975 with the maximum leader of Cuba. García Márquez had to content himself with interviewing the strongman of Panama, Omar Torrijos, a second-rank Caribbean dictator but a faithful reader of García Márquez. Torrijos had this to say about *The Autumn of the Patriarch*: "It's true, it's us, what we're like." "His comment left me astonished and delighted," said García Márquez. And "quite quickly," writes Martin, "the two men would come to build a friendship based on a deep emotional attraction which evidently turned over time into a kind of love affair."

In 1976 García Márquez returned to Cuba, and after waiting for a month (like the legendary colonel) at the Hotel Nacional for a call from the Comandante, the meeting that he had been anticipating for almost two decades finally took place. Once accepted by Castro, and under his personal supervision, he wrote *Operación Carlota: Cuba in Angola*, a chronicle that won him an award from the International Press Organization. Mario Vargas Llosa (who had written and published a doctoral thesis on *One Hundred Years of Solitude*) bluntly called him Castro's "lackey." Two years later, García Márquez declared that his adherence to the Cuban way was in a sense similar to Catholicism: it was "a Communion with the Saints."

"Ours is an intellectual friendship," García Márquez said in 1982. "When we get together we talk about literature." And it was not just literature that united them. "They began to have an annual vacation together at Castro's residence at Cayo Largo," Martin records, "where sometimes alone, sometimes with guests, they would sail in his fast launch or his cruiser *Acuaramas*."

García Márquez's wife "particularly enjoyed these occasions because Fidel had a special way with women, always attentive and with an old-style gallantry that was both pleasurable and flattering." Martin also informs us of Castro's culinary skills, and of Gabo's taste for caviar and Castro's for cod. When Gabo was awarded the Nobel Prize, Castro sent his friend a boatload of rum, and upon the family's return he put them up at Protocol House Number Six, which, just a few years later, would become their Cuban home. There García Márquez "overwhelmed" guests such as Debray with bottles of Veuve Clicquot. "There is no contradiction between being rich and being revolutionary," García Márquez declared, "as long as you are sincere about being a revolutionary and not sincere about being a rich man."

To this vein—not of socialist realism but of socialite realism—the book *Fidel & Gabo* by Ángel Esteban and Stéphanie Panichelli contributes the testimony of the Cuban poet Miguel Barnet, a friend of García Márquez and president of the Fernando Ortiz Foundation. Barnet gives a detailed account of the parties at the "Siboney mansion," describing even the attire of Gabo, who was the host. Fidel and Gabo, says Barnet, "are true specialists in culinary matters, and they know how to appreciate good food and good wines. Gabo is the 'great sybarite,' because of his love for sweets, cod, seafood, and food in general." And Manuel Vázquez Montalbán, a Spanish writer and friend of Castro, collected the following testimony from the "great Smith," who was perhaps Cuba's best chef: "Gabo is a great admirer of my cooking and he's promised me a foreword for my cookbook, which is almost finished." In that cookbook, each of the dishes is dedicated to the person for whom it was created. Gabo's is "Lobster à la Macondo," and Fidel Castro's is "Turtle Consommé." (In those days the Cuban ration book—which had been introduced in 1962—contained, per month and per person, the following delicacies: seven pounds of rice and thirty ounces of beans, five pounds of sugar, half a pound of oil, four hundred grams of pasta, ten eggs, one pound of frozen chicken, and half a pound of ground meat—chicken—to which fish, mortadella, or sausage could be added as an alternative in the category of "meat products.")

IN *The Autumn of the Patriarch*, the Patriarch looks down on the man of letters: "they've got fever in their quills like thoroughbred roosters when they are molting so that they are no good for anything except when they are good for something." García Márquez, now with a house of his own on the island, was good for a great deal. In December 1986, he established a film academy in San Antonio de los Baños: the New Latin American Cinema Foundation. The new institution—financed by Gabo—was important to the regime, because culture in Latin America has always been an essential source of legitimacy. Among its guests would be Robert Redford, Steven Spielberg, and Francis Ford Coppola. The academy, as Martin describes it, was a clever and exciting idea: "Cinema was convivial, collective, proactive, youthful; cinema was sexy and cinema was fun. And García Márquez lived every minute of it; he was surrounded by attractive young women and energetic and ambitious but deferential young men, and he was in his element."

All of it resembled a reconstruction of Gabo's Macondian paradise from before the leaf storm, with the advantage that now it was Gabriel García Márquez who lived on the other side, the privileged side, the "American" side. For ordinary Cubans, his Siboney mansion, the lavish meals, the champagne, the seafood, the marvelous pastas prepared by Castro, the yacht outings were—as García Márquez wrote about the "forbidden city" of the Yankees in Aracataca—"fleeting visions of a remote and unlikely world that was veiled to us mortals."

In 1988 García Márquez wrote a profile of the *caudillo* (as he calls him) that was published as the prologue to *Habla Fidel* (Fidel Speaks), a book by the Italian Gianni Mina. In this profile he furnished a sweeping literary homage to his hero ("He may be unaware of the force of his presence, which seems to take up all the space in the room, though he is not as tall or as solidly built as he seems at first glance"). That same year, living in Havana, García Márquez made progress on a book about Bolívar's final journey: *The General in His Labyrinth*. Martin suggests that his description of Bolívar was inspired by traits of Castro, and his descriptions of Castro by his image of Bolívar.

The following year began badly, with the reverberations of a public letter signed in December 1988 by several writers of international renown who demanded that Castro follow in the footsteps of the Chilean dictator Pinochet and dare to submit his regime to a plebiscite. For García Márquez—who in the 1970s had expressed his disdain for the institutions, the laws, and the freedoms of "bourgeois" democracy, and in December 1981 had mocked the "crocodile tears" of the "usual anti-Soviets and anti-Communists" after the repression of Solidarity in Poland—the letter was another chapter in the rise of the "right" fostered by John Paul II, Thatcher, Reagan, and Gorbachev himself. (In a visit to Moscow in the late 1980s, García Márquez had warned Gorbachev of the danger of surrendering to the Empire.)

Of the signatories to this letter of protest against the lack of political freedom in Cuba, Martin writes that "the American names are not especially impressive, apart from Susan Sontag, nor were the Latin American ones (no Carlos Fuentes, Augusto Roa Bastos, etc.)." Among the American authors who did not impress Martin were Saul Bellow and Elie Wiesel; among the Latin Americans, Reinaldo Arenas (who composed the document), Ernesto Sabato, Mario Vargas Llosa, Guillermo Cabrera Infante, and Octavio Paz; among the Europeans, Juan Goytisolo, Federico Fellini, Eugene Ionesco, Czesław Miłosz, and Camilo José Cela. But his reaction is understandable. For the biographer and for his subject, "1989 would be the year of the apocalypse."

Even more of a blow to Cuba's prestige (though not to its economy) than the downfall of communism in Eastern Europe was the much-talked-about verdict against Division General Arnaldo Ochoa and the brothers Antonio (Tony) and Patricio de la Guardia, on charges of drug trafficking and treason against the Revolution. This dark episode came to public attention in June 1989. According to the journalist Andrés Oppenheimer, the movement of drugs through Cuba began in 1986 and had the tacit blessing of Fidel, until the American intelligence services detected a compromised operation. Castro then took the opportunity to kill four birds with one stone: he could rid himself of a potentially serious rival (Ochoa was one of the supreme commanders of the intervention in Angola, a veteran of the incursions into Venezuela, Ethiopia, Yemen, and Nicaragua, and officially recognized as a "Hero of the Revolution") along with the de la Guardia brothers, both of them Castro's friends and attached to the Ministry of the Interior under another "implicated party," the division general José Abrantes. Fidel had entrusted Tony de la Guardia, his "protégé," with multiple intelligence operations (such as the laundering of $60 million for Argentina's Montoneros in 1975, in payment for a kidnapping). It is hard to believe that this new venture—expressly ordered by Abrantes—did not enjoy Fidel's blessing, like everything on the island. But the end justified the means.

The remarkable fact is that Antonio de la Guardia, a character out of an action film, was also a close friend of García Márquez. One of his paintings hung in García Márquez's house in Havana. In that same year, 1989, Gabo dedicated *The General in His Labyrinth* to him: "For Tony, may he sow good." On July 9, when the final verdict was about to be announced, Castro visited García Márquez at his house in Havana. Oppenheimer reconstructed fragments of the long conversation. "If they are executed," García Márquez is reported to have said, "nobody on earth will believe it wasn't you who gave the order." Later that night, the writer received Ileana de la Guardia, Tony's daughter, and her husband Jorge Masetti (the son of the late guerrilla leader Jorge Ricardo Masetti, an old friend and García Márquez's former boss at *Prensa Latina*). They had come to beg García Márquez to intercede on de la Guardia's behalf, to save his life. The writer said things like "Fidel would be crazy if he allowed the executions," and raised their hopes. He told them not to worry, and advised them not to appeal to any human rights organizations. Four days went by. Then, on July 13, 1989, Gabo's good friend Tony de la Guardia and Ochoa were executed. Patricio was sentenced to thirty years in prison and Abrantes to twenty. The latter died of a heart attack in 1991.

Although he left Cuba before the executions, according to testimony collected by Ileana de la Guardia herself, García Márquez attended "part of the trial, along with Fidel and Raúl, behind the 'great mirror' in the hall of the Cuban Revolutionary Armed Forces." In Paris, during the bicentennial celebration of the French Revolution, he told President François Mitterrand that it had all been just "a quarrel among officers." Publicly he claimed to have "very good information" that the charges of treason were justified, and he observed that, given the situation, Castro had no alternative.

A few months before the events, writing the final pages of *The General in His Labyrinth*, García Márquez had re-created Simón Bolívar raving in his sleep as he remembers his order to shoot the brave mulatto general Manuel Piar, who had been invincible in his battles against the Spaniards and a hero of the masses. "It was the most savage use of power in his life," García Márquez observes in his novel, "but the most opportune as well, for with it he consolidated his authority, unified his command, and cleared the road to glory." And at the chapter's climax García Márquez puts his grandfather's words in Bolívar's mouth: "I'd do it all over again."

"I don't publish any book these days," García Márquez said sometime in the mid-1980s, "before the Comandante reads it." Which is why, regarding the passage about Bolívar and Piar, Martin wonders, "Did he [Castro] remember it as he made his decision?" We can assume he must have read it. But given the "very good information" that García Márquez has always claimed to have about Cuba, and given his closeness to Antonio de la Guardia, the interesting questions concern not the Comandante but the writer. Was García Márquez unaware of his friend Tony's secret assignments? As he was writing his novel, did he even consider the possibility that his friend would be arrested on charges of purported "treason"?

And so an old cycle of complicity was complete. It began with an execution in the inner circle of the young García Márquez—his grandfather's shooting of his friend and military subordinate Medardo, the son of his lover—and it ended with another execution in his inner circle: the Comandante's sentencing of his friend Tony, the "sower of good." The writer who, from an early age, adopted his grandfather's "political morality," the one who "quite cold-bloodedly puts politics before morality," the one who saw Castro as "a representation of his own grandfather . . . against whom he could not, would not dare, would not even wish, to win," had been obliged to test his theory on himself as flesh and blood. And he had accepted the verdict of power.

THE FRIENDSHIP and the lobsters have gone on for almost thirty years. Panegyrist, court advisor, press agent, ambassador-at-large, plenipotentiary representative, head of foreign public relations: García Márquez has been all these things for Castro. In 1996, he dined with President Bill Clinton and told him that "if you and Fidel could sit down face to face, there wouldn't be any problem left."

Things were going fairly well for the writer and the Comandante, except at a few moments: 2003, for instance, when a movement more important and universal than democracy, the movement for human rights, seemed to come between them. In March of that year, in a sudden and devastating gesture, Castro's tribunal sentenced seventy-eight dissidents to anywhere from twelve to twenty-seven years in prison. (One of them was accused of possessing a Sony tape recorder.) Immediately thereafter, in the heat of the moment, he ordered the execution of three boys who had tried to flee the island on a ferry. Confronted with this state crime, José Saramago declared (though he later retracted his statement) that "this is as far as I go" in his relationship with Castro. But the writer Susan Sontag went further, and at the Bogotá Book Fair, she criticized García Márquez: "He's this country's greatest writer and I admire him very much, but it's unpardonable that he hasn't spoken out about the latest measures taken by the Cuban regime."

In response, García Márquez seemed to distance himself somewhat from Castro: "Regarding the death penalty, I don't have anything to add to what I've said in private and publicly as long as I can remember: I'm against it in any place, for any reason, in any circumstances." But almost immediately he distanced himself from his distancing: "Some media outlets—among them CNN—are manipulating and distorting my response to Susan Sontag, to make it seem like a statement against the Cuban Revolution." For emphasis, he repeated an old argument, justifying his personal relations with Castro: "I can't count the number of prisoners, dissidents, and conspirators whom I've helped, in absolute silence, to get out of jail or emigrate from Cuba over the last twenty years at least."

In "absolute silence" or in absolute complicity? Why would García Márquez have helped anyone leave Cuba if he did not consider their imprisonment unjust? And if he considered it unjust, to the extent of championing their cause, why did he continue—why does he still continue—to support a regime that commits such injustices? Wouldn't it have been more valuable to denounce the unjust incarceration of those "prisoners, dissidents, and conspirators" and help to focus international criticism on the Cuban treatment of political prisoners?

García Márquez does not write from an ivory tower. He claims to be proud of his work as a reporter. He promotes journalism at an academy in Colombia. He has asserted that the news story is a literary genre with the potential to be "not just true to life but better than life. It's as good as a story or a novel, but with one sacred and inviolable difference: novels and stories permit unlimited fabrication but news stories have to be true down to the last comma." How, then, to reconcile this declaration of journalistic ethics with his own concealment of the truth in Cuba, despite his possession of privileged inside information?

Eventually history makes both aesthetic and moral judgments. Aesthetically speaking, it is a little premature to say—as Martin does—that García Márquez is the "new Cervantes." But in moral terms, certainly, there is no comparison. A hero in the war against the Turks, wounded and maimed in battle, castaway and prisoner in Algeria for five years, Cervantes lived his ideals, his tribulations, and his poverty with Quixote-like integrity, and enjoyed the supreme freedom of accepting his defeats with humor. One does not see such greatness of spirit in García Márquez, who has avidly collaborated with oppression and dictatorship.

The beauties of the fiction of Gabriel García Márquez will survive the contorted loyalties of the man who created it. But it would be an act of poetic justice if, in the autumn of his life and at the zenith of his glory, he disassociated himself from Fidel Castro and put his influence at the service of the Cuban dissidents. There is no point in hoping for such a transformation, of course. It is the kind of thing that happens only in García Márquez novels.

9

Mario Vargaɔ Lloɔa

CREATIVE PARRICIDE

Peru's noted modernist painter Fernando de Szyszlo, a close friend of Mario Vargas Llosa, attended the wake for Vargas Llosa's father, who died in January 1979. He has given us a description of the behavior of the great Peruvian novelist on that occasion: "When he came into the room where they were holding the wake for his father, Mario spent only a few seconds before the man stretched out in his coffin and, without saying a word, without a single gesture, rushed away." Vargas Llosa is not only a novelist and short story writer but also an essayist, playwright, journalist, even a presidential candidate in the 1990 Peruvian elections. He is known throughout the world for the extraordinary quality of his writing but he is not fundamentally a happy man: "I write because I am not happy, I write because it is a way of struggling against unhappiness."

The cause of this unhappiness can be traced to a central event in his life: the appearance, when he was ten years old, of a father he had always been told was dead. It would be a terrible reappearance, whose ominous shadow would condition a large part of his life. Literature is the means through which Vargas Llosa has been able to confront not only the unfortunate reality of his own country (and elsewhere in Latin America) but his personal history of anguish.

Peru, where Vargas Llosa was born, the ancient viceroyalty whose image some authors in the seventeenth century identified with the biblical Ophir (site of King Solomon's mines) or with the Garden of Eden itself, also had a traumatic past. In the Conquest of Mexico (between 1519 and 1521 in central Mexico) the Conquistadores perpetrated massacres; epidemics of European diseases decimated the Indians, and their labor was delivered en masse to the estates (*encomiendas*) assigned by royal decree to the victors. But the Conquest was followed by a "spiritual baptism" that eventually would have beneficial results for the future of the country. The monastic orders, especially the Franciscans and Dominicans, incorporated the Indians into the new culture in a creative and generally peaceful way. The Spaniards and surviving Indians began to mingle in a process of "mixing the races" (*mestizaje*) that would eventually lead to a softening of racial distinctions. During the colonial period, explicit and multiple racial categories (the so-called *castas*) existed but would start to disappear in the nineteenth century. Mexico was not (and is not) free of racial prejudice, especially in an area like Chiapas with its heavily Indian population. But the idea of natural equality, fostered by the great "Apostle of the Indians" Bartolomé de las Casas (1484–1566), had penetrated the culture to the extent that a dark-skinned Indian—Benito Juárez—could rise to be president of the republic as early as 1858.

The Conquest of Peru, from beginning to end, was marked by extreme brutality. Its course was set by the assassination of the Inca emperor Atahualpa, garroted at Pizarro's orders after he had already accepted Christianity, and the later execution of his nephew and the last independent Inca leader, Túpac Amaru, beheaded in public before thousands of wailing Indians. The coast was settled by the Spaniards (later, African slaves and Chinese laborers would arrive). In the mountains and the cold highland plateau, most of the population remained Indian. Not the ideas of Bartolomé de las Casas but the doctrine of his famous opponent, the scholar Juan Ginés de Sepúlveda, was the guideline for the Spaniards of Peru: the Indians were "slaves by nature." Peru is not the only country of Latin America with distinct cultural and racial enclaves, but it has been historically one of the worst in maintaining the divisions, the distrust, the prejudice, and the ever-renewed violence, echoes of the extreme violence that gave birth to the Viceroyalty.

In his memoir, *El pez en el agua* (The Fish in the Water), Vargas Llosa describes the *variopinta* ("multicolored," a frequent adjective in his writings) society of Peru:

> White and cholo [the usual, somewhat disparaging word for a mestizo in the south of Latin America] are terms that mean more things than race or ethnicity . . . White (*blanco*) and cholo always apply to someone in comparison with someone else, because one is always worse or better situated than others, less or more poor or important, with features less or more western or mestizo or Indian or Asian than others, and all that savage nomenclature that decides a great part of the destinies of individuals is maintained thanks to an effervescent edifice of prejudices and feelings—disdain, contempt, envy, rancor, admiration, emulation—which is—underneath the ideologies, values and condemnations—the profound explanation of the conflicts and frustrations of Peruvian life.

His judgment of his country is harsh, both of its history and its people (by which he primarily means its non-Indian citizens), whom he describes as marked by "an 'I' that is hidden and blind to reason, that is sucked in with its mother's milk and begins its formation from the first cries and stammerings of the Peruvian." He both loves and despises Peru. At times he has promised to abandon the country and never write another word about it. Viewed from abroad, it has shamed him but no matter how angry he can be with his country, it is always present before his mind's eye. And he has wanted to liberate his country, first through literature and later through political action.

The complex, tumultuous, "multicolored" story of his life reads like one of his own novels. He was born in Arequipa, in the south of Peru, a city in an Andean valley and known for both its religious and revolt-prone nature. His mother, Dorita, was only nineteen years old when, on a visit to the city of Tacna, she met Ernesto J. Vargas, a minor employee of a radio station, ten years older than her. She rapidly fell in love with the man. Back in Arequipa, she began an intense, amorous correspondence that led to marriage, in 1935, a year after their initial meeting.

The newlyweds moved to Lima and, from the very beginning, Ernesto began to show disturbing traits of character. He practically imprisoned Dorita, forbade her to see her friends and especially her relatives. He would launch into jealous fits of rage. But even worse and more destructive was his pervasive social resentment. Though he was white-skinned, well built and blue-eyed, he was consumed with the conviction (in Vargas Llosa's words) that he came from "a family socially inferior to that of his wife." And he manufactured a ferocious antipathy to his wife's family, which spilled into physical abuse of Dorita herself. Even within the context of Ernesto's twisted values, the antipathy had no basis. The Llosa family in Arequipa, though respected, were very far from being aristocrats. Very shortly after their marriage, Dorita became pregnant. Ernesto one day, in a casual manner, told her that she should go to her family in Arequipa, where her pregnancy could be better attended. He then never called her in Arequipa, never wrote, never attempted any contact. Four months later Mario was born. Some of Dorita's relatives finally found and spoke to Ernesto in Lima. His reaction was to send her a letter of immediate divorce. Besieged by the gossip and innuendoes of a closed-minded Catholic and provincial city, the family—Dorita with her baby of less than a year—moved to Cochabamba, in the fertile eastern valley of Bolivia, where Mario's grandfather raised cotton and was the Peruvian consul for the area.

The boy grew up "spoiled and pampered," swathed in the love of the Llosa family. They told him his father was dead. He was given a photo of Ernesto and, each night after being put to bed, he would kiss the picture, saying good night "to my dear father who was in heaven." There in Bolivia, he wrote his first childish verses, lavishly praised by the family. A man "whose memory I turn to whenever I feel very despairing about our species and am prone to believe that humanity, in the end, is a big heap of garbage," his beloved grandfather Pedro taught him to memorize the poems of Rubén Darío. His mother, who was still, despite everything, in love with Ernesto, did not remarry.

In 1945, one of his uncles, the respected lawyer José Luis Bustamante y Rivero, was elected president of the republic. For the young Mario, he was a living example of decency and civic dedication:

> The admiration I had as a child for that gentleman with a bow tie . . . I still have, because Bustamante . . . left power a poorer man than when he gained it, was tolerant with his adversaries and severe with his followers . . . and respected the laws to the extreme of committing political suicide.

Bustamante's election excited the Llosa family and changed their situation. Grandfather Pedro was named prefect of the city of Piura and the family returned to Peru. Living with his mother and his grandfather, the boy turned ten and would remember those days as a very happy time.

Recorded in his memory as nearly perfect, which often happens when one remembers a period immediately preceding a catastrophe, that pleasant world was torn apart one morning when Dorita informed the child that his father had not really died. On a visit to Lima, she had accidentally encountered Ernesto Vargas. The sight of him seemed to wipe away Dorita's memory of five and a half months of a miserable marriage and the ten years of silence. When Mario finally met his father, he had the feeling that it was a hoax. The man did not resemble the father he had imagined when he had thought the man was dead. It was in reality a prescient foreboding. Without any explanation, his parents loaded him into a car and swept him off to Lima, far from the Llosa family and ten years of a happy and protected life. The nightmare was barely beginning.

In Lima, for the first time in his life, he was lonely. "Fog-bound Lima, horrible Lima," wrote the poet Sebastián Salazar Bondy. The boy read and read to escape his solitude during those first "sinister" months of

1947. Ernesto still nourished his irrational hatred for Dorita's family and could work himself up over the imagined slight of their mere existence: "when, turned furious with rage, he would launch himself against my mother, and would beat her, I really wanted to die, because even death seemed preferable to the fear I used to feel. He hit me too, sometimes." Together with the terror his father inspired in him from those early days on, another emotion was stirring in him: hatred, though at the time he could not fully accept the word. Ernesto Vargas commanded Mario never to visit his relatives. And it greatly disturbed him when the boy went to Mass (which made Mario, for a time, turn religious to oppose his father). And the situation kept getting worse:

> When he would beat me, I would totally lose control. Often, be-
> cause I was terrified, I would humiliate myself before him and beg
> his pardon, clasping my hands together. But it wouldn't calm him.
> And he would go on beating me, screaming at me and threatening
> to put me in the army.

At various times, between 1947 and 1949, the mother and the child tried to escape from that inferno. Each time, Ernesto managed to persuade them to return. There would be a few days of calm. Then the rages and beatings would resume. One day, with Mario in the car, Ernesto pulled up at a corner and picked up two boys. "They're your brothers," he said. They were the children of an American wife whom he had met during his separation from Dorita and had also abandoned (or she had left him).

These frustrated attempts at flight had one positive result. His father finally allowed Mario to spend weekends with his uncles and cousins who lived in Miraflores, a wealthy area of Lima. Those weekends were the best days of his adolescence. He attended dances, went out with girls, saw films, and socialized with boys from Miraflores. These friends and his mother's relatives became a second, much more welcome family.

Near the end of 1948, General Manuel Odría led a military coup that overthrew the democratic government of Mario's uncle Bustamante y Rivero and began the Ochenio de Odría (Eight Years of Odría), with its dictatorial emphasis on modernity and unmitigated nationalism. When Mario's uncle went into exile, his father celebrated the coup as if it were a personal victory. That same year, another decisive event occurred, connected in its way with religion. On the last day of courses in his preparatory school (run by the Salesian Fathers), Mario went to collect his grades and one of his teachers, Brother Leoncio, tried to sexually molest him. Mario left the room running and the event was enough to turn him permanently away from religion.

He would write love poems for one of his girlfriends (secretly, as a way of resisting his father, who would get angry when the boy wrote verses). As might be expected in a brutal (and certainly deeply insecure) macho like Ernesto, such sensitivity for him was the mark of a "queer." It is likely that, without his father's contempt for literature, Mario might never have persevered in his writing, which began as a form of play but in time would become his vocation. Predictably, following the pattern of many a tyrannical Latin American father, Ernesto enrolled the boy, not yet fourteen, in a military school, to force him away from literature and "make a man out of him." But for Mario, it was, in part, an opportunity: "enclosed within those bars corroded by the dampness . . . during those gray days and nights, amid the deeply depressing fog, I read and I wrote as I never had before and I began to be (although I didn't know it as yet) a writer."

II

In his two years at the Leoncio Prado Military School (1950–51), Mario was enveloped in the "multicolored" society of Peru. There were boys with the faces of cholos, whites, Indians, boys from the mountains and the coast, from rich and poor homes. To make a little money (since he was twelve, his father had stopped giving him money) he composed little pornographic novels for his classmates and with the income earned, on his days off went to brothels and bought books in bulk, including the works of Alexandre Dumas, about whom he writes in his memoir: "From the images in those readings stemmed, I am sure, my preoccupation with learning to speak French and one day to go live in France." For a time he thought of becoming a journalist, of making a living by writing, and did some reporting on crime for *La Crónica*. After two years in military school, Mario—in what can be justly be termed a Freudian slip—forgot the time limit on registration for the third and final year. And it was too late to register at any other school in Lima. Through his uncle Lucho in Piura, he was accepted at the Colegio San Miguel, where he would complete his high school (*secundaria*) education. In Piura he would grow close to his uncle Lucho, through whose influence he would combine a new social dimension with his growing commitment to literature. In his conversations with Uncle Lucho, he imbibed a consciousness "that Peru was a country of ferocious contrasts, of millions of poor people" and "a very vivid sense that such an injustice had to change and that the change would come through what was called the left, socialism, the revolution." That year in Piura, free of military school and his abusive father, gave him respite and a creative impetus, central to the beginning of his development as a journalist and creative writer. It was the first stage for his personal liberation through literature. In Piura, he worked for the newspaper *La Industria*. At the same time, attracted by a newspaper announcement of a competition, he poured himself into writing a play: *La huida del Inca* (The Flight of the Inca), which would win a prize and be performed at the Teatro Variedades of Piura, directed by Mario himself, at the age of sixteen. And then, disappointing his family, who had hoped to see him enter the Catholic University of Lima, he chose (in 1952) to study law and literature at the public University of San Marcos, where he expected to make contact with revolutionaries "and become one of them."

POLITICS HAD entered his life "at a gallop and with the burst of idealism and confusion it usually involves for a young man." In the university he joined a communist cell. Under the Odría dictatorship, the party had been banned, and the communists, hiding their organization under the cover name of Cahuide (for an Inca warrior famous for having leaped to his death from the heights of the fortress of Sacsayhuamán rather than surrender to Pizarro), were trying to reconstruct the party in secret. Mario's group met in small cells, printed leaflets attacking the dictatorship, got into fights with student Apristas (militants of APRA, Alianza Popular Revolucionaria Americana, the nationalist revolutionary party of Raúl Haya de la Torre, also banned at the time), and tried to move the university toward support for workers' strikes. Mario took the covert name of "Comrade Alberto," read the classic (and some heretical) Marxist works, and participated in a workers' strike (which he would later transform into literature in his first published work of fiction, in 1959, a collection of short stories titled *Los jefes*, and translated into English as *The Cubs and Other Stories*). But he soon found himself at odds with the dominating leftist dogmas of that period, the absolute dominion of Stalinist rigidity in politics and of social realism in literature. When he praised the prose of *Les nourritures terrestres* (The Fruits of the Earth) by André Gide, his comrades called him a "sub-man":

It was that, in part, that got me fed up with Cahuide. When I stopped going to cell meetings, around June or July of 1954, I had been bored for a long time with the inanity of what we were doing. I didn't believe one word of our class analyses, and our materialist interpretations—though I didn't say this in any emphatic way to my comrades—seemed to me puerile, a catechism of stereotypes and abstractions.

He describes his political enthusiasm in those years as "considerably greater than my ideological coherence." Perhaps for that reason, when a Christian Democratic Party was formed in 1956, he joined it. He even wrote speeches for Fernando Belaúnde Terry, the party's presidential candidate. His political passion was based on eclectic reading and admiration for individuals; he venerated Sartre just as he did Bustamante y Rivero. About his time as a Christian Democrat, he would later comment:

What the hell was I doing there, among these unbelievably respectable people, light years away from the Sartrean priest-bash-
ers, me a lefty, not completely cured of all the Marxist notions
. . . I still kept feeling? . . . Nevertheless, I stayed with the Christian Democrats because their fight against the dictatorship and in
favor of the democratization of the country was impeccable.

Vargas Llosa has always shown a consummate ability to transform
the events of his life into enduring literature. He used his experiences
at Leoncio Prado, the student violence he witnessed there, for his novel
La ciudad y los perros (The City and the Dogs), and his apprenticeship
as a reporter—with the free-living life that accompanied it—in one of
his earlier, most respected works, *Conversación en la catedral* (Conversation in the Cathedral), published when he was thirty-three years old, in
which he also began to exact literary vengeance on his father, through
the character of a selfish and overbearing father figure who takes his
place in a gallery of the fundamentally evil, life-destroying rulers of
Peru (and also a secret homosexual, as if to fling Ernesto Vargas's gibes
back in his face). The book is perhaps the culminating literary product
of his time as a leftist (his politics would change radically as he grew
older), a period that really began in 1952, while he had been reporting
on crime for *La Crónica*. There he became friends with Carlos Ney Bar-
rionuevo, director of the newspaper's literary supplement, and through
Ney was introduced to the work of two writers who would become essential influences: André Malraux, a man of action and beautifully sonorous prose, and most especially Jean-Paul Sartre, whose ideas on the
need for political and social commitment in a writer would leave deep
traces on Mario's future life. Much later, in 2001, in his book of essays
Literature and Politics, he would describe his feelings in those days:

What did it mean to be committed—a key word of the period
in which I began to write my first texts—to commit ourselves
as writers? It meant to assume, before anything else, the conviction that by writing we not only were materializing a vocation,

through which we would realize our most intimate longings, a mental and material predisposition that existed within us, but that we were also, by means of that vocation, exercising our obligations as citizens and, in some way, participating in that marvelous and elevating enterprise of resolving problems, of bettering the world.

A MUCH more serious matter for his family was his ill-timed elopement with his maternal aunt (by marriage) Julia Urquidi in 1955. Mario was nineteen, Julia ten years older. It seemed like another characteristic event in the heated emotional universe of the Llosas, an amorous rapture, a festive and almost crazy transgression, as if he were inverting (he seemed the one most madly in love) and compensating for the disaster of his father and mother's entanglement. Faithful to his character, Ernesto reacted "like a rabid dog," and Julia had to flee, for a time, to Bolivia. Twenty-two years later, Vargas Llosa would give his fictionalized version in hindsight of this passionate affair in a novel full of humor and feeling—in a very different vein, though no less intelligent and creatively impressive than his great, deadly serious masterpieces: *La tia Julia y el escribidor.* The title and work have been translated as "Aunt Julia and the Scriptwriter," though *escribidor* is more properly "scribbler" or "third-rate writer," and the novel intercuts the narrator's love for an "older woman" with the story of a noted hack writer of immensely successful radionovelas, as formulaic and sentimental as present-day telenovelas, who gradually goes insane and starts to confuse and muddle together the wildly disparate banalities of a number of soap opera scripts he had previously managed to produce almost simultaneously but still maintained as separate narratives. Material for this second thread also came from Mario's experience laboring for a time—among his many jobs—on radionovelas.

With his wife, Julia, still in Bolivia to avoid Ernesto's frenzied determination to prosecute her legally, Mario published his first stories, worked as a journalist, and continued his studies in literature while the law component of his university concentration interested him hardly at all. He would work many temporary "jobs that feed you," some of them supremely dull (behind the counter of a bank or registering graves in a cemetery). Others were truly valuable to him, even fruitfully formative. For three and a half hours a day, across a period of four and a half years, he worked for the eminent historian Raúl Porras Barrenechea and learned Peruvian history from the ground up, more thoroughly and profoundly than he could from any classes he attended at San Marcos. Then came the chance to realize a long-held dream. Thanks to a short story competition sponsored by the *Revue Française,* he earned a trip to the "city of light," Paris itself. On his return, he graduated in literature, with a thesis on the poetry of Rubén Darío. And more important than his academic experience was his ever-widening path through the world of letters. He explored various genres (including another play) and established friendships with noted Peruvian authors. Though at first he had disdained the "formalism" of Borges, he soon began to admire him. He continued to be dazzled by the skills of Malraux, and Sartre had converted him to the ethic of "commitment." But his discovery of William Faulkner was much more important to his development. The American southerner offered him the gift of a new conception of form. From him Vargas Llosa absorbed "the serpentine language, the chronological dislocation, the mystery and profundity and the restless ambiguities and psychological subtleties which that form [of Faulkner's] can lend to narratives."

In 1959, news arrived from Spain. His first published book, the short story collection *Los jefes,* had won the Leopoldo Alas Prize. That same year, he moved with his wife to Paris, where he would work teaching Spanish at a Berlitz school and produce journalistic pieces for Agence France-Presse and Radiodiffusion-Télévision Française. A new world was opening for the couple and Mario launched himself into his writing.

III
——

Mario Vargas Llosa was, at first, an enthusiastic partisan of the Cuban revolutionary victory: "considering Cuba as a model that could be followed by Latin America . . . never before had I felt an enthusiasm and so powerful a feeling of solidarity for a political event." Already, in 1958, he had written manifestos in favor of *los barbudos*. He was in Paris on the night of the triumph of the Cuban Revolution and he went out into the streets to celebrate the new year and the new era. In 1962, he made his first trip to the island and then went to Mexico, as a correspondent for Radiodiffusion-Télévision Française, when the Cuban Missile Crisis erupted onto the front pages and television screens. The French asked him to return to Cuba, where he spent some anxious days as the prospect of an American invasion (or bombardment) seemed imminent. He saw the American planes flying low over the island. The prospect of immolation flew through the air with them and Mario donated blood for the possible victims. Fortunately, America and Russia (over the heads of the Cubans) reached a resolution that forestalled an armed, perhaps nuclear confrontation. When he returned to France, his first novel, *La ciudad y los perros,* won the Biblioteca Breve Prize, awarded by the prestigious Spanish publishing house Seix Barral. Two years later, he would return for some months to Peru, make a brief but intense trip into the eastern jungle (it would give him material for his novel *La casa verde,* The Green House), and use the opportunity of distance from Paris to divorce Julia Urquidi. Shortly afterward, he would marry another family member, his cousin Patricia Llosa, who would be his faithful companion from then on.

In the beginning, the Cuban Revolution had shown a breadth, pluralism, and flexibility in the area of culture that drew the respect of most of the intellectual and artistic world. But there were disturbing omens, even at the outset. The cultural publication *Lunes de Revolución* (Monday of Revolution), directed by Guillermo Cabrera Infante, had closed in November 1961. And yet, Vargas Llosa would remember, "nobody talked about it, there was a kind of pact of silence in the air. Cabrera Infante himself behaved like a diplomat in Paris in 1965." Vargas Llosa would visit the island five times and gradually begin to distance himself from the Cuban Revolution. In the end he would come to see its government as an "authoritarian system, vertical, without freedom of the press" and "in no way what image, publicity and hope wanted to make us see."

In 1966 he visited the Soviet Union, where he attended a meeting of the Writers' Union that surprised him with its bureaucratic rigidity. And he noticed the long lines in front of stores, the privileges accorded to the bureaucrats, the ugliness of the architecture. Nevertheless, when he made his third trip to Cuba, in 1967, he was still under the spell of the revolution and agreed to join the Board of Contributors to the influential publishing house Casa de las Américas. The decision marked the high point of his commitment to revolutionary Cuba. He participated in a collective interview with Fidel Castro, who displayed his most likable persona, promising to rapidly correct whatever his critics pointed out to him. Vargas Llosa was impressed. In his collection *Sables y utopías* (Sabers and Utopias), of 2009, he writes:

Fidel, as he spoke, referred many times to Marx, to Lenin, to historical materialism, to the dialectic. Nevertheless, I have never seen a Marxist less attached to the use of formulas and crystallized schemes . . . If there was one thing about which I was absolutely convinced during that sleepless night, it was Fidel's love for his country, the sincerity of his conviction that he was acting for the benefit of his people.

Then an incident occurred that somewhat dimmed his fascination with the Cuban Revolution. Without his knowledge, his editors had nominated him for Venezuela's Rómulo Gallegos Prize. Venezuela had been invaded in that year, unsuccessfully, by a small guerrilla force linked to Cuba. Vargas Llosa, learning about his nomination for the literary prize and maintaining his sympathy for the Cuban regime, was disturbed by the possible connection of his name with Venezuela and its liberal president, Raúl Leoni. He mentioned his dilemma to Alejo Carpentier, who was then the Cuban cultural attaché in Paris. Carpentier proposed that Vargas Llosa, if he won the prize, should make a donation to the struggle led by Che Guevara, who was then somewhere in the mountains of Bolivia. Carpentier argued that it would make a great impression throughout Latin America. He then read him a letter from Haydée Santamaría, whose status as a comrade of Fidel Castro in the attack on the Moncada Barracks in 1953 (an action that foreshadowed the Cuban Revolution) had earned her near mythical fame and who was now a very powerful bureaucrat in the Cuban cultural ministry. She indicated that if Vargas Llosa made the contribution, the government, which understood that "a writer has needs," would return the money secretly to him, so that he would lose nothing. Vargas Llosa was surprised and indignant at this request for a charade. But when he did receive the prize, he included praise of the Cuban Revolution in his acceptance speech and explicitly stated his commitment to socialism.

Nevertheless, the incident initiated (or furthered) a distancing from the Revolution. The year 1968 brought two much more serious problems. In that year of widespread dissidence in both the communist and capitalist worlds, Cuban intellectuals were beginning to be hounded by the government. And the Russians reacted to the Prague Spring of rebellion within Czechoslovakia by pouring troops across the border in an August invasion. Fidel Castro, in a speech, justified the Russian onslaught. Vargas Llosa wrote a critical piece titled "The Socialism of the Tanks" and gave an interview in which he criticized Fidel's support for the Soviet intervention. In October of that year, a number of distinguished (and almost all, until then, pro-Castro) Latin American and Spanish writers including Vargas Llosa put their names to a letter "on the problems of intellectuals in Cuba." In November, García Márquez, then Mario's close friend, wrote him to say that the letter was in Fidel's hands:

> Nevertheless, I don't believe it will do any good. Fidel will answer, with the greatest delicacy he can muster, that what he does with his writers and artists is his own business and therefore we can go to hell. I know from a good source that he is not pleased with our attitude on Czechoslovakia and now he has a good opportunity to let off steam.

A long process followed that would lead to Mario's estrangement from the Cuban Revolution (and eventually from any form of socialism). Vargas Llosa did not attend a meeting of the Board of Contributors to Casa de las Américas in 1969, essentially because of a schedule conflict. In Cuba his nonattendance was interpreted as a deliberate distancing from the Revolution. He was sent a letter signed by the entire board asking him to come immediately to Cuba to discuss "your attitudes and opinions." Instead Vargas Llosa wrote to the magazine's editor in chief, Roberto Fernández Retamar:

My adherence to Cuba is very deep but it is not nor will it be that of someone who unconditionally accepts, in an automatic way, all the positions adopted on every issue by the revolutionary power. That kind of adherence, which seems to me deplorable even for a bureaucrat, is inconceivable in a writer since, as you know, a writer who stops thinking independently, or dissenting or loudly stating his opinions, is not a writer but a ventriloquist's dummy. With the enormous respect I feel for Fidel and for what he represents, I continue to deplore his support for the Soviet intervention in Czechoslovakia, because I believe that intervention did not suppress a counter-revolution but a movement for democratization within socialism in a country that was aspiring to make of itself something resembling what Cuba, precisely, has made of itself.

But he did not go to Cuba to discuss his "attitudes and opinions" and when, in 1971, Heberto Padilla was arrested (along with other intellectuals) and a falsified or extorted "confession" was circulated, Vargas Llosa resigned from the board of Casa de las Américas with a letter to Santamaría:

Using methods that are repugnant to the dignity of human beings to force certain comrades to accuse themselves of imaginary betrayals and to sign letters where even the syntax sounds like a product of the police is the negation of what made me, from the first day, embrace the cause of the Cuban Revolution: its decision to fight for justice without losing respect for individuals.

Though he continued to issue statements in favor of socialism and insisted that his disenchantment was directed toward specific actions, the Cuban government and its devotees abroad saw only betrayal. He composed and published a letter to Castro, signed by a star-studded international gallery of intellectuals, including Sartre, in which Vargas Llosa expressed their "duty to communicate ... our shame and our anger" over the case of Padilla. The letter was a turning point, an end to the season of love between intellectuals and the Cuban Revolution. For Vargas Llosa, it precipitated a torrent of antagonism and verbal abuse:

From having been a very popular figure among leftists and rebels, I turned into a leper. The same people who used to applaud me with so much enthusiasm when I gave a lecture would insult me ... and hurl fliers at me.

IV

Beginning in 1966, Vargas Llosa would live in Peru and London (though he would later give lectures or teach for a time in English or foreign universities). His sons Álvaro and Gonzalo were born in 1966 and 1967, his daughter Morgana in 1974. A scholarship permitted him to take a doctorate at the Universidad Complutense of Madrid for a thesis on García Márquez's *One Hundred Years of Solitude*. When the thesis was published, the Spanish literary critic Ángel Rama wrote a harsh review, which drifted off into an attack on Vargas Llosa for his "romantic and individualist" reading of the novel, contrary to "the idea of art as human and social work, which Marxism contributes," while in Latin America, the intelligentsia of the left had begun to turn their backs on him, as a result of his own turning away from the Cuban Revolution. (For months Carlos Rincón, in the journal *Casa de las Américas*, had been severely criticizing his theoretical ideas.)

Disenchanted with politics, he completely immersed himself for a time in the universe where he was strongest, most accurate, most completely at ease—literary creation. His fourth novel, *Pantaleón y las visitadoras* (Pantaleon and the Lady Visitors, the title loosely translated into English as *Captain Pantoja and the Special Service*), is a picaresque treatment of prostitution tolerated (and organized) by the Peruvian army for soldiers serving in the jungle. In 1976 he was chosen to be president of the writers' advocacy group International PEN and the following year he would publish *Aunt Julia and the Writer*. (Years later, in 1983, Julia Urquidi herself, now the abandoned woman, would write her personal account of the long-ago passion, *Lo que Varguitas no dijo* [What Little Vargas (his nickname at the time) Didn't Say], which both praised and dispraised Vargas Llosa. It was for once a criticism and evaluation of him that had nothing to do with politics but was reputed to have angered him. In it she claimed that her urgings and sacrifices had made him into a writer.)

In his theoretical essays of the 1970s he would devaluate the Sartre he had so admired, for the very real limitations of Sartre's literary skill but also in reaction to the Sartrean interpretation of "commitment," which he had begun to distrust and assign to the ambit of Marxism and socialism from which he was moving further away. Albert Camus surged in his estimation, for his independence from mechanical Marxism, his hatred of authoritarianism, and his praise for individual liberty. As for his father, Ernesto, after the last twist of his cruelty had failed to dissolve the elopement with Aunt Julia, the physical and psychological aggressions against his son had ended decades ago. Nevertheless, "even though I always tried to be polite with him, I never showed more affection than I felt (which was none). The terrible rancor, the fiery hatred I felt toward him as a child, was vanishing with the years." They last met in January 1979, by chance, in Lima and Mario accompanied the old man to his home where, while eating lunch, Ernesto collapsed. He died in the ambulance on his way to the hospital.

BY THEN Vargas Llosa had discovered liberalism. But his movement away from the left (and the expansion of his creative interests into broader and more universal themes) became definitive after the death of his father. A kind of personal liberation, exclusive of its specific content, seems to have dawned for him with the death of Ernesto Vargas and a closure came, at least in part, on the abuse he had suffered and that had formed (and would continue to form) an inextricable element of his inner being. In politics, he would experience something similar to a conversion.

A few months after Ernesto's death, Vargas Llosa attended an international conference organized by the Peruvian economist Hernando de Soto, where he heard Friedrich Hayek, Milton Friedman, Jean-François Revel (whose book *The Totalitarian Temptation* particularly impressed him), and other advocates of economic liberalism, with its emphasis on the open market, small government, and the elimination of virtually all controls on business and finance. By then he had read the philosophical and historical essays of Isaiah Berlin, including (in Berlin's *Against the Current*) essays on socialists like Alexander Herzen who had been influenced by classic liberal ideas. In time he would read Karl Popper and his arguments for classical liberalism, especially *The Open Society and Its Enemies*. Octavio Paz's approach to liberal and democratic positions also had its impact upon him: Vargas Llosa had written for the magazine *Plural* and became an even more frequent contributor to *Vuelta*. But in contrast to Paz, Vargas Llosa's criticism of socialism was not only aesthetic, ideological, and political but also economic. His adoption of the tenets of economic liberalism would be relentless. In time, it would lead him to support some of its highly questionable proponents in the United States and garner continuous criticism from adversaries in Latin America. At the time, as a mark of his new outlook, Vargas Llosa published an enthusiastic text centering on the ideas of De Soto, in which he advocated making squatter-occupied public land the private property of the migrants who had raised their temporary dwellings there; and, against conventional opinion, he defended street vendors, the "informal market," terming them microbusinesses and a dynamic force within the Peruvian economy.

Galvanized by his political and economic conversion, he would publish, in 1981, a long, magnificent novel, *La guerra del fin del mundo* (The War at the End of the World) about an episode in nineteenth-century Brazil that foreshadowed some of the manifestations of modern fundamentalism. With the flow of an epic, the book deals with the same events made famous by the Brazilian author Euclides da Cunha in his *Os Sertões* (Rebellion in the Backlands), a historical-sociological account of the war waged to resist the new Brazilian republic by a millenarian cult (drawn mostly from the poorest of the poor) in the nineteenth-century backlands (the *sertão*) of northern Brazil. This rebellion took its place in a string of similar Latin American events, before and after, a constant historical blockage within ancient, backward, and oppressive societies: the ferociously violent reaction of the masses—usually led by a charismatic savior who revives or manipulates atavistic myths—against a sudden attempt at modernization. In Peru, in 1780, the rebellion of the mestizo Túpac Amaru II against the Bourbon reforms was such an event. So to a certain extent was the initial Mexican revolt, under the leadership of Father Hidalgo in 1810, against the Spaniards, and, even more clearly, Emiliano Zapata's peasant revolution within the Mexican Revolution. In the remote, desperately impoverished, largely illiterate *sertão*, between 1893 and 1897, a messianic preacher claiming divine inspiration (and divinity itself in his status as a prophet), Antônio Conselheiro drew the loyalty and blind faith of many thousands of the dirt poor (including large numbers of recently freed Afro-Brazilian slaves) and led them to a remote area of Bahia where he offered them a safe haven, a collective colony of their own called Canudos, a rudimentary paradise where they could live and feed themselves and be safe from the "enemies" of religion. But the newborn republic (with the approval of the Church, for whom Conselheiro was a dangerous heretic) launched a series of

campaigns against the separatist settlement. Antonio urged his followers to defend "the truth of Jesus" against the "demon" incarnated in
the Brazilian Republic. The final war was to the death, with no quarter
given or expected from either side. The mobile guerrilla-like forces of
the Conselheiro overwhelmed a series of small government forces until
a large army, equipped with heavy artillery, finally broke through de-
fenses and massacred all the men (male prisoners had their throats cut)
and delivered the young women, after raping many of them, to brothels.

The novel certainly reflects the sea change in Vargas Llosa's political
opinions. Fanaticism and factional rigidity (here religious and atavistic)
lead their adherents to utter disaster. But equally important is the fascinating mosaic of multiple characters and intense action on both sides of
the war, which the author's genius enables him to depict from an almost
Olympian vantage point as the tragedy unfolds, step by step, before his
creative mind, not only the major themes and the carefully developed
moral judgments but the power of brilliantly fashioned details that linger
in the mind of the reader. There is, for instance, the moment in *The War
at the End of the World*, involving the "Lion of Natuba," a grievously de-
formed and crippled young man who moves like an animal on all four
limbs. A former human castaway in his native village who has found a
place of respect in Canudos and with the power to read and write some-
how acquired (by an utterly ignorant but obviously intelligent mind) has
become the Boswell to Antonio Conselheiro, copying down his every
word. When Canudos is overwhelmed by the troops of the republic,
rather than wait to have his throat cut, he rises up on his "rear extremi-
ties," takes the dead body of a child who has been shot from its weakened
mother who has begged him to throw the body into a flaming hut, and
saying, "This fire has been awaiting me for twenty years," scurries, singing a psalm, toward the flames that will absorb him.

v

The 1980s in Peru opened with an uncommon burst of hope. After
twelve years of de facto rule, the military stepped down and called new

elections, which returned to power the same president, Fernando Belaúnde Terry, they had unceremoniously deposed in 1968. At the time few recognized the dark symbolism of another new, and utterly different, development: the emergence of a Marxist guerrilla organization known as the "Shining Path" (Sendero Luminoso). Its first public manifestation—the curious practice of hanging dogs from lampposts with signs attached bearing the name of Teng Hsiao-p'ing, the "running dog" whom the Sendero accused of betraying Mao Tse-tung—aroused repugnance rather than fear. But the rapid plunge into fiercer activity very quickly demonstrated that this was a guerrilla group to be taken with the utmost seriousness.

Led from a secret command post by Abimael Guzmán—a university professor who, in his own estimation, was "the fourth sword of Marxism," along with Marx, Lenin, and Mao—the Senderistas had been preaching a form of "pedagogic terror" inspired by the Chinese Cultural Revolution and the terror of the Khmer Rouge in Cambodia. In contrast to all known revolutionary traditions, where the target is always the "class oppressor," the Shining Path singled out the people themselves for their attacks: peasants who chose not to cooperate with their putative liberators, workers who dared to defy calls for a strike. To these expressions of "false historical consciousness," the Shining Path responded not with pamphlets or wall posters, but with guns and knives: mutilation as warning, summary execution as punishment.

In 1983 Mario Vargas Llosa had the opportunity to learn precisely how this "pedagogic terror" had taken hold in parts of Peru. The government of Belaúnde Terry was being held responsible by the radical press and the parliamentary left for the mysterious death of eight journalists in the province of Ayacucho, the mountainous center of Sendero operations. By way of response, the president appointed a blue-ribbon commission—consisting of three members (one of them Vargas Llosa) and eight advisors—to look into the matter. After investigating the scene of the crime for thirty days, and after hearing testimony that would eventually fill a thousand pages, the commission concluded that "the journalists were murdered by the peasants of Uchuraccay, with the probable complicity of residents in neighboring communities, in the utter absence of the Peruvian armed forces."

Shortly thereafter Vargas Llosa published his own account of the affair in Western periodicals (including the *New York Times Magazine*), in which he explained the origins of the problem. The Indians of Uchuraccay, whose thousand-year-old culture had been under attack for some time by the guerrillas, had mistakenly assumed that the journalists were members of the Shining Path. Vargas Llosa's visit to Uchuraccay seemed to offer him an insight into the true nature of guerrilla movements in Latin America:

Perhaps this story helps to clarify the reason for the mind-shattering violence that characterizes guerrilla warfare in Latin America. These guerrilla movements are not "peasant movements." They are born in the cities, among intellectuals and middle-class militants who, with their dogmatism and their rhetoric, are often as foreign and incomprehensible to the peasant masses as Sendero Luminoso is to the men and women of Uchuraccay. The outrages committed by those other strangers—the Government forces of counterinsurgency—tend to win peasant support for the guerrillas . . . The fact is that the struggle between the guerrillas and the armed forces is really a settling of accounts between privileged sectors of society, and the peasant masses are used cynically and brutally by those who say they want to "liberate" them. The peasants always suffer the greatest number of victims: At least 750 of them have been killed in Peru since the beginning of 1983.

By then his philosophical and moral convictions had been most clearly defined through his long and intense polemic with the Latin American intelligentsia, whom Vargas Llosa defined as "a decisive element in our political underdevelopment." He referred specifically to the case of the Chilean poet and Nobel laureate Pablo Neruda (author, wrote Vargas Llosa, of "the richest and most innovative poetry in the Spanish language . . . and also, of hymns of praise to Stalin"), and to the

Cuban novelist-diplomat Alejo Carpentier (whose "elegant, skeptical tales" Vargas Llosa contrasted with his uncritical reverence for Castro). His criticism was aimed at others as well—for example, at the Argentine novelist Julio Cortázar, who had begun his career as a supporter of Francisco Franco. And, of course, at Gabriel García Márquez. For Vargas Llosa, García Márquez perfectly embodies the Latin American intellectual who insists that the choice in South America "is not between democracy and dictatorship (Marxist or neofascist) but between reaction and revolution, embodied in those infamous archetypes, Pinochet and Castro." In Vargas Llosa's view, the Latin American intellectual, far from representing a fearless tradition of criticism, has been a guardian of the most rigid orthodoxy, "preventing the democratic option, which is actually the one preferred by our peoples, from acquiring an original expression of its own . . . adapted to the complex realities of our societies."

This lengthy process of disenchantment, for which Vargas Llosa (like Octavio Paz in Mexico) was widely vilified, reached something of a climax in his report on the events in Uchuraccay, which he held up as a macabre metaphor, expressing the perverse limits to which ideological zeal can lead. At that moment, overcome with, in his own words, "amazement, indignation, and regret," he conceived *The Real Life of Alejandro Mayta*. It was a novelized anatomy of the archetypal Latin American guerrilla of the 1970s and '80s, the portrait of a redeemer.

VI
———

Zavalita, the principal character in Vargas Llosa's *Conversation in the Cathedral* (1969), memorably opens that novel by asking, "When did Peru get screwed up?" The question seems almost upbeat compared with the vision of their country shared by the protagonists of *The Real Life of Alejandro Mayta*. The novel takes place in a fictitious locale afflicted by both civil and international war. The book begins and ends with a description of the garbage "that's invading every neighborhood in the capital of Peru," symbolizing not waste but social decomposition:

drugs, hoarding, prostitution, and acts of violence committed by the poor against each other. Every character registers this horror, which grows by leaps and bounds as the story advances. "Things will get worse and worse . . . We thought we had touched bottom." In *The Real Life of Alejandro Mayta* the memorable phrase is not a question, but a dark affirmation: "There are no limits to our deterioration."

An alter ego of Vargas Llosa, a Peruvian novelist and former leftist who has spent fifteen years in Europe, returns home to investigate the circumstances surrounding the life of one Alejandro Mayta, who at the beginning of 1958—a few months before Castro's victory in Cuba—participated in a failed guerrilla insurrection in Jauja, which had been Peru's provisional capital after the Spanish Conquest. (Though Mayta is a wholly fictitious creation, the rebellion itself did occur, in 1962.)

Using the same methods that Vargas Llosa employed in his investigation of the events in Uchuraccay, the writer in the novel tries to reconstruct Mayta's life through a series of individual testimonies, which taken together are partial, inconsistent, or simply unclear: "With each new fact, more contradictions, conjectures, mysteries, and incongruities crop up." And finally, as in the real-life case of Uchuraccay, many details of the event remain unresolved. But unlike the real Vargas Llosa, the novelist in *The Real Life of Alejandro Mayta* is searching for something more than "the facts of the case." He is after "a certain symbolic presence embodying what came later, an omen whose meaning no one was capable of interpreting at the time." The unsuspected reality—ideological violence—was then a daily fact of life in Peru, Colombia, and various Central American countries. The author wants to identify the human archetype at the heart of this new phenomenon, the revolutionary personality consecrated to an absolute ideal and therefore capable of dying or causing others to die. The fact that Vargas Llosa himself spent some years pinning his hopes for Peru on just such people, and then many more years rejecting their solutions, imparts a deeply personal note to the narrative.

Alejandro Mayta comes to revolution not through social or economic deprivation, but from a truncated religious vocation. Like so many Latin American radicals, he has studied at a religious high school (technically a seminary), though his instructors were not Jesuits (as is commonly the case with educated radicals) but Salesians. Though it is not explored in the novel, the difference between the two religious orders is important. In those days, the Jesuits prepared the children of elites for the exercise of power. The Salesians, an order created at the end of the nineteenth century, concentrate on young men from the humbler social classes, to whom they teach the kind of skilled trades that put them in direct contact with workers, peasants, or (in the case of Peru) inhabitants of the shantytowns that surround the capital and other cities. The Jesuits specialize in rhetoric and dialectics: they are the legitimate sons of the sixteenth-century Council of Trent (though under the influence of Pope John XXIII, the Jesuits would alter their orientation between the 1960s and 1990s). The Salesians, in contrast, exalt the dignity of manual labor: they are the product of Leo XIII's late nineteenth-century encyclical *Rerum novarum*.

Mayta starts out preparing for the priesthood. He attends Mass every day. He crosses himself with conspicuous devotion. He takes Communion frequently. His friends call him "a little saint." The experience of an intensive religious education awakens within him a sense of piety laced with guilt. But in his youth, Mayta experiences a process of conversion not very different from that undergone by Chernyshevsky and other Russian revolutionaries, like Stalin himself—a change of catechism by which ex-seminarians pass, with no inner doubts, from one dogmatic creed to another. Mayta's new faith becomes the revolution; his new prophet, Leon Trotsky.

The seven members of the Trotskyist sect that Mayta finally joins read and reread the sacred texts (Marx, Trotsky's *Permanent Revolution*, Lenin's *What Is to Be Done?*) and argue interminably about the precise implications for Peruvian society of every chapter, passage, and idea. At times they resemble the Byzantine theologians who used to argue over the gender of angels, and at others they parallel—in a weaker form, and without being at all aware of the fact—some of the tensest moments in the history of messianism, the expectant wait for the savior who will restore harmony to the universe. In the Peruvian case, as in all others, the prospect of the millennium offers a rich utopian vision, one that dates back to the ideas of Mariátegui. The peasants will become owners of the land they work; the industrial proletariat will acquire the factories where they labor. There will be an end to all exploitation, inequality, fanaticism, and ignorance. Political bosses and their imperialist masters will be no more. Banks, private schools, businesses, and urban real estate will all be nationalized. Popular militias will replace a professional army based on class distinctions. And in accord with the Trotskyist critique of Stalinism,

> worker and peasant councils, in their factories, on their collective farms, and in government ministries, would prevent the outsized growth and consequent ossification of a bureaucracy that would freeze the revolution and use it for its own benefit.

"The assault on heaven . . . ," Mayta thinks to himself, somewhat anticipating what would later become the Theology of Liberation. "We shall bring heaven down from heaven, establish it on earth."

Some come to regard him as an agent of the CIA; others imagine he has connections with the KGB. (To accentuate Mayta's compulsion toward marginality, Vargas Llosa decides, perhaps unnecessarily, to make him also a closet homosexual, seeking in some undetermined way to achieve through social revolution his personal sexual redemption.) All of this tends to overpower the narrative with an atmosphere of factionalism and intolerance. Mayta celebrates his fortieth birthday sharing a garret with rats; he is the object of a police dragnet, is wholly absorbed in "sterile polemics," and spends time composing "masturbatory pamphlets."

Lieutenant Vallejos, an army officer (who in fact existed in real life), offers him the concrete possibility of revolutionary action by inviting him to join in the Jauja insurrection with other conspirators, including a high school teacher and a justice of the peace. Fifteen years later each has a different—and generally contradictory—view of "Mayta,

the Trotskyist" and his role in the events, but all agree that for him the
Jauja experience had a "purifying, redemptive" character.

The reality of revolution is, of course, far less lofty than its ideal.
Stupidity, misjudgment, ignorance, fear, treason, innocence, and bad
timing—all abort the insurrection. Vallejos and some of his younger
collaborators, a few hardly into adolescence, are killed. Mayta is cap-
tured and sentenced to a lengthy prison term.

In the final chapter of the novel, the author and Mayta finally meet.
Fifteen years have passed since the futile attempt at insurrection in
the mountains. Not a trace remains of Mayta's earlier unsettling characteristics. He quietly tends a small ice-cream parlor in Miraflores, a
prosperous suburb of Lima, and supports a wife and four children.
In confinement he was a model prisoner. Indeed, his pride and joy is
not the attempt at social upheaval years before (although neither is he
ashamed of it), but rather the tiny revolution of order, cleanliness, and
good conduct that he had championed in prison. He has no wish to
speak of events past. ("You don't know how strange it is for me to talk
politics, to remember political events. It's like a ghost that comes back
from the pit of time to show me the dead and make me see forgotten
things.")

His interlocutor is mistaken, perhaps, in consigning all of this to
apathy, moral irresponsibility, cynicism—to the great black hole of disenchantment. For Mayta expresses no anger or regret for what he has
been. He manifests a genuine interest in the affairs of daily life—in his
family, in his neighborhood, in tangible things, not in the abstractions
of the ideal. Perhaps without being fully aware of it, he has returned to
the humble, slightly anarchistic philosophy of the Salesian Fathers: to
work with one's hands among the poor. Having discarded his youthful conviction, Mayta appears to have experienced—along with Vargas
Llosa himself—yet another conversion. He has exchanged the absolute
for the real.

Mayta—the hero of the novel, and the many models for him in
recent history—failed in his one serious attempt at social upheaval. But

that failure was by no means inevitable. The Jauja insurrection might well have had a different outcome. "Over the years," one of the skeptical witnesses tells the novelist, "I've come to realize that he wasn't so crazy . . . If the first action had lasted longer, things might have turned out the way Mayta planned." Mayta himself, much older and wiser, denies that the rebellion was a suicidal gesture.

The terrain, the possibility of making contact with other centers of provincial rebellion, the role of a determined vanguard—these were elements common to other struggles more successful elsewhere. Mayta's failure was due to accidents and bad timing. "The Cuban Revolution . . . killed that superego that ordered us to accept the dictum that 'conditions aren't right,' that the revolution was an interminable conspiracy," a communist leader tells the novelist. "With Fidel's entrance into Havana, the revolution seemed to put itself within reach of anyone who would dare to fight." Similarly, in the 1960s, "daring to fight" in Bolivia, Che Guevara chose poorly, in terms both of human and physical geography. Ten years after his death, however, revolutionaries who belonged to the same universe as the youthful Mayta would attend more carefully to the details and hope to gain the power that had eluded him.

UPON COMPLETING *The Real Life of Alejandro Mayta*, where he exorcized his demons dating back to the guerrilla wars, Vargas Llosa undertook another exorcism, that of the most profound collective ghost in his own history: the racial hatreds of the "Peruvian archipelago," ancestral hatreds of unprecedented intensity in Hispanic America, rooted in history, geography, religion, cultural barriers, prejudice, color, and immigration, but sustained throughout the twentieth century by an indigenist ideology that Vargas Llosa—not without cause—rated as passé, reactionary, collectivist, magical, irrational, antimodern, and antiliberal. Such was the weight of this "beautiful lie" (the concept of an indigenous Arcadia) that Vargas Llosa did not want to approach it by writing yet another beautiful lie (a novel) but rather a painful truth.

The result was an extraordinarily serious and well-documented book of historical interpretation, *The Archaic Utopia*.

His critique of Peruvian indigenism delves back into its remote colonial origins, then discusses in detail its modern reappearance in the 1920s (in Valcárcel and Mariátegui). But it is centered above all on the life and works of José María Arguedas (1911–69), a noteworthy Peruvian novelist and anthropologist who took indigenism to new literary heights and to the greatest extremes of radical ideology. Sympathetically, without a trace of animosity, Vargas Llosa takes up the tragic life of this man, whom he knew, and whose life was torn apart by the confrontation between the modern world and his love for a mythicized version of ancient Peru.

Vargas Llosa argues that the idyllic Inca Empire depicted by various authors—allegedly fraternal, homogeneous, suffused with a "happy collectivist promiscuity," and crystallized above all in Arguedas's work—was a romantic idealization. All in all, these "traditions and customs" passed down across time had developed into a reverse racism (against *mestizos* of mixed heritage, blacks, whites, and Chinese), accompanied by isolation, passivity, machismo, regionalism, and brutal underdevelopment. In contrast to the figure of Arguedas, Vargas Llosa offers the ideas of the sociologist Uriel García (who makes a defense of "spiritual miscegenation," in other words, a Mexican solution for the Peruvian condition) and above all the Marxist criticism of Alberto Flores Galindo (1949–90), who analyzed the "despotic and dominating" character of the Inca Empire and the current developments—in large part transforming the old Peru—of Indian farmers committing themselves to the lure of private property and the market. These trends were already visible at the moment when Arguedas decided to end his life. In the opinion of Vargas Llosa, by 1986 "the Indian of flesh and blood has been emancipated from the Ghetto in which he was traditionally kept by exploitation, discrimination and prejudice—both social and ideological—and he has chosen modernity." But soon enough, Vargas

Llosa would find out for himself that this transition to modernity was much slower than he had imagined, and that these ancestral hatreds remained almost intact.

VII

Vargas Llosa would gradually return to active politics, eventually aspiring to the highest level of power, riding the wave of his now firmly democratic convictions and with the strong faith of a convert in the value of the free market. The Aprista Alan García won the presidency of Peru in 1985 (the first time APRA had triumphed), defeating a candidate to the left of him in a run-off election. His presidency (1985–90) was in numerous ways a disaster, marked by hyperinflation, careless spending on mega-projects often left uncompleted, a huge increase in poverty, and the constantly growing violence of the Sendero Luminoso, ineffectually countered by a "dirty war" studded with government atrocities. When García tried to nationalize the banking system, his attempts were frustrated. The drive against nationalization was spearheaded by three parties who, in 1988, formed a coalition called the Frente Democratico (FREDEMO). Vargas Llosa seemed a natural leader for that coalition, opposed to the statist populism of García, to outmoded militarism and to the Marxist guerrillas. One year later, FREDEMO nominated him for president of Peru. With all the vast power of his creative imagination, Mario Vargas Llosa could not have foreseen what was in store for him:

> . . . each time I have been asked why I was willing to move from my vocation as a writer into politics, I have answered "For a moral reason." Because the circumstances put me into a situation of leadership at a critical moment for the life of my country . . . [My wife] Patricia does not agree. "Moral obligation was not the decisive thing," she says. It was the adventure, the hope of living an experience full of excitement and risk. Of writing, in real life, the great

novel . . . I don't discount that, in the dark background where so
many of our actions are pieced together, it was the temptation of
the adventure, before any altruism, that pushed me into the life
of politics . . .

This honest evaluation of his motives comes from *El pez en el agua*
(The Fish in the Water), an elegantly written memoir published in
1993 that ranges across his entire life and includes his perceptions and
experiences along the route of his political adventure. After the various failures of the García administration, Peru was clearly in need of
strong, innovative government action. Vargas Llosa's proposals were
in line with his political philosophy: fiscal austerity (which many
feared would negatively affect the country's social programs), a commitment to free trade, and a thorough privatization of government
enterprises. It was a program that attracted a significant segment of
Peruvian opinion but not the left nor a considerable proportion of the
disadvantaged. It was branded, negatively, using the English word,
as a *shock* approach to the needs of the country. In the first stage of
the election (it was followed by a run-off, since no one gained more
than 50 percent of the vote), Vargas Llosa led the field but only with
27.61 percent of the vote while his closest opponent was a candidate
opposed to his sweeping austerity proposals, Alberto Fujimori of the
Cambio 90 (Change 90) Party, close behind him with 24.62 percent,
followed by a much smaller percentage for other candidates to the left
of FREDEMO.

The campaign was a vicious one. His opponents attacked Vargas
Llosa for his politics, his personal life, and even read sexually charged
passages from his novels over the radio in an attempt to discredit
him "morally." But along with the confrontation between neoliberal
economic philosophy and its opponents, along with the personalized mud-slinging of bare-knuckle politics, a curious blend of Peru's
endemic, pervasive, and "multicolored" racism also figured into the
campaign. Some of Vargas Llosa's supporters contended that Peru
had to be governed by a "real Peruvian" (they meant a white *criollo*).

Fujimori's partisans (and other parties) seized on the theme of racism and expanded it, in a reverse direction and to their great advantage. Anti-Chinese racism, for instance, is one of the country's strains of that particular psychological disease. Although they called him *chinito* ("little Chinaman," normally a disparaging term used for all people of Oriental descent), the people knew that Fujimori was the son of Japanese immigrants and that "Japan" meant wealth, power, possibly (in the minds of many uneducated people) a lifeline for Peru that could be established with Japan by a president of kindred ethnic origin. Fujimori argued that he represented not only "chinitos" but "cholitos," Peruvians of mixed descent. Vargas Llosa, on the other hand, was presented as a "white man," a "Spaniard," a "rich" member of the dominating race. In the final pages of *The Fish in the Water*, Vargas Llosa describes a profoundly painful experience with this reverse racism. It happened on a morning of intense heat, on his campaign trail, near a small village in the Valley of Chira:

An infuriated horde of men and women came out to meet me, armed with sticks and stones and every kind of blunt weapon. Their faces were twisted with hate, they seemed to have come from the depths of time, a prehistory in which human beings and animals were blurred together. Half naked, with very long hair and nails . . . surrounded by skeletal children with swollen bellies, shouting and screaming to encourage themselves, they launched themselves against the caravan as if they were fighting for their lives and wanted to immolate themselves, with a boldness and a savagery that said it all about the almost inconceivable levels of deterioration to which life had descended for millions of Peruvians. What were they defending themselves from? What ghosts stood behind those menacing clubs and knives?

There were many ghosts, of course, behind these raging villagers, dating back to the first apparition, the Spanish Conquest. "Spaniards out!" shouted the menacing crowd. And there it was: the heritage, intact, directed against a man blamed for being a member of the "ruling race," one of whom was now the victim of all that "primitive racial nomenclature that decides a great part of the destinies of individuals" in Peru.

VIII

In the second round, Vargas Llosa would be routed by Fujimori, who took 56.5 percent of the vote to Vargas Llosa's 33.9. (Fujimori would eventually implement the austerity measures Vargas Llosa had championed, beginning the economic revival of the country. He would later carry out a coup against a Congress dominated by his opponents, which [unfortunately] would be strongly supported by Peruvian voters in his 1992 reelection. And he would go on to break the back of the Sendero Luminoso—finally capturing its maximum leader, Abimael Guzmán—and engineer yet a third term in office, but would then fall into abject disgrace, charged with encouraging massive corruption and a slew of human rights abuses in the antiguerrilla campaign. Finally, he would be sentenced to jail for a long prison term.)

For Vargas Llosa, the great political adventure was over. He would continue emphatically affirming his political opinions but his road from now on would be the continuing process of creation and, as an integral part of it, his encounters with the past. In The Fish in the Water, he would finally offer a direct portrait of his own vicious personal dictator and family terrorist, his father Ernesto Vargas. He had already treated him indirectly in his novels, where the rebellion against the authority of the father is a constantly recurrent theme. But now he faced Ernesto head-on, and in the slowly unfolding details of the narrative, he would relive the "terrible rancor" aroused in his confrontation with an arbitrary, absolute, unpredictable, and brutal power.

In literature and in life, Vargas Llosa had faced all the fanaticisms of identity: of race, religion, and class. What demon remained to be exorcized? The principal cause of so much of Latin American misery, the "cruel father" of an entire country, the archetypical dictator, the despot who, in different ways, has often reduced the history of those countries to a mere biography of power. It would be the culmination of Vargas Llosa's creative process of parricide.

Dictatorship has been a central theme not only of Latin American history but of its literature. Almost all the novelists of the "Latin American Boom" had written a novel about or based upon their own local dictator. Vargas Llosa, since 1975, had been interested in treating the figure of Rafael Trujillo, absolute master of the Dominican Republic from 1930 until his assassination in 1961. Now that he had personally experienced his own political travails and accumulated new perceptions of the variegated evils of tyrannous men and tyrannous thoughts, he felt himself prepared to enter the hallucinatory realm of *The Feast of the Goat* (in Spanish, *La fiesta del chivo,* where *fiesta* carries connotations richer than those of a mere "feast," the notion of unbridled celebration, while *chivo,* "goat," refers to Trujillo's sexual appetites).

Two ideas crisscross and confront each other in the novel with the inevitability of Greek drama. Vargas Llosa dissects Trujillo himself with a clinical scalpel, not only his psychology but the anatomy of his personal exercise of power. There are the physical traits of domination: a paralyzing gaze, the myth of the man who never sweats, the mania for uniforms and gold and silver braid, but above all the unbridled sexual vanity, at the furthest extreme of our Latin macho culture, that Trujillo practiced for his own pleasure (his *fiesta*) and to impose and express his total control over the subjects of his royal will. Subjection through sexuality stands at the very center of the Trujillo phenomenon. In his own version of the ancient droit de seigneur (the supposed sexual right of a king or a noble to the first night with the virgin wives of his serfs), Trujillo would demand the services of his ministers' wives with the knowledge or at least the silent complicity of their husbands, not only to test the unconditionality of their servitude and obedience but to set himself up as a father to every family, a man with patrimonial rights over his entire island kingdom. This obsessive persecution, this enslaving of the woman to the male, which he himself had witnessed in the heart of his own family, touched a sensitive chord in Vargas Llosa's imagination. The principal character in the book (among a majority of real personages) is the fictional Urania, the daughter of one of Trujillo's loyalists, whose tragic violation represents the suffering of many Dominican women. The plot is driven by her return to Santo Domingo decades after the fall of the regime.

La fiesta del chivo picks its way through that sordid mob of courtiers, some of them grotesque, some of them atrocious, which every dictatorial regime produces. Some of them truly existed and appear under their real names. Others are fictitious but composed of sadly true details. They include Trujillo's favorite killer and torture specialist, Johnny Abbes García, his economic administrator (the cynical and corrupt Chirinos), his political advisor and crooked lawyer (the fictional "Cerebrito" Cabral, Urania's father), a dressmaker and pimp named Manuel Antonio, and the strangest of all, the man who briefly succeeded Trujillo in power (and would later be elected to a much longer term), Trujillo's poet and house intellectual Joaquín Balaguer. Vargas Llosa reports on Balaguer at his most craven when, in a speech, he asserts that God had protected the Dominican Republic from historical and natural disaster and then had passed on the task directly to Rafael Leónidas Trujillo Molina, a judgment promptly approved by the dictator. But did Balaguer believe it? "I did in politics what I was able to do," he confessed to Vargas Llosa in an interview. "I shunned women and corruption." He was unmarried and a solitary man, a modernist versifier and a person of culture. Machiavelli would have appreciated the shrewdness of Balaguer's survival across the Trujillo years, and also the adroit political clockwork he put into motion after the assassination. He permitted Trujillo's heirs to take revenge on the conspirators (most of them died under extreme torture superintended by Trujillo's sons Ramfis and Rhadamés Trujillo, or else were summarily shot—except for a few who survived in hiding and emerged as heroes), but afterward he honored the conspirators and—implacably and delicately—drove Trujillo's bloodstained sons into exile. "This is politics," he said in his interview with Vargas Llosa: "finding a way through among the corpses."

Perhaps the greatest mystery was the voluntary, almost hypnotized submission of most of the population. Certainly they were controlled by fear, since Trujillo had total power of life and death within his realm, but also, Vargas Llosa thinks, "Trujillo drew from the bottom of their souls a vocation for masochism, of beings who fulfilled themselves by being spat upon, maltreated and feeling themselves abject." He finds "something more subtle and indefinable than fear" in the paralysis of the will, not only of the ordinary Dominican citizen, but even in brave people like General José Román, who, after participating in the conspiracy, hesitates to commit himself after the actual death of the tyrant. He enters a state of psychic paralysis, which will result in his slow and horrible death by torture and a final gunshot from Ramfis. Vargas Llosa says that Trujillo, who had reigned for more than thirty years, continued living within the minds and feelings of many Dominicans, dominating them, continuing their vassalage. One of his major incentives in writing this novel was to reveal the mechanisms of such an acceptance of slavery.

Both stylistically and emotionally, Vargas Llosa's Trujillo is a very different figure from the dictators who move through the equally great novels of García Márquez. The well-made realism of Vargas Llosa's writing is far removed from the prose poetry of the Colombian. García Márquez's elegiac fascination with the inner life of the tyrant, and the atmosphere of power expressed in surreal or expressionistic images, is light-years from Vargas Llosa's harsh realism, which draws its strength not primarily from rhythm and image (though they are effective) but from devastating detail. The Colombian offers the complexity of the archetypical Latin American *caudillos* and *coronels*, our dictators, in works that use a range of devices and even humor for his indulgent portrayals of an "incontrovertible and devastating authority." *La fiesta del chivo*, on the other hand, is a blistering indictment of the tyrant and anyone willing to serve him. There is no possibility of sympathetic identification with the malevolent "father of his country," no trace of humor in this world of tyranny. *The Feast of the Goat* is a return to the moral universe of *Conversation in the Cathedral*, to the rage against patriarchal authority and its infinite possibilities of evil. And Vargas Llosa's great skill as a novelist allows him to give concrete form to this evil in even tiny details. In *The Feast of the Goat*, for instance, at a festive party in the open to which the abominable Ramfis Trujillo has sequestered some of the conspirators who were supposed to have been freed (instead they will be shot dead), one of Ramfis's cohorts runs, eager to participate, toward the men about to be killed, "without letting go of his shot glass of whiskey," a strangely chilling and psychologically convincing detail.

Only the martyrs merit the author's sympathy, from Urania (delivered unwitting, an early adolescent decked out in her best dress, by her father to Trujillo, who has aged into impotence and raging against his sexual failure, rapes her manually and destroys her future emotional life) to those who die in agony or the few who live to be welcomed as heroes, or the moving figure of Salvador Estrella Sadhalá, a committed Catholic who discovers, within his own tradition, in the writings of St. Thomas Aquinas, the right to tyrannicide as a last recourse for the benefit of "the common good." And Vargas Llosa continues to oppose the fantasies that lead to the quest for power, for absolute power, as they continue to plague the life of Latin America. "If there is anything I hate," Vargas Llosa has remarked, "anything that profoundly disgusts me and enrages me, it is dictatorship. It is not just a political conviction or a moral principle: it is a twisting inside me, a visceral reaction, maybe because I have endured many dictatorships in my own country, maybe because as a child I experienced in my own flesh the brutal imposition of authority."

In the year 2010, Mario Vargas Llosa finally received the Nobel Prize for Literature, an honor he has long deserved, and reached the apogee of his literary reputation. He is admired by millions of readers, a multitude of friends, and, with Patricia Llosa and his children, has created a warm and intimate family life. In a sense he has rewritten his family history and reconstructed the Eden of his childhood years in Bolivia, before the Fall that ensued through the reappearance of his father. For the son of Ernesto Vargas, scarred in his youth by parental abuse, it may be time, at last, to be happy.

PART V

Religion and Rebellion

10

Samuel Ruiz

THE APOSTLE OF THE INDIANS

Four days after the Zapatista uprising in the impoverished Mexican state of Chiapas on New Year's Day, 1994, a reporter interviewed one of its peasant soldiers, a prisoner of the Mexican army, and asked, Why are you fighting? "I want there to be democracy, no more inequality. I am looking for a life worth living, liberation, just like God says."

John Womack, Jr., uses these words as the epigraph to his book *Rebellion in Chiapas, An Historical Reader.* The speaker was José Pérez Méndez—a Mayan peasant like all the common soldiers of the Zapatista Army of National Liberation—and his statement conveys much of the impetus of the rebellion, whose leaders—at the highest level—were originally not Mayan *chiapanecos* but urban university graduates, like their chief, Subcomandante Marcos himself. They had been planning the uprising for ten years, with the original intention of establishing a guerrilla *foco* in Chiapas, a territory under their control from which revolution could spread. But the rebellion became something quite different: an event and movement that could go nowhere militarily but won extraordinary national and international attention.

The Zapatista soldier José Pérez Méndez had good reason to "want democracy." For the *Partido Revolucionario Institucional* (PRI), which still governed Mexico at the time of the rebellion and had done so uninterruptedly for nearly seventy years, the state of Chiapas was a secure reserve of votes in national "elections," giving the PRI, on average, 97 percent of its ballots. The electoral victories were engineered through efficient methods of fraud: vote buying, false ballots substituted for the real thing in areas where the government party felt threatened, and strong pressure from powerful local interests to vote the right way. The machinery of the corporate state had links with all levels of power in Chiapas, from the Indian *caciques* (political bosses) of small villages and communities all the way up to the dominant class—the owners of the coffee plantations and the cattle ranches, the lumber barons operating in the tropical forests, and other interests.

Pérez Méndez was justifiably protesting against the extreme social inequality in Chiapas. The state has immense natural resources. It is the primary producer of coffee, cattle, and cacao in Mexico, it is third in hydroelectric power, fourth in natural gas resources. And yet, in its population of 3.7 million as of 1994 (27 percent Indian, with four major groups of ethnic Mayans), 50 percent were undernourished, 75 percent earned less than the Mexican minimum wage (defined then as 1,500 U.S. dollars per year), and 56 percent were illiterate. In Los Altos ("the Heights") and the Lacandón Jungle—centers of Zapatismo—the conditions were even worse, intensified by a population density of 76 inhabitants per square kilometer, almost double that of the rest of the state. And in these areas, close to 80 percent of the population was Indian.

Perhaps the greatest impetus for Pérez Méndez's militancy lay in the daily affront to his dignity (Womack's "a life worth living" translates to *una vida digna,* which also carries the overtone of "a life with dignity"). Mexico is a country that for four centuries has undergone the most successful process of ethnic and cultural mixing in the Americas, but the ancient region of Mayan civilization (in Mexico comprising primarily Chiapas and Yucatán) has been an exception to the rule from the very beginning of the Spanish Conquest. Racial discrimination, exploitation, and servitude flourished through the centuries in its haciendas and cities. And they have bred ferocious ethnic wars.

There is no doubt that the movement gave the image of the Indian (about 10 percent of the total population of Mexico) greater dignity, returning his problems at least for a time to the center of the national agenda. And the shock of the Zapatista uprising of 1994 surely helped to intensify the demand for democratic change in the country. Faced with the threat that Mexicans might renew their historical inclination toward revolutionary action, the power structure of the Mexican corporate state, for the very first time, genuinely opened up the possibility of democratic electoral competition. At the same time, the political left, represented by the *Partido de la Revolución Democrática* (PRD)—a coalition of various forces including socialists, former communists, and dissident defectors from the PRI—could cleanly distance itself from the idea of armed revolution (strongly favored, and implemented in urban and rural guerrilla actions, by some sectors of the left since the late 1960s) to take on clearer form as a social democratic party contending politically for power.

The leadership of the internationally famous Subcomandante Marcos should not obscure the great importance in the Zapatista uprising of another individual whose work in Chiapas preceded Marcos by twenty-five years, Bishop Samuel Ruiz of San Cristóbal de las Casas and his diocese. Without a consideration and understanding of Samuel Ruiz's long years of evangelical labor, the Zapatista rebellion cannot really be comprehended or evaluated. Bishop Samuel Ruiz carried out what was probably the most successful practical application in all Latin America of the Theology of Liberation that developed out of the Second Vatican Council (Vatican II), convened by Pope John XXIII in 1962. Hundreds of thousands of Indians in the state of Chiapas "became conscious" of the conditions of oppression under which they live. This is obviously a great good, but the pastoral work of Samuel Ruiz had other results as well, some perhaps less desirable, or at least more controversial.

II

Hanging on a wall of Bishop Samuel Ruiz's office in the episcopal building in the highland city of San Cristóbal de las Casas was a "primitive" folk-style painting that depicts an imaginary encounter between Ruiz and his remote precursor: Fray Bartolomé de las Casas, the great Apostle to the Indians of the sixteenth century. The artist had presented the pair almost as twins, except for the eyeglasses Samuel Ruiz is wearing.

Bartolomé de las Casas, the "protector of the Indians," was the third bishop of San Cristóbal. The painting obviously fused the two men and recalls as well the traditional filial relationship in Mexico between priests and Indians, originating with the Franciscan missionaries summoned to Mexico by Hernán Cortés in 1524. Hidalgo and Morelos, the nineteenth-century leaders of the War of Independence against Spain, were both priests. Their armies—at least in the first stage of the rebellion—were primarily Indian. In many villages (both Indian and mestizo) throughout the Mexican republic, the village priest continues to be a figure of significant authority, both spiritual and secular. Chiapas, which is a living museum of Mexican history, seemed the perfect place for the resurgence of a very Mexican figure—the rebel priest who invokes the Thomist doctrine of the "just war" as a last resort of the oppressed against their oppressors.

The Dominican priest Las Casas was the victor in a theological dispute that had far greater importance than any mere change in the formulation of doctrine. He argued fervently that the Indians of the New World had souls, combatting the theologians who would define them as less than fully human and therefore natural slaves. The king of Spain was persuaded and in 1542 issued the New Laws of the Indies, through which the Indians officially became the wards of the Spanish Crown and not the brute property of the new Spanish rulers.

Parallels and echoes between the lives of Ruiz and Las Casas are many and resonant: "He was a good theologian and a consummate jurist . . . his soul was deeply troubled by the treatment of the Indian slaves who were bought and sold like flocks of sheep . . . he preached like an apostle teaching the means to their salvation, in order to put an end to such unlawful treatment," wrote a chronicler of the period about Fray Bartolomé. According to his twentieth-century counterpart, Samuel Ruiz, the grim reality that he himself encountered when he arrived in Chiapas in 1960 was not "generically distinct" from what had profoundly shaken the soul of his great predecessor. In one community he was informed that all the children had died almost overnight, as the result of an epidemic wrongly diagnosed by the official health services. In some haciendas, owners whipped their resident peons. In San Cristóbal de las Casas, bastion of the *coletos* (a term used for the white upper-class, especially within this city), Indians would still step off the sidewalks to let whites pass and could still hear themselves addressed with the same words of racial contempt that had assaulted the ears of Fray Bartolomé four centuries ago: "Indian dogs!"

An aggressive racism has long been characteristic of Chiapas, and the regions where Mayans live have a long history of confrontation between whites and Indians. It is by no means typical of Mexico itself, with its overwhelmingly mestizo population, though regional pockets of strong anti-Indian feeling (as well as more pervasive and subtle forms of racism) certainly do exist.

"To put an end to such unlawful treatment," both bishops took energetic action. They brought priests to the diocese who shared their concern for the Indians. Both would call on members of the Dominicans, which was a preaching order actively seeking converts. They showed a greater critical awareness of the injustice and cruelties inflicted upon the Indians and were the first to voice any doubts about the moral legitimacy of the Conquest.

Las Casas and Ruiz both had to deal with significant resistance from local ecclesiastics: Fray Bartolomé from members of other preaching orders, Ruiz with the old monsignors and other conservative priests of his diocese who were shocked when he would refuse to sleep in the "big house" of a hacienda and choose to spend a night in the modest home of a peon. Both would come to praise (and idealize) the values and customs of the Indians, arguing that they had lived in a better, harmoniously organized society, a harmony that had been subverted by the Conquistadores or—in this century—by exploiters and power brokers from outside the Indian communities.

In the words and actions of both men, you hear echoes of biblical prophecy. Before the Royal Court of Spain, Bartolomé de las Casas questioned the legitimacy of the Spanish Conquest, describing it as an action "unjust, iniquitous, tyrannical and worthy of all the fires of Hell," and prophesied that "the wrath of God" would turn against Spain and destroy it. With similar zeal and single-mindedness, Samuel Ruiz showed the same condemnatory view not only of the period of the Spanish Viceroyalty but also of the Liberal state of the nineteenth century and the nationalist-revolutionary Mexico of the twentieth. His strong criticism concentrated on the specific issue of the treatment of Indians and the poor.

Ruiz's attacks on government were also a chapter in Mexico's long history of rivalry between the state and the Church, the "two majesties." During the Spanish Empire, the power struggle between the Church and the Bourbon rulers would eventually spill over into the Mexican War of Independence, and throughout the nineteenth century, Conservatives and Liberals struggling for control of Mexico were fighting over the weight of secular or religious power. With the Liberal victory in the War of the Reform (1858–61), the vast properties belonging to the Church were expropriated and a constitutional separation of church and state was enforced. The conflict between them, however, has remained latent, and sometimes explosive. It surfaced most violently in the Cristiada uprising of the late 1920s when Catholic peasants (the Cristeros), especially in the west of Mexico, rebelled against the anticlerical measures of President Plutarco Elías Calles.

Bartolomé de las Casas was involved in a great moral confrontation more than 450 years ago. But he also achieved the victory of the Church over one aspect of secular power, the will of the local Spanish conquerors to make unlimited use of what was considered a material resource: the Indian as slave. Raúl Vera, while assistant bishop to Samuel Ruiz, was preparing arguments for the canonization of Las Casas and saw Ruiz as his direct descendant. Of Ruiz, he said, "He is a man who cannot be silent . . . who has assumed his responsibility mystically and mysteriously before the eyes of God."

"He is a prophet who creates prophets," said Miguel Concha, then provincial head of the order of the Dominicans in Mexico. And Samuel Ruiz did produce many prophets in his diocese: thousands of lay teachers of doctrine, called "catechists," the great majority of them Indians, who for three decades sowed (they would say received) the "Word of God" in their small communities.

III

During the sixteenth century, throughout Meso-America, the Franciscans and Dominicans, Augustinians, Jesuits, and others did the work of converting the Indians. As part of the process of persuasion, they used not only words but theater, music, sculpture, and paintings in the churches; but they also depended on instruction or catechism. The new catechist movement in Chiapas is a variation on this function, the propagation of doctrine by personal teaching in the effort to make the Indians conscious of their oppression.

This evangelical effort was at the very base of the political transformations and revolutionary turmoil that have shaken Chiapas before and since 1994. Fray Toribio de Benavente Motolinía, a famous Franciscan opponent of Bartolomé de las Casas, expressed his fear that the ideas of Las Casas would someday be "read by the Indians." This is precisely what Samuel Ruiz and his catechists had succeeded in accomplishing.

Samuel Ruiz was the center, the motive force of this peculiar catechetical movement. It is a role he came to play partly through his own origins, partly through the impact of a transforming conversion in the course of his life. He was the firstborn son of poor parents. His mother and father had met as braceros, migrant grape pickers in California. His mother was there illegally, as a "wetback." They married and returned to Mexico, where their son Samuel was born in 1924, in Irapuato, within the highland basin of the Bajío, to the north of Mexico City. This zone (along with Jalisco to the west) forms the heart of Catholic Mexico. During the late 1920s (the era of the Cristero uprising of Catholic peasants) and into the '30s, his father, now a small grocer, was not only pro-Cristero but also a Sinarquista, member of a homegrown Mexican movement that can legitimately be described as deeply Catholic but also, in its racism and exclusivism, as fascist. The movement was quite strong in the city of León, where Samuel Ruiz entered a seminary in 1937, at the age of thirteen. The young Samuel Ruiz saw Sinarquismo as "a movement that shook things up, a necessary step in the civic and political education of society." Later he moved very far from that position. The direct ideological descendants of Sinarquismo—the profoundly antidemocratic movements of the Catholic far right—were opposed to social Catholicism and Samuel Ruiz and liberation theology. But the fact that he came from a Sinarquista family surely did mean an early influence toward the rejection of the secular state in favor of a primarily religious affiliation.

The bishop's first thirty-five years did not clearly foreshadow the conversion that would make him a second "apostle of the Indians." At the seminary he showed considerable intelligence and application. In 1947, he entered the Collegio Pio-Latino-Americano Pontificio in Rome, a key center for the training of Latin American priests. He seemed well on his way to a relatively cloistered career as a church theologian when, at the Pontifical Biblical Institute in Rome, he studied biblical exegesis and began, as he would later say, "to half understand that the Bible is the only book written for a poor people in search of the promised land."

He returned to Mexico in 1951 and in 1954 was appointed dean of the Seminary of León where he had once been a student. In 1959, Rome chose him to become bishop of Chiapas. The bishopric entrusted to Ruiz comprised two-thirds of Chiapas, one of the poorest, most socially backward states in the Mexican Republic.

He was formally ordained in January 1960, and in 1962 he became one of the 2,692 bishops to attend the historic council that changed much of the direction of the Catholic Church, the Second Vatican Council convoked by Pope John XXIII. Shortly before the proceedings began, he had his first transforming revelation. It was his emotional response to one of the major themes Pope John presented as a preamble to the conference: the declaration that it was to be in the arena of developing countries, in the "Third World," that the Church would discover what it really is and what it really had to do. For the bishop of Chiapas, this exhortation implied a mandate: "it clarified and determined the essential mission of the Church: if it does not maintain an adequate relationship with the structural world of poverty, it is no longer the Church of Jesus Christ."

In 1964, Ruiz decided that his diocese was much too large for him to deal effectively with social problems. The poorest, overwhelmingly Indian area was what interested him most. Rome divided the diocese in two: the diocese of Tuxtla Gutiérrez (administered by Bishop José Trinidad Sepúlveda Ruiz Velasco) and what would become Ruiz's own, that of San Cristóbal de las Casas, which makes up 48 percent of the state and includes the great majority of its Indian population.

A year earlier, Ruiz had invited Dominicans and other groups into Chiapas, most of them dedicated to the new directions within the Church. In 1966, these "apostles" established the Mission to the Chamulas, which would undertake—along with normal priestly duties—the construction of a health center and workshops for arts and crafts, a night school for domestic science instruction, and the establishment of a communal farm. In 1967, Ruiz would restructure his diocese into six administrative zones, based in part on the ethnic identities of the Indian populations. But it was the opening of schools for the training and organizing of Indian catechists that was the decisive step in implementing the new evangelism. Ruiz celebrated Mass at one or another of these schools every Sunday. By the 1970s, more than seven hundred of these catechists had already been trained, and there would be many more in the years to come. It was an effort that, for the most part, met with approval from the higher authorities of the Church.

The "Preferential Option in Favor of the Poor" received its classic articulation at the 2nd Conference of Latin American Bishops—held in Medellín, Colombia, in the critical year of 1968. Ruiz attended the conference. The new theology incorporated some aspects of Marxist analysis: the class struggle as an objective fact, capital as the product of alienated labor, and especially the explanation of the underdevelopment of the so-called Third World as a direct product of the development of the so-called First World. In addition, the liberation theologists would try to discover, in their own way, "the Plan of God" in the Bible, and attempt to "activate the transforming energy" of biblical texts. And finally, the new theology would call for peaceful struggle to resolve the problems of the poor and the oppressed but would not exclude violence as a last resort.

IV

The communities of Las Cañadas—the area within the Lacandón Jungle that was to become a center of the Zapatista movement—had been a site of immigration from elsewhere in Chiapas ever since the 1950s. Most of these immigrants had been peons on estates directly bordering the jungle who were forced out when the government began to encourage the spread of cattle ranches by giving the landowners financial incentives to switch from farming. Little attention was paid to the fate of the peons, who were dismissed en masse. The local oligarchy, the landowners and the politicians of the PRI, who were deeply imbued with a master-servant notion of the economy and a racist view of society, lobbied locally and nationally against government land distribution, and they used their hired gunmen to prevent peons settling on unused lands within their estates. Other workers lost their places on the coffee plantations in the south of the state as the growers began to hire cheaper, Guatemalan labor. For many Indians, emigration to the jungle seemed to offer the only opportunity for bettering their lives. Between 1950 and 1980, the population of the Lacandón Jungle, originally fewer than 80,000 souls, nearly tripled, growing to about 225,000.

Diocesan catechists also moved into this area and began to apply a new method for "sowing" questions and "harvesting" responses, partly inspired by the ideas of the Brazilian (Jesuit-trained) educational reformer Paulo Freire—especially in his key work, *Pedagogy of the Oppressed* (1970). Freire's ideas involved eliciting original thought and verbal contributions from illiterate peoples in order to teach literacy and self-sufficient (potentially transformative) thinking and judgment. A truly liberating education was to center around "the appropriation of the Word . . . The Word of God summons me to re-create the world not for the domination of my brothers but for their liberation." Put into practice in Chiapas, the process came to be called "The Word of God" and the catechizer would be termed a *tijuanej*, which in the Tzeltal Mayan language means "the animator, the provoker, the stimulator."

Javier Vargas, a member of the Marist Brothers order and a leading teacher and director of the catechists, was traveling on one of his frequent inspection tours through the Ocosingo region near the Lacandón Jungle when it occurred to him that the experience shared by all the new inhabitants of the area, including the catechists themselves, was that of a new Exodus: the departure from the estates, the long and dangerous period of wandering through the jungle and the eventual building of new villages. Inspired by this idea as well as by Freire's thinking, Ruiz and Vargas, along with other workers of the diocese, conceived of replacing the traditional Catholic catechism of fixed doctrinal questions and answers with a new catechism, more in accord, as they thought, with Vatican II, which would express "all the sources of the Word of God, the Bible and tradition" but also "the history of the Indians as they record it, their traditions, their culture, wherein is the seed of 'the Word of God.'"

The result was a document fundamental to the conversion of many Indians to an indigenous form of liberation theology: *We Are Seeking Freedom: The Tzeltales of the Jungle Proclaim the Good News*. The text was based on collective conversations between catechists and Indians,

originally in Tzeltal Mayan and later translated into Spanish, to form a
printed book of a little more than a hundred pages (issued by the diocese in 1971). It contained prayers, songs, and readings of various kinds
organized around the theme of four types of oppression: economic,
political, cultural, and religious. There were many citations from the
New Testament and the prophetic books of the Old Testament, used
to support specific arguments. The economic oppression that the emi-
grants to the jungle had experienced was compared to Pharaoh's Egypt
within the context of an appeal to God:

> You said to the ancient Israelites when they were living as slaves:
> "I have seen the sufferings of my people. I have heard them weep
> and ask me for aid. I come to liberate them from their oppressors
> and carry them to a fine and spacious land that offers many fine
> fruits" (Ex, 3.7–8). Because of this we have come together to ask
> you, O Lord, to help us as well, to be of aid to us!

Oppression was also seen as political because the laws favor the
rich; it was cultural because the *caxlanes* (non-Indians) despised the
languages and cultures of the Indians, who as a consequence fell into
the error of despising themselves. And it was religious because conventional religious practice concentrated far too much on external
acts of worship, undermining the strength of men and doing no real
honor to God. The only valid response and reaction was to fortify
the community: "We live in community, we have a culture, we are
worth a great deal . . . the community is life, it carries me to freedom . . . the good Christian is he who makes the world grow for the
good of his brothers . . ." And more. God Himself was present in the
community. He spoke through those who speak and, in a sense, He
was the community.

This Catechism of the Exodus concluded with the question: "What
are we to do?" In 1974, to honor the five hundredth anniversary of
the birth of Bartolomé de las Casas, the state government of Chiapas

inadvertently set the stage for a further step toward action. The state authorities convoked a National Indian Conference (*Congreso Nacional Indígena*), undoubtedly meant to be one of the feel-good cultural events that are a common feature of Mexican official calendars. The state authorities asked for organizational help from the diocese, which Samuel Ruiz provided. The results were unexpected.

Months before the conference, six representatives of the diocese visited numerous villages and settlements, encouraging their participation. Fourteen hundred delegates attended, representing more than five hundred communities, most of them from Chiapas. The sessions dealt with specifically Indian problems and were conducted in Chiapas's four major Indian languages. Translators worked to reduce the language barriers. For many it was the first contact they had ever made outside their closed worlds. It was also the first major public conference in Chiapas at which the Indians themselves discussed their own problems without the restrictive presence and interference of the government. During one session, an old man wept, because "no one had ever asked him anything in his whole life."

The delegates agreed on statements about areas that required major improvement: the protection of Indian land rights, far better programs in health and in education, and a call for cooperative economic organizations to protect the Indian communities against exploitation. A speaker linked the conference to the labor of the catechists and dubbed this assembly "the son of the Word of God." It was followed by a series of conferences and meetings and journeys meant to encourage solidarity throughout the country and even abroad. A newspaper was started and a hymn was composed with versions in all four languages: "we advance as a single heart, as a single heart we are building our liberation."

A small number of political organizers attended the conference, men of the left, many of them radicalized by the massacre of students at the Plaza of Tlatelolco in Mexico City before the Summer Olympics in 1968. They had been in Chiapas, says Javier Vargas, "more invisible than visible . . . not that they were living there clandestinely—it was that they smelled, they felt the social force of the Chiapas Indians." They were in a sense the older brothers of men like Subcomandante Marcos, who was eleven years old in 1968. It was they who were mostly responsible for the Marxist phrases and ideas in some of the documents produced by the conference, but they were by no means its leaders. The overwhelming force of language, argument, and moral will clearly came from the Church. Given the societal abandonment of Chiapas and the resultant weakness of all its political institutions, it was natural enough that the leadership be taken by a more archaic institution, by the Church and specifically by a bishop who was a "convert" and on a mission to protect the Indians.

Inspired primarily by the catechist movement and stirred to a higher degree of social consciousness charged with the certitudes of religion, many of the Indians of Chiapas—especially in the newly settled areas of the Lacandón Jungle—began to seriously consider that the government was their enemy. Faced with a growing wave of requests for the partition of lands or formal acknowledgment of small land tenancies, the local authorities responded with threats, often carried out, of expulsion and violence. They did not understand that a new kind of community was forming in the jungle—more austere, more united, and much more combative. An absurd decree issued in 1972 by the national government of President Luis Echeverría contributed even more to its cohesion. The decree was presented as an act of "historical restitution" to the "last survivors" of the Maya culture: the Lacandón tribesmen living as hunters and gatherers in the jungle. An area of about 1.5 million acres was made the exclusive range of the Lacandón, a total of sixty-six families. But the decree was—at least in large part—a smoke screen for the gift of exclusive rights to large Mexican lumber companies that could reap the valuable tropical woods of the jungle. The welfare and lives of almost four thousand Indian families now settled in the region were threatened by this decree. The new communities began the hard struggle against its implementation.

Toward the end of the 1970s, the Church allowed (in Chiapas and elsewhere) another important structural innovation. A new category of church workers was established among the Indians, with new theological-political responsibilities. These were the deacons (*tuhuneles*, "servants") who, while laymen like the catechists, could, unlike them, offer the sacraments of baptism, extreme unction, and the Eucharist, and could serve as marriage witnesses in the name of the Church. This new office, which could be filled for life and was open to married men, was greeted with great enthusiasm. It responded to a centuries-old aspiration of the Indians—the desire, in the words of a *tuhunel*, "to have our own leaders, our own priests, our own religion." A drive to accomplish this aim of "spiritual autonomy" had been one of the reasons for the Indian rebellion of 1712, when the Tzeltal Maya not only struggled to overthrow the local government and reject burdensome taxes but also—an unusual objective during most of the colonial period in Mexico—fought to end Spanish domination and regain control of their religious life.

The historian Juan Pedro Viqueira argues that this war left an indelible trace on the Tzeltal zone of Los Altos, one of the two strongest centers of Zapatismo along with the Lacandón Jungle. The rebellion served to discourage the growth there of a mestizo population (called *ladinos*, especially in Chiapas) and helped to create the desire among its Indians to maintain themselves as a group apart. And it strengthened the fear and contempt in which they were held by the *coleto* and *ladino* population of San Cristóbal.

For Samuel Ruiz, and for his diocese, the *tuhuneles* were an important step toward the future, imagined largely as a return to primitive Christianity, to the Church before the Council of Nicaea (325 A.D.), the watershed moment when it adopted an institutional structure and turned away from its origins as a communitarian constellation of apostles and congregations. "Without vainglory," Don Samuel said to me in an interview, "I can affirm that if an anthropologist were to visit these communities, he would see that the figures of the catechist and the *tuhunel* almost belong to the tradition and form part of [the communities'] own culture."

In practice, Samuel Ruiz reflected a longing for both the communitarian primitive Church and a commitment to the Church's structure
as it later developed. By the 1970s, Ruiz was fully exercising the three
implicit aspects of his office: prophet, priest, and king. As a prophet,
his preaching lashed out at injustice and announced the hope of liberation. As a pastor and priest, he cared for his flock, offered them consolation, and guided them toward an awareness of the holy. As king, he
accepted a measure of treatment as a sovereign to whom his people
rendered homage. He had become known among the Maya—and addressed in person and writing—as *Tatic*, the Tzeltal Mayan word for
"father." Villages would prepare a month in advance for his visits. The
women sewed special dresses for the occasion, while the men worked
to prepare, as is usual in Mexico, a proper house for Tatic's stay. On
the day of his arrival, a line of men and a line of women formed to kiss
his ring. They slaughtered cattle for a large meal in honor of Tatic and
when he celebrated Mass, they sang praises for the prospect of liberation through God and the Gospels.

In 1974, when Ruiz turned fifty, he published a brief book of glittering erudition: *The Biblical Theology of Revelation*, in which he described the Indians of Chiapas as the collective body of Christ, devoted
to saving society and themselves; he envisioned reality (or at least the
reality of Chiapas and the Third World, the heart of his liberation theology) as involving on the one hand, oppression and oppressors, and on
the other a poor, oppressed people and a God who deals with injustice
and offers them liberation.

But the teaching of the Word of God also excluded those who disagreed. In some of the annual reports submitted by the catechists of
the Tzeltal area and stored in the diocesan archives, there were various
references to those groups who could easily form part of the growing
community, but who must "change" in order to be included. There
were, for instance, those who resisted the teaching method, those who
had ideological blockage, those who were being influenced by Protestant sects, those who disagreed politically, those who did not speak

their minds in discussions, those who thought the mere letter of the Bible was to be followed, "which does not give us life."

v

The expanding movement of the catechists and, later, the deacons—both involved not only with sacred matters but with the harsh daily problems of the poor—seemed to point to the need for a political organization capable of harnessing the increasing energy within the Indian communities. This was clear enough to a man as intelligent as Samuel Ruiz. Early in 1976, during a visit to Torreón, in the border state of Coahuila in the north, Bishop Ruiz met a group of young militants who called themselves ideological "maoists," having been influenced by the Chinese Marxist belief in the importance of organizing the peasantry (but not a commitment to armed revolution). Their leader was Adolfo Orive, a left-wing economist who had spent time in China. His organization, *Política Popular*, advocated the transformation of social relations rather than armed struggle. These young militants were university graduates who had worked as organizers among poor squatters living in Torreón, Durango, and Monterrey. They focused mostly on practical matters, such as trying to improve the squatters' housing, increase their water supply, and bring electricity to their colonies. "It seemed to me that he [Orive] possessed clarity of thought," Ruiz remembers. He was impressed.

He invited the group, some thirty young activists, to Chiapas. Orive's group began to work in the villages, alongside representatives of the diocese. Orive told the priests they could dedicate themselves to pastoral work while his "brigade" of workers would take care of political organization. They began small projects, such as helping the peasants to produce honey that they could sell, and negotiating with the federal government to enable the Indians to sell coffee without the participation of rapacious *coyotes* (middlemen).

By the middle of 1978, Orive's *brigadistas* or "northerners" had won the support of a few thousand catechists, who felt that these people could make tangible social improvements. But problems arose between the diocese and the *brigadistas*. The northerners at first had relied upon the structure of the diocese and its representatives in order to gain the confidence of the local population. But then they began to bypass the agents of the Church and move directly into the communities. Moreover, the diocese saw any contact with government as "compromising." They accused the *brigadistas* of being *reformistas* and compared their projects to the Golden Calf of Exodus, a "deception" that would only delay the struggle of the communities to liberate themselves from "the system" of oppression.

In the battle for the peasants' liberation, another small group, the CIOAC (*Central Independiente de Obreros Agrícolas y Campesinos*), some of them Communist Party members, succeeded in organizing hundreds of peasants. In contrast to "the struggle step by step" (*lucha paso a paso*) of the *brigadistas,* they favored a "struggle by forceful action" (*lucha al golpe*), such as occupying land that formed part of the haciendas.

The *brigadistas* continued their activity into the early 1980s, despite the distrust with which they were now regarded by Ruiz and his followers because of their willingness to work with government and their increasing distance from the Church. They founded the *Unión de Uniones,* which was able to conclude agreements with the government for a credit union to help finance grassroots projects for the production and sale of coffee. Many Indian peasants became small stockholders. But the crisis of 1982 (which bankrupted the Mexican government in the wake of a collapse in the oil boom) destroyed the project's economic basis, as the price of Chiapas coffee plummeted. The *brigadistas* lost much of their popular support; Orive (and some of his comrades) would go back north, but behind them they would leave a functioning organization in place, which would prosper again—with government aid—under the Salinas administration (1988–1994).

The political radicalization within the diocese intensified. Events in Central America during the late 1970s and '80s seemed to make an ever stronger argument for the *lucha al golpe*: the growth of military terror in Guatemala, the victory of the Sandinistas in Nicaragua, the upsurge of guerrilla action in El Salvador, and the assassination there by a right-wing militant of Samuel Ruiz's friend, Archbishop Óscar Arnulfo Romero (while he was celebrating Mass). In 1980, the diocese created a more radical doctrinal arm, known as SLOP ("root" in Tzeltal Mayan) and drawn from among the catechists closest to Samuel Ruiz and his teachings. They had the major assignment of organizing armed "self-defense" for the Indian villages but, lacking expertise in weapons, they would eventually turn to another group of outsiders, who established themselves in the Lacandón Jungle in 1983. They were the remnants of a guerrilla movement, the FLN (*Frente de Liberación Nacional*), founded in 1969 in the northern city of Monterrey. Once in the Chiapas jungle, they created the Zapatista Army of National Liberation (EZLN) and for six years (1983–89) SLOP and the Zapatistas worked together. Many catechists began to believe in the prospect of an armed uprising, in the idea that "the Word of God," the need to change society, led naturally toward a religious imperative to take up arms. In her book *Religión, política y guerrilla en Las Cañadas de la Selva Lacandona*, María del Carmen Legorreta Díaz, who was an advisor for many years to the *Unión de Uniones*, collected statements by former partisans of Zapatismo that show how the preaching of catechists was sliding toward a call for armed rebellion: "You would come to the conclusion that the people of God fought with weapons, not because it said so in the Bible but because that's the direction they developed out of the questions, about arms, about all the old prophets, they also struggled in Egypt, they rescued the native peoples who were suffering in their work like servants, like slaves; so, what could they do to liberate themselves? Why were they able to free themselves? Because they believed in God, they believed in the armed struggle."

Lázaro Hernández, the most important Indian leader of the diocese (he had been the "deacon of deacons"), joined the EZLN in 1983, taking the nom de guerre of "Jesús" while remaining a leader of SLOP (he would leave the Zapatistas in 1988). Soon many Zapatistas adopted biblical names: David, Daniel, Moisés, Josué—and, of course, Marcos. Within a few years, a new confrontation would develop between the diocese and this new movement of Zapatismo.

By 1988, Subcomandante Marcos was the second in command within the clandestine Zapatista hierarchy. Aside from the obvious question of where the power would rest (similar but much more serious than the problem a decade earlier between the Church in Chiapas and the *brigadistas*), the problem with the Church had much to do with the "unmasking" of Subcomandante Marcos' antireligious attitude. Marcos was known to have officiated at "revolutionary marriages" and to have commented frequently that "God and his Word aren't worth a damn" (*valen madres*). According to Legorreta, the diocese, faced with the growing influence of Zapatismo, decided to turn SLOP itself into an armed organization for "self-defense" to offset the influence of the Zapatistas. Bertrand de la Grange and Maite Rico, in their *Marcos, la genial impostura*, a book highly critical of Zapatismo, said that the SLOP leaders intensified their criticism of the Zapatista leaders, asserting that "Marcos is a *mestizo*, he is not poor, and why should we let him give us orders?" SLOP tried to buy more arms, to strengthen their position for whatever the future might hold and so as not to leave the armed option (the *lucha al golpe*) as the sole prerogative of the Zapatistas, but Marcos acted forcefully against those who doubted or opposed Zapatismo. Whole families were expelled from their villages or shunned by their neighbors, even to the point of pro-Zapatista deacons refusing the sacraments to some Indians who refused to join or support the EZLN. As for Ruiz, there is no evidence that he ever directly preached in favor of the armed struggle, but the activities of SLOP, led by those closest to him, clearly indicate that he was not totally opposed to the *lucha al golpe*. In the most radical official document issued by the diocese, the *plan diocesano* of 1986, there is a mention of present unjust conditions pointing toward "a new explosion . . ."

The Zapatista movement would go into crisis after the fall of the Berlin Wall, which undermined faith in its traditional Marxist ideology, not yet fully charged with its later "indigenist" arguments. But it still retained its strength among the young, the sons of those who had made the great exodus to the jungle. These young men dreamed of a transformation in their lives: "After the war, it is we who will give the orders." As for Samuel Ruiz, Marcos is said to have called him a *modista*, a word that can mean "seamstress" or "fashion designer," because the bishop followed the "fashions"—*modas*—of the moment. Marcos was implying that Ruiz in 1986–87 had looked with some favor on the possibility of a "just war" in order to move his flock to the Promised Land but had changed his mind with the fall of Eastern European communism. It is perhaps more accurate to say that Ruiz now saw the world differently and was reacting to the new geopolitical context of Central America, with the prospects growing weaker for a successful *lucha al golpe*.

Shadowing their relationship was the old conflict between the armed prophet and the prophet without arms, between Marcos and Don Samuel, the knighthood and the clergy, two medieval orders and both of them critical of the modern world, of the civil order—which of course was virtually nonexistent in the feudal state of Chiapas.

VI

Events were steadily moving toward January 1, 1994. Marcos had made his famous statement back in 1990: " . . . here there will be no Word of God, here there will be no government of the Republic, here there is going to be the Zapatista Army of National Liberation." Samuel Ruiz, speaking of the Zapatistas, lamented that "these people have arrived to mount a saddled horse." Some of the acts of the Salinas government gave the Zapatistas verbal ammunition. They argued that the North American Free Trade Agreement (NAFTA) with the United States and Canada threatened to flood Mexico with cheap farm products from the

north, cutting the income of Mexican peasants. The changes in Article
27 of the Mexican Constitution, permitting members of the collective *ejidos* to sell their land to private owners, seemed to be even more
threatening. The Mexican *ejido*, a form of land tenure dating back to
the last years of the Revolution but firmly established during the agrarian reforms of the 1930s, involved a combination of collective ownership and individual family farming; land could not be sold, nor could
creditors seize the land to pay off debts. In the eyes of some, laws that
permitted sale or debt seizure of *ejido* lands were a "betrayal" of the
Agrarian Reform, the "supreme achievement" of the Mexican Revolution. The Zapatistas spread the idea that the government was deliberately provoking the impoverishment and "collective death" of the
peasants and Indians of Mexico.

On August, 6, 1993, five thousand Zapatistas had staged battle ma-
neuvers in the jungle. By now Don Samuel was preaching against "that
cursed organization which advocates war and death" and urging his
catechists and deacons to teach that "the armed project is a project of
death, contrary to God, who chooses a road of life." But much of the sophisticated diocesan radio network remained available to the Zapatistas before, during, and after the outbreak of the rebellion.

The Salinas government began to funnel money into Chiapas. A
moderate organization, the ARIC (*Asociación Rural de Interés Colec-
tivo*), the new name for the *Unión de Uniones*, tried to carry on the
reformist goals of the *brigadistas*, with some success: they created a
new educational network, introduced new coffee-growing projects,
and came to the aid of twenty-six communities hurt by the legislation assigning exclusive privileges to the Lacandones in their area of
the jungle. Some Indians continued to believe in the *lucha paso a paso*.
But others sold their cattle to buy arms, and the Zapatistas retained
40 percent of their followers, despite government money and Ruiz's
now open opposition.

The newsmagazine *Proceso* had published an interview in September 1993 with Father Mardonio Morales in which he warned of

the existence of a guerrilla army in Chiapas and complained that the modern radio communication equipment purchased years ago by the diocese was being used by these guerrillas. But he exonerated Samuel Ruiz of any blame: "he suddenly realized the existence of a whole military organization. He has clearly denounced it . . . I think that the situation moved out of his control." In the next issue of the magazine, another cleric, Fray Gonzalo Ituarte, said: "it's a crazy fantasy, that a group of radicals from outside Chiapas arrived and through secret meetings manipulated and deceived the entire diocese, where we have people who are well educated, university trained, and among them no less than Don Samuel Ruiz."

Both opinions had truth to them. Ruiz and his diocese were perfectly aware of the ideas and actions of the Zapatistas. SLOP had at least considered the possibility of an armed uprising since 1980 but then, with the repression of rebellions in Central America and of course the collapse of the Soviet Union, they realized "it was not the way, an armed struggle is dangerous."

In some of their teaching sessions in the villages, Don Samuel and his vicar Ituarte used drawings of a tree to illustrate world and national politics. One drawing shows representations from the roots up of the elements of "the capitalist government which controls," beginning with different types of potentates (landowners, bankers, businessmen, etc.), passing through the trunk of political parties and institutions, and rising to the crest, where the various forms of media—as the instruments of ideology—are represented. Another tree is much simpler. The diocese organization SLOP forms the root; the peasants are the trunk. And the summit of the tree is plagued by a *majanté*, a "parasite" strangling fig vine marked "Z" for *Zapatismo,* which threatens to consume both trunk and roots.

But the Church's visual and verbal admonitions were fruitless. The Zapatistas began their rebellion on New Year's Day of 1994. In his first public statement after the uprising, Samuel Ruiz seemed to give legitimacy to the movement, which had acquired considerable national and international sympathy: "The truth is that for the Indians, tired of the promises made by the government, there was no other way out but that of the gun. They were driven beyond what they could stand, though we do think that there are alternatives." When the Salinas government unexpectedly declared a cease-fire after almost two weeks of fighting, both the government and the Zapatistas requested the mediation of Samuel Ruiz in the peace talks. He had spoken strongly in the preceding years against the armed rising, but his long-term pattern, while clear enough in the shifting policies of the diocese, had been one of ambiguity in relation to the *lucha al golpe*, a position that had a double and positive result. The Zapatistas still respected him, while the government recognized Ruiz as a valid intermediary. In 1994, Mikhael Gorbachev recommended him for the Nobel Peace Prize, which he might have won if peace had really come to Chiapas.

More than twenty-two thousand Indians opposed to Zapatismo, as well as members of the moderate ARIC, fled their villages in the Lacandón Jungle shortly after the uprising. Many of them later wrote to the diocese asking for protection of their property or complaining about Zapatista abuses. When I asked him whether this also was not an Exodus, Don Samuel replied, "They didn't understand. They thought the Zapatistas wanted to drive them out while in reality they wanted to defend them."

Although the stalemate between government and Zapatistas dragged on well into the twenty-first century, the quarrel between the diocese and the EZLN now seems a thing of the remote past. Ruiz once referred to "guerrillas with peaceful tints" as an immense communitarian assembly, a new People of Israel on the march toward the Promised Land. Gonzalo Ituarte said to me, "Marcos still has the confidence of Don Samuel. There is an identity between them, except on the option of arms. Marcos has learned to respect the faith and the Zapatistas lift their masks to take communion."

Samuel Ruiz himself, when I asked him directly about his involvement in the genesis of the guerrilla war, responded, "I knew all about the causes. The Indians lost their fear." Was there a recruitment of cat-echists by the EZLN? "There is no mystery about that. The Zapatista cause deserved support. The country saw it that way. A direct order was given to the catechists: they had to resign if they joined the EZLN. Some of them sent in their written resignations. They were seeking the establishment of the Kingdom of God." His statement seemed a return to the years when the diocese worked directly with the Zapatis-tas, in the belief that the Church could remain the leading force. As he had said to De la Grange and Rico: "We worked with them for six years. They trained the young men, and even women, for the armed struggle."

Bishop Ruiz had shown no affection for electoral democracy. When I first met him, in 1994, he had commented on the impending national and local elections: the center-right PAN was a party that represented the interests of the upper and middle classes, he said. The center-left PRD claimed to speak for working people, but the experience of England showed that workers were fully capable of voting for con-servatives. As for the governing party, the PRI, it wasn't even worth discussion. "There are no acceptable schemes," he said quietly but in a prophetic tone; "we have to search for national articulation beyond the political parties. What is most important is that 'civil society' manifest and express itself. I am hopeful that a miracle will happen. Or if not, there will be an immolation." In 1998 he still believed that the electoral process in Mexico offered no reasonable alternative: "The PRD is the same as the PRI. They use the same methods of co-optation. As an advertisement for themselves, they used a picture of me embracing a female Zapatista soldier."

Of himself, Ruiz spoke humbly: "Anyone who sees himself as a saint is no saint . . . All I have done is give a voice to those who had no voice, to the real subject of history, to the Indians." When I said good-bye to Don Samuel, it was with the feeling that we belonged to two very different worlds. His was a world of redemption. His struggle for social justice had been impressive but his attitude toward violence had been ambiguous, occasionally in word and very clearly in action and practice. In my view, in societies where the sacred is absolute, the sanctification of violence by a sacred authority exacerbates intolerance and sows death. I also felt that I had stood before a true incarnation of Isaiah or Amos, the righteous prophets of God. There is no doubt of the appeal of his person, and his character. I had the strange sensation that if I stayed to speak with him a few more days, perhaps I would have become a convert.

The similarities between Samuel Ruiz and Bartolomé de las Casas perhaps extend beyond the issue of their true social fervor and commitment, their courage and their effect on history, to the ambiguity of their heritage. Without the "holy rage" of Las Casas, Indian slavery might have been established as the norm in Latin America. But there remains the paradox that it was Fray Bartolomé who advised the king of Spain to import the first black African slaves to Latin America, so as to relieve the burden on the Indians. He would later regret this petition. But from his famous dictum "Humanity is one" he had excluded Africans.

The danger I saw in a redemptionist doctrine such as Bishop Samuel Ruiz's preaching of the "Word of God" in Chiapas, despite its positive effects in awakening the consciousness of people suffering from deeply oppressive social conditions, is that it leaves little room for dissent. And it could also serve to intensify the exclusiveness of traditionalist communities like those of the Indians of Chiapas. A lack of goodwill toward the acceptance of difference and compromise leads to potentially explosive situations.

In the election year 2000, the armed Zapatistas and the unarmed followers of the "Word of God" could have allied themselves with forces on the Mexican left and struggled, electorally and democratically, for legislation that could have helped the many poor of Mexico and particularly the Indians, who are often the poorest among them. It did not happen. That year Mexico and Chiapas went to the polls. But neither Samuel Ruiz nor Subcomandante Marcos believed in democracy. They opted for redemption. And that commitment has led to the political demise of Zapatismo.

Samuel Ruiz himself retired from office in the year 2000 and would die on January 24, 2011. His memory is still respected, even revered by many. Given the present direction of the Church, there will be no official proposals to canonize him after his death. But for many of the Indians of Chiapas he will, like Bartolomé de las Casas, long be remembered as their Apostle.

11

Subcomandante Marcoɔ

THE RISE AND FALL OF A GUERRILLERO

On January 1, 1994, the Mexican public woke up to disturbing and amazing news: the sudden violent outbreak of the Zapatista movement in the southern state of Chiapas, led by a mysterious man in a mask who would later come to be known as Subcomandante Marcos. Decades after the military defeat of the short-lived guerrilla uprisings of the 1960s and '70s in Central America, five years after the fall of the Berlin Wall, it was hard to believe in the reappearance of a guerrilla force in Mexico. The country had just concluded the NAFTA agreement with the United States and Canada and appeared to be on a fast track to modernity. Perhaps an even greater surprise was the fact that this was more than a political rebellion: it was a classical revolt and, as Octavio Paz has described the peasant movement within the Mexican Revolution, it was a "return to roots"—a resurgence of the past, and a resurgence of the most ancient of all pasts, Indian Mexico.

In the years after the uprising, news of the Zapatista movement, and the writings of its leader, appeared regularly on the front pages of national newspapers and in the international press. The character and ideas of this masked crusader are vital to understanding the nature, achievements, and failures of Zapatismo, as has been true of other moments in Mexican history, a narrative that at times has seemed like a social projection of the personal stories of its leaders, its men of power. And one must also understand the state of Chiapas.

"Everything in Chiapas is Mexico," proclaimed a tourist slogan coined by the government of Chiapas at the beginning of the 1980s. One of the positive effects of the Zapatista rebellion that began in January

1994 was that it alerted the Mexican consciousness to the falseness of that statement. It is true that Mexico is not, except in some areas, a genuinely modern country, but very little in Chiapas is characteristic of Mexico. A truer assertion would be "Everything in Chiapas is Peru," the other great viceroyalty of the Spanish Conquest.

Seen from a limited historical perspective, Mexico and Peru may seem very similar in their origins and their trajectories: both were the cradles of great civilizations, and both suffered traumatic conquests. Both endured a long colonial siesta, during which they were materially and spiritually dependent on Spain. In the nineteenth century, Peru and Mexico experienced independence movements, drafted liberal constitutions, lost wars with their neighbors, and alternated dictatorial regimes with democratic interludes. But the differences between Peru and Mexico are great and deep. Throughout most of Mexico, the gradual process of *mestizaje* (the "mixing of races") greatly reduced the differences of color and ethnicity while in Peru such divisions continued to be very marked, and the source of conflicts and prejudices. And in Peru, fueled by geographical separation and a far more brutal history of conflict, the indigenous culture maintained its strength and its powerful myths. In 1956, José María Arguedas documented the persistent legend of the "Incarri" (the word is a fusion of *Inca* and *rey*, or king), which presents the image of the battered head of the Inca emperor lying on the surface of the earth while, buried deep below, the body silently reshapes itself to avenge the bitter defeat of its people and to reconstitute an archaic utopia.

The Peruvian José Carlos Mariátegui, in an essay dealing with the early twentieth-century rebel Rumi Maqui, or Stone Hand, described his own experience of a revelation: an indigenous rebellion (despite the defeat of Stone Hand) could happen again, on a far broader scale, firmly based on "our oldest traditions." Years later, Mariátegui worked out his central contribution to Latin American political thought, the linking of indigenism with Marxism. "We certainly do not wish socialism in America to be a copy and an imitation. It must be a heroic creation," Mariátegui proclaimed. "We must give life to an Indo-American socialism reflecting our own reality and in our own language." His objective was "the reconstruction of Peru on an Indian foundation." But the revolution that Mariátegui proposed was not only economic, it was also spiritual. "The strength of the revolutionaries," he wrote in 1925, "does not lie in their science but in their faith, in their passion, in their will. It is a religious, mystical, spiritual force. It is the force of myth." He would never have suspected that his projected uprising would occur not in the Peru of his day but in late twentieth-century Mexico.

IN CHIAPAS, the Peru of Mexico, the Marxist-indigenist program devised by Mariátegui was finally acted upon. In the region of Los Altos of Chiapas and the Lacandón Jungle (*Selva Lacandona*), Indians (which in Latin America means people who consciously live as Indians) comprised 79 percent of the population in 1990, similar to that of Peru at the time of Rumi Maqui. By contrast, 33 percent of the population of San Cristóbal de las Casas (the Lima of Chiapas) was Indian. The conditions were comparable: the same dual demographics; the geography of hate between the white city and the Indian highlands; the weak historical role played by the Catholic Church; the same hierarchical and bigoted nomenclature. And Chiapas had witnessed, in 1712 and 1867, two bloody Indian rebellions against the white minority, aimed at restoring the ancient Mayan government and religion. Elsewhere in Mexico, except in a few places, and despite the vast machinery of indigenist mythmaking (which is as exaggerated and as false as the mythmaking of Hispanicism), the purely racial problem has been resolved, to a reasonable degree, since the nineteenth century, by a process of mingling and convergence that is not just ethnic but also cultural. Economic nationalism and the drive for social equality, rather than race, were the central forces in the decade-long social upheaval that was the Mexican Revolution.

And nearly everywhere else in Mexico except Chiapas the problem of the land—"the elimination of feudalism," as Mariátegui called it—was attacked at the roots in the way that the Peruvian thinker had hoped it would be, so that there was even a restoration on public land

of "the elements of practical socialism that [existed in] indigenous agriculture and life." And if the great land reform that President Cárdenas
initiated in 1936—by expropriating the large landowners and dividing
17 million hectares, 10 percent of the country, among three million
landless peasants—fell short of achieving a state of general well-being,
at least it provided a measure of social and moral compensation for
peasants of remote or recent indigenous origin. To understand the rebellion in Chiapas properly, it is important to recognize that *mestizaje*
and agrarian reform occurred late and only partially in Chiapas, as in
Peru. And in both places, unfortunately, ethnic prejudice still, up to a
point, disrupts the course of daily existence.

II
———

After New Year's Day of 1994, Peru and Chiapas had something else in
common: the almost mythical presence of a Mexican Rumi Maqui as
foretold by José Carlos Mariátegui, the evangelist of the "spirit of the
dawn." In Chiapas, this "savior of the Indians" bore the pseudonym
of Subcomandante Marcos. "The hopes of the indigenous peoples are
absolutely revolutionary," wrote Mariátegui. This is precisely what
Marcos understood, and this is precisely what he put into practice.

It was clearly not his original intention. "Before 1994," Marcos had
declared, "no one had conceived of an indigenous movement." The
future subcomandante was born Rafael Sebastián Guillén Vicente, in
Tampico, a port city on the Gulf of Mexico, in 1957. In his own words,
he "grew up and was educated" in the "traditional left of the catacombs." His intellectual training in Althusser, Foucault, and the other
radical scriptures of his student years, and his youthful association with
the *Frente de Liberación Nacional* (FLN; the National Liberation Front)
predisposed him to the rigid categories of academic and revolutionary Marxism. Yet early in his life—if we may trust the meager information that is available about the masked, pipe-smoking superstar of
Chiapas—there were certain somewhat offbeat elements in his development (of a kind that would have pleased Mariátegui) and they would

come to be very useful to him in his revolutionary career. He had a Don Quixote–like dreamer of a father, who was a reader of Balzac and also a humanist businessman, the owner of a chain of furniture stores that fell on hard times. (Rafael devised a mildly anticapitalist slogan for his father's business: "Visit us and relive the old-fashioned pleasure of giving.") Like Mariátegui, he received a strict Catholic education (though for Marcos it was with the Jesuits), and also like the great Peruvian, he showed strong artistic and cultural interests.

The young Guillén made speeches, performed as a magician, and published a literary magazine premonitorily titled *The Hidden Root*. He sang songs by the popular Catalan singer Joan Manuel Serrat and devoured the socially and morally engaged work of the Spanish poets León Felipe and Miguel Hernández. He showed films, built sets, directed plays, and was an accomplished actor. He already had a strong sense of humor—rare in a revolutionary—and it was not mere irony, but a gift for the discovery of the ridiculous in human beings, beginning with himself.

Guillén's graduate dissertation on textbooks as instruments of power (signed and dated "somewhere very near the university campus") and his shift toward graphic design—the making of posters, the composition of bulletins and pamphlets, and later the teaching of design in support of popular causes—may be seen as the embryonic beginnings of a revolutionary practice based on cultural criticism and artistic creation. Perhaps the subcomandante's great popularity with the Italian left owes some of its strength to a similar emphasis in Italian leftist history.

Guillén was in Nicaragua at the beginning of the 1980s, first with his teacher Alberto Híjar (a professor of aesthetics and Marxism) as a participant in a series of cultural courses, and later in the village of San Juan, where he is remembered for his austerity: "he was reserved and well-educated . . . almost priestly." His next port of call was Cuba, where he appears to have acquired not only his knowledge of the art and the "science" of guerrilla warfare, but also his acquaintance with the revolutionary icon he apparently wished to emulate. A veteran of the Cuban Revolution who met him at the time, a friend and comrade of Che in his adventures in Africa and Bolivia, has said that Guillén "wanted to know every little thing about Che's life in the mountains, in Bolivia, in Africa: what he read, how he wrote, what he ate, how he distributed food, how he smoked his pipe, what tobacco he used, how he practiced medicine in the villages . . . He even wanted to know how he breathed!"

An important Cuban official, upon meeting him in Havana in 1982, remarked that "this is a new Che." In fact, when he arrived in the Lacandón Jungle in 1983, Guillén (who had probably already adopted the name of Marcos in honor of a guerrilla fallen in battle who had formerly taught him Mexican history) wore the Che beret, smoked a pipe, told the Indians that he was a doctor, and dispensed medicine. But his Guevaran inspiration went beyond mimicry; it was the very essence of the guerrilla movement that he founded in Chiapas. This time the spark of rebellion, the *foco*, would catch fire—not just because of geography (the impenetrable jungle), but also because of the human environment. The indigenous community of the Chiapas highlands and especially of Las Cañadas was ripe for the ferment of revolution.

Marcos did not have to preach a gospel of indigenous redemption. For more than ten years he could concentrate on the military objective, which in Mexico was Marxist revolution, because the political-theological ground had already been prepared. Since 1971 the ideological instruction of the Indians had been the work of the diocese of San Cristóbal de las Casas, which was headed by Bishop Samuel Ruiz. In what became the most successful experiment in liberation theology in Latin America, Don Samuel, assisted by Dominican, Marist, and Jesuit priests, created a network of eight thousand Indian "catechists" who carried "the Word of God"—in essence, a Marxist interpretation of the gospel—around the region.

The pamphlets that they distributed called the indigenous communities "the new children of Israel," a people oppressed by world capitalism and its lackeys, the Latin American governments. In many cases these writings explicitly supported the guerrilla fighters of Central America. When Marcos, with the support of Don Samuel, came to the communities of the Lacandón Jungle, the Indians were mentally and spiritually prepared to embark on a long guerrilla campaign. Without this local indigenous elite, trained to struggle for salvation, the *foco* in Chiapas would likely have been extinguished before it had a chance to grow.

III
———

To his literary mentor, the writer Carlos Monsiváis, Marcos declared in 2001: "The EZLN prepared for January 1 1994, but not for January 2." It was the truth, stripped of any masks. When a fascinated Marcos video-taped the Indians who, on October 12, 1992, pulled down the statue of the conquistador Diego de Mazariegos in San Cristóbal, he did not yet realize that he was a character out of Mariátegui. He still believed that he was a revolutionary descended from those bred in the Russian universities of the nineteenth century, or a latter-day Che in training. And yet he was already writing texts suffused with the rhetoric of redemption, which owe their tone and even their imagery to the indigenous world that for almost a decade had surrounded and welcomed him.

In the first EZLN communiqués the indigenist message was not stressed. The Zapatistas talked about socialism. Then, all of a sudden, just after the January 1 announcement, to his own astonishment and to the astonishment of a broad cross section of the Mexican public, Marcos noticed that "something new has been born," "something else." This something was not just the growing public sympathy or at least understanding toward the rebels, or the repudiation by those, such as Fidel Velázquez, the old working-class leader of the PRI, who called for "the extermination of the masked men." It was the sudden recurrence at the end of the twentieth century of an old theme, an old Latin American or Indo-American prophecy (or melody): not only the "Word of God" but also, and primarily, the indigenist and revolutionary words of Mariátegui.

Marcos had surely read Mariátegui. His writings would have been on the required list in courses on Marxism or Latin American history.

But Marcos may not at first have consciously and deliberately adopted the Peruvian's premise of indigenism. It may have been a natural result of the situation as it stood on January 2. From that time on, Marcos and the Zapatistas, brilliantly sensitive to the power of the media and capitalizing on the fortuitous blossoming of the Internet, made a truly amazing use of high-tech communications (their hostility to capitalism notwithstanding) and placed the question of Indian rights squarely on the international agenda. They also succeeded in linking indigenism directly to two powerful currents: multiculturalism and the worldwide antiglobalization crusade. In 1996, in a message from the EZLN to the American planning committee of the Intercontinental Meeting for Humanity and Against Neoliberalism, Marcos proclaimed: "We are neoliberalism's maximum defiance, the most beautiful absurdity, the most irrelevant delirium, the most human madness." For Marcos, neoliberalism is the great evil of the postcolonial world. In his closing remarks at that meeting, he castigated it in biblical terms as a supra-totalitarian power: "In the world of those who live and kill for power there is no room for human beings . . . slavery or death is the choice their world offers all worlds."

Mariátegui would have welcomed the use of the media to advance the cause of the Indians. It fits in perfectly with the surrealist techniques for the "demolition" of bourgeois society, and with Mariátegui's proposal for a creative return to indigenous origins. There are many other elements of Zapatismo that he would have applauded within the Gramscian creativity of Marcos's cultural revolution. The use of the mask is one example. The black wool ski mask that Marcos always wore is an extraordinary conception, a symbol with all the advantages of a magnificently successful brand: different, mysterious, simple, cheap, useful, reproducible in itself or on posters and T-shirts. As an instrument of revolutionary marketing, its success was assured, because this was an instrument truly "made in Mexico," a country in which the mask has been a vital cultural artifact for centuries. And yet until Marcos, no one in Mexico had thought of using it to achieve such effects.

The next surprise took place in the discourse itself, especially in response to a question that was the title of a significant statement by Marcos published in newspapers on January 18, 1994, after the government had offered him a pardon and amnesty. His message was simple and thoroughly indigenist: the Indians, oppressed for five hundred years, had done nothing that required forgiveness. "What do they have to forgive us for?" The echo in the left-wing press and from university podiums was immediate, and it lingered more or less intensely for years. Here was a writer somewhere out in the jungle, a storyteller and a weaver of intricate moral fables (some of his writing praised by Octavio Paz), a powerful pamphleteer in the eighteenth-century tradition, uneven, overly prolific, emotional, incisive, hilarious, at times (as Fidel Castro noted) far too focused on death, but always a writer. Given the degree to which the Mexican left (even up to the present day) has been more cultural than social and more social than political, the discourse and symbols of Marcos had a truly revolutionary impact.

His writing often had a strong biblical tone and his use of quotations, especially from poetry, seemed natural and effortless, ranging from Shakespeare to Lewis Carroll, from Paul Éluard to Neruda, the indigenous oral tradition, Walt Disney, comic books, and the Latin American writers of the left: a real postmodern cocktail. Despite his talent, however, the writer in Marcos was only incidental. His literary skills were entirely at the service of his cause. The opposite was true of his master Mariátegui, who was an authentic writer of the avant-garde: rigorous, well informed, original, and whose writings on literature and art read just as well now as they did in 1928. They have not lost interest or relevance.

Within Mexico's borders, Marcos's words stirred the feelings of several indigenous groups in other southern states, though nothing similar to the events of January 1, 1994 occurred elsewhere. Outside Mexico, and especially in Italy, they energized the Western left for a time, after the trauma for many socialist movements that followed the fall of the Berlin Wall. The writer José Saramago wrote a rapturous prologue to the collection of Marcos's writings called *Our Word Is Our Weapon*. For

Saramago, Chiapas was the new Jerusalem, the Zapatistas were the
children of Israel, Marcos was their savior, Don Samuel was John the
Baptist. He was not alone in this belief. Highly respected intellectuals
from all over the West were of the same mind. "Marcos has earned his
indignation like few men alive," Norman Mailer noted on the jacket of
Our Word Is Our Weapon. Kurt Vonnegut likened Marcos to "our own
Tom Paine."

Saramago, at least, visited Chiapas many times. But in his wanderings he had seen only what he wanted to see: a polarized society of
Indians and soldiers. What he did *not* observe was the complicated reality of the place, a predominantly Indian society sharply divided for
many political, religious, economic, and cultural reasons. Mexico was
not and is not a country split between exploited Indians and non-Indian
exploiters. The truth lies elsewhere: Mexico is very much an ethnically
mixed country. Its biggest problems were and are decidedly not racial.

In keeping with the doctrine of his Peruvian predecessor, Marcos
had brandished a direct appeal to Mexican history, which he called
"our historical protection," creating an explicit link with the original
Zapatismo (1910–19) but also with many other moments, figures, and
episodes of the Mexican Revolution. The congress that he convoked
in 1994, for example, took place in a village in the jungle that Marcos
renamed Aguascalientes. Acting as the editor of living history, Marcos
was seeking to re-create the convention of 1914 in the city of Aguascalientes, a high point in the struggle of popular leaders Pancho Villa
and Emiliano Zapata against Venustiano Carranza's more conservative
forces.

He regularly situated himself within the Mexican tradition of revolution, as if to borrow legitimacy from the very country with which
he is at war. Since his first communiqué from the Lacandón Jungle on
January 2, 1994, his historical references had been constant: the coman-
dantes are "insurgents," they are like Hidalgo and Morelos, the leaders of the independence movement and the country's founding fathers.
Marcos's own models were the leaders of the Revolution: Villa, but
especially Zapata, around whom Marcos created his own innovative

legend. Merging Zapata's struggle for land with an ancient Mayan belief about the first man (called "Votán," which means "the hearth of the people") sent by God to divide up the earth, Marcos tried to create a myth that would be both Indian and Zapatista. He postulated a spirit called "Votán Zapata," who incarnates all the popular heroes of Mexico: "He is and he is not everything in us . . . he is walking . . . Votán Zapata . . . keeper of the night . . . master of the mountain . . . he is one and all. No one and all. The guardian and hearth of the people."

"A postmodern guerrilla," the writer Gabriel Zaid called Marcos. There was a movie director behind this rebel's mask, a filmmaker waiting to seize his opportunity and exchange his mask for a camera. His life is his best movie. In his interview with Monsiváis, Marcos made this explicit. He called for a Gramscian program for the regeneration of the left that will enable it to confront the neoliberal hegemony: "The problem facing the left is the construction of a cultural, historical, intellectual, and political framework. That is where there is a need for intellectual labor . . . We believe that the intellectual, progressive left must work to clear a path for itself. The challenge is great and richly rewarding," and so on—all rather banal assertions, except that it ends on the subcomandante's distinctive note: "And not just on an intellectual level, but on a cultural level as well, in film."

IV

La Realidad: this is the name that Marcos gave to the small village where he had his headquarters. The appellation expressed a certain hope and a certain arrogance. The problem is that La Realidad was not the same thing as reality. It was one thing to create a myth, and quite another thing to operate in a demythified world. Marcos's La Realidad was real enough. The indigenous people who built it and lived in it were actual and aggrieved, and they were led by an extraordinarily creative and determined man. But how did La Realidad translate into reality?

Marcos had been many things, but he was not an ideologue. Mariátegui prescribed agrarian reform for Peru as a first step in the adoption (the re-adoption, he would have called it, given the Inca antecedents) of socialism. But Mariátegui was a product of his time: he could admire the Russian Revolution as the dawn of history. Such radical idolatry was not available to Marcos and his generation, who have witnessed the final collapse of Eastern European communism. Marcos too was a product of his time, and the Marcos who was a conventionally pro-Soviet Marxist probably expired, belatedly, on January 1, 1994, three years after the Soviet Union. A day later the other Marcos was born, the indigenist Marcos, the media Marcos, the Marcos we knew.

The collapse of Soviet communism could not be denied by Marcos, his training in revolutionary Marxism notwithstanding. And so this expert in revealing the hidden and in hiding the obvious settled on another utopia, on a different salvation: "The essence of our struggle is the demand for the rights and culture of indigenous peoples, because that is who we are. Here we stand, we hold to our path, we resist." With the weight of these and similar words, Marcos—like such currents as the Black Power movement in the United States of the late 1960s—aimed at transforming identity politics into a revolutionary program.

But what did his assertion, floated from La Realidad, mean concretely, in reality? It expressed an admirable moral standpoint, but in practice it seemed to be confused and contradictory. "We don't need anyone to give us anything," Marcos had said, disdaining "handout politics," which yields only "one more store, one more clinic." The old criticisms of "reformism," of "economicism," of those who "sell their soul and dignity for a few coins" resounded in pronouncements that tended toward the spiritual and the messianic, and away from anything practical and possible. This suspicion of politics was the consequence not only of Marcos's radicalism, but also of his indigenism. He wanted his people to be saved but to stay the same, to experience a transformation without being transformed. It is no coincidence that Marcos had nothing to say about the Indians who had chosen not to stay the same, who did not accept his politics.

The late Alberto Flores Galindo, a brilliant writer of the Peruvian left, warned against visions that fail to breed effective economic and social progress—the kind of progress that involves investments, schools, stores, clinics—and instead assume the permanence of archaic ways of life that are supposedly superior but actually oppressive. "Only those who have never been at risk of contracting typhus," he wisely observed, "lament the arrival of a highway or the establishment of a medical center in a town." Of course Marcos had known human suffering—he had been surrounded by it in the jungle for almost twenty years—but his rejection of restitution that he considered unworthy ("we want things to change, we don't want charity") made it difficult to bring his struggle to a satisfactory conclusion. After all, who decides when an act of reparation—the sort of justice that most of Mexico desires—is genuine or sufficient? Had all the Indians of Chiapas been freely consulted?

v
—

This brings us to the heart of the matter: the question of democracy. Beginning with their first communiqués, Marcos and the Zapatistas had constantly reiterated their commitment to democracy. Almost all their statements ended with the phrase "democracy, justice, liberty." But their support for democracy remained abstract. They constantly interfered with the electoral processes in the corrupt local elections of 1995 and 1997, and Marcos urged his followers to abstain from two national elections, even the critical and closely contested presidential campaign of 2006, when the left-of-center candidate appealed for his support. From the viewpoint of Zapatismo, democracy meant that the nation should constitutionally recognize the right of the indigenous communities to be different, and up to this point their reasoning was democratic, since it appealed to the basic respect that majorities (in Mexico mainly mestizo) owe minorities, in this case, the Indians of Mexico. But what happens when some essential aspects of the cherished "practices and traditions" of communities infringe on those of their resident minorities, such as women, and Indians of other ethnic origins, and those of different religious faiths?

Questioned about this issue by Carlos Monsiváis, Marcos replied that "some practices and traditions do indigenous communities no good: prostitution, alcoholism, the exclusion of women and young people from collective decision-making processes—processes that are actually more collective than in urban areas but also discriminatory. Alcoholism, prostitution, machismo, and domestic violence must all be eliminated." He insisted that these changes should not be forcibly imposed, a position that showed respect and understanding for the way traditional cultures function, since some of these evils are rooted in strongly felt, religiously supported custom. But if they damage lives, by what process are they to be changed? And by acknowledging the need for such changes, Marcos shifted his ground. If the Mexican majority must concede to the indigenous minority their right to difference, then the indigenous majority in any region or community must concede the same rights to their own internal minorities: the inalienable individual rights of freedom of religion, expression, movement, and residence. Yet frequently in Indian communities, these rights are not honored, and people of differing faiths or opinion may be excluded, ostracized, or even killed.

Marcos preferred to avoid such issues. His concerns were different, and directed to the future: "The balance sheet of my role is still pending." And he was right. In 1994 there had been dead on both sides. (Even Marcos, obsessed as he was with death, sometimes seemed to forget them.) But at the beginning of the new century, his historical balance turned remarkably positive. Without the upheaval of January 1, 1994, the national government would not have provided schools, roads, and medical services to those communities, at least not to anywhere near the extent it did.

And then, in the year 2000, forty million Mexicans went to the polls and ended seventy years of one-party rule. It was a triumph for the idea of democracy but Marcos did not join the tide of change, though a million Mexicans had signed their names to a request that he move from his guerrilla bastion in the jungle to an open life in politics. What options remained to him? In 2001 a Zapatista "long march" arrived in

Mexico City and enjoyed a carnival of media coverage; its indigenous spokespeople gave speeches before the Mexican Congress. Marcos himself declared in an interview with Gabriel García Márquez that armed resistance was no longer viable. The march was his moment of glory, but it also demystified his image and his movement, and made him ordinary. And public opinion noted and approved President Vicente Fox's change in policy from that of his predecessors. Behaving like a true fox, the president unilaterally withdrew the army from its posts in the area of conflict. But the Zapatistas did not negotiate. Even the legislation on autonomous indigenous rights that Congress approved was rejected by them.

Marcos was still free to attempt a transformation even more exciting than the one he underwent in the 1990s from conventional guerrilla to Internet guerrilla. He could become a political leader of the Mexican left, which was sorely in need of leaders. In that role he could have pressed for an economic policy that addressed the needs of the poor, and especially the poorest of the poor, the Indians of Mexico. Marcos preferred to cling to his myth, until the myth began to wither. And the leadership of the left fell to a man no less charismatic, Andrés Manuel López Obrador. When Marcos refused to support López Obrador and even verbally attacked him (thereby surely stripping him of votes that could very well have given him the victory in a very close election), much of the left simply turned their backs on the subcomandante. For the Zapatistas, certainly, the alternative was grim: the public, in the early years of the new century, was tiring of them. And as democracy in Mexico continued its process of consolidation, the movement became increasingly isolated.

Marcos remained popular among young Mexicans, but as a celebrity, not as a role model. Other leaders of Mexican and Latin American rebellion had died violently at the hands of the enemy (Túpac Amaru II, Che Guevara) or at the hands of their own comrades. Marcos chose the most romantic ending: disappearance into anonymity, the passage into legend. For many reasons—political, philosophical, generational, cultural—Marcos (now fifty-four years old, living more or less anonymously in Mexico City) could have led the Zapatistas into the civic life of the nation. But instead he held fast to Mariátegui's gospel of indigenist redemption. In 2009 an old friend of his sent a photo of him without the mask to various Mexican newspapers. Nobody cared.

And the lack of attention is due to the many changes, for better or for worse, that have come to the state of Chiapas and to Mexico. On the good side, there has been palpable improvement in Chiapas, economically evident in the growth of public works, politically in the advance of democracy. The PRI and the PRD have won power in various townships and in some cases, a peaceful state of joint government exists between one of these parties and the Zapatistas. But many Chiapenecos have emigrated to the United States. And those who remain are preoccupied with the same problems as the rest of Mexico: crime, insecurity, and the ravages of the drug trade.

They say that Marcos is ill and that he frequently visits La Realidad, but the village is very different without international floodlights. And Mexico is different today, harsher than that era fifteen years ago but more sensitive to the condition of the Indians. That newfound sensitivity is due, in large measure, to the repercussions of January 1, 1994, and the flamboyant passage (and performance) of Subcomandante Marcos across the stage of history.

PART VI

The Postmodern Caudillo

12

Hugo Chávez

THE HERO WORSHIPPER

Turning history into scripture is an old practice in Latin America. Within the region's Catholic countries, stories of the past, with their heroes and their villains, became instant paraphrases of the Holy Story, complete with martyrologies, holy days, and iconic representations of secular saints. But in Venezuela, where the presence of the Church has been less fecund and influential than in Mexico, Peru, or Ecuador, the transformation of the profane into the sanctified has been more intense, perhaps because of the lack of "competition" with strictly religious luminaries such as the Virgin of Guadalupe or the patron saints of Mexican towns. Venezuela's civic worship is also unusual in being monotheistic. It has centered on the life and practical "miracles" of a single deified man: Simón Bolívar, the Liberator.

In addition to parades, speeches, ceremonies, competitions, inaugurations, commemorations, unveilings of monuments, official publications, and other formal events in veneration of Bolívar that successive Venezuelan governments of all political varieties have instituted, there arose, already in 1842, a spontaneous and enduring popular cult of Bolívar just twelve years after his death. It was fueled by a kind of collective penitence for the sin of letting Bolívar die on Colombian soil. And so the Liberator came to be relentlessly exalted by the same nation that, through rejecting his project for a Gran Colombia (which would have unified Venezuela, Colombia, Ecuador, and Panama), caused him to be ostracized. This sacralization of Bolívar was blessed within the Church itself, by the cardinal of Caracas in 1980, who declared from the seat of his diocese that all of Venezuela's misfortunes, the countless civil wars (more than 150 during the 150 years of independence), and the dictatorships of the nineteenth and twentieth centuries (longer periods of ferocity than in any other country of Latin America) all sprang from the "treason" that was originally committed against Bolívar.

Official, popular, manufactured, spontaneous, classical, romantic, nationalist, internationalist, military, civil, religious, mythic, Venezuelan, Andean, Ibero-American, Pan-American, universal: the cult of Bolívar became the common bond of Venezuelans, the sacrament of their society. Other sanctified heroes shared the altar, but they stood in Bolívar's shadow, and they were not always beloved: Francisco de Miranda, an early champion of independence; Antonio José de Sucre, Bolívar's loyal grand marshal; and General José Antonio Páez (Bolívar's right hand in war, his adversary in peace, and the founder of the Republic of Venezuela). Even in scholarly circles his immaculate image prevailed until the 1960s. When, in 1916, a young doctor dared to suggest that Bolívar was probably an epileptic, he was harshly attacked for this gesture of "patriotic atheism" against the Bolivarian faith—an "august, admirable, sublime religion . . . How is it possible, that a Venezuelan should ascend to the empyrean to remove Bolívar from Caesar's side, and relegate him to the inferno, beside Caligula?"

From a very young age, Hugo Chávez revered Simón Bolívar. And not just Bolívar. He had always looked for heroes. In his modest childhood in the small western plains city of Barinas, Chávez also intensely admired Chávez—that is, Néstor "El Látigo" (the Whip) Chávez, a famous Venezuelan pitcher who was killed in a plane crash after a brief passage through major-league baseball. Chávez recounts that, when he entered the Military Academy in 1971 at the age of seventeen, he visited the tomb of El Látigo to ask forgiveness for his diminished devotion. New heroes were now demanding his attention: Che Guevara and Fidel Castro. His personal pantheon also included Ezequiel Zamora (the popular leader in the Federal War of the mid-nineteenth century) and his own great-grandfather, a rebel of the early twentieth century with a somewhat murky career.

In Chávez's epic imagination, the interesting thing about this past inhabited by heroes was that they spoke directly to him and ended up being reincarnated in him. "Let me tell you something I've never told anyone," he confessed to several friends. "I'm the reincarnation of Ezequiel Zamora." (Some say he has always feared he would die like Zamora, by treason and a bullet to the head.)

With his contemporary heroes too, he craved direct contact. In an interview in 2005, President Chávez recalled his first encounters with Fidel Castro. "My God, I want to meet Fidel when I get out and I'm free to talk," he prayed in prison, after his failed coup attempt in February 1992, "to tell him who I am and what I think." Their first meeting took place in Havana in December 1994. Castro stood waiting for him in person at the foot of the steps descending from the airplane. From then on, Chávez came to see Castro "as a father," and his children saw him as a grandfather:

The day he came to visit Grandma's little house in Sabaneta, he had to stoop. It's a low door, and he's a giant. I saw it with my own eyes, didn't I? And I remarked on it to [my brother] Adan. Seeing him there, as if it was a dream: "this is like something out of a García Márquez novel." In other words, forty years after the first time I heard the name Fidel Castro, there he was in the house where we were raised . . . My God!

During the fifteen years in which he patiently plotted his revolutionary conspiracy, forging his spiritual links between his own genealogy and the nation's heroes, Hugo Chávez would convert himself into a being cast in the mold of García Márquez's magic realism. He would be the redemption, the climax—the supreme text prophesied by other texts—of the Sacred Scripture of Venezuelan history.

CHÁVEZ THE cadet was a celebrant of this Bolivarian religion, not in a ceremonial or academic context but through his biography and his sense of theater. In 1974, as testified in his writings collected in 1992 under the title *Un brazalete tricolor* (A Three-Colored Armband), his outbursts of lyricism about the Liberator went beyond the reverential imagery (pictorial, verbal, sculptural) of neoclassical history, beyond the romantic and patriotic equation of Bolívar with Alexander, Caesar, or Napoléon, beyond even the grandiloquent official images of "the apotheosis of the demigod of South America." In that year Chávez the cadet wrote an encomium for the hero that began with this curious sentence: "On June 23, on the eve of the anniversary of the great Battle . . . of Carabobo, Simón Bolívar gave birth to the nation." As the Venezuelan historian Elías Pino Iturrieta has explained, Bolívar was, for young Chávez, God the Father; the nation was the Virgin; the Christ child—the offspring of this transcendental couple—was the liberating army, which, in a leap across the centuries, was the very army to which Chávez belonged. In 1978 this notion would produce a natural corollary: the Bolivarian army would return to the historical stage in order to redeem the honor "of the humiliated mother," to continue the country's historical struggle for Independence and complete the work still to be done:

> It [the army] is your child, Venezuela—and it gathers the people of the nation to its breast to instruct them and teach them to love and defend you . . . It is your seed, Fatherland . . . It is your reflection, country of heroes . . . your glorious reflection. As the years go by, our Army must be the inevitable projection of the social, economic, political, and cultural development of our people.

After that first very personal, filial, but still collective contact with the memory of Bolívar, his metahistorical father, Hugo Chávez gave a provocative, almost revolutionary speech on December 17, 1983, the anniversary of Bolívar's death. It earned him a reprimand from his superiors and was soon followed by the staging of a scene that has become famous in Venezuela: the Oath of the Samán de Güere. He urged four of his friends to put on a theatrical performance in which he connected his revolutionary project to the memory of the national hero. Under a very old tree, the Samán de Güere, beneath which, according to legend,

Bolívar once sat down to rest, he repeated the oath that Bolívar took in 1805, in the presence of his mentor Simón Rodríguez, at the Monte Sacro in Rome: "I swear by the God of my fathers, I swear by my fatherland, I swear on my honor, that my soul will not be at peace nor my arm at rest until I see the chains broken that oppress us and oppress the people through the will of the powerful." The year 1805 had been conflated with 1983. Chávez changed two words: instead of "the powerful," Bolívar's oration had restricted his range to "Spanish power."

In the military exercises under his command, Chávez would order his subordinates to begin the day with a thought selected at random from a book of Bolívar's sayings, and he repeated these phrases like quotations from a timeless and all-purpose gospel. His revolutionary movement had the same initials as Bolívar. In the first interview that he gave after his coup, gazing out from prison at the National Pantheon, under whose central altar the remains of his hero rest, the comandante uttered these words: "Bolívar and I led a coup d'état. Bolívar and I want the country to change." Those were not metaphors. He was speaking in earnest.

When he got out of prison in 1994, fully equipped with the imagery of history he had absorbed into his own person, Chávez threw himself into the political activism that five years later would lead him to the presidency by democratic election. But in meetings with his ministers, he then initiated one of those disconcerting and idiosyncratic practices that have become a natural component of the Chávez narrative. He would place a chair at the head of the table. No one was allowed to sit there. He would stare at the chair with concentration. Only he could hear the elusive guest: Bolívar the Liberator.

Though his admiration for Bolívar was genuine, his appropriation of the myth was carefully and thoughtfully considered. In interviews from the period, Chávez referred to the "mystification" of which "Bolívar the man" was the object. He then proclaimed himself "a revolutionary first and a Bolivarian second." Yet his revolution needed an ideology, and he needed one, too. And immediately. At the very least there had to be an "ideological banner." He found it in his own cult of the hero. The Nicaraguan revolutionaries had adopted the figure of Augusto César Sandino, the legendary nationalist guerrilla of the 1920s. In Mexico, Subcomandante Marcos had recently invoked Emiliano Zapata with great success. But Bolívar meant much more to the nation of Venezuela: he was more than a hero, he was a demigod. Chávez would declare: "If the myth of Bolívar helps to get people and ideas moving, that's good . . ." When Chávez as president first visited Havana, Fidel Castro would also give his blessing to this credo. In a very Fidelian statement, he would say, "If today's struggles are called Bolivarianism, I agree, and if they're called Christianity, I agree." But even Castro could never imagine the extremes to which Hugo Chávez, once securely in power, would carry the cult of his hero.

IN LATIN America, poets are prophets. When he took office in February 1999, Chávez quoted some famous lines from Pablo Neruda, made the quotation the linchpin of his address, and built around it the most impressive theological-political performance ever seen in Latin America. The sermon was a long discourse larded with citations from Bolívar applied to the present day, full of religious shadings and grandiloquent turns that were extreme even by the permissive standards of Latin American rhetoric. Chávez heralded (in the Christian sense) his arrival in power as something greater than just an electoral or political or even historical triumph. It was still more: a *parousia*, the return to life of the dead and of the nation, the resurrection announced by the apostle Pablo (Neruda):

> *It is Bolívar who comes back to life every hundred years.*
> *He wakes every hundred years when the peoples awaken . . .*

Later in the same speech, Chávez turned to the idea of historical guilt, centering it around his country's overwhelming poverty, and decreeing a new historical truth: the republic that was born in 1830 by "betraying the Condor" (another of Bolívar's holy names) had brought down upon itself a curse that lasted nearly 170 years. The nuances of this republican past (which, despite wars and dictatorships, also included periods of civil liberty and material progress) were left out of the picture, condemned to the same hell as liberal democracy, which, against all odds, had been a growing presence in Venezuela since 1959, confronting coups of the right and guerrillas of the left but—with respect for the rule of law, civil liberties, and the electoral process—encouraging social and economic progress. For Chávez, this "odious political model" also had to die. Venezuela was now face-to-face with the greatest miracle, the "return of the Condor," the "resurrection . . . which is nothing other than advancing the social revolution under the luminous beacon of Bolívar." It was his first official unveiling of the new Bolívar, a revolutionary Bolívar, already in embryo a socialist Bolívar.

The initial civic rite of this "national re-foundation" was a baptism of the nation blessed by the presence of Bolívar incarnate, "our infinite Father," "genius of America," "shining star," "shaper of republics," "truly great hero of our times," "true master of this process." In honor of Bolívar, Chávez declared, the Republic of Venezuela would add the word "Bolivarian" to its name, and the new constitution would be "based on the doctrine of Bolívar," omniscient, eternal, infallible.

From then on, the ceremonies of the cult of Bolívar—in official propaganda, in the media, in the marketplace—showed no limits. The Chavista masses would gather in the plazas of Caracas to stage the scene of the Oath of the Samán de Güere. They would chant "Watch out! Watch out! Watch out! Bolívar's sword is moving across Latin America! Bolívar lives! Bolívar goes on living!" The masses would hear Bolívar speaking through their president and across the centuries on every conceivable theme: oil, the labor movement, social revolution, the beneficence and necessity of socialism. They would begin to shop for Bolivarian plantains and rice, buy Bolivarian chickens, cut their hair at Bolivarian barbershops. "We have boldly sought a new frame of reference," explained Chávez, in an interview he gave in the 1990s. "Original and all our own: Bolivarianism."

Chávez's unquestionable boldness has been the subject of a number of anthropological studies that attempt to explain its success. Some scholars point to the popularity of various Bolivarian myths among the Venezuelan people. Pino Iturrieta has collected incredible accounts of these secret and magical Bolívars: the Bolívar possessed by the spirit of a supernatural being gifted with powers of healing and salvation, called Yankay; the Bolívar of popular legend, the purported son of a black slave woman from the cocoa plantations; the Bolívar of liberation theology, who died poor and promises redemption for the dispossessed; the syncretistic Bolívar of Venezuela's old African religions, who occupies the center of a "Liberationist Court" presided over by Queen María Lionza (incorporated into the Catholic Church as a saint), the major deity of the Venezuelan version of Santería. She is worshipped by those who seek love, health, money, and good fortune. In her ceremonies, the shamans invoke Bolívar to condemn "political parties," to bring equality, peace, and liberation, to "bless the neighborhood guerrillas and proclaim a kingdom of happiness ruled by the military."

Imbued with these strains of popular religiosity, and exploiting them instinctively but also with calculation to further his cause, Chávez has continued to play the role of a magician, saint, and messiah—but his most audacious move was to invigorate the Bolivarian cult by setting himself in the place of a High Priest, appropriating Bolívar's charisma. The historian Pino Iturrieta found a fitting metaphor within the history of Christianity: "Now a tropical Constantine has imposed the complete identification of a people with a national deity."

II

To what political tradition does Hugo Chávez's Bolivarian rhapsody belong? According to his own version, his destiny was revealed to him around 1977, when he read a book: *The Role of the Individual in History* by Georgi Plekhanov. He has more than once told the story of this moment of inspiration, his epiphany before the text: "I read Plekhanov a long time ago, when I belonged to an anti-guerrilla unit in the mountains . . . and it made a deep impression on me. I remember that it was a wonderful starry night in the mountains and I read it in my tent by the light of a flashlight." Again and again he turned to it "in search of ideas [about] the role of the individual in historical processes." He still has the same copy of "the little book that survived storms and the years; the same little book with the same underlinings . . . and the same arrows and the same cover I used as camouflage so that my superiors wouldn't say 'what are you doing reading that?' "

Herma Marksman, his mistress in the 1980s, has said, "He read everything, but he especially liked the stories of great leaders." The stories—and the theories. In an interview in 1995, Chávez remarked that "we men can situate ourselves . . . in leading roles that speed or slow the process, give it a small personal touch . . . But I think that history is the product of the collective being of the people. And I feel myself absolutely given over to that collective being." In colloquial terms, he has often referred to himself as a mere "instrument of the collective being." This is a highly idiosyncratic use of Plekhanov, but with it Chávez crafted his argument for the rule of the traditional Latin American military autocrat, the *caudillo*: "If they [the *caudillos*] develop a real awareness, if they detach themselves and view the process from a distance, if they devote their lives, their efforts, to collectivize through their 'mythical' power . . . then you can justify the presence of the *caudillo*."

This theory of the individual in history, which is really a theory of the great man in history, explains his admiration for Castro. Although at the time he still wondered whether it was "a curse or a spreading virus" for the historical process to rely on a single man, when he visited Cuba in 1995 Chávez was deeply moved by the way the people identified with the leader, the "collective" with the *caudillo*. While he was traveling in the eastern region of the island, a woman recognized Chávez in a restaurant and hugged him: "Caramba! you talked to the chief, you talked to Fidel." For Chávez, "that is the people's message, I get everything I need straight from the people, the people on the street." Apparently Chávez had made his decision. It was sufficient for the leader sincerely to declare himself a humble servant of the collective, and for the collective sincerely to accept him as its leader. "The role of the individual in history" could then unfold.

In practice, though, what was the "collective"? Did it have segments, or was it a homogeneous whole? And were those parts free to form judgments? Could they disagree with the *caudillo*? Was there a way of measuring how well the *caudillo* served the collective? Could the collective choose another *caudillo*, or no *caudillo* at all? These questions did not occur to the ambitious soldier. The important thing was the mystical union of the many and the one, the dissolving of the collective into the leader. That was why it seemed natural and even desirable to Chávez that Castro had "enormous influence over the island": that "generations have gotten used to Fidel doing everything. Without Fidel they would be lost. He's everything to them." Castro was an example of the way in which *caudillos* can "detach themselves, view the process from a distance and devote their lives . . . to collectivize through their 'mythical' power." And Castro had the historical right to be "everything": he was, after all, a hero—the great hero of Latin America.

Chávez also proposed to "detach himself," just as Castro had for more than fifty years. And he was a hero, too—maybe not a conquering hero, a triumphant and legendary guerrilla like Fidel, but still a soldier with the heart of a guerrilla: "The body of the nation is in pieces. The hands over here, the legs over there, the head on the other side of the mountains, the body of what is really the collective. Now, to go through life and get something done about putting that body back together, joining the hands to the arms and bringing it to life, giving the people, the collective, a motor, I think this justifies having lived." Marksman saw a transfiguration in her longtime lover: a "messianic glow" had descended upon him. According to another revolutionary friend, Chávez "was convinced that he was carrying out an earthly mission guided by a superhuman force." At the time, Chávez himself seemed to reject—but only halfheartedly—this vision. "I don't believe in messiahs or *caudillos*, although people say that's what I am, I don't know whether I am or not, maybe there's a little bit of that in me . . ."

PRESIDENT CHÁVEZ has been an assiduous reader of Plekhanov, but perhaps not the most astute reader. Georgi V. Plekhanov, who was born in Gudalovka, Russia, in 1856 and died in exile in 1918, was considered the father of Russian Marxism. He wrote *The Role of the Individual in History* around 1898, during the honeymoon period of his relationship with his disciple V. I. Lenin, with whom he edited the journal *Iskra*. Originally a Bakunian populist, Plekhanov fled czarist Russia in 1880, taking refuge in Geneva. He would not set foot on Russian soil again until 1917. It was he who coined the term "dialectical materialism." Plekhanov believed that there were immutable laws of history, and he thought that if Russia followed the same trajectory as the countries of Western Europe, it would emerge from feudalism into a state of mature capitalism, which was the necessary condition for its inevitable evolution into the ultimate and final dictatorship of the proletariat. In 1889 he made his first appearance at the Congress of the Second International. In 1895, Lenin traveled to Switzerland to meet him.

Following the lead of Thomas Carlyle, Plekhanov believed in the existence of "great men" as initiators or originators. "This is a very apt description," he wrote. "A great man is precisely a beginner because he sees further than others, and desires things more strongly than others." In this sense, the great man is a hero "not . . . in the sense that he can stop, or change, the natural course of things, but in the sense that his activities are the conscious and free expression of this inevitable and unconscious course." The leader is the supreme instrument of history's search for its conclusion. His freedom consists in his ability to choose a course of action in accordance with the fixed laws of historical progress:

> If I know in what direction social relations are changing, owing to given changes in the social-economic process of production, I also know in what direction social mentality is changing; consequently, I am able to influence it. Influencing social mentality means influencing historical events. Hence, in a certain sense, I

can make history, and there is no need for me to wait while "it is being made."

Plekhanov's concept of the "individual's role in history" might have been inspired by Hegel, who in his *Philosophy of History* speaks of "world-historical men." These beings with an essential role in the development of the universally valid "Spirit," these visionary agents of History, are followed by their sympathizers, who "feel the irresistible power of their own inner Spirit thus embodied." From this metaphysical-authoritarian premise Hegel concluded that the ordinary rules of ethics were not applicable to great men. "Heroic coercion," he noted in his *Philosophy of Right*, "is justified coercion." The moral equivalence of might and right was also a key doctrine of Thomas Carlyle: "Might and Right," he wrote in 1839, "so frightfully discrepant at first, are ever in the long run one and the same."

Lenin certainly agreed. But Plekhanov did not, and this was the irreparable difference between them. Against the backdrop of the Second International in Brussels in 1903, the disagreement between the two grew deeper, and led finally to a break. Lenin assumed absolute leadership of the movement, with the support of the group that would come to be known as the Bolsheviks. "This is the cloth from which Robespierres are cut," thundered Plekhanov, who would accuse them of "mistaking the dictatorship of the proletariat for a dictatorship over the proletariat." Shortly afterward he gave up the editorship of *Iskra*, leaving it in Lenin's hands. His final article was a prophetic *j'accuse* titled "Centralism or Bonapartism":

> Let us imagine that the Central Committee, recognized by all of us, had the right, still under consideration, of "liquidation." The following could then occur. A congress is convened, the Central Committee "liquidates" the elements with which it is displeased, selects at the same time the creatures with which it is pleased, and with them makes up all the committees, thus guaranteeing itself without further ado an entirely submissive majority at the

congress. The congress composed of the creatures of the Central Committee affably shouts "Hurrah!" approves all its acts, good or bad, and applauds all its projects and initiatives. In such a case, the party would really have neither a majority nor a minority, because we should have put into practice the political ideal of the Shah of Persia.

Over the following years, Plekhanov grew more and more isolated, disturbed by the new phenomenon of absolute power concentrated in a vanguard party, itself commanded by a person beyond appeal, a "Shah of Persia." This phenomenon struck him as contrary to the laws of history. That was why he called Lenin the "alchemist of the revolution" and considered him a "demagogue from head to toe."

In the standard manuals of Marxist-Leninist theory, Plekhanov figures as a wrongheaded dissident. According to Lenin, the attitude of his old ally was "the height of vulgarity and baseness." Plekhanov is remembered as the first leading intellectual before Trotsky to sound an alarm against Marxism-Leninism. Just months before his death, he came out in support of the ill-fated Menshevik prime minister Kerensky. Of Lenin, he said in his *Political Testament* that "not understanding the true goal of that maximalist fanatic was my greatest mistake."

IF PLEKHANOV had lived until the end of the twentieth century, chances are that his view of Castro would have been much the same as his view of Lenin. He would have denounced the Shah of Cuba. The Plekhanov who fought for humanist values, the Plekhanov who refused to subordinate society to its leader and represented the classic Marxist critique of the Caesarist and Bonapartist spirit of Lenin and Leninism, is not the Plekhanov whom Comandante Chávez has been reading and rereading for thirty years. He may consider himself a Plekhanovist, but Plekhanov would not have been a Chavista.

And judging by his political writings, Plekhanov's teacher would also not have supported Chávez nor his mystique. In Marx's writing after his famous attack on Bonapartism (*The Eighteenth Brumaire of Louis Bonaparte*) there is an unexpectedly direct connection to President Chávez's epic script. In London, around 1857, Marx received a request from his New York editor, Charles A. Dana, to write an article on Simón Bolívar for *The New American Cyclopaedia*. Although military affairs were Engels's specialty, and although Marx felt a marked and racist distaste for what he regarded as the backward and barbarous countries of Hispanic America, he accepted the assignment. He wrote hastily, with his usual sarcasm, drawing on just a few sources, all hostile to the Liberator. The final version of his biographical sketch made Dana uncomfortable, though he published it anyway in 1858.

In Marx's account, Bolívar is pilloried—among other negative qualifications—as a yokel, a hypocrite, a clod, a womanizer, a traitor, a fickle friend, a wastrel, an aristocrat putting on republican airs, a liar, a social climber who surrounded himself with the show of a court and whose few military successes were due to the Irish and Hannoverian mercenaries whom he hired as advisors. That Marx's animosity toward Bolívar was almost personal is clear. In a letter to Engels he repeats his opinions, calling Bolívar "the most dastardly, most miserable and meanest of blackguards," comparing him to Faustin-Élie Soulouque, the flamboyant Haitian *caudillo* who in 1852 had himself crowned emperor under the title of Faustino I.

Marx's assault on Bolívar stems directly from his devastating critique of Louis Bonaparte (who reigned as Napoléon III of France between 1852 and 1870). Marx compared Bonaparte's huge bureaucratic and military apparatus to "a frightful parasitic organism that, like a net, constricts the body of French society and stops up all its pores." He felt that Bolívar showed similar authoritarian tendencies, and his criticism has always been a nightmare for the Latin American left. How to explain it? And what to do now that President Chávez has decreed Bolívar a prophet of "twentieth-century socialism"? In 2007 a book was published in Caracas, *El Bolívar de Marx*, which consists of facing texts by two serious Venezuelan writers of opposing views— the liberal historian Inés Quintero and the Marxist philosopher

Vladimir Acosta. They conduct an elegant debate on the subject of Marx's portrait of Bolívar.

Quintero documents the authoritarian side of Bolívar, which has served as an ideological inspiration not only for the Latin American and Venezuelan right, but also for Italian and Spanish fascism. Both Mussolini and Franco identified themselves with Bolívar's Caesarism. The Latin American left had a great need to rehabilitate him—but given its own authoritarian history, it had little to say on this essential point, and could only continue to cite the errors in the text or its Europeanist slant. Then a new apologetic strategy developed, meant to reclaim the hero under the rubric of Ibero-Americanism, and slowly proceed (except for a few isolated objections) toward an anti-imperialist Bolívar. The next step came with the rise to power of Hugo Chávez: "the Return of the Condor."

Acosta and Quintero both honor the empirical truth of the past. But when they turn to the present, and to the use that the Chavista regime makes of history, their views radically diverge and become a reflection of the intellectual polemic now raging in Venezuela. Acosta explains Marx's reasons for attacking Bolívar, but he does not explain his own reasons for adopting Chávez's Bolivarian narrative. The omission triggers a contradiction. After justifying Bolívar's concentration of power into himself as a wartime imperative, Acosta maintains that historians "on the Right" have denied Bolívar his historical reality—and then he immediately goes on to deny Bolívar the same protection on the left by validating Chávez's idiosyncratic interpretation and appropriation of the Liberator. Acosta calls the Chavista act of faith a "rescuing for the people" of the "human political greatness and enduring Ibero-American significance of Bolívar." He fails to note the resemblance between his president's "Bolivarian" project and the ahistorical and "sacralizing" perspective for which he takes the rightists to task. He speaks for *his* Bolívar and *his* Chávez:

His exploits and much that survives of his thought have been actively incorporated into this struggle of the majority of the

Venezuelan people and other South-American peoples to achieve the democracy, equality, independence and sovereignty that his liberating actions offered them and that were denied them by the Creole oligarchies, the only ones that benefited from the process of Independence and whom now it seems possible to defeat.

In response, Quintero cites a speech by President Chávez in which he scolds those who take Marx's *Capital* as gospel, divorced from its temporal context. "You have to realize," said Chávez, "that this was written over there in eighteen-something . . . you have to realize that the world has changed." The words of Chávez himself underline a contradiction implicit in the use that he has tried to make of Bolívar as a prophet of twenty-first-century socialism. Quintero then offers detailed evidence of Chávez's "arbitrary, selective, and anachronistic use of Bolívar's discourse, without considering the specific historical circumstances Bolívar had to live through."

This dispute between Acosta and Quintero is not merely academic. Acosta completely understands what Chávez is doing with the memory of Bolívar, and he defends it. In his view it is an objective, genuine, and historically valid renewal of an old process, the interrupted liberation of the continent. For Quintero, the problem is not just the falsified and self-interested use that Chávez makes of Bolívar's life and ideas, but something more pervasive: the ever increasing political application of Chávez's version of the Liberator:

If Bolívar serves to justify the "socialism of the twenty-first century," he can just as usefully endorse the end of the democratic transfer of power and the installment of a dictatorial regime, based on the claim that the example and the word of the father of the nation are being implemented point by point.

Beyond the specifics of this polemic, it is clear that Karl Marx, the critic of power, saw the concentration of power in the hands of one man as a historical aberration, in whatever context, whether "bourgeois"

France or "barbarous" Latin America. Since his doctrines presupposed a collective affirmation of civil society that would be emancipating and egalitarian, Marx not only rejected personalized political power, he refused any hint of it for himself. Much later in time than his book on Napoléon III and his article on Bolívar, he wrote to his friend Guillermo Bloss in November 1877:

Engels and I wouldn't pay a penny for popularity . . . because of my repugnance toward any cult of personality, during the existence of the International, I never permitted them to publish the numerous and bothersome messages I used to receive from many countries, in recognition of my merits. We never answered, except to reprimand them. The first affiliation of myself and Engels to the secret society of communists involved the single condition that they eliminate from their statutes anything that might contribute to the superstitious prostration before authority . . .

Marx had been much more than a historical visionary; he had changed the history of the world. But the far-reaching role he played did not include the cult of individual power, or anything resembling Carlyle's cult of heroes, still less any cult of himself. For that reason, despite its prejudices and errors, the polemical text of Marx on Bolívar can be explained by his political convictions against the concentration of authority. And they are valid for any time and place.

III

"I don't know anything about Marxism, I never read *El Capital*, I'm not a Marxist or an anti-Marxist," Hugo Chávez said in 1995. He was telling the truth. Chávez was never, in any strict sense, a Marxist, nor was he familiar with what would have been the uncomfortable side of Marx for him, the critique of power. And Marx had also specifically criticized a political use of the past: "The social revolution of the nineteenth century cannot draw its poetry from the past, but only from the future . . .

In order to arrive at its own content, the revolution of the nineteenth century must let the dead bury its dead."

Whether he knows it or not, Chávez is the progeny not of Plekhanov or Marx, but of Thomas Carlyle. It was Carlyle's historical and political doctrine, condensed in 1841 in the series of lectures published as *On Heroes and Hero-Worship*, that envisioned and legitimated charismatic power in the twentieth century, the same power that Chávez represents, with unequaled incandescence, in the Latin American twenty-first century. Despite what the post-Marxist theorists who now focus upon him might wish to be the truth, Chávez comes from a more anachronistic tradition of ideas. He does not see history in terms of the struggle of classes or masses, or of races or nations, but of heroes who guide "the people," who incarnate them and redeem them.

Bolivarian Venezuela and its maximum leader have a number of reasons to recognize themselves in Thomas Carlyle. Unlike Marx, Carlyle admired Bolívar, whom he dubbed "the Washington of Colombia":

Melancholy lithographs represent to us a long-faced square-browed man: of stern . . . consciously considerate aspect, mildly aquiline form of nose, with terrible angularity of jaw, and dark deep eyes, somewhat too close together (for which latter circumstance we earnestly hope the lithograph alone is to blame) . . . Bolivar has ridden, fighting all the way, through torrid deserts, hot mud-swamps, through ice-chasms beyond the curve of perpetual frost—more miles than Ulysses ever sailed; let the coming Homers take note of it . . . Under him was gained the finishing "immortal victory" of Ayacucho in Peru, where old Spain, for the last time, burnt powder in those latitudes and then fled without return. He was dictator, liberator, almost emperor, if he had lived. Some three times over did he in solemn Columbian parliament lay down his dictatorship . . . and as often, on pressing request, take it up again, being a man indispensable . . .

The writings of Thomas Carlyle were a strong influence on Latin American authoritarian thought in the late nineteenth and early twentieth centuries. His relevance to the Bolivarian regime, and to the thinking of its leader, lies in his concept of the hero as a central actor in history. Revolutions, Carlyle insisted, require a hero to give new meaning to collective life. On the subject of his transcendent faith in great men (inspired by Fichte, who maintained that the "Divine Idea" manifests itself in only a few individuals), Carlyle coined his famous phrase: "'Hero-worship' becomes a fact inexpressibly precious; the most solacing fact one sees in the world at present . . . No sadder proof can be given by a man of his own littleness than disbelief in great men." And in *Sartor Resartus* he summed up his philosophy of history:

> Great Men are the inspired (speaking and acting) Texts of that divine Book of Revelations, whereof a Chapter is completed from epoch to epoch, and by some named History; to which inspired Texts your numerous talented men, and your innumerable untalented men, are the better or worse exegetic Commentaries . . .

Through the many speeches by the maximum leader of the Bolivarian Revolution, traits originally ascribed to Bolívar have been gradually transferred to the man who seems to be Chávez's greatest hero: himself. Chávez too believes in modern Latin American history as a Sacred Text populated by heroes on a holy and urgent mission, for which they are gifted with divine fire. In our time, they have been Che Guevara and Fidel Castro. Since his youth, Chávez has felt that the history of his country and the hopes for its future (at least until his arrival, until "the return of the condor" and the "national resurrection") are reflected in the biography of Bolívar. And in his inaugural address of 1999, an apotheosis of his principles and of himself, one more life story was inscribed in the Sacred Text: his own.

From the end of the nineteenth century, the positivist historical schools of Latin America invoked Carlyle to justify the military *caudillos* that the region—supposedly "ungovernable" through "Anglo-Saxon" democracy—"required" to make any significant progress. José Enrique Rodó had applied (in his *Motivos de Proteo*) that idea in relation to Bolívar. In the no less influential book *Las democracias latinas de América* (1912), the Peruvian Francisco García Calderón also had found the heroic key to Latin American political history in Carlyle. But it was in 1919, with the Venezuelan sociologist Laureano Vallenilla Lanz, that the use of Carlyle reached its apogee. In his book *Cesarismo democrático* (Democratic Cesarism) he presented the theory of the "necessary gendarme," with reference to the Venezuelan dictator Juan Vicente Gómez (who was termed "Carlyle's man" by the historian José Gil Fortoul).

But in the 1930s a new political dimension was added to the "cult of the hero." It was Jorge Luis Borges who discovered a troubling key to Latin America in Carlyle. As a young man, Borges learned German, inspired by Carlyle's Germanophilia. More than thirty years later, rereading the last lecture in *On Heroes and Hero-Worship*, he noted that "Carlyle reasons like a South American dictator in his defense of the dissolution of the English parliament by Cromwell's musketeers." Borges was referring to the passage in which Carlyle describes how, in 1653, four years after the beheading of King Charles I, the Puritan revolutionary Oliver Cromwell—Carlyle's favorite hero—loses patience with Parliament, made up of "little legalistic pedants" with their "worn-out constitutional formulas" and their "right of Election," and finally dissolves it to become, with the "power of God," the Lord Protector of England.

Borges read Carlyle with Latin American eyes, detecting Cromwell's resemblance to our antidemocratic prototypes: *caudillos,* revolutionaries, dictators. Curiously enough, Carlyle would find his next great hero in one of the most remote corners of Latin America. During the years in which he compiled the unpublished speeches of Cromwell, Carlyle bemoaned the fact that the nineteenth century had not produced a leader like that "great, earnest, sincere soul who always prayed before his great undertakings." "Our age shouted itself hoarse," Carlyle wrote, "bringing about confusion and catastrophe because no great man did heed our call." Then suddenly, around 1843, Carlyle discovered, by chance, a "hero" worthy of the name, a "savior of his age," a "phoenix of resurrection": José Gaspar Rodríguez de Francia, the lifelong dictator of Paraguay (from 1814 to 1840) after it won independence from Spain. Francia was at first a fervent Jacobin, who in some ways modernized his country and then locked it away in paranoid and destructive isolation. He was probably insane and his absolute personal rule, accompanied like a dirge by random and unrelenting cruelty, threw his country into a slough of backwardness from which it is barely emerging in this, the twenty-first century.

Based on a few reports by German travelers, Carlyle began to write a biography, the only one he wrote that dealt with a contemporary: the biography of that "one veracious man," the "Cromwell of South America," a "man sent by Heaven," a "fierce condor." Carlyle admired Francia's scorn for the intellectual forms and political institutions of eighteenth-century rationalism. And, above all, he applauded the tyrant's desire to perpetuate himself: "My lease of Paraguay . . . is for life," Francia had said. Through him, Carlyle declared, "Oliver Cromwell, dead two hundred years . . . now first begins to speak." A South American dictator had given Carlyle new faith in the present and future possibility of heroes.

When Borges was writing in 1949 (under the dictatorship of Perón in Argentina) it had become clear, even along the spectrum of Latin American intellectuals, that Carlyle was a direct ancestor of fascism.

Hugo Chávez, in his political ideology (though it is not likely that he has ever read Carlyle), is a descendant in Carlyle's lineage. He is the "hero," the real protagonist of his regime, and hero worship is his central ideology. Can one throw the charge of "fascist" at him?

A man eminently qualified to judge, one of the most respected members of the Venezuelan democratic left, and a critic of Chávez on various fronts, most intensely for his mishandling of the economy and his disdain for the rules of democracy, the former guerrilla fighter Teodoro Petkoff says that he is not yet a fascist but that he shows some disturbingly similar traits:

Chávez is not a fascist but he has fascistoid elements: the cult of
the leader sent by providence . . . the manipulation of history for
political ends, the disregard for legality and republican forms in
the name of the voice of the people, his permanent and oppressive
presence in the media, his brutal and aggressive speech-making
against his adversaries . . . Chávez, for his enemies, neither bread
nor water. And also he's a soldier, a man trained to annihilate the
enemy.

IV

The purpose of the Bolivarian Revolution, according to Chávez, is to
confront head-on the problems of poverty that afflict the majority of
Venezuelans and (as Chávez would likely say) to rescue them. And the
route toward that rescue leads through Venezuela's oil. The pride (and
curse) of modern Venezuela has been its "black gold." Rómulo Betancourt, the Father of Venezuelan Democracy, in his first term as president (1945–48), succeeded in negotiating rather favorable terms with the
foreign oil companies, and in his second term (1959–64) he and his minister of energy resources, Juan Pablo Pérez Alfonzo, were driving forces
behind the formation of OPEC and its impressive capacity to maneu-
ver for the benefit of "Third World" oil-producing countries. But after
fifteen years of economic growth, expansion of social benefits, and an
exemplary democratic political process, the oil boom of the mid-1970s
brought a new generation to power that combined positive actions (like
the nationalization of the oil industry and a vastly increased support
for culture and education) with widespread and growing corruption.
The collapse of oil prices in the latter half of the 1980s called for budget
adjustments. When cuts were imposed rapidly and drastically in February 1989 (through various means, including sudden price increases in
gasoline), rioting broke out in Caracas over a three-day period, with
the police facing the populace and hundreds of dead. This "Caracazo"
was, in retrospect, a fatal blow to the democracy that had been solidly

evolving since 1959 for the first time in Venezuelan history. A collapse of confidence began that eventually brought Hugo Chávez to elected power, in February 1999.

After 1999, the oil was in the hands of the Bolivarian Revolution in the person of its leader, hundreds of billions of dollars' worth, gushing from the wells at a time when oil prices were soaring day after day. Venezuelan oil is the property of the nation, under the stewardship of the government oil company, PDVSA (Petróleos de Venezuela S.A.). The oil had been fully nationalized in 1976 and the company, at the operational level, had been perhaps the most efficient state-run oil enterprise in Latin America. For Chávez, the revenues from Venezuelan "black gold" would nourish two essential currents of his enterprise, one flowing downward to the Venezuelan people, the other across his borders to support and influence other Latin American countries. By the year 2008, he had spent $62 billion in subsidies to fifteen countries.

Chávez essentially ruined Petróleos de Venezuela. As with many other aspects of the nation, he wanted his faithful loyalists in charge. After an unsuccessful coup attempt against him in 2002, from which he was rescued by General Raúl Isaías Baduel (whom he imprisoned in 2008) and by popular protest, he moved against the management of PDVSA. The managers called a strike that collapsed after two months. The eventual result was the dismissal of virtually all trained management and a third of the skilled work force: 18,765 workers, technicians, and engineers. Many left the country. The march of political loyalty had trampled down efficiency. PDVSA became an inefficient, corrupt, and dependent bureaucratic monster. By 2008, production of oil had declined by 34 percent, exports by 50 percent, while the president, between 1999 and 2008, was dispensing, on average, $122 million in oil revenues per day.

The flow abroad was in large part liquid—the oil itself at bargain prices or direct donation—to countries with left-wing governments aligned in varying degrees with Chávez's worldview, whether Cuba with its own president-for-life or the elected governments of Bolivia or Nicaragua. It was an unprecedented (and for his purpose effective) ideological use of Venezuela's oil riches, and Chávez felt certain that he could combine this huge exterior outlay with a massive expenditure on social programs within the country. But much depended on the worldwide price of a barrel of oil. Venezuela was immersed in the magic realism of an economy that now produced less and consumed more, all thanks to the exponential increase in oil prices, which between February 1999 and 2008 went up, from $10 to $140 per barrel. In mid-2008, Chávez's ministers considered it "impossible" for the price to come down for the time being. The Comandante boasted that he could raise it to $250 a barrel. The near collapse of the world economy in the autumn of 2008 put brakes on his bravado, as the price of oil plummeted along with the decline in world industrial production.

WITHIN VENEZUELA, his social programs have been extensive, though their success is debatable. They have gained him the loyalty of large segments of the poor. Chávez created the Bolivarian Missions, a parallel system meant to bypass formal government structures so as to rapidly reach the poor in areas like health and basic education. Venezuela was meeting the Cuban need for oil and Castro made good-neighborly use of Cuba's considerable investment in medical education by dispatching doctors and nurses and technicians (and military specialists in state intelligence) to Venezuela. The social programs implemented through the different "Missions" (subsidized food, free medical assistance, literacy training, and general education) did in fact have a strong period of growth between 2004 and 2006. But by 2007 they were in decline, and their loss of credibility was perceptible: empty shelves in stores as well as problems of supply, staff, and low quality in both medical and educational services. The deterioration has recently grown worse, including the scandal of ten tons of chickens discovered rotting in warehouses.

The whole program has suffered from its pell-mell inefficiency, the rapid attempt to replace traditional institutions with new forms intimately connected with the Chavista mystique and its empowerment. The government hospitals, for instance, have suffered from reduced investments—with the money channeled instead to the Missions—and as a direct result, mortality in childbearing has increased. The expropriation of strategic assets such as electricity, telecommunications, iron and steel, aluminum and cement went hand in hand with the deliberate exclusion of private enterprise, which, unsurprisingly, reduced investment to historic lows. But the effect of this weakening of the means of production was postponed because the gap in supply was filled by unparalleled imports of consumer goods. There was, for a time, a growth of per capita income in Venezuela—14.6 percent between 1999 and 2006—attributable of course to oil revenues, but since 2007, real income has fallen substantially as a result of inflation, which reached 31 percent in 2008 and was then the second highest in the world after Zimbabwe. In 2009, the rate of inflation stood at 25.1 percent, the highest on the continent and second globally only to the Democratic Republic of the Congo. And in 2010 the economy shrank by 19 percent.

As for corruption, its magnitude is hard to measure given the system's total opacity. But there is external evidence, based on numbers from the Central Bank of Venezuela itself. Of the $22.5 billion that left the country between 2004 and 2008, $12 billion was never accounted for. Something similar happened at PDVSA, with $5 billion vanishing in 2005. Venezuela ranks quite low in the Corruption Perceptions Index (CPI), an international measure not of corruption itself, which because of its criminal nature is always largely hidden, but of a nation's internal perception of corruption. In 2009, Venezuela was ranked at number 162 of 180 countries assessed, the lowest in Latin America except for Haiti.

WITHIN VENEZUELA Chávez is omnipresent. Every Sunday he appears on television for a minimum of five hours, live from the palace of Miraflores. It is his weekly show, *Aló presidente* (Hello President!). Presiding over his silent, acquiescent ministers, all dressed in red, the Comandante tells stories from his life and unleashes a stream of consciousness about romantic adventures, gastric ailments, baseball games; he also sings, dances, recites, prays, laughs, and most of all bashes Yankee imperialism and capitalism in general. In these sessions Chávez may also announce electoral strategies, huge transfers of fiscal resources, petroleum subsidies, social initiatives, troop movements, diplomatic ruptures, business expropriations, cabinet changes.

Chávez is an aggressive, dominating presence who sometimes has guests on his show but rarely leaves them any room to speak. He rants against his enemies, unreservedly praises his own initiatives, and fills his language with colloquialisms and profanities. But for many, *Aló presidente* may be more than just a clown show. He gives them at least the appearance of contact with power, through his verbal and visual presence, which may be welcomed by people who have spent most of their lives being ignored. Teodoro Petkoff remembers that during the marches against the unsuccessful coup that temporarily imprisoned Chávez in 2002, he saw an old woman carrying a sign she had obviously made herself, with spelling and grammatical errors in its tiny quota of words and that read "Give me back my crazy guy!"

The main key to Chávez's enthronement lies not in his economic measures (though they have been truly disastrous) or even in the impact of his social programs, but in his handling, through the media, of his colossal persona. His takeover of the Bolívar myth is complete. All the fantastic strains of popular religiosity in Venezuela, its folk political theology, are now centered around him. Of course, demigods do not share power. From the moment he was first elected president, Chávez has used democracy to undermine democracy. Venezuela still holds elections but he has taken numerous measures to undermine all independent sources of power and to crush the opposition.

After the recall referendum in 2004 was defeated, he introduced what Petkoff has called "political apartheid"—job discrimination against, and the political harassment of, more than 2.3 million people who voted against him. In May 2007, he shut down RCTV, the oldest and most popular open TV station, and three years later he did the same to its cable TV affiliate. He has systematically harassed the other remaining independent network, Globovisión.

In December 2007 a referendum proposed by Chávez was defeated at the polls. It included a great number of constitutional changes (including the legalization of his possible reelection) and would have moved Venezuela more rapidly toward a Cuban model of government (there was even an article about the possible political integration of the two countries). In the following year, Chávez disqualified hundreds of possible opposition candidates for mayoral and gubernatorial office. After the opposition nevertheless made surprising gains in those elections, and aware that the global economic crisis would soon reach Venezuela, Chávez decided to wager everything on another referendum to be held in February 2009. The proposals were greatly slimmed down from the 2007 portmanteau referendum. The primary objective was to legalize the possibility of unlimited reelection to the presidency. The electoral process that culminated in the vote on February 15, like all such ballots since Chávez has been in office, was thoroughly unequal. On one side was the opposition, without economic resources, exhausted after years of intense protests; and, on the other side, Chávez, with all the economic and propagandistic power of the state and hundreds of thousands of state employees working illegally for his cause. In the weeks leading up to the vote, the abuse of power was not hidden. The government seemed to flaunt it as an instrument of intimidation. Having closed, harassed, or fined the few media outlets that opposed him, Chávez devoted the impressive media network that he has assembled (three hundred radio stations, a number of subsidized newspapers) to relentless propaganda for him and his regime. The opposition, barred from these outlets and slandered in them, was left with only one truly independent opposition channel (in which the Chávez government is now the majority stockholder and he may soon shut it down).

v
───

Among the sixty-nine articles of his constitutional reform rejected by plebiscite in 2007 was the possibility of indefinite reelection, which could give him a lifelong lease on Venezuela. Now, with the victory of his 2009 referendum—which reduced the bewildering variety of the 2007 plebiscite to only a single issue: eliminating term limits—he may have achieved this goal. It was approved by 55 percent to 45 percent, in a 70 percent voter turnout, though many constitutional lawyers thought the proposal was illegal.

Even before he assumed power, Chávez defended the need for a charismatic leader: "The *caudillo* is the representative of a mass with which he identifies, and he is recognized by that mass without any formal, legal process of legitimization." As president he proclaimed himself "a revolutionary first and a Bolivarian second" and preached the need to wipe clean the slate of the past from Bolívar's death to his own ascension. The military dictatorships of the past (including the brutal one of Juan Vicente Gómez, from 1908 to 1935) were no better than the country's experience with "stinking democracy." For him, all of Venezuela's military regimes before his own were "essentially the same" as the democratic governments of Rómulo Betancourt (1959–64), Raúl Leoni (1964–69), or Rafael Caldera (1969–74). With or without braid, "on horseback or in a Mercedes Benz," they all represented "the same prevailing economic and political thinking, the same denial of the people's right to be the protagonist of their destiny." The revolution that he stood for would bury the "ruinous political model . . . of the last forty years" and put the people back in control of their destiny.

For Chávez, another factor, his identity as a soldier, is almost as important as his faith in the role of the *caudillo* and his revolutionary convictions. "Our movement was born in the barracks. That's a factor we can never forget, it was born there and its roots are there." From the beginning it was clear that he loved military parades, and that he saw the country and the society from the idealized point of view of an orderly and hierarchical military structure. On the subject of liberal democracy, his opinions have always been emphatic: "Liberal democracy does not work, its time has passed, new models must be invented, new formulas . . . Democracy is like a rotten mango: it has to be taken as seed and then sown." Speaking about the opposition parties represented in parliament, Chávez went so far as to exclaim, at a rally before he was first elected, that "we, you and I, are going to roll the [social democratic opposition] up in a giant ball of . . . I can't say what because it's rude." And the crowd responded: "Of shit!" Years later he would declare that "the opposition will never return to power, by fair means or foul." On the question of his tenure in office, if not eternal or for life, still conceived as very long indeed, he suggested, when he visited Cuba in 1999, that his presidency would last "twenty to forty years."

On a continent where European ideas from the right and from the left have sometimes been fused into bizarre mixtures, one influence on the development of Chávez's authoritarian ideas is likely to have been a man he once described as his "great friend," the Argentine sociologist Norberto Ceresole. One month after his first election, Chávez would expel him from the country because Ceresole's paranoid, neo-Nazi anti-Semitism had become an embarrassment to many Chavistas, in a country where a Jewish community had long lived in peace and prosperity. Chávez had met Ceresole shortly after being released from prison in 1994. He had spent two years behind bars for leading, as a paratrooper colonel, an abortive coup attempt against the democratically elected government of Carlos Andrés Pérez, under whom the Caracazo had exploded in 1989. (Pérez would be impeached in 1993.) The coup had little support in the Venezuelan military and never got off the ground. But it was the beginning of Chávez's status as a "hero" for many Venezuelans who saw him as their would-be champion against corruption. When he was allowed to appear on television, after his surrender, so that he might instruct all his supporters to lay down their arms, he threw in a remark that the movement had failed *"por ahora* (for now)."

Hugo Chávez was impressed with Ceresole's energy and apparent learning. And the meeting came at a delicate moment in Chávez's life, when the future seemed uncertain and he was ripe for the influence of a powerful personality. Ceresole's adventurous résumé involved oscillations through time and space and formal ideologies. He was essentially an authoritarian leftist, with an abstract Argentine-style hatred for the United States, a loyalty to Peronism, and a strong dose of neo-Nazi ideology thrown into the rest of the mix and eventually dominating his ideas. He had been a left-wing Peronista Montonero guerrilla, an advisor to the extreme right-wing Carapintadas (who had hoped to overthrow one of the

democratic regimes that had succeeded the Argentine military terror of
1976–83), a member of the Soviet Academy of Sciences, and a professor at
the Soviet Military Academy, then a representative in Madrid of the Leba-
nese Shiite group Hezbollah, and so on. By the time he arrived in Venezuela explicitly to seek out Chávez, as a rising military star, and to become
for a time his advisor, he had settled into obsessive raging at the politics
of Israel and, far worse, neo-Nazi Holocaust denial (though he always rejected the label), spinning his paranoia into the myth of a worldwide Jewish
conspiracy out to dominate Latin America. One of his major influences on
the future comandante would be his focus on the necessary union of Latin
American countries to oppose the United States of America, Bolivarian in
form but—unlike Bolívar's entirely practical dream—intensely ideological. He also may have strengthened the future comandante's military inclination toward the central importance of the *caudillo*. In *The Caudillo, the
Army and the People: The Venezuela of Comandante Chávez* (1999), the last book
he would produce before his expulsion from Venezuela, Ceresole wrote:

> In Venezuela, the change will be channeled through one man, one
> "physical person," not an abstract idea or a party . . . the people
> of Venezuela created a caudillo. The nucleus of power today lies
> precisely in the relationship established between the leader and
> the masses. The unique and differential nature of the Venezuelan
> process cannot be distorted or misinterpreted. What we have here
> is a people issuing an order to a chief, a caudillo, a military leader.

The question of anti-Semitism (and accusations of it) really entered
into Chavismo as an offshoot (albeit a disturbing one, with frequent
anti-Jewish or anti-Israel remarks made on official TV by his spokesmen) of the Comandante's foreign policy and his strong views on foreign affairs, which may have been partially influenced by the lingering
shadow of Ceresole.

———

CHÁVEZ HAS persecuted select and sometimes collective enemies but
his actions have not been brutal. Verbally, though, he certainly has

been brutal and abusive beyond all limits. Those who are not with him are "against Venezuela," are "imperialists," "pitiyanquis" (little Yankees), "filth." A climate of psychic hatred has been encouraged, working to further divide a nation that was not historically divided. And the mismanagement of the economy is not only due to the evident problems of corruption, the placement of often incompetent Chavista loyalists, and the diversion of resources toward the imperatives of Chávez's foreign policies, but also to his insistent demonization of the market economy, oriented toward the creation of "21st-century socialism" obviously based on Cuban policies about which Fidel Castro himself now expresses his doubts. They also stem from Chávez's impulsiveness and his impatience. One prominent feature has been his urge to "bypass" the formal institutions of government and "go directly to the people." The result has often been—as with PDVSA and the Missions—the ruination of irreplaceable institutions.

With his victory in the second referendum—and his growing control over the electoral apparatus and the Congress, fiscal, judiciary, and electoral branches of the state—Chávez may be able to win the series of reelections he considers essential to his project. But there are a number of barriers that may derail the runaway train of the Bolivarian Revolution. Most important perhaps is the continued existence of an active and vibrant civil society in Venezuela. Six million people voted for the Chávez proposal to abolish term limits, but five million abstained, and another five million voted against him. The present opposition is based on a democratic value structure that was several generations in the making and still retains institutional and legal weight. It is a dissident mass and is made up of elements from a wide social spectrum: workers, housewives, union leaders, small and medium-size business owners, intellectuals, academics, artists, writers, priests, journalists, and by now a significant segment of the poor.

Anti-Chavista students in particular have been at the forefront of this public and nonviolent resistance. The great majority of students are opposed to Chávez, as evidenced by the multitudinous marches that have taken place in Venezuela since 2007 and by the fact that most

of the elected leaders of student government organizations are partisans of the opposition. These students are in favor of a shift of resources
and the strengthening of programs and institutions to help the poor.
They oppose Chávez for a number of reasons, but what most angers
them is Chávez's cult of personality and one-man rule. They want their
political freedom to choose and the idea that a *caudillo* may govern
their children and grandchildren is totally unacceptable.

AND FINALLY, it should be added that if Bolívar was the hero, for him,
of the nineteenth century and Castro of the twentieth, Chávez will
surely seek the same glory in the twenty-first. And he may let tensions
build to the breaking point. He very well might, as some socialists used
to say, sharpen the contradictions. And then Venezuela, as has happened too often in its past history, could be plunged into a new world
not of redemption but of blood.

Epilogue

In 1984 I had a conversation on Mexican television with Octavio Paz, who had just turned seventy. Although we spoke about many things, I was especially interested in the tension (and, in a way, the contradiction) that I perceived between his relatively late commitment to political liberalism and his ongoing admiration for the three ancient traditions of Mexico: the Spanish, the Catholic, and the Indian. In his *The Labyrinth of Solitude*, he had characterized the nineteenth century as the time of an unfortunate rupture with these traditions. In Mexico (and throughout Latin America) the nineteenth had been the century of classic liberalism and, for Paz, an age of loss, preceded by the "communion" (*comunión*—an important word in Paz's poetic vocabulary) of the Colony (the three centuries of New Spain), when, Paz asserted, "all men and all races had found a place, a justification and a meaning."

Twenty-five years later, he still had his doubts about the liberal tradition into which he had been born. He had just published his great book on Sor Juana Inés de la Cruz and her entrapment within the pressures of Catholic orthodoxy. He could not ignore the darker aspects of the long colonial period—its despotism, its corporate and hierarchical structure, the absence of freedom and criticism, the power of the Holy Inquisition—but he still felt a nostalgia (which he considered characteristic of his generation) for the "living, social and spiritual order" of Catholic and monarchical New Spain. He was fully aware of the social progress that nineteenth-century liberalism had brought to Mexico, separating church and state, abolishing many unjust privileges, establishing the legal equality of all Mexicans. But liberalism, by itself,

could not lead to "the birth of a new order." It was for him a "superfi-
cial revolution" spurred by intellectuals and a minority of the middle
class. It could not be compared to the "much deeper revolution" that
resulted from the introduction of Christianity. It had not penetrated
to the depths of Mexican life (*al país profundo*). It had not created a new
"order . . . a harmony between beliefs, ideas and actions."

For decades, Paz had believed that the Mexican Revolution and,
most especially, an expected socialist revolution could reestablish an
organic and humanly beneficial state of "order." Nor was he alone
in his hopes. Various generations of thinkers, teachers, students, and
Latin American guerrilla fighters had shared this conviction, and
they thought of themselves not as mere reformers but more truly as
redeemers.

The twentieth-century criticism of nineteenth-century liberalism
spread through Europe after World War I, not only in leftist voices but
from thinkers as diverse as T. S. Eliot, Oswald Spengler, and Sigmund
Freud. It would reach Latin America in the 1920s, merged with the prestige of the Soviet Union and the aura of Marxism, which had inspired
the imagination and expectations of much of the world, like a new religion. In Latin America it encountered especially fertile ground, due
to ancestral social problems like poverty, inequality, and racism as well
as grievances arising from the crisis of 1898 and the long sequence of
conflicts (cultural, political, economic, and military) between the two
Americas—in José Enrique Rodó's terms, Ariel and Caliban. But the
attraction, across the twentieth century, of redemptive ideology and
growing anti-Americanism cannot be explained solely by a "nostalgia
for order" that has lingered (though with diminished force) right up to
our own time. It is also in part due to the survival of that antique order
itself, the mental imprint upon us of the "two Majesties," the Monarchy
and the Church, the sword and the cross.

The influence of the monarchy survived in our countries, in a reduced but evident form, a half-buried state of mind, a political culture
endowed with the terminology of "State," "people," "popular sovereignty," and "Revolution," though with a significance quite different,

often directly opposed, to the Anglo-Saxon usages of these terms. The American historian Richard Morse (1922–2001) deeply explored this context of contradictions, especially in his important and influential book *El Espejo de Próspero* (Prospero's Mirror), in 1982, which has never been published in English. He pointed to the essential conflict between Latin American and Anglo-Saxon political philosophies. In the nineteenth and early twentieth centuries, English and American thinkers for the most part had based their ideas on John Locke and (to a lesser degree) Thomas Hobbes. They argued for the force of human reason, for the individual conscience as the source of political power, for civic tolerance and a social contract that could limit naturally occurring violence and organize a life in common for society. Some Latin American theorists had adopted these imported ideas, but far more central and pervasive was the tradition stemming from the Catholic neo-scholastics, like the Jesuit Francisco Suárez (1548–1617), who had renovated the current of analysis emanating from St. Thomas Aquinas.

In contrast to the Hobbesian assumption of a state (if unregulated) of individual egos in automatic conflict, Suárez sees "an ordered whole in which the will of the collectivity and that of the prince are in harmony, illuminated by natural law and in the interest of civil felicity and the common good." The state is seen as paternal, protective, and corporative, an "organic architecture," a "mystical body." It is a father, dominating its subjects for their own good and kept in order not by the dictates of free individuals but by objective, external precepts of natural law. And the most important point is that "the people" are the original reservoir of sovereignty (delegated to them by God) but, as the consequence of a primal political pact, they in turn not only have delegated this sovereignty but have transferred it entirely to the prince or monarch, who then (in a process similar to the transubstantiation accomplished by the Mass) becomes the coordinating center of society.

This alienation of power from the people to the monarch is total and extremely difficult to revoke. The monarch can act according to his "royal will" and the people must accept it, provided that the monarch does not violate the original conditions of the pact and keeps to

the recognized norms of justice. And this proviso leaves a tiny opening through which the pact may be terminated. If the people judge
the prince to be a "tyrant," the option exists (in a society where public
criticism could not occur and a popular vote was inconceivable) of de-
position, insurrection, and, in the most extreme need, the killing of
the tyrant: "tyrannicide," an extreme and very unlikely action, never
implemented in the monarchical history of Spain (though it occurred
in France and England).

But two and a half centuries before Rousseau, Suárez had elaborated a theory similar to the Swiss Frenchman's notion of the "general will," which decisively influenced the outbreak and development
of the French Revolution. The Jesuit specifies that a ruler can only be
executed if his acts of tyranny and injustice are "public and manifest."
Action would be taken by a collective "we," not at all resembling the
free and democratic decisions of a collection of individuals but rather a
kind of "all" that was indivisible and not subject to appeal, the Voice of
God, the Will of the Nation united and expressed in the public square.
And this concept has been passed down through the centuries most
clearly by the great Spanish playwrights of the Golden Age. Only in
the Spanish language does a great literature exist that contains, almost
as a genre, the repeated theme of a people insurgent against its rulers,
though the revolts are not directed against the monarch himself, the
original beneficiary of the primal pact, but against his governors and
other local powers. There are at least ninety-four plays whose plotting
incorporates this kind of insurrection.

The other colonial Majesty, the Catholic Church, has oscillated
between the commitment to a closed and intolerant hierarchical society and a populist collectivism, directed toward relieving a society
oppressed by poverty, inequality, and injustice. This second tendency,
embodied most remarkably in Father Bartolomé de las Casas, the original protector of the Indians, was passed on to university-educated elites
of the twentieth century, transferred from the redemptive fathers to
the modern civic and revolutionary redeemers.

Latin American Marxists, both theorists and men of action, found fertile soil in this old idea of the sovereign people in insurrection. Our countries in the twentieth century sometimes seemed to be a fresh stage for the dramas of the Spanish Golden Age, with its peoples (legitimately) in revolt against the "evil government" (*mal gobierno*) of military dictators, frequently supported by Washington. (These military governments, it should be stressed, were criminal seizures of power and generally replete with authoritarian outrages while at their very worst—in Argentina, Chile, and elsewhere—they were regimes of mass murder.) But once the process of overthrowing a tyrant has been completed, the redeemers have too often (as happened in Nicaragua) given power to a modern version of the absolute monarch, individual or collective, rather than instituting a liberal democracy with a social or even socialist direction.

NOT ALL the redeemers treated in this book have felt a nostalgia for the ancient order. The monarchical tradition is completely alien, for instance, to the ideas of José Martí. Only at a tangent was his life and work touched by the cultural universe of Catholicism. But without considering the underlying Catholic culture within which he lived and died, one cannot understand the impact of his martyrdom nor the myth that has survived his short life. And it may be an exaggeration to find elements of a new Catholicism in the writings of Rodó, but it is nevertheless certain that he was so read and interpreted both in his own lifetime and later.

In Vasconcelos, the ancient inspiration is abundantly clear. His emphasis on education was explicitly inspired by the redemptive labors of the sixteenth-century missionaries. The indigenist Marxism of Mariátegui (which he himself described as a new "religion") cannot be understood without considering Latin American Catholic culture; nor the connection of Eva Perón, in life and death, with her "shirtless" loyalists intent on the righting of wrongs; nor the Christlike impact (and postmortem sanctification) of Che Guevara; nor the original Marxism of Octavio Paz and his subsequent conversion away from these ideas, assumed with the guilt of the convert and the passion of a Crusader.

Liberation theology was of course for Bishop Samuel Ruiz a natural development of this tradition and even in the histrionic Subcomandante Marcos (pupil of the Jesuits, Marxist, storyteller, and guerrilla) the aspiration is discernible toward an earlier order, an archaic indigenous utopia.

Little trace of Catholic schemata appears in the work of our two greatest novelists, but in both there is a crucial confrontation with the First Majesty, the all-powerful monarch who is "of the same substance" (in the words of the neo-scholastics) as his people, a figure of power toward which García Márquez, in both his literary and personal life, has directed his veneration and Vargas Llosa has criticized and condemned.

Hugo Chávez is something other, a person with no nostalgia at all. He is a postmodern mélange of redemptive ideologies, theories of heroism and Caribbean authoritarianism, without a trace of liberal or democratic conviction. His dream is of a monarchy erected on the base of "21st-century socialism," a new and definitive consubstantiation of the *caudillo* and his people, which he sees as having been already achieved only by Fidel Castro. Chávez envisions himself as a continental redeemer and has come perilously close to the claim of being not only the earthly representative of a divinized Bolívar but his reincarnation.

It is a strange aspiration and opposed to the nature of Bolívar himself (despite his authoritarian tendencies), who rejected the monarchical past, refused to be crowned emperor, was opposed to social revolution, and feared that the centrifugal tendencies of the new federalist republics would nourish *caudillos,* popular insurrections, and even anarchy. He favored a government that would be "paternal" and centralized but within a strong republican context, in a sense the Thomist paradigm limited and controlled by laws.

SINCE 1989, for the first time in our history, all the countries of Latin America, with the single exception of Cuba, have adopted the procedures of electoral democracy. Many now show a marked dedication to competitive economic growth along with programs that further social justice. Such governments, when truly committed to democracy, are in line with Octavio Paz's final position: "a reconciliation of the two great political traditions of liberalism and socialism . . . the theme of our time." The phrase reflects the present-day consensus in Latin America. And in general, the region seems to have freed itself of our two most endemic evils, militarism and the cult of the *caudillo*. But the influence of the ancient order has not died. The temptation of political absolutism and ideological orthodoxy, emanating above all from contemporary Cuba and Venezuela, is still alive and dangerous.

As long as there are nations immersed in poverty and inequality, redeemers will appear and seek to lead and liberate those peoples. Some of them will propose extreme solutions. But the process of democracy—often fragmentary and gradualist and perhaps less exciting than other alternatives—has shown more success in confronting such problems. And whatever solutions are proposed and instituted, the people of a country must have the absolute right to affirm or reject programs and leaders in the privacy of the voting booth, within the simple but profoundly moving atmosphere of honestly conducted elections.

Sources

EPIGRAPH

The epigraph is from "La letra y el cetro," *Plural* 13, October 1972.

JOSÉ MARTÍ

My major sources were the writings of Martí himself: his letters, articles, and to a lesser degree his poems. I worked with the electronic edition of his *Obras Completas* (Centro de Estudios Martianos y Karisma Digital, Havana, 2001, on CD-ROM) but also with the print edition (Lex, Havana, 1946) and other collections, especially his *Epistolario* in five volumes (Colección Textos Martianos, Editorial de Ciencias Sociales, Havana, 1993) and the three-volume edition of his *Obras Escogidas* (Editorial de Ciencias Sociales, Havana, 2002), his *Nuestra América* (Biblioteca Ayacucho, 1985), and his *Poesía completa: Edición crítica* (UNAM, Mexico, 1998). I also drew biographical information from *El diario del soldado*, a biographical account by a close friend of Martí, Fermín Valdés Domínguez, available at www.josemarti.org/temas/biografía/amigos.

For his ideas on democratic government and republics, I consulted his *El presidio político en Cuba* and *La República Española ante la revolución cubana*. Both can be found in *Obras completas*. Most of his articles written in the United States (often dealing with his life in New York and including his pieces on the death of Marx and on revolutionary violence) are in the five volumes of *En los Estados Unidos: Escenas Norteamericanas* (volumes 9–12 of the *Obras Completas* and also volume 13: *Norteamérica, Letras, pintura y artículos varios*).

Among the considerable number of biographies and biographical articles on Martí, I found the following particularly relevant: *Martí, escritor*, by Andrés Iduarte (Joaquín Mortiz, México, 1982); on his period in Mexico: *Martí en México, recuerdos de una época*, by Alfonso Herrera Franyutti (Conaculta, 1996); for his place in the history of literary modernism: *Las corrientes literarias en la América Hispána*, by Pedro Henríquez Ureña (Fondo de Cultura Económica [hereafter FCE], 1949) and "La poesía de Martí y el modernismo: examen de un malentendido" by Emir Rodríguez Monegal in *Número*, 1a. época, n 22, January to March 1953. The record of his unhappy love life and his relation to his daughter are detailed in José Miguel Oviedo's *La niña de Nueva York* (FCE, 1989). Hugh Thomas in *Cuba: The Pursuit of Freedom* (Da Capo, New York, 1998) discusses his role in Cuban history, as does Rafael Rojas in *José Martí: la Invención de Cuba* (Editorial Colibrí, 1997). How his image was used by the modern Cuban Revolution is analyzed in an article by Enrico Mario Santi, "José Martí y la Revolución Cubana," in *Vuelta*, no. 121, December 1986. For the role of Martí within Caribbean culture, I consulted the great book by Gordon K. Lewis: *Main Currents in Caribbean Thought: The Historical Evolution of Caribbean Society in Its Ideological Aspects, 1492–1900* (University of Nebraska Press, 2004). Very useful on the literary and spiritual impact of Martí were the letters and notes of Miguel de Unamuno (Archivo José Martí, Ministerio de Educación, Cuba, núm. II, Tomo IV, Enero Dic. No. 1, 1947). Guillermo Cabrera Infante, in *Mea Cuba* (Vuelta, Mexico, 1993), provides a moving description of his tragic death.

JOSÉ ENRIQUE RODÓ

I based my study primarily on the writings of José Enrique Rodó himself: *Obras completas*, with an introduction, excellent prologue, and notes by Emir Rodríguez Monegal, 2nd ed. (Aguilar, Madrid, 1967), and on *José Enrique Rodó: La América Nuestra*, compilation and prologue by Arturo Ardao (Casa de las Américas, 1970). I also consulted the Ayacucho edition (1993) of *Ariel* and *Motivos de Proteo*. His letters can be found in *Obra póstuma*, volume 17 of the *Obras completas*.

Biographies and interpretations of Rodó that I found of value included *Rodó: Medio siglo de Ariel (Su significación y trascendencia literario-filosófica)* by Carlos Real de Azúa, the foremost specialist in the works of Rodó (Academia Nacional de Letras, Uruguay, 2001) and *Marmoreal Olympus: José Enrique Rodó and Spanish American Nationalism*, by David Brading (Centre for Latin American Studies, University of Cambridge, 1998). On the final collapse of the Spanish Empire: *El fin del imperio español (1898–1923)*, by Sebastián Balfour (Crítica, Barcelona, 1997). An important landmark in anti-imperialist criticism is "To the person sitting in darkness," by Mark Twain, published in *North American Review* in February 1901, to be found in *Tales, Speeches, Essays, and Sketches* (Penguin, New York, 1994). On the American influence on Mexico's 1824 Constitution and Lorenzo de Zavala: *La Independencia de México. Textos de su historia. Vol. II. El constitucionalismo: un logro* (SEP-Instituto Mora, Mexico, 1985). The quotation from Simón Bolívar is in *Discursos y proclamas* (Biblioteca Ayacucho, Caracas, 2007). Also relevant is his "Carta de Jamaica" in *Doctrina del libertador* (Biblioteca Ayacucho, Caracas, 1976). The quotation from Faustino Domingo Sarmiento is in his *Viajes* (Unesco, ALLCA—F.C.E., Archivos 27, Nanterre, France, 1996). The texts by Justo Sierra are in his *En tierra yanquee* (Tipográfica de la impresora del Timbre, Mexico, 1897). For the Spanish reaction to their defeat in 1898: Ángel Ganivet, *El porvenir de España*, en *Obras completas*, volume 2 (Aguilar, Madrid, 1957). Useful on the ideological and cultural misunderstandings between the two Americas are the articles by Tulio Halperin Donghi ("Dos siglos de reflexiones sudamericanas") and Enrique Krauze ("Mirándolos a ellos"), both to be found in the collection *La brecha entre América Latina y Estados Unidos* (FCE, 2006). Kipling's "The White Man's Burden" first appeared in *McClure's*, February 12, 1899. On the image and uses of Shakespeare's Caliban within Latin American culture: Rubén Darío in *El Tiempo*, Buenos Aires, May 20, 1898, collected in *El Modernismo visto por los modernistas*, edited by Ricardo Gullón (Labor, Barcelona, 1980) and "Caliban," by Ernest Renán in *Drames philosophiques* (Calman-Lévy, Paris, 1923). The quotation from Groussac is from *Del Plata al Niágara* (Administración de la Biblioteca de Buenos Aires, 1897).

On the influence of Rodó's *Ariel* in Latin America: the books of

Pedro Henríquez Ureña, *Las corrientes literarias en la América Hispána* (FCE, 1949); *Obra crítica* (FCE, 1981); and *La utopía de América* (FCE, 1989). Also Emir Rodríguez Monegal's "El maestro de la Belle Epoque," in *Revista de la Universidad de México*, vol. 26, no. 2, October 1971. On Rodó in Spain: Rafael Altamira, prologue to *Liberalismo y jacobinismo de José Enrique Rodó* (Editorial Cervantes, Barcelona, 1926).

The poem "A Roosevelt," by Rubén Darío, is in his *Poesías completas* (FCE, Biblioteca Americana, 1984). On Alfredo Palacios: the essay by Mariátegui: "Alfredo Palacios" in *Temas De Nuestra América*, in *Obras completas*, vol. 12. On Manuel Ugarte, I consulted his article "El peligro yanqui," in *El País*, Buenos Aires, October 19, 1901, in the Biblioteca Nacional de la República Argentina, while his "Carta abierta al presidente de los Estados Unidos" was published in many Latin American newspapers. His writings have been collected in *La Nación Latinoamericana* (Ayacucho, Caracas, 1978). On the university reforms of 1918: *La Reforma Universitaria (1918–1930)* (Biblioteca Ayacucho, Caracas). On Deodoro Roca: *Entre influencias y olvidos*, by Fernando Pedró (Asterión XXI, *Revista cultural*). On Thomas Carlyle in the writings of Rodó, see Rodó's *Motivos de Proteo* and *El mirador de Próspero*. On the influence of Carlyle in Latin America: *Las democracias latinas de América*, by Francisco García Calderón (Biblioteca Ayacucho, Caracas, 1985). My description of Rodó's final years is based on the above-mentioned biographies.

JOSÉ VASCONCELOS

The major source for information on Vasconcelos continues to be his classic autobiography in four volumes: *Ulises criollo*, 1935; *La tormenta*, 1936; *El desastre*, 1938; and *El proconsulado*, 1939, which I used in its original edition published by Ediciones Botas. I also made use of his collected letters, especially *Las Cartas políticas de José Vasconcelos*, edited by Alfonso Taracena (Editora Librería, Mexico, 1959) and *Vasconcelos–Alfonso Reyes: Correspondence* (IFAL, Mexico, 1976), compiled by Claude J. Fell.

For the cultural environment before, during, and after the Mexican Revolution, I applied and expanded the research already done for my books *Caudillos culturales en la Revolución Mexicana* (Siglo XXI, Mexico, 1976) and *Daniel Cosío Villegas, Una biografía intelectual* (Joaquín Mortiz, Mexico, 1980). On his childhood, youth, and family life, I conducted interviews in 1988 with his daughter Carmen and son José Ignacio Vasconcelos. I also consulted two articles by John Skirius: "Génesis de Vasconcelos" (*Vuelta* 37, December 1979), and "Mocedades de Vasconcelos" (*Vuelta* 43, May 1980). For his time as Secretary of Education: the book by Claude J. Fell, *Los años del águila, 1920–1925* (UNAM, Mexico, 1989). On the Vasconcelos movement of 1929, I interviewed Andrés Henestrosa and Alejandro Gómez Arias in May 1989 and explored the exhaustive work of Skirius: *José Vasconcelos y la cruzada de 1929* (Siglo XXI, 1978) and Henestrosa's article "La campaña presidencial de 1929," in *Excélsior*, February 1982.

From Vasconcelos's vast production and his work as an editor of magazines, I made ample use of his *Obras completas*, published between 1957 and 1961 (Libreros Mexicanos Unidos, Mexico), and the anthology *Páginas escogidas* (Ediciones Botas, 1940). I also consulted "Cuando el águila destroce a la serpiente," *El Maestro*, 1921; "Un llamado Cordial," *El maestro*, 1921; *El movimiento educativo en México* (issued as a pamphlet, Mexico, 1922); and his "Discourse on the Day of the Teacher," 1924; the magazine *La Antorcha*, Segundo Período, 13 números: abril de 1931 a abril de 1932. For his connections with Nazi Germany, *La revista Timón y José Vasconcelos*, Itzhak Bar-Lewaw (Edimex, Mexico, 1971). Also: "La inteligencia se impone," in *Timón*, June 8, 1940, num. 16. On his final years: "Siempre he sido cristiano," Sergio Avilés Parra, (*Mañana*, Mexico) January 24, 1948; "Vasconcelos, voz clamante en el desierto," Emmanuel Carballo in the "México en la Cultura" supplement to *Novedades* (January 4, 1959); Interview with Vasconcelos, in *Señal, semanario católico* (July 5, 1959).

Among the most useful books that deal with him are *Ensayos y notas*, by Daniel Cosío Villegas (Editorial Hermes, 1966); Jorge Cuesta's

Poemas y ensayos. Tomo III (UNAM, Mexico 1964); Manuel Gómez Mo-rin's *1915* (CULTURA, 1927); Alfonso Reyes, his *Obras completas*, volumes 12, 2, and 4; *Diálogo de los libros*, by Julio Torri (FCE, 1980).

JOSÉ CARLOS MARIÁTEGUI

Mariátegui's collected works fill twenty volumes: *Obras completas de José Carlos Mariátegui* (Amauta, Lima—cited below as *O.C.*), a collection that includes (in volumes 10 and 20) texts by various authors about Mariátegui and about the project of Mariategui's magazine *Amauta*. I also frequently consulted his works at http://www.patriaroja.org.pe/docs_adic/obras_mariategui/, and the facsímile edition of the magazine *Amauta* (Editora Amauta, 1926–30, nos. 1–32).

The major sources on his life: *Etapas de su vida*, by María Wiesse (*O.C.*, vol. 10, Amauta, 12th ed., Lima, 1987); *Introducción a Mariátegui*, by Aníbal Quijano (Ediciones Era, Mexico, 1982); and *Mariátegui y su tiempo*, by Armando Bazán (*O.C.*, vol. 20, Amauta, Lima, 1969). *La Creación Heroica de José Carlos Mariátegui, T. I. La Edad de Piedra (1894–1919)* by Guillermo Rouillon (Editorial Arica, Lima, 1975) supplied a great deal of information on his childhood and youth. Also of use was a biographical documentary, produced by TV Perú, *Sucedió en el Perú: José Carlos Mariátegui*, http://www.youtube.com/watch?v=20Uc6TQgjjo&p=AED877BBD07839A7&playnext=1&index=1).

The fatal encounter between the poet José Santos Chocano and the young intellectual Edwin Elmore was recorded by his colleagues, including Mariátegui, in issue no. 3 of *Amauta*. The quarrels about Vasconcelos are documented in "Poetas y bufones," in the *Obras completas de José Santos Chocano* (Aguilar, Madrid, 1972), and reconstructed by José Emilio Pacheco in "Leopoldo Lugones y el amor en la hora de la espada," *Letras Libres*, no. 10, October 1999.

The famous speech of Manuel González Prada is available at http://es.wikisource.org/wiki/Discurso_en_el_Politeama; and the writings of María Wiesse and Aníbal Quijano treat the influence of González Prada on Mariátegui and Haya de la Torre. The period that Mariátegui called his "stone age" (his connections with Abraham Valdelomar, the magazine *Colónida*, and his work for various newspapers) is described by his biographers, especially Guillermo Rouillon. It is the time when he first turns his attention to Rumi Maqui, for which see *La utopía arcaica: José María Arguedas y las ficciones del indigenismo*, by Mario Vargas Llosa (FCE, Mexico, 1996).

The influences upon him (and Mariátegui's insights) in Europe, first in Paris and then in Italy, are treated in his *La escena contemporánea* (*O.C.*, vol. 1, Amauta, Lima, 1957), where he discusses his aesthetic and moral reactions to fascism, World War I, and his encounters with (among others) Barbusse, Sorel, and Rolland, whose ideas deeply impressed him. These years are also presented in his *Cartas de Italia* (*O.C.*, vol. 15, Amauta, Lima, 1969). The quotation from Richard M. Morse is from *El espejo de próspero. Un estudio de la dialéctica del nuevo mundo* (Siglo XXI, Mexico, 1982). Also during this time, Mariátegui began to develop his particular form of Marxism: see his *Defensa del marxismo* (*O.C.*, vol. 5, Amauta, Lima, 1959), in which he also describes his intellectual contacts with Croce, Gentile, and Gramsci. From his *Cartas de Italia*, I drew his comments on fascism. His interpretation of surrealism can be found in his *El artista y la época* (*O.C.*, vol. 6, Amauta, Lima, 1957).

The relations between Mariátegui and Víctor Raúl Haya de la Torre, and their differing attitudes toward APRA, are dealt with by his biographers (already cited) and Mariátegui's final position on this issue is in issue no. 17 of *Amauta* (Facsimile edition, Lima). Also relevant are the comments of Víctor Raúl Haya de la Torre in his *Obras completas* (Juan Mejía Baca, Lima, 1985) and two books by other authors: *Víctor Raúl. Biografía,* by Felipe Cossío del Pomar (Pachacútec, Lima, 1995) and *El pueblo continente. Ensayos para una interpretación de América Latina,* by Atenor Orrego (Centro de Documentación Andina, Lima, 1987). In Mariátegui's *Temas de Nuestra América* (*O.C.*, vol. 12, Amauta, Lima, 1960), he delineates his views of the Mexican Revolution.

His analysis of Peru is inextricably linked with his indigenism, Marxism, and utopian thinking. For his masterwork, the *7 ensayos de interpretación de la realidad peruana*, I used the edition of Aníbal Quijano, with notes and chronology by Elizabeth Garrels (Biblioteca Ayacucho, 2nd ed., Caracas, 1995) and the relevant material (as well as other themes) in his *El alma matinal y otras estaciones del hombre de hoy* (*O.C.*, vol. 3. Amauta, Lima, 1959), his *Defensa del marxismo* (*O.C.*, vol. 5, Amauta, Lima, 1959); *Peruanicemos al Perú* (*O.C.*, vol. 11, Amauta, Lima), *Temas de nuestra América* (vol. 12, Amauta, Lima, 1960) and finally *Ideología y política* (*O.C.*, vol. 13, Amauta, Lima, 1957). Some of his important interpretations of politics are to be found in his *Historia de la crisis mundial. Conferencias pronunciadas en 1923* (*O.C.*, vol. 8, Amauta, Lima, 1959).

The central treatment of the publishing house Amauta is in volume 19 of his *Obras Completas*. It contains a narrative description of the enterprise, from its origins to its demise after the death of Mariátegui and contains a general index.

For the quotation abut myth and the religious aspects of Marxism, see his *El alma matinal*, while his comment on Roosevelt and Thoreau is from "El Ibero-americanismo y Pan-americanismo," in *Temas de Nuestra América*.

Along with his *7 Ensayos*, *Peruanicemos al Perú* is the principal site for his indigenist ideas. Also relevant on this theme is *Tempestad en los Andes*, by Luis Valcárcel (Polémica, Lima, 1927), from which book Mariátegui drew his description of the *ayllu* and the *curacas*. His debates with Luis Alberto Sánchez are amply discussed in Alberto Flores Galindo, *Buscando un Inca* (Horizonte, Lima, 1986). The same author describes Mariátegui's divergences from more orthodox Marxists in his *La agonía de Mariátegui: la polémica con la Komintern* (Centro de Estudios y Promoción del Desarrollo, Lima, 1980).

OCTAVIO PAZ

For Paz's view of his own life, I found the following material especially useful: his short autobiographical book *Itinerario* (FCE, Mexico, 1993) as well as the series of interviews published in volume 15 of *Miscelánea III, Entrevistas*, from his *Obras Completas* (Círculo de Lectores and FCE, Mexico, 2003). Also the interview (with Claude Fell) in the magazine

Plural (November 1975) titled "Vuelta a *El laberinto de la soledad*" on the genesis of his most famous work of prose, and my own biographical interview with him (in March 1984) collected in my book *Travesía liberal* (Tusquets, 2003).

Important autobiographical material comes directly from his poems, collected (along with all his prose writings) in the fifteen volumes of his *Obras completas* (FCE). A good selection of his poems, mostly from his later work, has been edited and translated by Eliot Weinberger in *Collected Poems of Octavio Paz* (New Directions, 1991), though all selections from Paz's poems and prose used here have been newly translated from the Spanish by Hank Heifetz.

My information on Paz's grandfather Ireneo comes from his memoirs, *Algunas campañas* (FCE, Mexico, 1996), dealing with Ireneo's long period as a rebel and fighter on the liberal side in the nineteenth-century Mexican civil wars; from Napoleón Rodríguez's *Ireneo Paz: Letras y espada liberal* (Ediciones Fontanara, 2002); and especially from the prologue of Felipe Gálvez, *Hoguera que fue* (UAM, 2004). I also consulted facsimiles of Ireneo's magazine *El Padre Cobos* and his newspaper *La Patria*, as well as Octavio Paz's memories of his grandfather in his own poetry and prose and his preface, "Silueta de Ireneo Paz," to *Algunas campañas*.

Octavio Paz Solórzano, the poet's father, left no memoir but a number of articles on the Zapatista Revolution and one biography of Zapata, published in 1986 by his son Octavio, "Tres revoluciones, tres testimonios," and *Zapata* (EOSA, 1988). I also examined various articles by him in magazines and newspapers of his time, such as *Crisol*, *La Prensa*, and *El Universal* and drew information on his life as a rebel from the newspaper *La Patria*. The report of his death appeared in "El Licenciado Paz muerto bajo las ruedas de un tren," *El Universal*, March 13, 1935. His letters to Zapata can be found in the Archivo de Gildardo Magaña in the Centro de Estudios Históricos de Condumex.

The most important anthology of Octavio Paz's articles on Mexico is *México en la obra de Octavio Paz* (FCE, Mexico, 1987), in three volumes: *El peregrino en su patria*, *Generaciones y semblanzas*, and *Los privilegios de la vista*. Another major anthology (compiled by Enrico Mario Santí) is *Primeras letras* (Vuelta, 1988), which contains his major essays and articles written between 1931 and 1944. I am also grateful to Hugo Verani for his excellent *Bibliografía crítica de Octavio Paz, 1931–1996* (FCE, Mexico) and I made frequent use of Paz's various books of essays, especially *Octavio Paz en España: Antología de textos y poemas* (FCE, Mexico, 2007); two editions of *El laberinto de la soledad* (Cuadernos Americanos, 1950; and FCE, Mexico, 1960); *Las peras del olmo* (Biblioteca Breve, Barcelona, 1971); *Corriente alterna* (Siglo XXI Editores, 1967); *Posdata* (Siglo XXI Editores, 1970); *Los hijos del limo* (Seix Barral, Barcelona, 1974); *El ogro filantrópico: Historia y política 1971–1978* (Joaquín Mortiz, Mexico, 1979); *Sor Juana Inés de la Cruz o las trampas de la fe* (Seix Barral, Barcelona, 1982); *Tiempo Nublado* (Seix Barral, Barcelona, 1983); *Hombres en su siglo* (Seix Barral, Barcelona, 1984); *Poesía, mito, revolución* (Vuelta, 1989); *Pequeña crónica de grandes días* (FCE, Mexico, 1990). Also of interest are Paz's discourses at the conference "Encuentro Vuelta: La experiencia de la libertad," proceedings of which were published in 5 volumes, and his articles on the conflict in the state of Chiapas, published in *Vuelta*: "Chiapas: Nudo ciego o tabla de salvación," February 1994; "Chiapas: hechos, dichos, gestos," March 1994; and "Chiapas: La selva lacandona," February 1996.

Essential to my presentation of Paz was a consideration of the magazines he directed and the articles he published in them, the earlier magazines reissued as a collection by FCE: *Barandal* (1931), *Cuadernos del Valle de México* (1932–33), *Taller* (1938–41), *El Hijo Pródigo* (April–September 1943), *Plural* (1971–76), and especially *Vuelta* (1976–98). I also refer to articles that appeared elsewhere, like the debate between Paz and Carlos Monsiváis in *Proceso*, December 19–January 23, 1978, which can also be found in *El pensamiento político de Octavio Paz*, by Xavier Rodríguez Ledesma (UNAM and Plaza y Valdés, 1996).

Paz was a prolific correspondent and many significant statements can be found in his letters. Unpublished correspondence that I was able to consult include his love letters to Elena Garro (June 22–August 10, 1935) and his correspondence with José Luis Martínez and Victor Serge.

Archived at the Benson Latin American Collection in the University of Texas at Austin are the letters to Octavio Barreda. In the Harry Ransom Center at the same university are his letters to Charles Tomlinson. His exchanges with José Bianco are in the Houghton Library of Harvard University. In the Archivo Condumex is his diplomatic correspondence with Antonio Carrillo Flores between 1964 and 1968, partially published in "Cartas a la cancillería," *Vuelta*, March 1995.

Published collections of his letters include *Correspondencia Alfonso Reyes/Octavio Paz* (1939–59), edited by Anthony Stanton (FCE, Mexico, 1998) and *Octavio Paz/Arnaldo Orfila, Cartas cruzadas* (Siglo XXI Editores, 2006). His connections with France are detailed in Octavio Paz, *Jardines errantes: Correspondencia con J. C. Lambert 1952–1992* (Seix Barral, Barcelona, 2008) and with Spain in Octavio Paz, *Memorias y palabras: Correspondencia con Pere Gimferrer, 1966–1997* (Seix Barral, Barcelona, 1999). For his connections with the magazine *Plural* and the tensions within the culture and politics of the 1970s, see his *Cartas a Tomás Segovia* (1957–85) (FCE, Mexico, 2008). For his critical distancing from the Cuban Revolution, I consulted two articles by Rafael Rojas: "Lecturas cubanas de Octavio Paz," *Vuelta*, June 1998, and "El gato escaldado: Viaje póstumo de Octavio Paz a la Habana," *Anuario de la Fundación Octavio Paz*, no. 1, 1999. For his position in Mexican literature during the 1970s, I found his correspondence with José Gaos useful: "José Gaos a Octavio Paz, 12 diciembre 1963," in *Obras completas de José Gaos* (UNAM, Mexico, 1992) and for his connection with José Revueltas, the latter's *Las evocaciones requeridas*, volumes 25 and 26 (Ediciones Era, 1983). I located materials on Paz's period as a teacher and a bureaucrat in the Archivo Histórico de la Comisión Nacional Bancaria and the Archivo Histórico de la Secretaría de Educación Pública.

The chapter contains various references to articles about Paz. Some by his mentors and several more by friends or colleagues, among them José Alvarado, Efraín Huerta, and José Luis Martínez, like "Imagen primera del poeta," by José Luis Martínez, in *Luz espejeante: Octavio Paz ante la crítica*, selection and prologue by Enrico Mario Santí (UNAM and Ediciones Era, 2009). Very important is the book by Elena Garro,

Memorias de España 1937 (Siglo XXI Editores, 1992). For Paz's relationship with Elena Garro (mainly for the unpublished material, not for its interpretation), I used Patricia Rosas Lopategui, *Testimonios sobre Elena Garro* (Ediciones Castillo, Monterrey, 1998). I also looked at the memoir by the daughter of Paz and Garro, Helena Paz Garro's *Memorias* (Océano, 2003).

The essays by Gabriel Zaid on the guerrilla war in El Salvador and the need for elections in Nicaragua (which provoked fierce debates between Paz—and *Vuelta*—with the Mexican left in the 1980s) can be found in *De los libros al poder* (Grijalbo, 1988) while their sequel, Paz's speech at the Frankfurt Book Fair, "PRI: Hora cumplida," which led to his being burned in effigy, can be found in *Vuelta*, November 1984,"El diálogo y el ruido." My own article, "Por una democracia sin adjetivos," which also provoked debate at the time, appeared in *Vuelta* in January 1984. A good deal of the debate took place between the magazines *Nexos* and *Vuelta* and was described in the newsmagazine *Proceso*.

There is no complete biography of Octavio Paz. Works of interest on his life include the prologue by Enrico Mario Santí to *Primeras letras*, and the same author's introductory study to *El laberinto de la soledad* (Cátedra, 1993); Froylán Enciso's *Andar fronteras* (Siglo XXI Editores, 2008), which focuses on his diplomatic career; and Elena Poniatowska's *Las palabras del árbol* (Joaquín Mortiz, 2009), which includes interesting interviews with Paz in the 1950s and '60s. But the book that comes closest to being a biography is the excellent work of Guillermo Sheridan, *Poeta con paisaje: ensayos sobre la vida de Octavio Paz* (Ediciones Era, 2004), especially useful and illuminating for the period 1929–43 and for Paz's time in Spain during the Civil War.

Various sources are especially relevant for different periods of Octavio Paz's long, varied, and productive life. For his childhood, I am indebted to conversations with his widow, Marie-José Paz, and articles by relatives (like Guillermo Haro) and the close friends of his early years (like Juan Soriano). The period of his young manhood (from his dropping out of law school to his time in Yucatán and Spain and his long stay in the United States and Europe) is described by Paz in *Itinerario*. I discussed this period with the sons of some of these early friends, especially David Huerta and Octavio Novaro Peñalosa. His time with Elena Garro is in her memoirs, which must be read with caution. My description of the Mexican intellectual milieu that followed the World War II is based on conversations with José Luis Martínez and articles he wrote at the time, such as "La literatura mexicana en 1942," in *Literatura Mexicana, siglo XX* (Antigua Librería Robredo, 1949). Also useful was Elena Poniatowska's "Juan Soriano, niño de mil años," *Plaza y Janés*, 1998; Paz's articles about Soriano, collected in *Los privilegios de la vista*; Paz's articles "Antevíspera: *Taller*, 1938–1941" and "Poesía e historia (Laurel y nosotros)," both of which can be found in *Sombras de obras* (Seix Barral, 1983) as well as my own book: *Daniel Cosío Villegas: Una biografía intelectual* (Joaquín Mortiz, 1980) and my essay "Cuatro estaciones de la cultura mexicana," in *Mexicanos eminentes* (Tusquets, 1999). Many other sources for various periods of his life are mentioned within the chapter.

I first met Octavio Paz on March 10, 1976, at the funeral of Daniel Cosío Villegas, who had been my teacher. I became deputy editor of the magazine *Vuelta* in 1976 and my connection with the magazine and Paz himself continued until his death in April 1998. Many of the events and much of the information that I present are from personal experiences I shared with Paz (as he shared his memories with me) across twenty-three years. I myself was present and heard the words to Marie-José that conclude the chapter.

EVA PERÓN

A previous version of this chapter appeared under the title of "The Blonde Leading the Blind" in *The New Republic*, February 10, 1997. The principal sources for the chapter were *Eva Perón: A Biography*, by Alicia Dujovne Ortiz, translated by Shawn Fields (St. Martin's, New York, 1996) and *Santa Evita*, by Tomás Eloy Martínez, translated by Helen Lane (Knopf, New York, 1996). Also of use was Michael Casey's *Che's*

Afterlife: The Legacy of an Image (Vintage, New York, 2009). For information and illumination on various aspects of Eva's historical period, I am grateful to the historian Enrique Zuleta Álvarez and to Dr. Vicente Massot.

CHE GUEVARA

A partial, previous version of this chapter appeared under the title "The Return of Che Guevara" in *The New Republic* on February 9, 1998.

The selections from Che's writings come from his *Obras completas*, in three volumes (Legasa, Buenos Aires, 1995–96). Other publications consulted were his *Diarios de motocicleta: Notas de un viaje por América Latina* (Planeta, Buenos Aires, 2004); *Otra vez: Diario inédito del segundo viaje por Latinoamérica* (Ediciones B., Barcelona, 2001); *Pasajes de la guerra revolucionaria: Congo* (Mondadori, Mexico, 1999); *El socialismo y el hombre nuevo* (Siglo XXI Editores, Mexico, 1977). A number of his letters are available on the Internet: *Che: Guía y ejemplo: Epistolario*, at http://www.sancristobal.cult.cu/sitios/che/epistolario.htm.

I consulted the three major biographies of Che Guevara: *Che Guevara: A Revolutionary Life*, by Jon Lee Anderson (Grove, New York, 1997); *Ernesto Guevara: también conocido como El Che*, by Paco Ignacio Taibo II, 9th ed. (Planeta–Joaquín Mortiz, Mexico, 1997); and *La vida en rojo: Una biografía del Che Guevara*, by Jorge Castañeda (Alfaguara, Mexico, 1997). Useful for a consideration of his ideas was *El pensamiento del Che Guevara*, by Michael Löwy (Siglo XXI, Mexico, 1997).

For Cuba's problems with the United States: "Rusia, Estados Unidos y América Latina," by Daniel Cosío Villegas, in *Ensayos y notas*, volume 1 (Hermes, 1966); and "Estados Unidos falla en Cuba," in *Ensayos y notas*, volume 2 (Hermes, 1966). For Che's youth in Córdoba and the family environment, I consulted with the historians Tulio Halperin Donghi and Carlos Sempat Assadourian, and drew some material from the useful script by Luis Altamira for the documentary *La infancia del Che* (Del taller de Mario Muchnik, Barcelona, 2003). For the books that interested him: *El último lector,* by Ricardo Piglia (Editorial Anagrama, Barcelona, 2005). On the ideological ferment in Córdoba: *Deodoro Roca, El hereje:* Selección y estudio preliminar, by Néstor Kohan (Editorial Biblos, Buenos Aires, 1999); and *"Manifiesto Liminar" de la Reforma Universitaria de 1918,* by Deodoro Roca (Editorial Universitaria de Córdoba, Córdoba, 1998).

Various articles by Hugo Pesce can be found in the archives of *Amauta,* Mariátegui's magazine. For Che's period in Mexico: *Retrato de Familia con Fidel,* by Carlos Franqui (Seix Barral, Barcelona, 1981). There is a discussion of Lázaro Cárdenas and the Cuban exiles in my book *Lázaro Cárdenas: El general misionero* (FCE, 1987). On Che in the Sierra Maestra, aside from the biographies and the work of Carlos Franqui mentioned above, I consulted Hugh Thomas's *Cuba: The Pursuit of Freedom* (Da Capo, New York, 1998). For a highly critical account of Che's period at the head of La Cabaña prison see "Una fría máquina de matar," by Álvaro Vargas Llosa, in *Letras Libres,* February 2007.

For Che's economic thinking, the following works were useful: "La creatividad en el pensamiento económico del Che," by Carlos Tablada, in *Nueva Internacional,* no. 2, 1991, pp. 71–99, and by Michael Löwy: *El pensamiento del Che Guevara* (Siglo XXI, Mexico, 2007). Also the articles by Carmelo Mesa Lago, "La gestión económica del Che" and "Availability and Reliability of Statistics in Socialist Cuba (Part One)" in *Latin American Research Review,* no. 4, 1969; and "Ideological, Political and Economic Factors in the Cuban Controversy on Material Versus Moral Incentives," *Journal of International Studies and World Affairs,* no. 14, 1972, and "Problemas estructurales, política económica y desarrollo en Cuba" (1959–70), in *Desarrollo Económico,* no. 13, 1973. Also Huber Matos, *Cómo llegó la noche* (Tusquets, Tiempo de Memoria 19 Barcelona, 2002); Héctor Rodríguez Llompart, "Che Comunista y Economista," in *El Economista de Cuba,* December 2007; *La revolución cubana: 25 años después* (1984), by Hugh Thomas, G. Fauriol, and J. Weiss (Playor, Madrid) and "Soviet Economic Aid to Cuba: 1959–1964," by Robert Walters, in *International Affairs,* no. 42, 1966. The conversations, presentations, and interviews of Valtr Komarek at the conference "Encuentro de Vuelta: la experiencia de la libertad," organized by *Vuelta* in 1990, gave me the chance to document, from a firsthand source, Che's economic ideas and perspectives.

I drew information on Che as a guerrilla from Carlos Franqui's *Cuba: El libro de los doce*, by Carlos Franqui; *Memorias de un soldado cubano: Vida y muerte de la Revolución*, by "Benigno" (Daniel Alarcón Ramírez) (Tusquets, Barcelona, 1997); *El Furor y el delirio*, by Jorge Masetti (Tusquets Editores, Spain, 1999); and the two books by Régis Debray: *La guerrilla del Che* (Siglo XXI, Mexico, 2004) and his more disenchanted *Alabados sean nuestros señores* (Sudamericana, Buenos Aires, 1999). On mercenaries in the Congo, *Congo Mercenary*, by their South African commander, Mike Hoare (Paladin, 1967). Simon Reid-Henry in *Fidel and Che: A Revolutionary Friendship* (Walker, New York, 2009) offers a penetrating description and analysis of the relations between Che and Fidel. "El ángel desalmado," by Alma Guillermoprieto, in *Historia escrita*, translated by Laura Emilia Pacheco (Plaza y Janés, Mexico, 2001), discusses his youthful vision of a revolutionary future. On the guerrilla action of university students: *De los libros al poder*, by Gabriel Zaid (Grijalbo, Mexico, 1988). On Che's heritage: *Che's Afterlife: The Legacy of an Image*, by Michael Casey (Vintage, New York, 2009). On his role as a martyr, *Mea Cuba*, by Guillermo Cabrera Infante (Editorial Vuelta, Mexico, 1993).

GABRIEL GARCÍA MÁRQUEZ

Most of this chapter appeared under the title "In the Shadow of the Patriarch," in *The New Republic*, November 4, 2009.

My major sources were Gabriel García Márquez's autobiography: *Vivir para contarla* (Editorial Diana, Mexico, 2002) and the biography by Gerald Martin: *Gabriel García Márquez: A Life* (Knopf, New York, 2009). Also of importance for biographical information: *Un García Márquez desconocido*, by Plinio Apuleyo Mendoza (Emecé Editores–Editorial Planeta Colombiana, Bogotá, 2009); *El olor de la guayaba* by Plinio Apuleyo

Mendoza and Gabriel García Márquez (Mondadori, Barcelona, 1996), *García Márquez: Historia de un decidio*, by Mario Vargas Llosa (Barra, Caracas, 1971), and *El otro García Márquez: los años difíciles*, by Pedro Sorela (Mondadori, Madrid, 1988), of particular value for its discussion of the culture of the Caribbean as reflected in the work of García Márquez. Also of some interest is *García Márquez: Writer of Colombia*, by Stephen Minta (Harper & Row, New York, 1987) and *García Márquez for Beginners*, by Mariana Solanet (Writers and Readers, New York, 2001).

Among García Márquez's novels, the most relevant for this chapter were *La hojarasca* (Editorial Diana, Mexico, 1986); *El coronel no tiene quien le escriba* (Ediciones Era, Mexico, 1968); *Cien años de soledad* (Mondadori, Barcelona, 1987); *El otoño del patriarca* (Editorial Diana, Mexico, 1991); and *El general en su laberinto* (Editorial Diana, Mexico, 1994). I consulted the following collections of his articles and journalism: *Obra periodística 1: Textos costeños* (Grupo Editorial Norma, Santafé de Bogotá, 1997); *Obra periodística 2: Entre cachacos* (Grupo Editorial Norma, Santafé de Bogotá, 1997); *Obra periodística 3: De Europa y América* (Grupo Editorial Norma, Santafé de Bogotá, 1997); *Por la libre: Obra periodística 4 (1974–1995)* (Mondadori, Barcelona, 1999); and *Notas de prensa: 1980–1984* (Grupo Editorial Norma, Santafé de Bogotá, 1995).

For the history of Colombia: *Del poder y la gramática*, by Malcolm Deas (Tercer Mundo Editores, Bogotá, Caracas, and Quito, 1993); *País fragmentado, sociedad dividida: Su historia*, by Marco Palacios and Frank Safford (Grupo Editorial Norma, Bogotá, 2002). For Uribe y Uribe: *El liderazgo de Rafael Uribe: La modernización de la Nación y el Estado*, by Edgar Toro Sánchez (Federación Nacional de Cafeteros de Colombia, Bogotá, 2008). For the record of the United Fruit Company: *Close Encounters of Empire: Writing the Cultural History of U.S.-Latin American Relations*, by Gilbert M. Joseph, Catherine C. LeGrand, and Ricardo D. Salvatore (Duke University Press, Durham, N.C., 1998); and *The United Fruit Company in Latin America*, by Stacy May and Galo Plaza (National Planning Association, Washington, D.C., 1958).

On Octavio Paz and García Márquez, see the interviews by Rita

Guibert and Julián Ríos in Paz's *Obras completas* (Círculo de Lectores y Fondo de Cultura Económica, vol. 15). The text by Mario Vargas Llosa comparing *One Hundred Years of Solitude* to the epic of Amadis of Gaul is in *Sables y utopías: Visiones de América Latina* (Aguilar, Mexico, 2009). On the Latin American novels dealing with dictators: *La palabra mágica*, by Augusto Monterroso (Ediciones Era, Mexico, 1983). A valuable article on *El otoño del patriarca* is "Vasto reino de pesadumbre," by Alejandro Rossi, *Plural*, September 1975. On García Márquez as a journalist: the review of *News of a Kidnapping* by Charles Lane, *New Republic*, August 25, 1997, and Gabriel Zaid, "Relato donde no se escucha a un náufrago," *Vuelta*, April 1979. For the connections of García Márquez with Cuba and Fidel: *Coto vedado: En los reinos de Taifa*, by Juan Goytisolo (Ediciones Península, Barcelona, 2002) and *La hora final de Castro: la historia secreta detrás de la inminente caída del comunismo en Cuba*, by Andrés Oppenheimer (Vegara, Madrid, 2001). For the friendship between García Márquez and Castro: *Fidel & Gabo: A Portrait of the Legendary Friendship Between Fidel Castro and Gabriel García Márquez*, by Ángel Esteban and Stéphanie Panichelli (Pegasus, New York, 2009). For the episode of the executed boat people see the newspaper accounts in *La Jornada*, April 2, 14, 28, 29, and 30, 2003. For the address by Susan Sontag in Frankfurt: http://www.stecyl.es/prensa/031015_ep_Sontag_titere_con_cabeza.htm.

MARIO VARGAS LLOSA

Some of the material in this chapter appeared in the following articles in *The New Republic*: "Revolution's Revenge," June 23, 1986 and "Exorcisms," February 11, 2002.

The primary biographical source on Vargas Llosa is his autobiographical account, *El pez en el agua* (Seix Barral, first reprinting in Mexico, 1993). Very important were my conversations with Fernando Szyszlo in Lima in 2003 and with Vargas Llosa himself in Mexico City, in March 2010. Another important resource was *Diálogo con Vargas Llosa*, by Ricardo A. Setti (Kosmos Editorial, Mexico, 1989). Among his other writings most relevant to this chapter were the novels *La guerra del fin del mundo* (Alfaguara, Barcelona, 1997), *Historia de Mayta* (Seix Barral, Barcelona, 1984), and *La fiesta del Chivo* (Alfaguara, Bogotá, 2000), and, among his nonfiction books, *La utopía arcaica: José María Arguedas y las ficciones del indigenismo* (FCE, 1996).

On Peru as a multiracial and conflict-ridden country, see his article "El país de las mil caras," in *Contra viento y marea III (1964–1988)* (Seix Barral, first reprinting in Mexico, 1990). On his early literary and political decades, see his *Literatura y política* (ITESM/Ariel, Mexico, 2001) and *Historia secreta de una novela* (Tusquets, Barcelona, 1971).

He discusses his relationship with Cuba in *Sables y utopías: Visiones de América Latina* (Aguilar, Mexico, 2009) and in his discourse on receiving the Rómulo Gallegos Prize, "La literatura es fuego," which can be found in the *Revista Nacional de Cultura (181)*, year 29, Caracas, July–September 1967. His exchanges of letters with García Márquez, Roberto Fernández Retamar, and Haydée Santamaría are in the Archives of Mario Vargas Llosa at Princeton and his "Carta a Haydée Santamaría" in *Sables y utopías*.

On his polemics with the Cuban Revolution, see "A propósito de *Historia de un deicidio*: Va de retro," by Angel Rama, in *Marcha*, Uruguay, May 5, 1972. The perspectives and opinions of his first wife on their matrimony: *Lo que Varguitas no dijo*, by Julia Urquidi (Ediciones Última Hora, La Paz, Bolivia, 1983). On his disenchantment with Sartre and his encounter with the thought of Camus, see his *Entre Sartre y Camus* (Ediciones Huracán, Puerto Rico, 1981) and "La rebelión perpetua," interview by Danubio Torres Fierro with Mario Vargas Llosa, *Plural*, August 1975.

On his redirection toward economic liberalism and his sympathy for the ideas of Hernando de Soto, see his article "La revolución silenciosa," in *Contra viento y marea III (1964–1988)* (Seix Barral, first reprinting in Mexico, 1990). His important reportage in the 1980s, "Sangre y mugre de Uchuraccay," can also be found in that volume. Some of my comments on his presidential campaign were gathered firsthand during my presence in Peru in March 1990. On various positives and negatives of his campaign, see the review of the translation of *El pez en el agua* (A Fish in the Water) by Alan Riding in the *New York Times*, May 15, 1994. For Vargas Llosa's current praise for the American Tea Party movement, see his column "Las caras del Tea Party" in *El País*, October 10, 2010. The discussion of Vargas Llosa's views on power and dictatorship is drawn from my interviews with the writer.

SAMUEL RUIZ

Most of this chapter appeared in the article "Chiapas: The Indians' prophet," in *The New York Review of Books*, December 16, 1999.

I drew much material for the chapter from my two visits to Chiapas (September 1994 and October 1998). On both visits I interviewed Samuel Ruiz, and on my second visit, some of the figures within the Church connected in one way or another with the theological and political ferment in Chiapas: Padre Diego Andrés Lockett, Fray Gonzalo Ituarte, Padre Javier Vargas. During that week I also spoke at length with two academic specialists on the history, society, and politics of that state: Juan Pedro Viqueira and Jan de Vos.

The most useful writings by Samuel Ruiz were his *Teología bíblica de la liberación* (Editorial Jus–Librería Parroquial, Mexico, 1975) and *En esta hora de gracia: Carta pastoral con motivo del saludo de S.S el Papa Juan Pablo II a los indígenas del continente* (Ediciones Dabar, Mexico, 1993).

Books and articles on the rebellion in Chiapas: *Chiapas, el obispo de San Cristóbal y la revuelta zapatista*, by John Womack, Jr. (Cal y Arena, Mexico, 1998) and his *Rebellion in Chiapas: An Historical Reader* (New Press, New York, 1999); *Marcos: la genial impostura*, Bertrand de la Grange and Maite Rico (Editorial Aguilar, Mexico, 1998); *El caminante*, by Carlos Fazio (Espasa-Calpe, Mexico, 1994); *La rebelión de Las Cañadas*, by Carlos Tello Díaz (Cal y Arena, Mexico, 1995); *Religión, política y guerrilla en Las Cañadas de la Selva Lacandona*, by María del Carmen Legorreta Díaz (Cal y Arena, Mexico, 1998); two texts by Xóchitl Leyva and Gabriel Ascencio Franco: *Lacandonia al filo del agua* (Mexico, 1996) and "Testimonio de don Eustaquio," in "Catequistas, misioneros y tradiciones en Las Cañadas," which can be found in *Chiapas: Los rumbos de otra historia*, by Juan Pedro Viqueira and Mario Humberto Ruz (UNAM and University of Guadalajara, 1995); *Proceso catequístico en la zona tzeltal y desarrollo social (un estudio de caso)*, by Reyna Matilde Coello Castro (Universidad Autónoma de Tlaxcala, Tlaxcala, 1991). An important article in two parts appeared in the magazine *Proceso*: September 13 and 20, 1993: "Estamos buscando libertad. Los tzeltales de la selva anuncian la buena nueva."

My historical sources on the Indian theme in Mexican history were *Historia General de las Indias Occidentales y particular de la gobernación de Guatemala*, by Fray Antonio de Remesal (Porrúa, Mexico, 1988); two works by Fray Bartolomé de las Casas: *Del único modo de atraer a todos los pueblos a la verdadera religión* (FCE, Mexico, 1992) and *Historia de las Indias* (FCE, Mexico, 1992). Also *Carta al emperador: Refutación a Las Casas sobre la Colonización Española*, by Fray Toribio de Benavente Motolinía (Jus, Mexico, 1949); *Noticias de la vida y escritos de Fray Toribio de Benavente o Motolinía*, by José Fernando Ramírez. On the Indians of Chiapas: "El encuentro de los mayas de Chiapas con la teología de la liberación," by Jan de Vos, in *Eslabones* (University of Colima, Colima, July–December 1997) and "El Lacandón: una introducción histórica" in *Chiapas: Los rumbos de otra historia*, by Juan Pedro Viqueira and Mario Humberto Ruz (UNAM and University of Guadalajara, 1995); "El Congreso Indígena de Chiapas: un testimonio," by Jesús Morales Bermúdez, in *Anuario 1991* (Tuxtla Gutiérrez, Instituto Chiapaneco de Cultura, 1992). Viqueira and Ruz's *Chiapas* is of outstanding interest, especially the essays by Viqueira: "Los altos de Chiapas: una introducción general" and "Las causas de una rebelión india: Chiapas, 1712." On the pedagogy utilized in Ruiz's educational project: *Misión Chamula: San Cristóbal de las Casas*, by Pablo Iribarren (edition printed in offset, 1980) and Paulo Freyre's *Pedagogía del oprimido* (Pedagogy of the Oppressed) (Siglo XXI, Mexico, 1984).

SUBCOMANDANTE MARCOS

Some of the material in this chapter appeared in the article "The View from La Realidad," in *The New Republic*, August 13, 2001.

From January 1, 1994, until the middle of 2001, Subcomandante Marcos and the Zapatista movement had a major impact on the political life of Mexico. At the time, I followed the movement closely, wrote about Marcos and Bishop Samuel Ruiz, and visited the state of Chiapas when it was in ferment. Some of the material presented in this chapter comes from articles I wrote then, collected in my book *Tarea Política* (Tusquets, Mexico, 2000). I also deal at some length with the latter-day Zapatista movement in my book *Mexico: Biography of Power* (Harper-Collins, New York, 1997).

My principal sources: *La rebelión de las Cañadas: Origen y ascenso del EZLN*, by Carlos Tello Díaz, corrected and augmented edition (Cal y Arena, Mexico, 2000) and *Marcos: la genial impostura*, by Bertrand de la Grange and Maite Rico (Aguilar Nuevo Siglo, Mexico, 1997). Also consulted: *Marcos: El señor de los espejos*, by Manuel Vázquez Montalbán (Aguilar, Mexico, 1999); *La guerra en el papel*, by Marco Levario Turcott (Cal y Arena, Mexico, 1999) and *Subcomandante Marcos: El Sueño zapatista*, by Yvon Le Bot (Plaza & Janés, Mexico, 1997).

For a discussion of Peruvian and Mexican indigenism, the myth of Incarri, and the figure of Rumi Maqui, see *La utopía arcaica: José María Arguedas y las ficciones del indigenismo*, by Mario Vargas Llosa (FCE, Mexico, 1996). For the history of Indian rebellions in Chiapas, see *María Candelaria: India natural de Cancuc*, by Juan Pedro Viqueira Albán (FCE, Mexico, 1993) and the volumes of the collection *Chiapas: Los rumbos de otra historia*, edited by Juan Pedro Viqueira and Mario Humberto Ruz (University of Guadalajara, Mexico, 1995).

For the specific history of the rebellion: *Rebellion in Chiapas: An Historical Reader*, by John Womack, Jr. (New Press, New York, 1999); *Our word is our weapon: Selected writings*, by Subcomandante Marcos, edited by Juana Ponce de León (Seven Stories, New York, 2001); and *EZLN: Documentos y comunicados*, edited by Elena Poniatowska and Carlos Monsiváis (Ediciones Era, Mexico, 1994).

For the perspectives of the Zapatista movement in relation to democracy: *Democracia en tierras indígenas: Las elecciones en los Altos de*

Chiapas (1992–1998), by Juan Pedro Viqueira and Willibald Sonnleitner (El Colegio de México, Mexico, 2000). For a criticism of the ideology of Zapatismo, see the article by Juan Pedro Viqueira, "Los peligros del Chiapas imaginario," *Letras Libres*, January 1999. For an overview of the present situation: *Los indígenas de Chiapas y la rebelión zapatista: Microhistorias políticas*, by Marco Estrada Saavedra and Juan Pedro Viqueira (El Colegio de México, Mexico, 2010).

A criticism of indigenism can be found in *Buscando un Inca: Identidad y utopía en los Andes*, by Alberto Flores Galindo (Horizonte, Lima, 1986). For a literary appreciation of Marcos's writings, I consulted "El prosista armado," by Christopher Domínguez Michael, *Letras Libres*, January 1999, and for a sociological consideration of neo-Zapatismo: "La guerrilla postmoderna," Gabriel Zaid, in *Claves de la razón práctica*, vol. 44 (July 1994).

HUGO CHÁVEZ

An earlier version of much of this chapter appeared under the title of "The Shah of Venezuela" in *The New Republic*, April 1, 2009.

The chapter is in large part a synthesis of my book on Chávez, *El poder y el delirio*, which was published in 2008 in two editions by Ediciones Alfa (Caracas) and Tusquets Editores. Particularly relevant are three chapters of the book: "Venerador de héroes: Biografía y mitología," "Marxismo o fascismo: crítica ideológica," and "La batalla por el pasado: historia y propaganda."

The most useful biographies of Chávez are, first of all, *Hugo Chávez sin uniforme*, by Cristina Marcano and Alberto Barrera (Debate, Mexico, 2007) and, though it is a hagiography, *¡Hugo! The Hugo Chávez Story from Mud to Perpetual Revolution*, by Bart Jones (Steer Forth Press, New Hampshire, 2007) for much relevant information.

On his political ideas before coming to power, the most important text is *Habla el Comandante Hugo Chávez Frías*, by Agustín Blanco (UCV, Venezuela, 1998). Also of value: "Entrevista a Hugo Chávez

Frías: Soy sencillamente un revolucionario," by Rosa Miriam Elizalde and Luis Báez (www.profesionalespcm.org/_php/MuestraArticulo2 .php?id=1872).

I made frequent use of the following writings by Chávez himself: *El libro azul* (Ministerio del Poder Popular para la Comunicación e Información, Venezuela, 2007); *Un brazalete tricolor* (Ediciones Vadell, Venezuela, 2004); and his speeches: "Discurso de toma de posesión," February 2, 1999, http://www.analitica.com/biblioteca/hchavez/toma .asp; "Discurso en el Paseo de los Próceres," February 2, 1999, http:// www.analitica.com/biblioteca/hchavez/los_proceres.asp.

Three excellent books on the Venezuelan cult of Bolívar: *El culto a Bolívar: Esbozo para un estudio de la historia de las ideas en Venezuela*, by Germán Carrera Damas (Alfa, Venezuela, 2003); *Nada sino un hombre*, by Elías Pino Iturrieta (Alfa, Venezuela, 2007); and by the same author, *El divino Bolívar* (Alfa, Venezuela, 2006). On Venezuelan history, I benefited from long conversations with three great Venezuelan historians: Simón Alberto Conzalvi, Germán Carrera Damas, and Elías Pino Iturrieta. I also consulted these books by Consalvi: *El precio de la historia y otros textos políticos* (Comala.com, Venezuela, 2007); *Reflexiones sobre la historia de Venezuela* (Comala.com, Venezuela, 2007); and *El carrusel de las discordias* (Comala.com, Venezuela, 2003).

On Plekhanov: *El papel del individuo en la historia*, the Spanish version of *The Role of the Individual in History* (Editorial Intermundo, Buenos Aires, 1959) and Samuel H. Baron's *Plekhanov in Russian History and Soviet Historiography* (University of Pittsburgh Press, 1995). On Carlyle in Latin America: *Las democracias latinas de América, la creación de un continente*, by Francisco García (Colección Biblioteca Ayacucho, Venezuela, 1979), and José Enrique Rodó's *Ariel* and *Motivos de Proteo* (Biblioteca Ayacucho, Venezuela, 1976). For Karl Marx, *El dieciocho Brumario de Luis Bonaparte*, the Spanish translation of *The Eighteenth Brumaire of Louis Bonaparte* (Progreso, U.S.S.R., 1981). Marx's evaluation of Bolívar is in the *New American Encyclopedia* of 1858, available in Spanish as "Bolívar y Ponte": www.marxists.org/archive/marx/works/1858/91/ bolivar.htm. For the polemic between Inés Quintero and Vladimiro

Acosta: *El Bolívar de Marx* (Alfa, Venezuela, 2007) and a consideration of the same theme in the article by Ibsen Martínez, "Marx und Bolivar," *Letras Libres*, no. 85, January 2006.

Chávez is criticized, especially for his economic record, by Teodoro Petkoff in *El socialismo irreal* (Alfa, Venezuela, 2007); "Sólo nosotros somos gente," *Peripecias*, no. 75, 28, November 2007; and "Pensamiento único," *Tal Cual*, April 3, 2008. Corruption within his regime is discussed in an article by Gustavo Coronel: "Corrupción, administración deficiente y abuso de poder en la Venezuela de Hugo Chávez," Cato Institute, November 27, 2006, http://www.elcato.org/node/2080; from an informational perspective in *Transparencia Internacional, Índice Nacional de Percepción de la Corrupción*, in http://www.transparency.org/. Also useful was the article by Reyes Theis, *Lucha contra la corrupción presenta escasos avances*, in the Mexican newspaper *El Universal*, March 2010, available at http://politica.eluniversal.com/2010/03/22/pol_art_lucha-contra-la-corr_1801920.shtml.

On issues of oil and the governmental role in the economy: "An Empty Revolution, the Unfulfilled Promises of Hugo Chavez," by Francisco Rodríguez, *Foreign Affairs*, March–April 2008, and Ramón Espinasa, "Desempeño del sector petrolero 1997–2007 y primer semestre 2008" and "Papel estatal en la economía venezolana es cada vez mayor," by Agence France-Presse (AFP), available at http://www.portafolio.com.co/archivo/documento/CMS-7415728; "Gobierno de Venezuela persigue a opositores," Amnesty International, April 5, 2010, available at http://www.amnistia.cl/web/ent%C3%A9rate/go bierno-de-venezuela-persigue-opositores; and numerous other newspaper and magazine articles.

On the Missions: "La Venezuela de Chávez," by Scott Johnson, *Letras Libres*, no. 79, Mexico, July 2005, and "Inside Chavez's Missions," by Álvaro Vargas Llosa, Independent Institute, January 23, 2008.

On the influence of Norberto Ceresole and the question of anti-Semitism in Chávez's Venezuela, see Ceresole's *Caudillo, ejército, pueblo* (Al-Ándaluz, Spain, 2000); "Hugo Chávez's Jewish Problem," Travis Pantin, *Commentary*, July–August, 2008. And on the net, "Judíos venezolanos:

¿en la mirilla de Chávez?" by Daniel Shoer Roth, February 6, 2006, http://www.analitica.com/va/vpi/9360288.asp.

On Chávez and Venezuelan students I found the following articles and information particularly useful: "Unidad gana elecciones estudiantiles en la UCV," by María De Lourdes Vásquez, in *El Universal*, available at http://rbv.info/es/archivado/6560-venezuela–100-unidad-gana-elecciones-estudiantiles-en-la-ucv; Comisión Electoral Estudiantil, "Resultados electorales," available at http://cee.fceusb.org/; "Situación de violencia en Luz dejó tres heridos," *El Universal*, May 15, 2009, available at http://boletin.uc.edu.ve/index.php?option=com_content&view=article&id=25107:situacion-de-violencia-en-luz-dejo-tres-heridos&catid=8:actualidad&Itemid=2; "Candidato de UNT y PJ gana las elecciones en la Universidad del Zulia," *Noticias*, May 14, 2009, available at http://www.noticias24.com/actualidad/noticia/46933/candidato-de-unt-y-pj-gana-las-elecciones-en-la-luz/.

Index